Spectrum Guide to
SEYCHELLES

Camerapix Publishers International

NAIROBI

Spectrum Guide to Seychelles

© 1991 Camerapix

First published 1991 by
Camerapix Publishers International,
P.O. Box 45048,
Nairobi, Kenya

ISBN 0 86190 405 2

This book was designed and produced by
Camerapix Publishers International,
P.O. Box 45048,
Nairobi, Kenya

The **Spectrum Guides** series provides a
comprehensive and detailed description of each
country it covers together with all the essential
data that tourists, business visitors, or potential
investors are likely to require.

Spectrum Guides in print:
Kenya
Pakistan
African Wildlife Safaris
Zimbabwe
Tanzania

Printed and bound in Hong Kong

Publisher and Chief Executive: Mohamed Amin
Editorial Director: Brian Tetley
Picture Editor: Duncan Willetts
International Projects Director: Debbie Gaiger
Editors: Adrian and Judith Skerrett
Production Editors: Catie Lott and Sally McFall
Typesetting: Kimberly Davis
Photographic research: Abdul Rehman
Editorial Assistants: Jennifer Trenholm and
Mary-Anne Muiruri
Design Consultant: Craig Dodd

4

Editorial Board

Spectrum Guide to Seychelles is another welcome addition in the popular series of high-quality, lavishly and colourfully illustrated *Spectrum Guides* to exotic and exciting countries, cultures, flora, and fauna.

This guide is largely the work of a group of dedicated Seychelles lovers, long-time residents in these remote and exciting Indian Ocean islands — and the photographic magic of **Mohamed Amin**, *Spectrum Guides* Publisher and Chief Executive, and colleague **Duncan Willetts**, who know the islands well.

The person responsible for the complex liaison and logistics was *Spectrum Guides* International Projects Director **Debbie Gaiger.**

Kenyan **Brian Tetley** provided editorial direction and contributed a significant amount to the "Places and Travel" section.

The editors of *Spectrum Guide to Seychelles,* **Adrian** and **Judith Skerrett,** worked long and hard to produce a fascinating, in-depth guide to their adopted home, ably assisted by such Seychellesphiles as **David Rowat, Glynis Sanders, Lindsey Chong Seng, Katy Beaver, Betty Beckett, Willy** and **Pam Kemp, Dennis** and **Susan Law,** and **Ron** and **Gill Gerlach.**

Adrian and Judith Skerrett, born in Stoke-on-Trent, England, have lived in Seychelles since 1980. Adrian, a dedicated ornithologist and co-author of *A Birdwatcher's Guide to Seychelles*, is Executive Officer of the Royal Society for Nature Conservation — RSNC — and a member of the board of trustees of the Seychelles Islands Foundation — SIF — managers of the World Heritage Sites of Aldabra and Vallée de Mai.

He is actively involved in all manner of conservation work in Seychelles and is managing director of Mahé Shipping Company.

Judith, an historical novelist, is secretary of the RSNC and the Aride Island Advisory Committee, and has carried out many years of research into all aspects of Seychelles life, particularly its history.

Welsh-born David Rowat, a zoologist who spent his childhood in West Africa, combines his love of nature with scuba diving.

He and Glynis Sanders, a Scottish-born trained midwife who shares his passion for diving, underwater photography, and fishing, have owned and operated the Seychelles Underwater Centre, in Victoria, Mahé, since 1985.

The balance of Underwater Seychelles including the best dive sites in the islands, was compiled by Willy and Pam Kemp, two more ardent underwater enthusiasts who made Seychelles their home in 1986 after years of professional diving in the Arabian Gulf and Red Sea.

Welsh-trained zoologist-botanist Lindsey Chong Seng, a Seychellois who spent more than a decade as an islands' conservation officer and is now Director of Tourism Support Services, contributed his great knowledge of natural history and the islands to verify and supply information.

It was a task in which he was assisted by another scientist and educator, Katy Beaver, who has wide-ranging experience in Africa and the South Pacific as well as Seychelles.

Kenyan **Colin Church**, Seychelles' Nairobi-based Tourism Officer, checked the manuscript for factual errors.

Maintaining *Spectrum Guides* in-house style and copy editing was the responsibility of **Catie Lott** and **Sally McFall**. Design was by **Craig Dodd**, one of Europe's leading graphic designers, while Kenyan **Abdul Rehman** oversaw photographic research.

Finally, Editorial Assistants Kenyan **Mary-Anne Muiruri** and American **Jennifer Trenholm** coordinated the preparation of manuscripts for typesetting, which was carried out by another American, **Kimberly Davis.**

TABLE OF CONTENTS

Half-title: Seychelles yacht rides a sun-dappled sea. Title page: Seychelles parasailer rides an azure sky. Overleaf: Nature's granite sculpture on La Digue. Following pages: The original tropical paradise — St. Pierre Islet off Praslin. Pages 12-13: Jade and silver set in turquoise — Bird Island (Île aux Vaches).

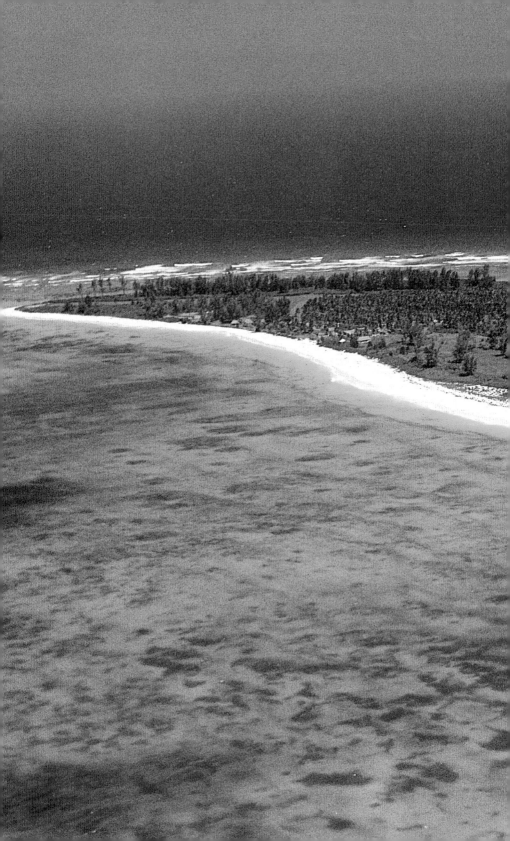

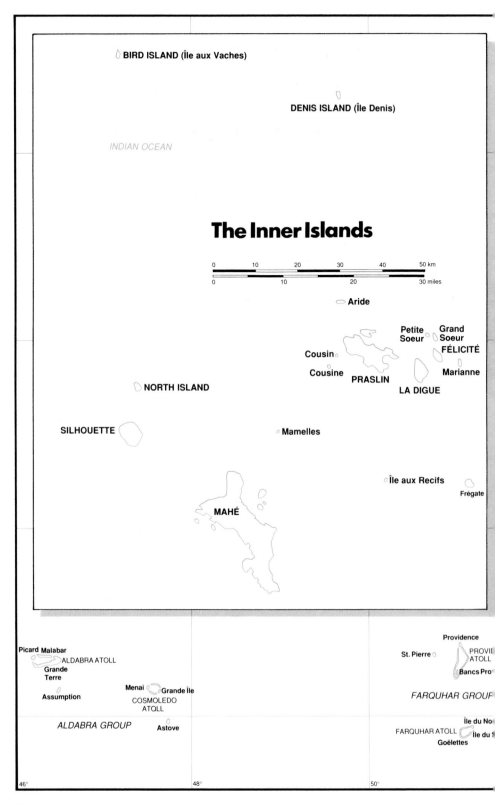

BIRD ISLAND (Île aux Vaches)

DENIS ISLAND (Île Denis)

INDIAN OCEAN

The Inner Islands

| 0 | 10 | 20 | 30 | 40 | 50 km |
| 0 | | 10 | | 20 | 30 miles |

Aride

Petite Soeur Grand Soeur

Cousin FÉLICITÉ

Cousine PRASLIN Marianne

NORTH ISLAND LA DIGUE

SILHOUETTE Mamelles

Île aux Recifs

Frégate

MAHÉ

Picard Malabar
ALDABRA ATOLL
Grande
Terre
Menai Grande Île
Assumption COSMOLEDO
ATOLL

ALDABRA GROUP Astove

Providence
St. Pierre PROVI
ATOLL
Bancs Pro

FARQUHAR GROUP

Île du No
FARQUHAR ATOLL Île du !
Goëlettes

46° 48° 50°

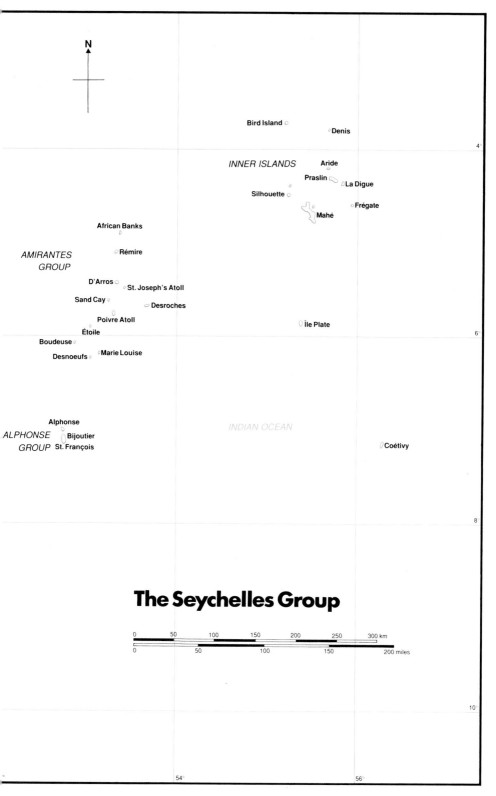

N

Bird Island ○
　　　　　　　　　○ Denis
　　　　　　　　　　　　　　　　4°

INNER ISLANDS　　Aride
　　　　　　　　　　○
　　　　　　　Praslin ◌ ◌ La Digue
　　　　Silhouette ○
　　　　　　　　　　　　　○ Frégate
　　　　　　　　　　Mahé

African Banks
　　　　○

AMIRANTES　　○ Rémire
GROUP

D'Arros ○
　　　　　○ St. Joseph's Atoll
Sand Cay ○
　　　　○ Desroches
Poivre Atoll
　　○
Étoile　　　　　　　　　　○ Île Plate
　　○　　　　　　　　　　　　　　6°
Boudeuse ○
Desnoeufs ○　○ Marie Louise

Alphonse
ALPHONSE　○
GROUP　(◌ Bijoutier
St. François　　　　　　　　　　　○ Coétivy

INDIAN OCEAN

The Seychelles Group

```
0        50       100      150      200      250      300 km
0            50           100          150          200 miles
```

　　　　　　　　　　　　　　　　　10°

54°　　　　　　　　　　56°

The Seychelles Experience

Seychelles! Its very name seems to whisper of Paradise. And for most it is as close as they can get on earth. As your plane homes in on those tiny specks of land a thousand miles from anywhere in the glittering waters of the Indian Ocean — and thousands of miles from the strains and pressures of modern life — prepare to witness a miracle.

The islands of the Seychelles are scattered with random perfection, like a fabulous neck-lace of topaz, emerald and turquoise in a setting of silver, each one a treasure, a discovery, a secret you will cherish the rest of your life.

No two islands are the same. In the high forests of Silhouette you will find a hint of mystery; on the footpaths of sleepy La Digue, perfect peace.

On Mahé, eccentric houses and crumbling walls, draped with ferns and lianas, tell the story of man's brief but eventful history there.

And on Aride you will experience the wonder of a natural miracle — an unrivalled spectacle of seabirds — while on Praslin you can simply stretch out on one of its fabulous beaches to forget the world for a while.

No one has been allowed to tamper with this idyll. Long after the Dodo vanished, Seychelles manages to keep the last flightless bird of the Indian Ocean alive on its remote natural treasure house of Aldabra. No other Indian Ocean island has conserved such a large proportion of its unique fauna and flora.

The magic persists, too, in that first sight of the elegant Vev in its black plumes, the endearing magpie robin with its sweet, falling song, and in the shy white-eye and secretive scops owl. Look out for them all — you will see their like nowhere else on earth.

Seychelles remains a natural paradise. It has no high-rise hotels nor fast food restaurants (indeed there is little about Seychelles that could be said to be swift), but there are deserted beaches of white sand washed by warm, clear seas, and shaded by leafy palms and kindly *takamakas*.

Now and then you may need to pinch yourself to remember that this is no dream.

Against the sigh of the waves and the wind you will hear the lively patois of the Seychellois — colourful and content, if a little shy, and happy to share their islands' secrets for, like the islands themselves, they remain unspoilt by the modern world.

Take a voyage either skimming over the waves in a speedboat or cruising the islands under sail. With the sun on your cheeks and the pleasant breeze in your hair, you may feel years younger and suddenly want to do something you had never dreamed of before.

So why not explore the amazing under-water world — a bizarre mirror image of the beauty on land — with its forests of white, red, blue, and orange corals, circled by vast shoals of fabulous reef fish, each trying to outdo the other in colour and design?

Rent a mask and snorkel — or take the opportunity of a lifetime and learn to scuba dive in one of the safest and most beautiful marine environments in the world.

You can take Seychelles from above as well. Let the experts on Mahé's Beau Vallon beach harness you to a parachute, and go parasailing. The experience is exhilarating, the views out of this world.

On Mahé or Praslin, you can hire a moke to explore either one of the two largest islands and experience the awesome hush of Mahé's rainforest, or the cathedral-like still-ness of Praslin's primaeval Vallée de Mai.

And if all this sounds too much like hard work (Seychelles soon weaves its soporific magic on even the most manic visitors) just follow the coast road until you find a beach you like; in all probability you will have it to yourself.

And if even the thought of driving is an effort, worry not. None of the other islands has a single road between them.

All this in a country where there is no need to fear about your health, tropical diseases, or dodgy drinking water. As you might well

Opposite top left: Senior Seychellois citizen. Opposite top: Mahé schoolgirl. Opposite left: Seychelles' famous welcoming smile. Opposite: Mahé schoolboy out of class.

Above: Victoria's floodlit bicentennial monument — known as Twa Zwazo.

expect of Paradise, Seychelles has none of these blights — not even malaria.

After each day of dreams come true you can relax with dinner by the beach, or in one of the excellent restaurants, most within earshot of the breaking waves.

The spicy food is delicious. And after a wonderful meal, say of curried octopus cooked in coconut milk, and baked breadfruit, you can *sega* (dance) into the night with the locals, or stroll along the shore by moonlight.

Seychelles' nightlife is as simple as that, for part of the magic of these enchanted islands is that everything winds down as gently as it begins. Anyway, the chances are that after a wonderful day in the sea and sun your bed will be only too welcome.

Tomorrow brings another sunrise of pastel pink on the eastern horizon of the Indian Ocean, luminous promise of another day of magic in these islands that so many think of as Paradise.

No matter how often you experience it, Seychelles never fails to surprise and delight with the breathtaking beauty of one of the most unspoilt holiday destinations in the world.

So welcome to Seychelles.

18

Travel Brief and Social Advisory

Some do's and don'ts to make your visit more enjoyable.

Sun, sand, and sea

Though it is a one-party socialist state, Seychelles has no currency controls and none of the restrictions or repression associated with some countries on the extreme left.

It remains a liberal society, with warm, easy-going people. Rare example among developing nations, it has free health services and there is a nine-year compulsory education programme for every child from the age of six.

It is also one of the loveliest travel destinations in the world. Even though often wet, the vacationer is guaranteed a great deal of sunshine, some of the most fascinating marine fauna and flora in the world, warm, crystal clear waters, idyllic beaches, and fine hotels.

The weather in Seychelles is generally warm and humid. The year divides into two seasons, influenced by the monsoon winds, with transition periods of unsettled weather in the interim, and an average of twelve hours daylight each day throughout the year.

The south-east monsoon, which blows fairly steadily from May until the end of September, is relatively dry. It builds up as the season progresses, causing choppy seas, but keeps temperatures at a pleasant average of between 24°–30°C (75°–86°F), with cooling breezes, lower humidity (around eighty per cent), and light rainfall.

Always be prepared for some rain. Seychelles owes much of its beauty to its year-round rainfall. The rainy season proper, however, when clouds settle on the hills, and the rain often thunders down for hours, even days, is during the north-west monsoon, particularly in December and January.

From October to April, this rather erratic wind brings high humidity, (sometimes nearly 100 per cent) and, when the wind drops away, higher temperatures (up to 31°–32°C [88°–90°F]).

During the transition periods (April and October) you can expect calm seas, but with little or no breeze it is often extremely hot and humid. There is generally less rainfall on Praslin than Mahé because of Mahé's higher mountains. Each island's weather varies — rain on Mahé, for example, does not necessarily mean rain on La Digue.

Getting There

Air Seychelles flies three times a week from London Gatwick via Paris, Frankfurt, and Rome, and once a week from Singapore; Air France from Paris via Djibouti, and Jeddah three times a week; British Airways from London via Bahrain twice a week; Kenya Airways via Nairobi twice a week; Lux Air via Johannesburg once a week; and Aeroflot via Moscow once a month.

It is strictly forbidden to import spearguns, which will be taken from you for the duration of your stay, arms, ammunition, non-prescription drugs, animals (Seychelles is rabies-free), seeds, flowers, fruit and vegetables (unless you have the necessary permits), radio transmitters, walkie-talkies, and pornographic literature.

Music and video tapes, and compact discs should be declared, and will sometimes be taken from you. You will be issued with a receipt and the items can be collected a few days later after they have been screened by the Security Department.

On leaving Seychelles, please remember that you need a special permit to export a *coco de mer* nut. This should be given to you at the point of purchase. The export of whole carapaces of the hawksbill turtle is forbidden, though tortoiseshell products can be exported.

However, remember most countries are signatories of the Convention on International Trade in Endangered Species (CITES) and it is therefore illegal to import such products into them.

Getting Around

By road

As a nation of fragmented islands, Seychelles' main avenues of commerce and travel are the waterways of the Indian Ocean. The only roads that exist are on the three main granitic islands, all generally in good condition, especially those on Mahé. They are fairly narrow, however, and bends, including some hairpins of almost 180 degrees, are frequent.

Usually there is a deep storm drain by the roadside and you need to take care to avoid these, specially when driving — or walking — at night during a tropical deluge.

In many places even these deep drains cannot cope with such torrential downpours and muddy waters swiftly flood across the road. Landslides may also occur at such times — and potholes can appear from nowhere.

Generally driving standards are sloppy, reflecting the laidback, *laissez faire* ambience of the locals and their attitude to life at all levels, although you do not meet the suicidal style of driving so prevalent in much of Africa and Asia.

You will meet many careless drivers, seemingly oblivious to the white lines in the centre of the road and the Highway Code, who cut corners and are laggardly in the extreme in returning to their own side when you approach.

The rationale seems to be that as long as the other driver has time to slam on his brakes it is perfectly in order to swing over to the wrong side of the road in the face of oncoming vehicles.

It is an attitude reflected in the phenomenal ratio — one-in-six — of accidents chalked up in 1989 when, with only 6,000 vehicles, there were more than 1,000 accidents.

Cars frequently stop without warning and two drivers, each heading in opposite directions, block the road as they stop to talk. One sensible precaution is to sound your horn before overtaking. At least it lets the driver ahead know you are there.

Parking on the wrong side of the road, often on double yellow lines, facing oncoming traffic, is a favourite habit. Pedestrians display even more *kamikaze* instincts — walking two or three abreast, backs to the traffic, on narrow roads without sidewalks. Many never even bother to glance left and right to check for oncoming traffic as they cross the road.

Holiday drivers introduce another unpredictable factor. Those from continental Europe often drive on the right and circle roundabouts in the wrong direction. Others infected by the soporific atmosphere dreamily drive in the wrong direction along one-way streets.

Almost all, overwhelmed by their first visions of this other Eden, tend to stop abruptly and without warning to admire the views.

Drunk driving is a hazard that is faced every Saturday night, on public holidays, and on payday at the end of the month. Note also that pedestrians bearing Seybrew beer bottles should be given a wide berth (for Guinness bottles allow an extra metre).

The speed limit, sixty-five kilometres (40 miles) an hour out of town and forty kilometres (25 miles) an hour in towns and villages, is largely academic. The many steep hills and twisting bends preclude all but the most suicidal from attempting to break the limit.

Seychelles has no permanent traffic lights and those you may see at road works have, in the past, been placed upside down.

Given all this, if you drive at a gentle pace and keep your eyes open you are unlikely to experience any major problems.

And when you drive over the mountains, even on Mahé, you may well wonder where have all the tourists gone.

There are many car rental companies in Seychelles and cars can be booked on arrival at the airport, through hotels and tour agents, or direct. Book cars on Praslin in advance. Vehicles are limited in number.

The standard of rental cars is extremely good: by law all are less than five years old.

Mini-mokes are popular. The average rate for a moke in June 1990 was around 285 rupees a day. Remember that open sides are fun in the sun, but uncomfortable in the rain. Saloon cars (about 300 rupees a day) provide greater security. Rates are cheaper for longer hire periods.

Vehicles can be delivered or pre-delivered to prearranged points for your convenience at no extra cost. Drivers are available if re-

Above: Seychelles International Airport on Mahé was built upon land reclaimed from the sea.

quired, but this can be expensive. The wearing of seat belts is soon to be compulsory.

There are no motor bikes for hire, but bicycles are popular on Praslin and La Digue. On La Digue you will find these for hire around the jetty, or at La Digue Island Lodge. Rates vary between twenty-five to forty-five rupees a day. On Praslin you should ask at your hotel for details.

Getting around by car is most certainly the best way to see Mahé and Praslin since you will not be tied to bus timetables.

But bus fares are extremely cheap and if you intend to use them do check times before you set out on what by Seychelles standards is a long journey.

Taxis are excellent but expensive. Almost all the 116 taxis on Mahé and all fifteen on Praslin now have meters. These were introduced in June, 1990. You should make sure that it is switched on before you drive off.

Rates on Mahé are fifteen rupees for the first kilometre and three rupees and twenty cents for each additional kilometre.

Praslin: eighteen rupees for the first kilometre and three rupees and eighty cents for each additional kilometre.

Waiting time is eleven rupees for fifteen minutes, and five rupees for each piece of baggage on Mahé and Praslin.

You can arrange an hourly rate privately with a driver, or have them pick you up at a prearranged time or place, but note that they sometimes hesitate to come out to places other than the obvious landmarks, e.g. hotels, restaurants.

Taxis are usually in good condition and drivers speak English. A tip is not expected.

By air

At least eighteen return flights a day operate between Mahé and Praslin, with an additional five flights on Sunday and two on Monday.

There are also regular return flights from Mahé to Frégate (twice a day), Bird (daily), Denis and Desroches (three times a week).

Many outer islands have airstrips, but charter flights are extremely costly.

The workhorse of the domestic flight network is the Canadian Twin Otter. Three planes, each with twenty seats, are operated by Air Seychelles. They also operate the smaller nine-seater and fifteen-seater Islander and Trislander planes.

Above: Air Seychelles domestic flight in landing circuit over privately-owned Denis Island (Île Denis).

By boat

Boat is the traditional means of inter-island travel and there are regular ferry services between Mahé and Praslin and La Digue. Check times of departure. This is by far the cheapest method of crossing between Mahé and Praslin.

Ferries are also available between Praslin and La Digue. Again times vary and time-tables are not strictly followed. Check times on the day of your departure to avoid being stranded. Island cruises can be arranged through the Marine Charter Association, in Victoria, Mahé (See "Listings").

By foot

Though the mountains of Mahé offer rugged and challenging walks you need have no fears of venomous snakes or the many predatory creatures found over much of the tropics. But take care to stick to marked footpaths. Even on so small an island you will be surprised — possibly alarmed — to find how easy it is to lose your way and your bearings.

Good training shoes or lightweight walking shoes are needed for most mountain trails,

but on the more gentle slopes of Praslin and La Digue you will feel more comfortable in flip flops or plastic sandals in the generally hot, humid conditions.

Never drink from mountain streams. The water may look crystal clear, but under a microscope it could be teeming with parasites. Carry your own water (and refreshments). There are no snack bars in the hills.

The south-east monsoon, when conditions are drier and less humid and paths are safer, is the best time to go walking.

Walking is at its most pleasant during the cool of early morning or late afternoon, but bear in mind sundown is between 18.00 and 19.00 and the swift shutter of Equatorial night-fall allows no twilight.

Take care to avoid the sharp spines on many of the endemic palms. *Pandanus multi-spicatus* is as spiky as it sounds (See "Forests of Mist and Rain", Part Three). Many tree trunks and branches are rotten, especially in the mist forest, so be careful about which handhold you choose.

The People

Out of town people generally are more

friendly and courteous than the townsfolk. The Seychellois, however, are reserved and diffident and it is difficult to strike up a conversation unless you know a few basic words of Creole, which is always appreciated.

Despite their seemingly frosty reserve you will find that most Seychellois are only too willing to help. There is none of the animosity that exists between tourists and locals in much of the Caribbean and other parts of the world.

With few exceptions, the Seychellois are not poor and do not resent a visitor's comparative affluence. Neither do they resort to crime, or begging, to maintain their homely lifestyle.

Many find tourists entertaining, even a little eccentric (especially those who spend hours gazing at birds through binoculars), and knowing that their country is exceptionally beautiful are quite willing to indulge them, pleased to see that their islands are appreciated.

The standard morning greeting is *bonzour*, and usually immediately after midday, *bonswar*. This can be followed by *komonsava* (How are you?), to which you reply *byen mersi* (fine, thank you, assuming of course that you are).

The police are exemplary. Bribery and corruption, so rife over much of Asia and Africa, have not crept into Seychelles' life and almost without fail the police are kind, helpful, and considerate. The same applies to other services.

Always ask before taking a person's picture. The colourful market in Victoria, for example, is a magnet for photographers, but after years of having cameras poked into their faces by complete strangers the stallholders have become understandably sick of this behaviour and rightly think it rude not to be asked for their consent.

Beggars are virtually unknown. Occasionally children, almost casually, may try the "give me one rupee" line, but they never persevere. Generally you see more poverty on the streets of western capitals than in Victoria.

A tip is not anticipated or demanded, even in restaurants, but given freely it is always appreciated.

Safety

Seychelles is extremely safe and mugging and violent crimes are as rare as the Seychelles warbler (See "Birdlife", Part Three). You can walk the streets and beaches with no fears of coming face to face with a hoodlum with a flick knife or a potential Jack the Ripper.

There is, however, a small degree of petty theft and some care of your valuables is needed. Careless tourists, lulled into a sense of false security by the rhythm of the changing tides and the happy, relaxed ambience, have left valuables on beaches or the seats of open mini-mokes.

This has proved too great a temptation for that tiny section of the Seychellois who have discovered that tourists are easy targets. So always lock your valuables in the boot of your car, or keep a close eye on them if you leave them on the beach to take a dip in the sea.

Keep money, passport, and airline tickets in a safe place, such as the hotel safe. Even in this Eden, petty theft exists, but you have no need to suffer from it if you apply a minimum of common sense.

Clothing

Lightweight, cotton clothes are standard — even essential — all year round. From the minute you step off your plane until you leave, you can forget about ties, suits, and pullovers and switch to wearing T-shirts, shorts, and flip flops or sandals every day.

Training or lightweight walking shoes are useful if you intend to explore the mountains. In the heat and humidity, heavy shoes are extremely uncomfortable.

Hats and caps are useful for all and essential if you suffer from baldness or thinning hair as the Equatorial sun is extremely deceptive and you need to protect your head. Sunglasses are also vital; the more so on the beaches where the white sand blindingly reflects the sun's glare.

Women should not go topless on any but the main tourist beaches, such as Beau Vallon. Although topless sunbathing has been accepted near the hotels, the conservative Seychellois have no wish to see semi-naked tourists on their quieter beaches and nude bathing anywhere is forbidden.

A good traveller respects local customs. Pay your hosts the respect they deserve and avoid walking around town in scanty bathing costumes. The Seychellois expect a certain standard of dress for a visit to town, but shorts are quite acceptable.

It may be your holiday, but remember that the Seychellois are going about their normal everyday working lives, and if you try to board a bus, or go into a shop without a shirt on you may be asked to cover up — or leave.

Shorts and T-shirts, acceptable everywhere, give sufficient freedom to most visitors, but some hotels and more formal restaurants may require men to wear long trousers in the evenings.

Below: Sea Gateway to Seychelles — bustling Victoria Harbour, Mahé.

What to take

Almost all western consumer goods are available, but occasionally things do run out because of the vagaries of shipping timetables. The distances involved, lack of economies of scale, and high import taxes mean that imported goods are expensive.

It is best to carry all the cameras, photographic equipment, and films that you will need. Films can always be purchased locally, but the price may be twice as much as at home.

If you wear spectacles you should also carry a spare pair. Contact lens solutions are not available in Seychelles and you should bring enough with you.

And if you are taking medication carry sufficient doses to continue treatment through the duration of your visit. Drugs are available locally but only on prescription and they are expensive.

Carry plenty of sun cream (high factor, ten or over, for real protection). Mosquito repellent is available, but you may want some before you have time to get to the shops.

Health

Some doctors recommend typhoid and polio jabs, but they are not essential. These are not endemic and public health standards in Seychelles are extremely high. There is no malaria and all planes are sprayed on arrival.

But the mosquitoes, like all the rest, do bite and the anti-coagulant they inject to help them draw your blood is extremely irritating. They are most active towards nightfall, when particular care should be taken. Used conscientiously, insect repellent and mosquito coils keep them at bay.

Should you fall ill, medical facilities are reasonably good, but clinics, and the hospital, are often crowded. Medical services are free to nationals, but tourists pay a small charge.

Even on overcast days never underestimate the strength of the overhead sun, perhaps the biggest single risk to the enjoyment of a healthy holiday, but easy enough to avoid if you are sensible.

Even in the shade you can suffer severe burns due to reflection, especially from the sea or sand. Avoid sunbathing in the middle of the day and build a tan slowly.

Sandflies, found on some beaches where seaweed collects, are irritating and can cause allergic reactions. Again, insect repellent is the answer. If the bites become infected use antihistamine or antibiotic cream.

When walking in undergrowth avoid the hanging, papery nests of yellow wasps. They are extremely aggressive close to home. Giant millipedes are harmless, but avoid large centipedes which have front legs adapted for biting.

Snakes and palm spiders are harmless, but avoid other large spiders (See "Maestros of

Disguise", Part Three). Scorpions are nocturnal and rarely seen unless you go looking for them.

Never walk barefoot on soil for you can easily pick up worms or other parasites, and if you are catering for yourself always wash fruit and vegetables carefully before eating. Water in hotels and most houses is safe to drink and it is not necessary to buy bottled water.

Never sit or park under coconut trees. These heavy nuts fall with considerable force. Always wear sandals when swimming over coral, or, better still, flippers.

Always wear something on your feet when you wander over exposed reefs at low tide. Coral cuts are slow to heal and difficult to keep dry on a beach holiday. Black sea urchins are the biggest hazard to snorkelers or divers. You remove the spines by applying pawpaw skin to them. It digests the offending material.

Some corals sting. If in doubt, look but do not touch. Cone shells can sting, and some are extremely dangerous; never pick them up by the thin end where the poisonous harpoon is located. To prevent ear infections, wash your ears with freshwater after swimming.

Chemists close on Saturday afternoon, Sunday, and public holidays. Your hotel or guesthouse will tell you which is the nearest clinic.

Tourists can be treated at any time at the Victoria Hospital.

Photography

One-hour processing is available for colour prints, and a same-day service for slides, in Victoria.

There are warning signs outside military installations and some government buildings where photography is forbidden. Do not ignore them.

The best light is in the early morning or late afternoon. The vertical midday shadows experienced on the Equator mar photographs.

When to go

The tourist season extends all year-round, with peaks corresponding to holiday time in Europe. May to September, during the drier, slightly cooler south-east monsoon, has the longest hours of sunshine, and the lower humidity makes walking more pleasant.

Strong winds blow during the peak of this monsoon, around July and August, when high seas make crossings rough. The cool sea breeze ashore, on the other hand, makes the climate refreshing.

Between October and April the north-west monsoon brings more humid conditions and at the peak, around mid-December to February, often heavy rainfall. One year is different to the next, however, and anyway a huge tropical downpour may actually add to the variety of your holiday.

For divers, visibility is best between the two monsoons, April–May or October–November, when the sea is calmest. However, conditions are normally good throughout the year.

For birdwatchers, most seabirds nest during the south-east monsoon. April, with the onset of a new breeding season, is often the most exciting month, while from October onwards can be good for migrants. Seychelles' unique land birds can be seen all year round.

Where to stay

There is a sophisticated tourist infrastructure. All tourist premises are licensed by law and their standards are high.

Options include hotels up to five star standard, some excellent small guesthouses, and self-catering flats. Camping is forbidden and there are no youth hostels. See Listings for "Hotels and guesthouses".

Communications

Letters vary in the time they take to come and go overseas, but when posting an airmail letter or postcard it is worth remembering that the Post Office displays a list of deadlines for various destinations.

Internal delivery to post office boxes is efficient but most people have no house address and finding people may take the postman time. Similarly, post between the islands is often quite slow, particularly to the outer islands.

The Central Post Office by the Clock Tower in Victoria is open weekdays from 08.00–16.00 and 08.00–12.00 Saturdays. Other mailboxes are located in police stations in the districts. Most hotels offer postal facilities and many small shops sell stamps.

Cable and Wireless in Francis Rachel Street

operates a twenty-four hour cable, telephone, telefax, and telex service. Most larger hotels will have telex and fax facilities. Direct dialling is possible to most countries and to Praslin, La Digue, and Desroches. Hotels add a markup to the cost. Public call boxes can be found outside many police stations.

Telephone calls are quite expensive. Rates are published in the telephone directory.

National Anthem

Avek kouraz ek disiplin nou ti briz tou baryer
Gouvernay dan nou lanmen nou pou reste touzour frer
Zanmen Zanmen nou pou aret lite
Plito lanmor ki viv dan lesklavaz
Zanmen Zanmen nou pou aret lite
Legalite pou nou tou
Laliberte pou touzour

Debout zonm lib
Fyer seselwa
Nou laport in ouver
Nou semen in trase
Nou soley in leve
Nou pa pou tourn deryer
Debout zonm lib
Debout seselwa
Annou reste dan linite dan laliberte

Avek dinyite nou later nou bezwen kiltive
Avec determinasyon lanmer nou pou eksplwate
Annou touzour mars nou tou ansanm
Pou rekolte tou sa ki noun senmen
Annou touzour mars nou tou ansanm
Fraternite dan leker
Nou lavenir devan nou
Debout zonm lib
Debout seselwa
Annou reste dan linite dan laliberte

Meaning of the National Anthem

With courage and discipline we broke our barrier
Government in our hands, we will stay forever brothers
Never, never will we stop the fight
Better die than live in slavery
Never, never will we stop the fight
Egality for all
Liberty for all

Stand free man
Proud Seychellois

Our door has been opened
Our way has been traced
Our sun has risen
We will not turn back
Stand free man
Stand Seychellois
Let us stay united in freedom

With dignity we must cultivate our land
With determination we will exploit the sea
Let us always march together
To harvest what we have sown
Let us always march together
Fraternity in our hearts
Our future lies ahead
Stand free man
Stand Seychellois
Let us stay united in freedom

National flower

An orchid, the *payanke* or tropicbird orchid, so named because the waxy white and green flowers have a long spur like the tail of a tropicbird, is the national flower of Seychelles.

National bird

The Seychelles Black Parrot, the only parrot found in the islands, is the national bird.

PART ONE: HISTORY, GEOGRAPHY, AND PEOPLE

Opposite: Simple but elegant lines of a Mahé Catholic church.
Above: Seychelles' national coat of arms.

Islands in the Sun

With more than eighty deserted, unspoilt, and uninhabited islands in the sun, jade jewels in the sparkling turquoise of the Indian Ocean just four degrees south of the Equator, Seychelles may well qualify as the world's best-kept secret.

Little more than 200 years ago all 115 islands in this archipelago were uninhabited. But in 1742, despatched by Bertrand François Mahé de Labourdonnais, French Governor of Mauritius, a French ship, under the command of Lazare Picault, sailed into the calm waters of a small bay in the south-west corner of one of these islands and anchored.

The captain took the ship's boat and stepped ashore on the white sands of Anse Boileau beach — one of the first to explore these then unnamed islands, with their rugged mountains, lagoons, coral atolls, splendid beaches, and curved, seductive bays.

His exploration finished, Picault sailed away and these deserted islands, the only oceanic islands in the world composed of granitic rock from a continental shelf, dreamed on, basking in their almost perfect climate under the Equatorial sun until fourteen years later when France took possession of the seven islands in the Mahé group.

An expedition under Captain Corneille Nicholas Morphey named them Sechelles, later anglicised to Seychelles, in honour of Vicomte Moreau de Sechelles, the French Controller General of Finance.

In the next few years these and other islands across more than 1,340,000 square kilometres (515,000 square miles) of the Indian Ocean were slowly populated — the first settlers arriving at St. Anne's Island in 1770.

Fifteen years later the population of Mahé was seven Europeans and 123 slaves: the founding families of today's generations.

There are almost 70,000 Seychellois, more than two-thirds of them under the age of thirty, of which the great majority, almost ninety per cent, live on Mahé. The rest are scattered throughout the archipelago in small communities on about thirty other islands and coral atolls.

A fusion of the people of three continents, Africa, Asia, and Europe, the Seychellois who speak three languages — Creole, French, and English — have created a unique culture.

Thought by many to be the original Garden of Eden, the islands are 1,600 kilometres (1,000 miles) from the nearest mainland — Africa. In fact, Seychelles is more sea than land.

Though their exclusive nautical economic zone extends across more than 1.3 million square kilometres (500,000 square miles), the combined land area of the islands adds up to just over 450 square kilometres (176 square miles): two-thirds the size of a capital city like Nairobi, Kenya.

Ringed by steep and magnificent mountains whose stark, granite walls counterpose the lush and ancient forests scattered with a profusion of palms and tropical plants, few capitals can claim a more beautiful backdrop than Victoria, in the north-east of Mahé, the largest of the islands.

The mountains sweep down to the narrow lanes and broad main mall of this fascinating town with its attractive mixture of modern and indigenous architecture, as Creole in inspiration as anything in the Caribbean.

Even though Seychelles lies on the other side of the globe, halfway across the world from the Caribbean, it is impossible to escape the feel of the West Indies — in both the culture and the pace of life, as well as in the music and the setting.

Focal point of Victoria is its deep-sea port and fishing docks which surround the yacht basin where schooners and luxury ocean-going cruising yachts gently bob at their moorings on the ebb and flow of the tide.

With a population of around 23,000 people, Victoria is also the political and administrative capital of Seychelles. Praslin, fifteen minutes flight away, is the second most populated island.

Satellite communications link this remote island nation instantly to the rest of the world and the Government has established a well-maintained network of asphalt roads on both Mahé and Praslin with villages and towns linked by frequent bus services run by the national transport company.

The social welfare systems, including state health services and compulsory education, are a model for many much larger and more resourceful nations.

Aiming for a ceiling of about 100,000

Above: Tomb of Chevalier Jean-Baptiste Queau de Quincy, State House Gardens, Victoria, Mahé.

visitors a year, hotel development has reached a peak. There are nearly 4,000 beds in the islands: enough to maintain a viable tourist population without damage. Only a few more hotels will be allowed.

This policy should ensure that Seychelles, while remaining tranquil and unspoilt, will also remain one of the most exclusive holiday resorts in the world and that hopefully its visitors will continue, in the words of one person, "to take only photographs and leave only footprints in the sand".

Since independence in 1976, the government has established an impressive record in, its conservation and management of Seychelles' terrestrial and marine ecosystems.

Its highest mountain, 905-metre (2,972-feet) high Morne Seychellois, forested by great and ancient trees, is its main national park on land, embracing a large area of the northern end of the island.

In the dark, cool shade of this rainforest it is hard to believe that the island's tropical beaches lie only a few kilometres away.

Another national park is on Praslin where the palm forest that produces the unique *coco de mer*, the largest seed in the plant kingdom, is preserved in the Vallée de Mai.

This strange, double coconut, with its uncanny likeness to the female pelvic region, has been surrounded by myths for generations — the principal one being that this must be the forbidden fruit and Vallée de Mai the original Garden of Eden.

Even stranger is the *bwa mediz* — a plant that was rediscovered as recently as 1970 and is so botanically distinct that a new family of plants had to be named to classify it. Then there is the pitcher plant, which has tendrils that develop into insect traps.

Above all, this natural paradise where temperatures rarely fall below 24°C (75°F) or rise above 30°C (86°F), forms one of the world's greatest treasuries of marine and avian life.

The national marine parks and bird sanctuaries of Seychelles ensure that these legacies will be preserved for future generations of islanders and visitors.

The marine parks can be explored by glass-bottom boat, scuba diving, and snorkeling, and the bird sanctuaries on foot. Strict laws prohibit interference with any fish, molluscs, corals, and marine flora of the parks — and of

31

the bird life and their island habitats.

Just over 1,000 kilometres (622 miles) from Mahé, the most southerly point of Seychelles, 420 kilometres (260 miles) from Madagascar, is Aldabra, one of the world's largest atolls.

The last remaining natural habitat of a rare and endangered species of giant tortoise, it was described by Sir Julian Huxley in 1970 as a unique "living natural history museum".

Now fully protected and managed by the Seychelles Islands Foundation, Aldabra also supports large colonies of seabirds and many endemic land birds.

It is home to the flightless white-throated rail, the last remaining flightless bird in the Indian Ocean following the extinction of the Dodo, solitaires, and other rails.

This unique ecosystem, a parallel of the Galapagos Islands, has been donated by the Seychelles Government to UNESCO as a World Heritage Site.

Other rare and astonishing birds — including forty surviving pairs of the paradise fly-catcher found only on La Digue island — make their home in these enchanted islands.

The magpie robin of Frégate Island and black parrot of Praslin are just two of them. Frégate is also the home of the incredible giant tenebrionid beetle, a unique insect.

Over a million sooty terns make their love nests each year on aptly named Bird Island.

Aride, most northerly of Seychelles' inner islands, was purchased for the Society for the Promotion of Nature Reserves (now the Royal Society for Nature Conservation) in 1973 by Christopher Cadbury. Known as the Seabird Citadel, it hosts the world's largest colonies of lesser noddies and possibly roseate terns.

It is also particularly famous for its Wright's gardenia — or bwa sitron — a beautiful flower.

Other unique bird species include the Seychelles warbler, which clings to life on Aride and Cousin Island, the Seychelles kestrel, scops owl, Seychelles cave swiftlet, and the distinctive blue fruit pigeon.

For scuba divers, there are more than 100 different species of living coral and hordes of exotic and indigenous tropical sea fish — more brightly coloured and exquisitely shaped than anything on land.

Even snorkeling in just a few metres of water reveals a Technicolor underwater world of fantastic coral and marine life.

Offshore, Seychelles offers some of the finest big game fishing in the world. The seas are bursting with sailfish, yellowfin, tuna, barracuda, and many more species, including marlin and fearsome sharks — a challenge that yearly draws such celebrities as best-selling author Wilbur Smith who has a holiday home in the islands.

No wonder Seychelles is known as the treasure isles of the world — offering all who visit them memories that will last a lifetime.

The Granite and the Coral

Written in the rock and coral, and the sand and seas that surround the 115 Seychelles Islands, strewn like a handful of pearls across the Indian Ocean, is the story of a nation unlike any other on the face of the earth.

Lost in the immensity of the Indian Ocean, like a remote nebula with the island of Mahé at its centre, the first people to sight the fantastic eroded granite formations and coral atolls of the Seychelles archipelago were probably Arab traders who began venturing farther south after the advent of Islam in the seventh century.

At the time when the Portuguese, captained by Vasco da Gama, landed in East Africa in 1498, Seychelles was indeed uninhabited.

And many years were to pass before Seychelles became attractive to countries seeking to expand their territories. Meanwhile, however, they served as ideal hideouts for the pirate ships who turned from the Spanish Main in the West Indies to the rich plunder of the Indian Ocean.

Much of this rich history must remain a mystery. Were the Polynesians, when they were making their long migrations across the seas, the first people ever to see these islands? If so, they lingered only long enough to seed a few useful trees, casuarina and coconut, perhaps in case they returned, before sailing on to Madagascar.

Arab traders from the coast of Africa, the Red Sea, or other Indian Ocean islands also visited Seychelles but nobody knows how often.

Arab graves have been found on Silhouette,

Above: 18th-century Possession Stone laid on 1 November, 1756, now in Victoria's National Museum.

and the well, coral foundations, and graves on Frégate may have more to do with these wandering merchants than with the pirates to which tradition links them.

One suggestion is that it was Arabs who discovered the *coco de mer* and exported it, careful to keep its origins shrouded in mystery so that the prices stayed high.

In fact, ancient manuscripts suggest that Seychelles was known to the Arabs as early as AD 851, and there seems to be another reference — to "the high islands beyond" Maldives — in AD 915.

Aldabra, for example, is named from the Arabic. Later, the granitic Seychelles themselves also had an Arabic name, *Zarin* or "Sisters".

The Portuguese were comparative latecomers. During the fifteenth and sixteenth centuries, they made several expeditions to the Indian Ocean, some led by the famous Vasco da Gama.

It is probable that they were sighted by Vasco da Gama's Portuguese contemporary Cabral in 1502, whilst a year later Joao da Nova named a group of islands, known today as Farquhar, after himself. And in 1502, when Vasco da Gama was appointed admiral, the Amirantes — "Islands of the Admiral" — were named in his honour.

From 1506 onwards Seychelles appears frequently on Portuguese charts as the "Seven Sisters" or "Seven Brothers".

In January 1609, two ships of the English East India Company anchored there, thinking they were in the Amirantes. John Jordain, who was aboard the *Ascension*, has left us with an evocative eyewitness account, the first real descriptive glimpse of Seychelles.

He noted "noe signe of any people that ever had bene there", and described the islands as "an earthly Paradise".

Man, of course, was ready to try and change that. Unfortunately for Seychelles, the crew of the *Ascension* also took good note of the "many coker nutts, both ripe and greene, of all sorts, and much fishe and fowle and tortells and manye scates with other fishe".

The giant land tortoises referred to were good news for hungry sailors since they could be kept alive on board ship for a long time, providing fresh meat.

Another ominous observation was made by William Revett, a sailor: "Here groweth such goodly shipp tymber as the lyke or better cannot bee seene, both for hayght, strayghtnes and bidgnes" ... and Europe was on the brink of several centuries of war — wars which, more than ever before, would be fought at sea.

After a pleasant stay, their ships anchored "as in a pond", the English sailed. Surprisingly they did not return with a view to settle for another 200 years. But the secret of Seychelles was out.

Treasure Islands

It was a secret that was particularly useful to the brigands and privateers who roamed the Indian Ocean, mainly to the north of Madagascar, at that time. The islands offered refuge and shelter from the hue and harry of the men o' war of the European navies.

From 1685 onwards attacks by the English pirates like Read, Williams, John Avery, White, Bowen, and Tew; the French, including le Vasseur; and the Americans, Burgess, Halsey, North, and Captain Kidd, constituted grave peril for the coasts of Mughal India,

Arabia, and Africa as well as for the ships of the East Indian Company.

Protests by the Great Mughals of India, who threatened to close their ports to European shipping, together with the continuous loss of ships, forced English and French warships into hunting the pirates down. As a result pirate raids began to diminish after 1718 before dying out completely by the middle of the eighteenth century.

Important relics related to pirates have been discovered in Seychelles: on Frégate, Plate, Astove, and at Bel Ombre. Many Seychellois are still convinced that fabulous caches lie hidden on Mahé, and the search is still going on for treasures believed to have been buried by le Vasseur — "La Buse" ("The Buzzard") — at Bel Ombre.

Prowling the Indian Ocean in search of prizes to seize and bounty and riches to plunder, the isolation of the islands gave them a chance to refit and careen their vessels, reprovision, and share out their booty far from prying, jealous eyes.

Little evidence of the pirates remains, although ruins on Frégate have long been associated with them, and legends of treasure buried on the islands have become part of the rich folklore of the Seychellois.

The pirate most often associated with the islands is Olivier le Vasseur, one of three men who made off with the largest haul of booty during the pirates' heyday in the area.

According to local belief, he buried his share, taken from an attack on a Portuguese ship, at Bourbon (now Réunion) in Seychelles. In particular, le Vasseur had prized the fabulous regalia of the Archbishop of Goa who was aboard.

After the successful visit to Réunion, however, the pirates were pursued by an English squadron, and spent some time off the coast of Mozambique in hiding. According to one source, the pirates had little joy there — and le Vasseur decided to abscond with his share of the Portuguese booty.

He was betrayed, arrested, and tried by his peers for attempted desertion. His share of the loot was confiscated but, until someone finds the treasure, the truth will remain a tantalising enigma (See "Pirates and Plunder", Part Three).

Le Vasseur is far from being the only

Above: Treasure artifacts found at Bel Ombre.

candidate for the ownership of Seychelles' treasure trove. Many other pirates, equally notorious, were in the area — they included Edward England, George Taylor, William Kidd, Tew, and Avery. Taylor and England were le Vasseur's companions during the attack on the Portuguese ship.

As trade and shipping increased in the area, piracy became more and more restricted. Eventually their plundering ended. Mauritius (then the Île de France) and Bourbon became French settlements — used for experiments in tropical cultivation — and it seemed natural enough that the scattering of islands to the north should also enter the colonial fold.

Seychelles possessed

Mahé de Labourdonnais, appointed governor of the Île de France in 1735, was a man of great energy and vision who worked hard to drag his colony into the modern age. It was he who introduced sugar to the Île de France — and it soon paid off.

He also thought Seychelles would make an excellent stopover for ships *en route* between the Île de France, the Cape, and India, which was now the hub of a vast trading empire.

In 1742, Labourdonnais equipped two ships and sent them to Seychelles to investigate the potential of the islands. In overall command was Captain Lazare Picault aboard the *Elizabeth*. Jean Grossin was captain of the *Charles*.

After sailing through the Cargados, past Agalega, Joao da Nova and Astove, they reached Mahé, anchoring at Anse Boileau (not Baie Lazare which now carries Picault's name).

Like others before, the visitors were impressed by nature's richness, so much so that Picault tentatively named the main island Île d'Abondance. On 26 November, well-laden with tortoises and coconuts, the expedition set off back to the Île de France.

The islands looked promising for new settlement, but Picault was not the best of cartographers, so in May 1744 he found himself back on the Île d'Abondance, this time in a more comfortable anchorage off what is now Victoria.

A skilled mapmaker was aboard to draw good charts, and Île d'Abondance was renamed Mahé in honour of Labourdonnais. They explored Frégate, St. Anne, and Île de Palme (Praslin), and left two weeks later.

Now the islands came to be known either as the Îles Labourdonnais, or Three Brothers. Picault thought there was room for 300 plantations. The climate seemed suitable for all sorts of crops. The timber was excellent, and the numbers of tortoise, turtle, and fish prodigious.

The only "serpents" in this Eden were the crocodiles — described by one visitor in 1769 as "monstrous" — which lived in the dense mangrove swamps that fringed the sheltered areas of the Mahé coast.

Victim of political machinations, Labourdonnais soon lost influence and in a sad saga of spite and jealousy was replaced in 1746, returning to France to face trial for maladministration. Although his trial eventually vindicated him, he was jailed in the Bastille. Weakened by the years of prison life he died in 1753, shortly after his release.

Meanwhile, what of Seychelles? René Magon, one of a series of governors who came and went on the Île de France, re-read Picault's reports and sent two ships — *Le Cerf* and the *St. Benoit* under the command of Corneille Nicholas Morphey (son of an Irish

Above left: Le duc de Praslin.

Above: Portrait of Jean Moreau de Séchelles.

father and Breton mother) — to claim them for France in 1756 under the new name of Sechelles.

It was planned to leave ashore a "Possession Stone", engraved with the arms of France, to prove ownership. The ships, which sailed in July, arrived at Picault's old anchorage in September.

After further exploration of the islands, there was a small ceremony on 1 November when the stone was laid, "facing the entry to the port", as Morphey read aloud the Act of Possession before several witnesses and the French flag was raised.

The flag was saluted with three salvoes of fire, cries of "Long live the King", and a nine-gun salute from the *Cerf*. The ships sailed away, and once again peace settled over the islands, but now Seychelles was officially "on the map".

Le duc de Praslin (hence the new name of the Île de Palme), then Secretary of State for the Navy, became interested in Labourdonnais' idea of using Seychelles as a depot for shipping and in 1768 another expedition set sail for the islands.

In command was Marion Dufresne with two ships, the *La Digue* and the *La Curieuse*. During this mission the origin of the *coco de mer* was officially noted.

The following year another expedition, commanded by Jacques Raymond Grenier, with Alexis Marie Rochon, arrived to take astronomical sightings. Now the French wanted to settle the islands, but at the smallest possible cost.

"To make there a settlement"

Brayer du Barre, who had done solid service in France as administrator of a state lottery in Rouen, was given permission to make a settlement on St. Anne for a probationary period of nine months.

The administrators of the Île de France, who granted him this right, were Francois Julien Desroches and Pierre Poivre who was particularly interested in the cultivation of spice plants at a time when the Dutch had a virtual monopoly on cinnamon, cloves, and pepper, and prices were high.

Poivre undertook many brave expeditions himself to obtain plants from Dutch settlements, which he tried to grow on the Île de France.

At best, du Barre has been seen as a loveable rogue, at worst a charlatan, but this is perhaps unfair. His enthusiasm for this new project, which exudes from his many letters, was undeniable. In this light, his later, erratic actions may be seen as those of a desperate man, rather than one with dishonest intentions.

On 12 August, 1770, the ink barely dry on his new concession, du Barre sent the *Telemaque* with fifteen white settlers, seven slaves, five Indians, and one negress to Seychelles to "sow the land and plant coffee". Their leader was Charles Delaunay.

This shipload of hopefuls disembarked on St. Anne Island on 27 August, 1770. Du Barre, a dreamer, had a quicksilver mind, falling on one idea after another with great energy, but he lacked the funds, knowledge, and backup needed to see his projects through.

Later, he envisaged a settlement with sixty to eighty slaves working on coffee plantations, raising cattle and poultry, growing spices, cassava, rice, maize, harvesting timber, fish oil, and tortoiseshell. But his dreams all came to nothing.

Although on a much humbler scale the settlement flourished at first, reports soon reached the Île de France that the settlers did nothing but "devastate the tortoises". Ships' captains complained they could not provision in Seychelles because the colonists grew nothing.

Du Barre, who was bankrupting himself trying to support his many projects, not surprisingly expected the French government to help him out financially. His letters grew increasingly desperate as he wrote to anyone who might help him — even the King of France himself.

He felt let down by the authorities on the Île de France who now seemed more interested in starting their own settlement in Seychelles, encouraged by the early success du Barre had enjoyed before Delaunay lost control of his men.

Poivre, who had always been keen to try and grow spices in Seychelles, and had encouraged du Barre, now sent his own man, Antoine Gillot, to set up a spice nursery on Mahé. The two settlements soon became rivals, Gillot and Delaunay accusing each

Above: Pierre Poivre, 18th-century French governor of Mauritius, who introduced the spice industry to Seychelles.

other of theft and negligence.

Finally, in August 1772, the original St. Anne settlers abandoned their colony. Du Barre was convinced that this project had been sabotaged by Hangard (who had arrived on a passing ship and decided to stay, quickly acquiring land and, according to du Barre at least, the harassed proprietor's house on St. Anne), the Île de France authorities, and Delaunay's incompetence.

But when he argued for the opportunity to start a new settlement, his pleas fell on deaf ears. Bankrupt and disillusioned, he died later in Pondicherry. Ironically, others who offered to take over du Barre's settlement asked for, and in some cases were offered, far more generous terms than he.

Gillot stayed on to create the spice garden at Anse Royale, where the soil was "black and deep" and there were "two fine rivers". He grew nutmeg, cloves, cinnamon, and pepper, shaded by banana and Indian coral trees.

Poivre and Desroches had been replaced by governors who had little interest in

Above: Elegant interior of Victoria's State House built in 1913.

Seychelles and Gillot's settlement was badly neglected. When his slaves ran away, he survived for more than a year on little else but maize because no supplies were shipped to him.

Once again it was war which highlighted Seychelles' strategic importance and after British ships were seen around the islands, the French decided to reaffirm their presence.

Lieutenant Charles de Romainville and a detachment of fifteen men arrived to bolster the hardy colonists who had struggled through the intervening years on Mahé and St. Anne. Among them were Hangard and Gillot.

The first Government House, some nine metres (30 feet) by 3.6 meters (12 feet), was built together with a shop, hospital, kitchen, prison, and guesthouse. Later a house was built for the doctor, and a tortoise pen, boat-shed, and battery added. The small outpost, called L'Etablissement, grew into what is now Victoria.

De Romainville, already ailing, was kept busy arbitrating the many disputes between the colonists, which did nothing to improve his health. Once, when what seemed to be a British ship approached Mahé, he uprooted and burnt the spice garden rather than let the precious plants fall into enemy hands. Unfortunately it was a French ship and his superiors were much displeased.

He was replaced in 1781 by Berthelot de la Coste — de Romainville died soon after his return to the Île de France — who was unenthusiastic about his new posting. De la Coste's relationship with the colonists was poor and he was replaced, as stand-in until a new commandant arrived, by Gillot.

But Gillot was also a sick man and could not command the respect of the civilian population of four. He was replaced in September 1787 by Caradec, who was more successful and managed to put things in order.

During this period, the geographer, agri-culturalist, and engineer, Jean Baptiste Philogene de Malavois, visited Seychelles with a surveyor to assess the suitability of the islands for settlement and report on the po-tential for crops and natural resources. De Malavois drew up a set of thirty decrees to conserve the precious timber and save the tortoises.

He wanted the turtles and coconuts sensibly

38

harvested, recommended the establishment of coastal forest reserves, and ordered that timber should only be taken for personal use.

Land should only be granted to responsible heads of families, married men — preferably those with agricultural or seagoing experience. Each man would be entitled to one concession only, and the colonists were to settle down to serious farming to end the rampant plunder which had gone before.

De Malavois estimated that in the four years before his arrival 13,000 land tortoises had been taken by visiting ships — an average of sixty a vessel. Gloomily he doubted if all the tortoises in the islands now numbered more than 6,000. He suspected that introduced cats and dogs had already caused losses among the young ones.

Sadly, like many visionaries, de Malavois was largely ignored. Although commandant, he remained powerless as paradise was plundered.

Now there was change in the winds that blew from France. Whispers of revolution hung in the air. It was the same breeze that helped to blow de Malavois and his conservationist aims back to the Île de France.

A quiet revolution

Before his departure, however, he called the settlers together in June 1790 to compile *cahiers de doleances*, or lists of grievances, as the population of the colonists' motherland had done. This Colonial Assembly had just ten members. After ten days, they reached several conclusions. The most important was the decision to administer their own affairs and draw up their own constitution.

New concessions would only be granted to the children of established settlers and the produce of the islands would no longer be at the disposal of a distant Governor General on the Île de France. They would answer only to the new National Assembly in Paris.

On the subject of universal equality, however, they remained silent. Slaves were their bread and butter and they could not contemplate life on the plantation without them. Thus did Seychelles experience its own version of the French Revolution.

The first representatives of the new order in Paris arrived from the Île de France, *en route* to India, in July 1791 by which time de

Malavois had resigned and Nageon de L'Estang was commandant.

Although Gautier and Yvon, the commissioners, were in a hurry, they found time to hold a short ceremony at L'Etablissement. On 1 August, 1791, the new French flag was unfurled and the assembled colonists (about eighty-five free settlers and 487 slaves) managed five cheers for "La nation, la loi et le roi". After this hurried visit, the Île de France sent two more commissioners.

Sieur Esnouf arrived as the colony's new administrator and Danile Lescallier, an appointee of the French National Assembly, responsible for the implementation of the revolutionary constitution on the Indian Ocean islands, was sent to Seychelles to explain the new way of doing things.

He came at a bad time — a slave ship had just arrived from Mozambique which was in the grip of a smallpox epidemic. Fearful of an outbreak on the islands, the settlers kept his ship, the *Minerve*, at anchor in quarantine and the Seychellois received the revolutionary message in a boat bobbing alongside his ship, Lescallier shouting down to them.

They could have their constitution, he agreed, but they must remain dependent on the Île de France for their administration. They would, however, have their own assembly, of which any French citizen over twenty-five could be a member — and it would report directly to Paris.

Esnouf tried to enforce Paris's new decree against slavery, but it was conveniently ignored by the new assembly.

Seven capitulations

In 1794 Chevalier Jean-Baptiste Queau de Quincy arrived as Seychelles' new commandant. Now in his forties, he had been a member of the household of Louis XVI's brother. Able and quick-witted, he had left France as an officer in the Pondicherry Regiment. But he was perhaps not always as honest as he claimed.

In Seychelles he found his métier and carefully steered his little colony through the difficult years of the French Revolutionary and Napoleonic Wars, wise enough to know when to change sides.

This was the era of the corsairs. Based on the Île de France, and in Seychelles, these

Above: One of the many French naval frigates that plied Seychelles' waters.

legalized pirates, operating under government licences or *lettres de marque*, preyed on enemy merchant shipping in the area.

Any prizes taken were supposed to be reported to the authorities and shared with them. The best known of these patriotic pirates was Robert Surcouf, who sheltered in Seychelles from time to time. There was also a home-grown privateer of some repute, Jean François Hodoul.

De Quincy did his best to help his countrymen in the *guerre de course*, but his colony was remote and ill-equipped and he did not want to attract British attention.

Despite his skilful footwork, however, the inevitable happened. A Royal Navy squadron, consisting of three well-armed ships, and two prizes — a captured corsair vessel and a Danish ship which had been found with military supplies bound for the Île de France — arrived.

Commodore Henry Newcome needed to do some repairs and land prisoners and wounded and Seychelles seemed as good a spot as any. Cautiously flying a French flag, he anchored his ships off St. Anne for the night.

Hodoul, who had just arrived back on his ship the *Olivette*, warned de Quincy that the warships were British but there was little to be done and at 08.00 on 16 May, 1794, the British ships entered port. The Marines landed and Hodoul's ship, with 400 slaves aboard, was seized.

Newcome asked for medical help for his sick and wounded, many of whom were French, but de Quincy told him he "could not render assistance to the enemy of the Republic".

Undeterred by this show of resistance, Newcome gave the settlers an hour in which to surrender. Given the odds against them, the colonists were all in favour of capitulation.

But de Quincy wanted a solution which would leave the honour of his nation and flag "beyond any reproach". He was also anxious that buildings and property ashore should remain intact.

Upon receiving such promise, at 09.00 the same day Seychelles yielded to the British. De Quincy had no other choice. The fire-

Above: 19th-century register of freed slaves.

power of the squadron amounted to 166 cannons. The commandant had eight. Newcome commanded between 12,000 and 13,000 men. De Quincy had only twenty "capable of carrying arms".

The affair was much more traumatic for de Quincy than for Newcome, who dismissed it with one sentence in his log: "A.m. at 8 the Marines of the Squadron under Lieutenant Matthews landed when the Island capitulated. Squally with rain." He set his men to making repairs and finding provisions.

All was "absolute tranquillity" during the squadron's sojourn in Seychelles' waters. The British disabled what firepower the colony had, but otherwise nothing was damaged.

De Quincy tried to stop approaching French ships from entering port — the devious British were still flying the French flag — and sent out pirogues to warn his compatriots. But the seas were rough, and no one could reach the slaver, *Deux Andres*, which was taken after a skirmish with the forty-four-gun *Resistance.*

On 1 June, at 06.00, the British sailed for the Indies, the squadron, including new prizes taken, now consisting of seven ships.

They left de Quincy with some explaining to do, and yet more headaches in the form of forty sick men Newcombe had landed on St. Anne and many French prisoners who had escaped overboard during the squadron's stay.

The little colony had 190 extra mouths to feed. After a meeting of the General Assembly on 5 June it was decided that two ships would be sent to the Île de France with as many prisoners as possible. The *L'Utility* was commandeered from Praslin, and another boat hauled out of the mud to make the journey.

De Quincy, who kept his ears open and sent as much information about British naval movements as he could, also asked for another ship to be sent urgently to take away the remainder of the prisoners. They were all on short rations — a pound of rice a man, sweet potato, turtle, and fish.

It occurred to the wily commandant that Seychelles could benefit from the situation prevailing in the Indian Ocean. Remaining neutral, the colony could profit by supplying ships from both nations, yet still provide a haven for French corsairs.

The British seemed disinterested in acquiring the islands. For one thing, they simply did not have enough men or ships to maintain a presence in Seychelles.

Now de Quincy flew the French flag as soon as the British turned their backs, ready to raise the Union Jack as soon as they were in sight again.

As a result the colony prospered. The population rose to eighty families with almost 2,000 slaves, producing all sorts of crops: "rice, maize, pineapples, bananas, sweet potato, manioc roots, lemons, nutmegs, cinnamon, vanilla pods and . . . very good cotton".

In September 1798 the *Centurion*, which had formed part of Newcome's squadron, revisited the colony. The British seized a slaver, the colonists sold the ships six bullocks, and everything passed off peacefully.

De Quincy had built himself a nine-roomed house at Pointe Conan where a pendulum clock ticked peacefully in his elegant drawing room. But in such time of war life did not remain tranquil long.

In August 1799, a French corvette, the *Surprise*, anchored off the islands on her way to France, with ambassadors from Tipoo Sahib, France's Indian ally, aboard.

Most inconveniently, she was still there in September when HMS *Braave* arrived.

Above: 1903 unveiling of Victoria's Clock Tower — a replica of one on Vauxhall Bridge Road, London.

Above: The Clock Tower and downtown Victoria today.

The *Braave* was the better-armed ship, and the French corvette surrendered. Embarrassed, de Quincy swore that the French flag had not flown in Seychelles since his capitulation.

He promised to give the British every assistance, and when the captain of the *Braave* insisted the ambassadors be handed over to him, de Quincy was ready to oblige. The ambassadors eventually surrendered, but had destroyed their despatches, and so the British let them go. The matter was settled peacefully, and the capitulation remained in force.

No doubt, however, the captain of the *Braave* would have been horrified to know how many French corsairs came and went through Mahé's Port Royale. They included the *General Malartic,* the *Hirondelle*, the *Iphigenie,* and Hodoul in his *Uni,* which actually captured a small British privateer just off St. Anne.

Unwelcome arrivals

It was some time before the British reacted, but at last HMS *Sybille* arrived to find the frigate, *Chiffone*, flying the French flag.

De Quincy had been as unhappy to see this ship arrive on 11 July, 1801, as the British were to find her in port. In more ways than one, the *Chiffone* meant problems for the commandant. She had a cargo of French prisoners, sent into exile in Seychelles by Napoleon after an attempt on his life.

Among them were men with fearsome reputations: Lefranc, who had helped massacre Louis XVI's guards, Saint-Armand, credited with strangling 100 victims, and others of equally dubious merit. Not surprisingly the Seychellois greeted these new settlers with dismay — only to be even more dismayed to hear from Captain Guiyesse of the *Chiffone* that another shipload of exiles was due.

Reluctantly de Quincy let the prisoners disembark. De Malavois, now back on Mahé, ran away at the very sight of them. They were left under guard as the crew of the *Chiffone* set about making repairs.

At this point, in August, the *Sybille* arrived and after a brief battle the *Chiffone* was taken, with the loss of thirty-five men and fifty wounded. A battery of guns from the French ship mounted on land were used against the *Sybille*. Naturally this angered the British.

The guns were located just below de Quincy's own house.

When Captain Macadam of the *Sybille* demanded an explanation, as usual the commandant managed to talk his way out of the situation. Luckily, Macadam was feeling generous, and yet again the capitulation was renewed.

Sybille sailed, and the second consignment of deportees arrived. Now their numbers totalled seventy, and terrible tales were told of the deeds they had done during the Revolution.

Assassins, fanatics, and mass-murderers (André Corchant sent over 1,500 citizens of Lyons to the guillotine and not a trial between them). As if this were not enough, the captain of the *La Flêche* which had brought them, reported that his ship had been seen on his way in and chased by a British sloop.

On 5 September, 1801, the self-same sloop, the twenty-gun *Victor*, headed towards L'Etablissement's harbour and a fierce battle ensued. The French corvette raked the *Victor's* rigging with fire, seriously disabling her. Nonetheless, she was able to get her broadside to bear on the French ship and opened up a "well-directed fire ... which was kept up incessantly".

When *La Flêche* began to sink, her spirited captain ran her aground on a reef, and set her on fire. French losses were heavy. The two officers met ashore, and Captain Collier of the *Victor* warmly commended his opponent, Captain Bonamy, for his valiant defence.

Despite this, Collier refused to take away the deportees, who now outnumbered the nervous settlers. Claiming the status of political prisoners, they did no work. They were there, they said, because of their love of liberty and equality, talk the planters did not want their slaves to overhear.

These hapless people were summoned to work before dawn by bells, ordered out of the town by a cannon shot at dusk, could be mutilated for running away, and executed for hitting their masters, or a member of the master's family.

Runaways were also shot, but all the same, many took the risk and lived *en marronage* in the hills. The settlers who lived in fear of these escapees imagined the deportees stirring them up to overthrow their island government.

In fact, the exiles were trying to do just that and de Quincy banished those he believed were involved to Frégate, begging the Île de France authorities to remove the pests.

He was able to relax a little when the *Le Belier* arrived to carry thirty-three off to Anjouan in the Comoros where the sultan promptly poisoned them. Six more who remained in Seychelles managed to escape aboard visiting ships, others were later sent to the Île de France, and a few settled in Seychelles.

At the start of the nineteenth century, Seychelles was a sizable colony of more than 1,800 inhabitants: 220 whites, 100 free blacks and 1,500 slaves.

The giant land tortoise, however, had not fared so well. It was becoming scarce. By now the islands were an established stop-off point for ships plying the Indian Ocean to stock up on fish, rum, fresh turtle, and freshwater. On the whole, the wars had been good to the settlers.

In March 1802, news came of peace in Europe, but by September 1803 fighting had resumed. And, because this was a "new start", the settlers decided they could legitimately return to the French fold.

The capitulation compromise had been unpopular with many in the community, and the new governor of the Île de France was unhappy too, even though he could never hope to protect this tiny, remote colony from the British who, sure enough, came back.

Last years of the war

When HMS *Concorde* arrived in September 1804, her captain demanded a new capitulation and de Quincy, who must have had a silver tongue, not only secured a renewal of the original, generous terms, but won additional privilege from the charmed Captain Wood.

In effect, since Seychelles was now a British possession, de Quincy maintained that Seychelles' shipping should not suffer from interference by the British.

It was agreed that local vessels should fly a special flag which would enable them to pass, unmolested, through the blockade Britain now imposed on the Indian Ocean.

Above: Surrounded by tropical trees, State House and its verdant gardens overlook Victoria, the capital of Mahé.

This blue flag bore white lettering which read "Sechelles Capitulation".

It was a triumph for de Quincy, whose shipowning colonists greeted the news with delight. But over on the Île de France his superior, de Caen, was disgusted and told de Quincy that he was "quite unable to approve".

Until the day the British actually garrisoned the islands, he refused to recognize it. However, de Caen was so many kilometres away, behind a British blockade, that de Quincy carried on doing his best to keep his colonists alive and prosperous, while still doing their duty by visiting French warships.

Indeed, when a squadron under the command of Rear-Admiral Linois arrived in 1805, he quite agreed with de Quincy's policy. The settlers had no hope of resisting a well-armed warship, and it was too risky to arm the slaves in case of rebellion.

Leaving the islands virtually defenceless, Linois sailed away again. In November of the same year the British frigate *Duncan* arrived in port, but her master had other things to occupy his mind. His crew deserted in large number and he was kept busy chasing them

around the hills of Mahé.

During the earlier visit of the *Terpsichore* and the *Pitt*, de Quincy had a bad time of it. Already cynical about Seychelles' "capitulations", they came in under French flags and, no doubt heaving a sigh of relief, de Quincy hoisted his own tricolour.

As soon as he realised they were British, de Quincy remembered de Caen's rebuke concerning "necessary steps" he should take against any "furious man or implacabe enemy". He even fired a few rounds to pacify his superior.

The frigates sent troops ashore to take him prisoner and held him aboard until they sailed next day.

Generally, however, the colony served two masters quite nicely indeed. When the British paid a visit, the Union Jack flew over L'Etablissement, when the French were in port the tricolour was hoisted, and under their blue and white flag Seychelles' slavers and trading vessels ran up and down the Indian Ocean with impunity.

When the *Duncan* returned it seized a slaver anchored off Île Thérèse, but the slaves had already been landed on the island. *Duncan* returned again in June 1806, but this third visit was less eventful. Captain Lord George Stuart was with them aboard the HMS *Russell* and he obligingly renewed the capitulation. It was all very civilized, agreement reached easily over a drink and a meal.

The final renewal of this remarkably elastic agreement was made in August the same year during the visit of three British ships, the *Albion, Drake,* and the *Pitt.*

The moment they sailed, Seychelles once again became a haven for French frigates, corsairs, and slavers, which ducked in and out of the British blockade. Ships now came to Seychelles to refit.

The corvette *Venus* and the twelve-gun *Gobemouche* were two which availed themselves of the service. Meanwhile, ships arriving directly from France kept the settlers up-to-date with the news at home.

These heady days were nearing their close, however. British colonists had lost patience with the French corsairs in the region and tightened the blockade until, inevitably, the French colonies surrendered — first Bourbon, then in December 1810, Île de France.

Keeping the enemy out

When de Quincy heard the news later the same month he hoped that his own, generous terms of surrender would remain, distinct from those under which the other colonies had fallen. But he had to remain in suspense until April the following year when Captain Beaver arrived aboard the frigate *Nisus.*

The captain had little time for the islands — he thought they had no use "other than of keeping the Enemy out of them" — but nevertheless tried to claim a few as prizes of war.

He and de Quincy reached a compromise: Seychelles would continue under the terms of its own capitulation, but the colony would also recognize the terms of the Île de France capitulation.

Lieutenant Bartholemew Sullivan, a wounded member of the Royal Marines, was landed to monitor this ambiguous situation while he recovered.

De Quincy remained in charge. When *Chlorinde,* a French frigate in need of repair, sailed into the port in May, Sullivan, who

was a guest of Hodoul, could not interfere.

Indeed, de Quincy suggested he look the other way when the ship, repaired and reprovisioned, left port to the cheers of the Seychellois despite the British flag fluttering from the town flagpole.

Although Sullivan was perhaps wise to turn a blind eye, he became increasingly frustrated by de Quincy's crafty schemes and when he took over as Civil Agent the earnest young man, who thought the settlers had "no sense of honour, shame or honesty", longed for revenge.

Certainly they were never averse to pulling the wool over his eyes, especially when it came to slave trading which was now illegal under British law (although the planters could keep the slaves they already had).

In June 1812, after a tip-off that a cargo of slaves had just arrived, Sullivan rowed through the night to Praslin and confiscated them. Despite this minor triumph, however, eventually he resigned from pure frustration. And for the Seychellois, life went on pretty much as always apart from the petty annoyance of interfering civil agents.

Under the terms of the capitulation, French laws, land rights, and customs all remained intact. De Quincy was Justice of the Peace and, whichever flag flew over the capital, those who had power in Seychelles were still Frenchmen.

The colony boomed. Its high quality cotton sold well, new settlers moved in (the 1810 population of 4,000 doubled within eight years), and there was now money to be made from whaling as well as slave-trading.

Though he knew of four cargoes of slaves brought in with his knowledge but against his will, Lieutenant Bibye Lesage, the new Civil Agent, was less vigilant against the slavers. If not a slave-trader, he was a landowner and at least sympathetic.

He and de Quincy struck up a good relationship, and when settlers complained against Lesage, de Quincy had one of them sent to Mauritius to answer for sedition.

But the slavers did not have it all their own way. Some ran aground, some were captured, and some lost their valuable cargos to smallpox epidemics. Yet the islands were never short of slaves. In five years — 1810 to 1815 — their numbers more than doubled from 3,015 to 6,950, an increase that was not all due to natural causes. The British continued to be ambivalent about the future of the archipelago and it was not until 1815, in fact, that Seychelles became a dependency of the new colony of Mauritius.

The year before — in 1814 — Lesage had moved on, selling his land in Seychelles to his successor, Captain Madge, who became proprietor of Poivre and Desroches Islands.

Louis Poiret, his estate manager, claimed he was Louis XVII of France and that he had been rescued from the Temple Prison and taken to the home of a cobbler whose name he assumed. Eventually he was brought to Seychelles where he settled as a planter at Cap Ternay. For a time he worked on Poivre, then returned to Mahé where he died in 1856.

Whatever the truth, he wrote letters in the name of Louis XVII, and called all his children "Louis" or "Marie" after his "father" and "mother".

Waging an ineffectual, half-hearted struggle against the slavers, one of which he seized in Mahé's harbour but lost again because, he claimed, he had no pistols to guard it, Madge stayed in the islands for twelve years.

De Quincy was little help. In 1816 after Madge arrested one of the leading traders, it seems certain that de Quincy connived at his escape: his distinctive white tenders were seen towing away from its anchorage the ship which carried the man to freedom.

In anger, Madge arrested de Quincy and took him to Mauritius to stand trial, de Quincy protesting his honour all the way. The court there described him as a "lump of Passion, Prejudice and Partiality", but gave him bail.

But de Quincy, who emerged from the trial unscathed, was losing popularity with his own countrymen because of his "partiality" as Chief Justice in Seychelles.

He remained unbowed, nonetheless, outlasting Madge who was removed in 1826 — condemned by a parliamentary commission for failing to stamp out slave-trading in Seychelles. A slave owner himself, Madge had more than 100 working his holdings.

The year after Madge's disgrace, de Quincy died. He was buried with full honours near Government House under the flag-

staff he had used to such good effect.

A clever man, who was seen as a real gentleman by virtually everybody he met, it is certain his diplomatic talents saved Seychelles from much unnecessary strife during the traumatic war years.

He cared more about his colony than pointless gestures on behalf of France, and he remains an attractive figure in Seychelles' history. After his death, however, his family, like many others, left the islands.

After de Quincy

The cotton boom had ended and although the number of whaling ships in the area had risen to seven by 1829, and the American fleet was also showing an interest, it was not enough to provide an income for everyone.

Besides, talk of emancipation was in the air everywhere, and not only the planters were aware of it. The slaves had also taken in "certain ideas of liberty".

As more and more ran away to live *en marronage*, stole boats to escape, and dared to make formal complaints about their treatment, slave owners mounted night patrols to protect themselves.

Yet for the planters life remained good. Madge's successor, Harrison, was easy-going, the climate was pleasant, they still had their house-slaves to carry them about in their hammocks and serve the guests at the dances they loved to hold.

But the breakdown in discipline affected the crops, fields were neglected, and by 1830 Seychelles relied on maize from Mauritius. Yet nobody seemed unduly worried. The landowners sold an occasional cargo of sugar to India, and some, such as Hodoul, turned to boat building.

Thus, on the eve of emancipation, the picture in Seychelles was one of decay. Fields had gone wild, houses had fallen down, and their proprietors predicted disaster.

Finally, in 1835, came the moment of truth — slavery was abolished. Mylius, the new Civil Agent, noted that Emancipation Day, 11 February, 1839, was celebrated in certain quarters of Seychelles with "peaceable demonstrations of joy".

There was little else to be happy about: still no church, no proper school, no market or hospital, although at least Mylius had made a start on a wharf in the area that in 1840 became the port of Victoria.

Pigs were uprooting the cemetery at Bel Air, but in Mauritius the authorities remained unmoved, although they would "determine how much can be spared without injustice to greater interests, for those of such a place as the Seychelles".

These were decades of decay but in 1861 a ray of hope glimmered on the horizon with the arrival of the first boatload of liberated Africans, rescued from Arab slave-traders in the Mozambique Channel. Since emancipation, plantation owners had found it impossible to coax, or bully, their former slaves back to work. They asked for a poll tax to be levied, so that former slaves would have to have cash to pay it.

They introduced the "*moitié*" system, under which workers were given land to squat on — but only in return for three days work a week.

These new arrivals, many of them young men and women aged from ten to twenty-five, the first of some 2,532 freed slaves brought to the islands in the years that followed, were hired at once as labourers.

Whatever the rigors of their employment on the new coconut plantations that sprang up, they later held a thanksgiving ceremony in 1897 where 2,000 of them presented a loyal address, in which they seemed pleased, at least, to be "freed from slavery". Due to their hard work, by the end of the century, the Seychelles' economy depended on the coconut.

But when investors arrived and bought up large plantations, eager to see their outlay quickly recovered, they worked the labourers so scandalously hard that even the bureaucracy in Mauritius was stirred sufficiently to appoint a protector to look after their interests.

Dr. William MacGregor was shocked by the "curtailed wages, stinted rations, insufficient clothing, bad houses . . . excess of work and maltreatment".

These were not the only hazards of Seychelles life. One wild night in October 1862, after two days of heavy rain, the upper part of Victoria was buried by an enormous landslide.

In all, seventy-five people, many of them sheltering with the Sisters of Charity, were killed. The only compensation was that the mud and rubble filled in an area later used as a sports field.

Slowly Mahé acquired other amenities. Good, gravelled paths were laid — one from Victoria to Cascade, another to the north, and a third over the hills to the north-west coast. There were Catholic churches, a convent school for girls, and a college for boys.

Now the Seychellois clamoured for freedom from their Mauritian apron strings. They were not alone in thinking they deserved better. Sir Arthur Gordon, the governor of Mauritius, prepared a petition which the locals signed, and sent it to the Colonial Office.

The reforms demanded, including greater independence, were accepted and Seychelles was given its own legislature — the Board of Civil Commissioners, which sat from 1872 onwards — and their own constitution.

Finances were separated from those of Mauritius, a Board of Education was established, a land tax imposed, and a hospital, cemetery, poorhouse, and lighthouse built, but it was never enough.

Finally in 1903, Seychelles separated from Mauritius to become a colony in its own right — celebrated by parades, a new crest, and a fully-fledged governor, Mr. Sweet-Escott, who decided that the town should have a clock tower. It was modelled on one in Vauxhall Bridge Road in the centre of London.

He also wanted the colony to feel more English. After all these years, the atmosphere was distinctly Gallic, a situation he hoped to influence by introducing English into the school curricula.

Copra remained an important crop, but in the 1890s the vanilla market boomed until a synthetic substitute was invented in 1902. Then cinnamon came to prominence and these were good times for Seychelles.

Although two attempts to establish banks in the colony failed, the government made long-term loans available to planters to encourage development, and initially the 1914-18 war benefited business. Nitroglycerine, essential to the war effort, was made from a derivative of copra and as long as the steamers still called to take it away there was a market for the crop.

Otherwise, except for those who went away to fight, the war touched Seychelles only

Above: John Karabega, King of Bunyoro, Uganda, exiled to Seychelles from 1901 to 1923.

lightly. Prices for goods were high, however, and if the wealthy planters had money, ordinary people found it difficult to survive. Wages fell and prices increased by about 150 per cent. Even the once free breadfruit and cassava that the people ate suddenly had a cash value.

As a consequence, crime also increased, and petty theft became common. Not surprisingly, some took the opportunity to escape by joining the Pioneer Corps and going off to war between late 1916 and early 1917. Sent to East Africa to put up telephone lines and dig ditches, they soon fell prey to beriberi, malaria, pneumonia, and dysentery.

At war's end the population stood at about 24,000, the majority suffering from an economic depression at a time when London seemed to forget about the colony completely, except when it wished to use it as a place of exile for troublemakers from other corners of the empire.

This trend had begun in 1877 with the arrival of the ex-Sultan of Perak, who was supposed to have been involved with the murder of the British Resident.

King Prempeh of Ashanti was sent there in 1900 to be kept in "La Roseraie", a house owned by the Adam family at Les Mamelles.

His exile "Europeanised" him in both dress and religion and he became a Protestant Christian. By 1901 a handful of detainees were in residence, and many more arrived in the following decades.

There was now local agitation for greater representation at Whitehall, and a Planters Association was organized. The Colonial Development Act of 1929 ensured a more liberal flow of funds to Seychelles, but another depression was just around the corner, and the price of copra fell so dramatically that finally it cost more to produce than it sold for.

Wages plummeted in sympathy and for the first time the silent majority, the ordinary workers, found a voice. They sent a petition to the government complaining about the treatment they were given by their employers. The taxation system also laid the heaviest burden on those least able to pay.

To sort out these mounting problems, Seychelles needed an efficient governor. He arrived in the body of Sir Arthur Grimble, who strove to restore social justice and reform income tax by exempting the lower income groups. He also wanted model housing, children's playgrounds, and smallholdings for the landless.

But, as the lively columns of the local newspapers showed, the planters were more concerned about their own interests than those of their workers.

With the creation of the League of Coloured Peoples in 1937, however, more was heard of the labourer's needs and hopes, including demands for a minimum wage, a wage tribunal, and free health care.

In 1938 the education system underwent reform and a proper administration was established. The Colonial Office was just beginning to set about implementing some of Grimble's enlightened suggestions — admittedly with ponderous deliberation — when war broke out.

This time Seychelles was in a good position to monitor shipping in the area, and a seaplane depot was established on St. Anne, a battery built to protect the harbour, and a garrison established. And once again a Pioneer Corps was raised to serve in the western desert.

But despite some precautions regarding

internal security, and the occasional blare of the trumpet used by the commander of the new Local Defence Force, life in Seychelles continued peacefully.

Times were changing for the better, however. Progress arrived on the islands in the form of electricity, a few motorcars, asphalt roads, and telephones.

With the rest of the world in turmoil, Seychelles kept busy with its own political upheavals. The embryo of Seychelles' first political party, the Taxpayers Association, which represented the employers and land-owners, had been formed in 1939.

Grimble called it "the embodiment of every reactionary force in Seychelles", and it was a sign that the Grand Blanc aristocracy were determined to retain their privileged status.

After the war, another governor, Sir Selwyn Clarke, acknowledging that self-government was inevitable, set about achieving the fulfil-ment of the long-held dream of universal adult suffrage. In the meantime the vote was given to literate property owners — just 2,000 out of a population of 36,000.

In the first election, held in 1948, most of those elected to the new Legislative Council were members of the conservative Planters and Taxpayers Association. Except on Praslin, the more progressive element fared badly.

The economy continued to develop and prosper and by 1960, 6,880 hectares (17,000 acres) of coconuts were under cultivation and the islands had a population of more than 41,000.

Four years later two political parties were formed, the Seychelles People's United Party (SPUP) under France Albert René, which campaigned for independence from Britain, and James Mancham's Seychelles Democratic Party (SDP).

Mancham's SDP pressed for closer inte-gration with Britain, whilst the SPUP favoured full independence. Britain was not keen on integration and remained neutral, while opinion in Seychelles appeared divided.

At the first election with full adult suffrage in December 1967, each party gained three seats with Mancham claiming a majority through the support of an independent.

Subsequent elections in November 1970 and April 1974 gave the SDP a slim majority in terms of votes cast, but a large majority in terms of seats, due to lack of proportional representation.

In March 1975, at a London constitutional conference, a coalition between SDP and SPUP was adopted, and independence set for June 1976. On Independence Day, 29 June, 1976, Mancham became President and René Prime Minister.

On 5 June, 1977, when Mancham was in London attending the Commonwealth Prime Minister's Conference, a coup took place and René assumed control. This day became known as Liberation Day.

A new constitution was adopted, and the Seychelles People's Progressive Front — SPPF — replaced SPUP and became the sole politi-cal party of the country. New elections were called and in 1979 René was elected President. He was re-elected at subsequent elections in 1984 and 1989.

During this period, with the opening of the international airport in 1972, tourism arrived as a new industry in Seychelles. About 3,000 tourists visited Seychelles that year, rising to 15,000 by 1973 and more than 30,000 by 1975.

Today the number of tourist arrivals is rapidly approaching the 100,000 mark, but the limits set on hotel building, and the regulation that hotels should not exceed the height of the palm trees, has ensured some things remain unchanged, and that Seychelles today is still much as it was in 1609 when John Jordain first saw this "earthly Paradise".

Above: Victoria's Zomn Lib monument.

49

The Land: A Continent in Mid-Ocean

Those who wonder why there is nowhere else on earth quite like Seychelles will find the answer lies, quite literally, under their feet, for the main islands are composed of granite. The great boulders which make Seychelles' mountains and beaches so picturesque are the building blocks of great continents, in fact.

With one exception, all the world's ocean islands are either coralline or volcanic in origin. Only the ocean islands of Seychelles are made of solid granite.

The dramatic cliffs that rise from the sea, carpeted with lush vegetation, and the boulders strewn about the island, are the debris of gigantic movements of the earth's crust long ago. Torrents of rainwater cutting their way to the sea over the millenniums have exposed granite ribs on the mountains.

There in mid-ocean stands a continent in miniature. It poses the riddle: where *did* these islands come from?

About 250 million years ago, the super-continent of Pangaea stretched almost from one pole to the other and combined all the world's continents.

Studies of magnetic rocks and modern dating techniques suggest that this single landmass was torn apart by continental drift, opening a space between Laurasia (modern North America and Eurasia) to the north, and the southern continents, known as Gondwanaland. This space, the Tethys, or Tethyan Ocean, includes much of the modern-day Indian Ocean.

As the awesome process continued, Gondwanaland itself split. South America drifted away from Africa, and Africa from Madagascar, and to this day the landmasses appear to fit together like a giant jigsaw puzzle.

India became an island off Africa. It pushed northward to join Asia, forcing the Himalaya mountain chain to rise in a process which continues, pushing the world's highest mountains still higher.

The Tethyan Ocean was gone and the Indian Ocean was born. In it, 1,600 kilo-metres (1,000 miles) to the south of India, 1,600 kilometres (1,000 miles) to the east of Africa, and 1,600 kilometres (1,000 miles) to the north-east of Madagascar stood an unknown and uninhabited set of castaway islands that time forgot.

The Seychelles archipelago lies between four and ten degrees latitude south and between forty-six and fifty-six longitude east, right in the middle of the Indian Ocean.

The islands carry remnants and reminders of the supercontinent to which they once belonged. Their insect fauna, rich with Gondwanaland species, continued to evolve into many different forms. No mammals roamed the islands because their golden era had not dawned. There, unchallenged, the reptiles still ruled.

The trees and plants also evolved in many ways, some remaining close to their African originals, others related more to species of the Orient, unheard of in Africa. In time the islands' flora and fauna began to take on unique characteristics, and Seychelles' species were born.

On **Mahé**, the dominant rock is an alkali granite, containing glass-like pieces of smoky quartz. In the **Praslin group**, the granites are often reddish grey, due to the presence of coloured alkali feldspars.

In some places, notably **Curieuse** and **La Digue**, you find wedges of coral well above the highwater mark — yet more evidence of the titanic forces which continue to shape these islands.

At one time, the landmass was a good deal larger. All three major banks of modern Seychelles — the **Saya de Malha Bank, Nazareth Bank**, and **Seychelles Bank** — were well above sea level during the last Ice Age when much of the world's water was trapped in frozen wastes.

At that time, the landmass was perhaps 130,000 square kilometres (50,200 square miles), or nearly 300 times the present size. No doubt this explains why some of Seychelles' unique flora and fauna, which cannot survive in seawater, came to spread between the various islands.

Today the Seychelles archipelago is made up of 115 islands, of which about thirty are inhabited. The islands cover a total of 455 square kilometres (176 square miles) of land

Above: Northolme, a favourite snorkeling area at the north end of Mahé's Beau Vallon beach.
Overleaf: Seychellois kids enjoy a sunny afternoon on the granite rocks unique to these Equatorial islands.

scattered over a maritime area of about 1,340,000 square kilometres (515,000 square miles).

The main island Mahé, twenty-seven kilometres (17 miles) long and between four and eight kilometres (two–five miles) wide, is also the largest. The capital, **Victoria**, and the international airport, are situated on Mahé.

The island lies 1,600 kilometres (1,000 miles) from Mombasa (Kenya), 3,200 kilometres (2,000 miles) from Bombay (India), 1,700 kilometres (1,050 miles) from Port Louis (Mauritius), 1,000 kilometres (620 miles) from Diego Saurez (Madagascar), and 2,500 kilometres (1,550 miles) from Colombo (Sri Lanka).

Seychelles is divided into several groups and two large categories — the "inner" and "outer isles".

The inner isles in the north, close to Mahé in the central part of the archipelago, are granite with tropical vegetation inland, like huge gardens rising out of the sea.

They represent forty-eight per cent of the land surface of the republic, including the larger islands of Mahé, Praslin, and La Digue, characterized by a narrow strip of coastline and higher ground and mountains inland, and **Curieuse**, **Frégate**, **Cousin**, **Cousine**, **Silhouette**, and **North**, together with thirty-two other tiny islands.

The distance to the outer isles in the west and south-west ranges from 100 kilometres (62 miles) to **Bird** and **Denis** to 1,090 kilometres (677 miles) to **Aldabra**.

The outer islands are also divided into two large groups: the **Amirantes**, consisting of twenty-four islands surrounding a central group which includes **Saint Joseph**, **Poivre**, **African Banks**, and **Alphonse**; and **Aldabra**, comprising twenty-two islands around **Providence**, **Farquhar**, **Cosmoledo**, and the immense atoll of Aldabra. Farquhar and its small archipelago is often considered a third group.

The distant islands are all coral, sandy, low lying, and covered with palm trees, often only a few metres above sea level, like the Amirantes, or higher with eroded ground like the moon's surface, such as the Aldabra group.

Above: L'Ilot Frégate, seen during the fifteen-minute flight from Mahé to Frégate.

The outer islands, little known to travellers, are used to cultivate coconut palms for copra and coconut oil, and some now have landing strips among the palm trees which has improved communications and ended their centuries of isolation.

Many are inhabited by only a few men who do contract work in rotation on coconut plantations or as fishermen and administrators for a few years. Development on far islands like Farquhar, Providence, **Coétivy**, **Astove**, Cosmoledo, Alphonse, **Marie-Louise**, and **Desnoeufs** is carried out under the auspices of the government's Island Development Company — IDC.

The low coral islands

Seychelles illustrates the geological history of the whole Indian Ocean. Apart from remnants of Gondwanaland, the chain of low coral islands west of Mahé is a continuation of the major fault lines east of Madagascar. None is more than three metres (10 feet) above sea level and their precise age is unknown.

Similar low platform islands stand to the north of Mahé (Bird and Denis), as well as to the south (**Plate** and Coétivy).

Atolls

Atolls are horseshoe-shaped, or roughly circular, coral reefs enclosing a lagoon. Their ring-like structure may be due to coral on the outside of the mass receiving more nourishment from the ocean than the coral inside, so that it grows faster. Sometimes parts of the reef grow more quickly and a ring of islands is formed.

There are several atolls in Seychelles of which Farquhar, with its ten islands, is the largest. There are also atolls in the Amirantes, at Alphonse, **St. François,** and **St. Joseph**. **Desroches** is a drowned atoll, the island itself a linear sand cay on one edge of a huge atoll, twenty kilometres (12 miles) in diameter.

Raised limestone islands

In the western corner of Seychelles' waters lies the Aldabra group. Aldabra, **Assumption**, **Cosmoledo**, and **Astove** are "high" limestone islands, probably volcanic in origin.

All but Assumption are atoll-like, with a basaltic basement less than one kilometre (half a mile) below the ocean, capped by a pinnacle of limestone rising to about eight metres (26 feet) above sea level.

Aldabra, the best studied island, appears to have emerged and disappeared several times in its history. The last emergence was around 125,000 years ago, or about the time of the last interglacial period. There are two distinct terraces at four metres (13 feet) and eight metres (27 feet) above sea level marking different stages in the island's history.

Three land form types have been recognized on Aldabra: the pinnacle mushroom-shaped surfaces (a product of intensive solution and erosion), the flat platform areas (probably old lagoon floor), and the uneven surfaces (comparatively smooth, but broken by deep potholes, probably representing an old marine erosion surface).

Another raised platform limestone reef occurs at **St. Pierre**, a considerable distance east of the Aldabra group.

With its white sandy beaches, spectacular scenery, rich coral reefs, and tropical climate, this corner of Gondwanaland is forgotten no longer.

The number of tourists which arrive each year is rapidly approaching 100,000, but Seychelles has realised its future lies in preserving its natural riches.

This treasure house, created over hundreds of millenniums, should be around for some time yet for those who wish to discover one of the most beautiful countries in the world.

The People: A Culture Called Creole

Seychelles has about 70,000 people. European explorers did not land on these islands before the seventeenth century, and the first settlement dates back to 1770: these were French colonies with African slaves.

During the nineteenth century the population increased substantially because thousands of Africans freed from slave ships were set down on the islands by the British Navy.

Other new colonies had also been established; many settlers were of French origin from nearby Mauritius. Others came from south-west India and from the Canton region in China.

Over many years, all these different races of immigrants with different cultures formed a racial mixture which is the population of the Seychelles today: a population which has a very special charm of its own.

Almost all are concentrated on the cultivated granite islands, which are more hospitable and developed than the remote "Robinson Crusoe"-like islands to the south and west. Mahé has the most inhabitants and, together with Praslin and La Digue, accounts for ninety-nine per cent of the total population.

Considerably more than half of the population is under twenty-five. The working people go about their daily business in shops, hotels, in various government ministries, and in the agricultural sector which is being successfully developed.

The Seychellois are never in a hurry, especially when on foot, and even modern influences have been unable to seduce them from their traditional lifestyle, a style of life characterized by a certain happy-go-lucky way.

Lively and colourful, this polyglot nation of many different cultures and complexions is still in the process of creating a culture. The forbears of most came as slaves, and based their cultural identity in Africa or Madagascar.

White settlers who arrived of their own volition, brought with them the expatriates longing for what they *thought* they had left behind, an idealised France. To this uneasy alliance of slave's and master's culture was added the colonial influence of Britain and France.

Only comparatively recently have the Seychellois been able to take their destiny in their own hands and explore the remarkable heritage of their diverse origins.

There is still a balance to achieve between the novelty of a distinctly Seychellois culture, and the ancient wealth of its components: the legacies of Africa, Europe, and Asia combined. That heady mixture has still to be assimilated, and time alone can make the synthesis.

In the interim, young Seychellois live in a society which faces the challenge of juggling the compact disc player with the **bom** and **zez**; the remnants of African magic with modern medicine.

Language

Most Seychellois speak three languages: Creole, English, and French. Creole has been the official language since 1981, but the usual language of business and the law is English. Many families of French descent still use French in the home.

Children are taught in Creole for their first years of schooling, and thereafter in English. French is taught later.

Seychellois pick up languages quickly, and those dealing with tourists often speak German or Italian.

Creole is a French patois which originated during the days of slavery as a means for African and Malagasy slaves to communicate with each other, and with their French masters.

It has a more straightforward grammar than French, though much of the vocabulary remains the same. It is a lively and interesting language, but the pronunciation is harsher than French.

Words have been borrowed from the Arabic, from original tribal languages, and more recently from English, whole phrases often entering into common usage.

The language has only had a written form for the last few years, and spellings have varied during that time, but the basic aim is a phonetically-spelt language. The Kreol Institute is responsible for the development of written and spoken Creole.

Names

Glancing through the pages of a Seychelles telephone directory tells a great deal about the story of the country's birth. It contains the grand French names of the descendants of the planters, such as St. Jorre, Marel, and du Boil, and the Indian and Chinese names that came in the late nineteenth century — an influx of workers and traders seeking a new life in Seychelles.

Top: Fashionable island headgear.

Above: An Easter bonnet adds to the holiday sunshine.

Most evocative of all are the names given to liberated slaves by the crews of the British ships which rescued them from Arab slave-traders and brought them to the islands as free men.

Thanks to them, Cesar, Romeo, Adonis, and Figaro became common local surnames. Some slaves took the names of their owners, and children took their mother's Christian name, so that Josephine and Elizabeth, among others, were also adopted as surnames. Some names commemorate special events.

There is a record of children being christened "English Frigate" after the visit of a British warship, though perhaps this also had something to do with the number of sailors visiting the town.

Class

Class barriers are crumbling, but although races and colours now happily blend in Seychelles, it used to be colour that defined class. The grand *blancs* were the plantation owners, the *noirs* were labourers, and the *blancs brûlés* somewhere in between.

Whites married whites. Coloureds who married into a white family were considered to have bettered themselves. But such inflexibility is now a thing of the past, another sign of a truly emergent Seychelles society.

Families

Yet family trees, and family ties, continue to arouse great interest in Seychelles for, as you might expect in such a small population, relationships are far-reaching and complicated.

The English language runs out of nouns in its efforts to describe some of these relationships, but Seychellois are usually aware that they exist.

A great deal of confusion arises because of the relaxed attitude to partnerships and wedding formalities. Despite the influence of the Catholic church, to which the vast majority belong, relationships between men and women remain, for the most part, casual and temporary — *en passant* is the local description.

Usually, a Seychellois family is a matriarchy. Fathers come and go, but the mother is constant. Brothers and sisters may have different fathers, which has helped create

Seychelles' multinational population and which often puzzles tourists.

The origin of this cheerful indifference to "regulation" perhaps goes back to the days of slavery, when the slaves were not allowed to form lifelong partnerships.

A couple might be separated and sold at any time. In the lean years after the world wars, big weddings would have been out of the question because of the expense, and it is part of the national character that anything

Top: Young Seychellois beauty.

Above: Hats on to Seychelles' summer fashion.

less than a real celebration is not worth the bother.

This helped to establish the common practice of *vivre en menage*, and there is no stigma attached to living together, nor to being the child of such a relationship.

Many men drift in and out of different partnerships. In fact, it used to be the practice for mothers to encourage their sons to do this as a preliminary to settling down in later years. This was known as *marche marche*.

The extended family is still common in Seychelles, with grandparents, aunts, older sisters, cousins, children, and grandchildren sharing the same home, or living close by.

Architecture

Visitors are often charmed by the architecture of Seychelles. Even the rusting tin roofs have mellowed to provide a pleasant autumnal patchwork along the Victoria skyline.

The atmosphere is colonial, reminiscent of those distant brick-built homes in Europe, modified by climate and materials to produce sagging wooden buildings huddled against the hillsides.

Glimpse beyond the billowing door curtain into the most humble wooden house, balancing precariously on its columns of blocks or boulders, and nowadays you will most likely see a TV, stereo, and fridge.

Rooms are crowded with furniture, chairs, and little tables — a gauge of status, as are the glass-fronted sideboards bulging with much-esteemed glassware.

The interiors are spotlessly clean, the floor swept and polished, dotted with rag rugs. Much of life is spent on the verandah, watching passers-by, or listening to the radio in the evenings.

The kitchen is usually separate due to the risk of fire as many cook over kerosene stoves. Gardens are sometimes untidy, with old cars and bits of scrap strewn about, but the ground in front of the house will be swept clean every day, and many Seychellois fill their old milk tins with plants and line them up outside.

This picture is not static, of course, and newly-built bungalows are springing up in the hills, where perhaps a more Western style of family life is followed.

Church

If it is not so important to have married parents, it is important to dress well, and this is particularly noticeable on Sunday mornings when most women flock to church, immaculately dressed, as keen to see what everyone else is wearing as to be seen in their finery themselves.

In Seychelles, where entertainment can be a scarce commodity, churchgoing is a great social occasion. Seychellois have made a happy compromise with church rules.

They simply ignore those they feel they cannot live up to, so that marriage is not essential, and it is no sin to consult a *bonhomme di bois* if you want a love potion. Yet they love their Catholic faith deeply, and Seychellois are seen at their best when walking to the church.

Little girls dress up in frothy nylon party dresses, their hair decorated with bows and ribbons. Little boys are smart in long trousers, long-sleeved shirts, and bowties.

Sisters, giggling together behind their prayer books, are often dressed alike. The church is largely the preserve of the women.

Younger men who *do* attend would not look out of place on a sunny day in London, but watch for the representatives of an older generation, dignified in long trousers, dazzling white long-sleeved shirt, and straw hat.

It is not so common these days to see the older women in their traditional outfit of a long-sleeved, loose-fitting smock blouse worn over a long skirt.

Apart from general church festivals, there are also local feasts that celebrate saints important to the individual parishes and islands, especially one in La Digue in August. A child's first communion is an important family event. Little girls, in particular, wear their finest for the occasion — white lacey dresses, white socks and shoes, and elaborate hairdos.

On a more sombre note, the Seychellois honour their dead on 2 November, visiting the cemetery to lay flowers on the graves.

Washing

One thing you are sure to notice is that these clothes will be bright and clean. This is partly due to the elbow grease the women use when slapping them against the rocks in the river during laundering. A good place to see this is at the river opposite the **Bel Air cemetery.**

As you drive around the island, you will notice washing spread out over boulders, hedges, and grassy places. Often this is not drying, but being "washed" the Seychellois way. Soaked in soapy water, the clothes are spread in the sun for the heat and bright light to do the work of the washing machine.

Food

Eating is not simply a matter of staying alive in Seychelles, an attitude that owes much to their French past. Usually up before dawn for a simple breakfast, with tea or strong coffee (sadly, rarely made in the traditional way these days), many people have relatively long and complicated journeys to work, which usually means getting to Victoria.

Lunch might be a takeaway curry, or a samosa and a piece of heavy cake (which often has a liberal amount of pink or green food dye in it).

Supper is the real treat of the day. At about five o'clock in the evening, as the heat of day fades, the whole of Mahé smells of frying garlic and fish. Men often shop for the family, stopping off on the way home at the market, loading their produce into their white, red, and blue-striped shopping bags (See "Tastes of Seychelles", Part Three).

They may also carry home the fish for dinner, a large *bourzwa* on a string, or a packet of mackerel. The pavements of Victoria are spotted with blackened drops of fish blood.

Fishing

Seychellois know all there is to know about local fishing conditions. They have adapted and evolved boats to suit their local needs: the elegant *pirogue*, usually built of *takamaka* and painted black and trimmed in white; the *katyolo* with a narrow beam and banana-like shape, often brightly painted; the more robust *welbot* with inboard engine, mast and sails; and finally the one-masted schooners which ply the outer islands and more distant fishing grounds.

The fish which most often provide the daily meal, *kordonnyen*, *kakatwa*, and *rouze* are caught in locally-made traps or *cassiers*.

These are made out of entwined bamboo strips in the shape of the letter W.

The fish swim in through the central cone-shaped entrance, making it difficult for them to find a way out again. The trap is weighed down on the sea-bed with stones, and marked on the surface by a polystyrene float.

In season, mackerel is popular. They are caught in large seine nets. Tourists are often fascinated to see these being hauled ashore at Beau Vallon, and sometimes lend a hand. Larger fish, such as *bourzwa, zob, karang, bekun,* kingfish, and marlin are taken on handlines.

In some areas it is still customary to announce the arrival of fresh fish on the beach by blowing into a conch shell like a horn.

Entertainment

As early risers, ten o'clock is the normal bedtime, although during weekends young Seychellois make the most of clubs and discos. Until the advent of radio and television, Seychelles evenings were spent in story-telling or gossiping.

The slaves brought with them well-loved tales of crafty *Soungoula*, the monkey or half-monkey, and his dupe, *Makoupa*.

True stories from the past have become folklore. They recall the avalanche of 1862 in which seventy-five people died, and the giant who grew three metres (nine feet) tall in the 1870s, and was poisoned because people were afraid of him. He is still feared by the washerwomen who work near his burial place in the Bel Air cemetery.

Then there is the story of Louis Poiret, whose descendants still claim that he was the missing dauphin, smuggled out of the Temple Prison in Paris during the revolution and brought to Seychelles to live out his life in safety. And, of course, there are stories of pirate treasure.

Now that Creole has a written form, such tales can be saved, but increasingly the Seychellois are writing novels and poetry in their own language, creating a new literary heritage for the future.

Gossip, known locally as *radyo banmbo* or *can can,* is a Seychelles mainstay, as might be expected in such a small community. Speculation about *any* event, however trivial, is rife, and rumours of the most outrageous improbability spread like wildfire from one end of Mahé to the other.

Some rumours, at least, are invented under the influence of potent local brews such as *toddy*, *bacca*, and *la purée*, and passed on above the din of a game of dominoes. In some ways, dominoes may well be the national sport.

You often see men playing the game huddled around a table outside shops and community centres. The object seems to be to make as much noise as possible in slapping the pieces down.

For the more energetic, soccer has become Seychelles' official national game, and basketball, volleyball, and boxing are all popular. Until recently, swimming was uncommon. Even people who made their living on boats often could not swim, but now this is changing. The government has introduced a programme to teach all children the skill.

Weddings

For a real treat nothing beats a wedding. These are usually big affairs with rarely fewer than fifty guests who drive in procession to the reception, tooting the horns of their cars.

The atmosphere is more informal than in Europe, often because the happy couple

---

Below: A rickshaw for two at a Seychellois wedding.

have been living together for years and have saved up to have a big wedding reception later in life.

After the meal, which will include the local specialities, the toasts begin, and almost every guest has to make a speech, tell a story, or sing a song — *Ave Maria* being a particular favourite — or else one of the bittersweet ballads, known as romances, which tell, appropriately, of love but are usually sad.

After hearing a romance, there may be tears in the eyes of grandmothers and aunts, but the mood quickly brightens again as someone else comes to the microphone.

Sometimes a *salle vert* or archway of palm leaves decorated with flowers is erected, and the newlywed couple lead their guests around the room and through the arch to the strains of a cheerful piece of music well-associated with the ceremony, which is called *Serenade*.

A tradition now largely ignored is the **levers de chambre**, when family members visit the newly-married couple at dawn the morning after the wedding to check that all is well. The entire wedding party used to descend on the couple eight days later to carry on the celebrations.

Funerals

Local burials are hedged about by superstition. Perhaps it was the watchful silence of the forests the early settlers found which incubated the fear of ghosts and spirits, or a legacy of their Malagasy forbears. Even today, death rituals and ancestor worship are important aspects of Madagascan culture. Whatever the reason, most older Seychellois have a feeling for the supernatural.

Traditionally, the body of the deceased is shown in the main room of the house, head towards the mountain and feet towards the sea. Candles are lit and people come from all over to visit the bereaved. This is known as *viellees mortuairs*.

Those closest to the deceased may keep up a vigil for hours, while others play cards or dominoes outside, making as much noise as possible to keep evil spirits away.

The coffin is later pushed to church on a handcart, family and friends following in procession. These traditions have not entirely died out, but of course times are changing.

Magic

In this atmosphere of fear of the unknown, *gris-gris,* or local magic, has thrived for centuries. Improvement in education has meant the fading of such beliefs, but Seychellois still consult a *bonhomme* or *bonfemm di bois,* seeking spells or potions to secure a lover, change their luck, or bring about revenge.

Gris-gris has always existed alongside the Catholic faith, although there have been conflicts and times when the priests have been driven to distraction by members of their congregations taking communion wafers to use in *gris-gris* ceremonies.

It is still a sensitive subject, and few people speak openly about it, even though these days *gris-gris* is not supposed to be used for anything sinister. In the past, however, *bonhomme di bois* have been associated with some strange deaths.

The ceremonies involve some unlikely ingredients: old bottles filled with blue water, rusty tobacco tins, well-thumbed playing cards, face powder, dried coconut, chicken bones, herbal extracts, pebbles, and mirrors.

Seychellois intent on revenge need a lock of hair or a scrap of clothing, so that a potion can be made up and left somewhere near the victim for them to come into contact with it.

A *gris-gris* can be spread over the doorstep to influence that person, perhaps during a court case. A chicken bone placed under the pillow of the desired man or woman will win their heart.

Another form of sorcery is *Ti Albert,* which has its origin in Europe. *Ti Albert* was an author who in 1800 wrote two volumes on magic which became popular both in France and in the French colonies.

One or two copies arrived in Seychelles, and minor spells and potions from them have been used occasionally in the past.

Superstitions

A rich legacy of superstition has built up over the years. The *katiti* or Seychelles kestrel, brings bad luck or — if it roosts in your roof — death. A dog barking on a moonlit night could mean the return of an evil spirit, such as a *dondosias* (zombie) or a *nam* (ghost).

A turtle dove flying into the house could bring great sorrow. A house should not be swept after dark or you will never be rich.

The Seychellois also have their own sayings. One of these reflects their easy-going attitude to work, "Larzen I bon, me I trdser (money is good but it is too expensive)".

Others recall folk memories. Older people, convinced of ill-treatment at the hands of their offspring, might cry, "Temps de Malavois", referring to an eighteenth-century governor who was considered particularly strict, or in a mood of self-pity they might say, "Put me outside and let the avalanche take me".

The avalanche of 1862 made a deep impression, and for years afterwards it was common to give a date of birth as so many years before or after this event.

Herbal medicines

There is an interesting tradition surrounding the use of herbal medicines in Seychelles, and of course local faith in some of these remedies is now shown to be justified. This knowledge is called *raspail-terme* after a French chemist whose book on home medicine was much prized in Seychelles.

Madagascar periwinkle has long been used medicinally and now doctors are using it to

Below: *Gris-gris* charms work their magic.

Above: Seychellois group performs the traditional *sega* dance of the islands at the Sheraton Hotel.

cure childhood leukaemia. *Citronelle* tea is taken to settle stomachs. *Toc Marie*, made into a tisane with boiling water, is good for sore throats and chests. *Yapana*, mixed with honey, is a local cure for coughs and chills.

There are many more and, in fact, there is now a research project to investigate these herbal medicines. The project, coordinated by the Ministry for Community Development, will collect and analyse the chemical properties of local medicinal and aromatic plants, and an herbarium will be established.

Music

Music and dance are the most obvious expressions of local culture. Old rhythms have been adapted to the guitar and keyboard to give Seychelles its distinctive style of popular music.

In the old days the music was made on simpler instruments. The **bom** is like an archer's bow, with a calabash, or **sok**, fixed to the curved wooden shaft, which acts as a resonance chamber. The player plucks the string or **ligne** to play the instrument, varying the sound by altering the *ligne*, or positioning the calabash against his stomach or holding it

away. Usually, he also plays a rattle, containing seeds or grit, at the same time.

The **makalapo** is also an instrument based on a bow, but the wooden arch is attached to a piece of corrugated tin, partially buried in soil or sand, held down on one side with a piece of coral, and on the other by a section of palm tree trunk. The player sits with a leg on either side of the tin and produces strange, discordant sounds by hitting the tin.

Both these instruments used to accompany chants and dances. The dances are lost, but some of the chants survive, now mostly unintelligible because the meaning of the tribal words has been forgotten, the pronunciation distorted. The *makalapo* had a spiritual purpose too, to summon spirits and make them dance.

The **zez** and **mouloumba** are zithers of Madagascan origin. The *zez* has a single string attached to a **baton** which is notched at one end.

Again, a calabash which has holes in it is used as a sounding box; these holes are stopped or opened to change the tone. The calabash rests on the player's shoulder and the string is plucked at the notched end of the baton.

The *mouloumba* is a kind of megaphone with strings. The cone is made of bamboo, and the strings, made from bamboo bark, are strung along the outside and scraped with a stick, whilst the megaphone is placed against the player's mouth to amplify his voice. Again, these instruments were used to accompany chants. Those sung to the *mouloumba* are almost indecipherable today because they are mostly of Madagascan origin, delivered very rapidly, interspersed by gasps and grunts and sung with a nasal intonation.

The drums include the African **tamtam** and two varieties of **tambour**. One is made from a hollowed-out tree trunk, the other looks like a large tambourine, covered with goat or ray skin that is heated to tauten the skin before the drums are played. They are associated with the performance of the *moutia*. No one who hears this eerie music easily forgets, and it would be a pity if the Seychellois were to lose this particular heritage.

"Ton Pa" is the musician most associated with these instuments and the ancient chants which go with them.

Although such music is unlikely to become commercially popular, it could be preserved and explored by the many excellent local singers and bands.

The popular music scene in Seychelles is lively, most of the songs based on the jaunty rhythms of the *sega*, with Creole lyrics that extol the beauty of the islands or the joys of love.

Others take a wry look at life, or have a political bent. Amongst the most famous names are Patrick Victor and Joe Samy, The Tropiks, Saturn, and many more.

Dances

At some time you are bound to see one of the local dances. A **sega** is the basic rhythm, and to this the locals do the *sega* dance. It is based on a very simple step — simple that is until you try to do it.

If you watch a maid polishing floors the old-fashioned way, with half a coconut husk under her foot, one arm behind her back, and the other wielding a grass brush in front of her, then watch her feet. She is doing the *sega* step, which seems to depend on a great deal of movement in the hips.

This dance is of African origin, but the Seychellois have made it very much their own. The movements are lascivious, the couples facing each other, but not touching.

Sega is traditionally danced to the throb of the drum, with accompanying chants based on small everyday incidents.

There is a less light-hearted *sega* of Madagascan origin called the **sega tremble**, in which the dancers seem to enter a trance, but this is not often seen.

The **moutia** is more than simply a dance, it is an event, one which tourists are unlikely to see outside cultural displays. Seychellois are still sensitive about their *moutias*, which are very personal affairs.

For years, shocked members of the church and government tried to stamp out the *moutias*, believing them to be little less than orgies, and at best a threat to public morals. It is certainly true that the dancers' movements are sensual, and the atmosphere electric.

Moutias are held at night, preferably under the moonlight, on a beach or in a

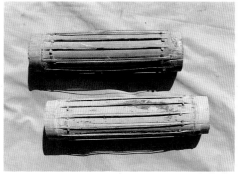

Traditional Seychelles music instruments.

Top: The *zez* .

Above: *Mouloumba*, two zithers of Madagascan origin.

Above: Carefree Mahé youngsters — children of the sun.

clearing. A bonfire is lit to heat the drums in order to tune them. Things get off to a slow start, with what seems to be an unenthusiastic shuffling around the clearing.

The simple, but evocative music makes it clear that the *moutia* is all African in origin, brought by slaves whose only escape from drudgery were these impromptu gatherings.

The men begin by chanting songs in a hypnotic monotone. These songs can be composed on the spot, but many have survived from tribal times. This is a preparation for the dance itself. The audience will sit around talking and drinking while the musicians beat their drums to tune them. Eventually one of the men will approach his chosen partner, arms extended, opened towards her.

Man *(cavalier)* and woman *(dame)* dance back to back, turning only occasionally to face each other. Everything is slow and rhythmic, but their movements and gestures are blatantly provocative, and even though the partners do not actually touch, the atmosphere is one of sensuous tension.

Soon the women join the chanting, answering the phrases called out by the men. The women's full skirts are raised above

their knees to reveal their shuffling steps.

All movements are strangely controlled, as though played out in slow motion, bodies are held stiff, expressions are serious.

A *moutia* is a fascinating glimpse into a past which seems unbelievably distant from modern Seychelles, but survives still in folk memory. One rarely seen dance is the **madio** or **galoupilon** during which two women jump over two poles held parallel to the ground in the shape of the letter X.

Again, a **kamtole** is more than just a dance, it is a social evening during which several dances are performed, usually in the order of a **valse**, **ecossaise**, **masok**, **polka**, **contredanse**, **berline,** and finally a **pas-de-quatre**. As you may guess from the names, these dances are of European origin.

The contredanse is the highlight of the evening, the dancers moving in and out, performing complex figures to the orders of a **komander** who shouts them out in a sing-song, nasal tone, telling them to **balancez**, **maillez à gauche**, or perform the **chaine anglais**, **rond salon,** or **promenade-galop**.

The chants these days are made in Creole or a mixture of French and Creole. The music is provided by a Kamtole band, with violins and a triangle being the essential instruments. Some bands also have banjos, mandolins, accordions, and a drum.

With the formation of a Cultural Troup, entertainments in the hotels and regular dance competitions for young people keep the Kamtole alive in Seychellois' hearts and it should not be missed by any interested visitor.

Chants

In many ways, the chants which accompany the dances are equally fascinating. *Moutia* chants are often composed "on the spot", but a few have survived in Seychelles from the early days.

This is reflected in some of the strange words included, dating from a Creole no longer used, from tribal languages, and from archaic French and Malagasy.

Usual topics are bawdy love stories, satire (often aimed at a rival, or a lover in the audience), or some grievance the performer has against someone, often those in authority, so that in the early days the slave master or plantation owner would be the target.

The chants at a *moutia* also related the everyday dramas of life on the estates. Because they are made up spontaneously, *moutia* chants include many repetitions, refrains, and breaks while the singer thinks up his next line. Naturally, this spontaneity has meant that most *moutia* chants are instantly lost forever.

Other types of songs are the **romances** performed at weddings, usually of French origin, and traditional **roundsongs** which used to entertain people in the evenings before the advent of radio and television.

Naturally, fishermen and *piroguiers* who used to row their canoes between the islands developed chants to help them keep rhythm.

These songs often told of shipwrecks and storms at sea. Back on land, mothers sang lullabies to their children about the dangers facing their fathers out at sea, catching the fish for supper.

Theatre

Seychellois street-theatre, or **sokwe**, also has chants associated with it. Sadly these impromptu displays are never seen today. The participants, (usually men), covered themselves in a disguise made out of creepers and vegetation, and wore masks and green beards.

It seems to have been reminiscent of English mummery, but again there are African and Madagascan influences. Another form of theatre has a strong suggestion of mummery.

The **boya** tells a story of healing or resurrection. A sick person is healed or a corpse raised from the dead. The National Archives are capturing some of these stories, chants, and songs on audio tape for the future, in an ongoing project to record the memories of older Seychellois. Modern theatre in Seychelles is also benefiting from increased interest in the Creole language. Adaptations are made of classic plays from all over the world, but plays are also being created locally.

There are tragedies, (*Adelaid Demrez*), comedies (*Bolot Feray*), farces (*Rimer lo Teodor*), and 'musical spectaculars such as *Temwayaz Lalit*, to name but a few of the recent successes created locally along the lines of European theatre, but wholly Seychellois in character. These are an exciting new development in Creole culture.

From these tangled skeins, young Seychellois are creating a culture of their own, and establishing a substantial body of national art and literature.

It is possible to buy paintings from a number of artists whose work might carefully document Seychelles' scenes, or merely give impressions of the country by use of bold colour and simplified outlines, greatly influenced by Michael Adams. Visual arts are thriving in Seychelles, with diversity of style, form, and content (See "Arts and Crafts: A Heritage in the Making", Part Three).

Antoine Abel, the poet, has led Seychelles' literature into the present, and there is a Seychelles Authors' Society.

Two hundred years is no great length of time in the history of a nation or the never-ending process of creating a culture but what is now emerging is recognizably — and distinctly — Seychellois in character.

It has excitement and a sense of discovery about it which visitors will find refreshing, while the older traditions, still honoured even if modified to suit modern conditions, have another sort of mystique.

In the cultural melting pot of these exotic islands who knows which way things will move next?

PART TWO:
PLACES AND TRAVEL

Above: Graceful facade of the Kreol Institute, Victoria, where the language of the islands is updated, revised, and researched.

Opposite: Cool stream falls over lichen-covered rocks in Mahé's Morne Seychellois National Park.

Mahé: The Isle of Abundance

Covering an area of 152 square kilometres (58 square miles), **Mahé** is the largest island in the Seychelles archipelago. Rising to a height of 905 metres (2,969 feet) above sea level at its highest point, it stretches twenty-seven kilometres (17 miles) from north to south. And at its widest it is eight kilometres (five miles) across.

One of the first to explore this once remote island cloaked with a lush mantle of tropical vegetation that gave verdant flesh to its granite bones named it the Isle of Abundance, for marvellous and many were the wild and wonderful plants that flourished in its flatlands and thrust their roots deep into the mountainsides.

Even more exotic were the creatures that inhabited the depths of these liana-draped jungles — insects and birds separated from their own kind and left to evolve in a time-forgotten world many thousands of millenniums ago when Gondwanaland, the supercontinent, broke up.

In the flickering blink of time since man first set foot on Mahé just over 200 years ago, much has gone — felled or destroyed by his wilful hand. But much also remains to delight and astonish on what is perhaps one of the most beautiful islands (certainly one of the most remote) in the world.

With its high inland mountains counterposing its sixty-eight glistening white palm-fringed beaches, Mahé is indeed an island of abundance, and of surprise and discovery around every bend in the trail, with its many striking contrasts of landscape and natural life.

Climb the mountains for stunning panoramas over the Indian Ocean to Mahé's many sister islands. Pause for a break in one of the tea, coconut, or mahogany plantations. Skirt the mangrove forests of hidden creeks. Or stop to ponder the power of the sea where spectacular waves create fountains of foam and fury as they break on granite cliffs.

Beyond the international airport, built twenty years ago on land reclaimed from the sea, immense beaches of gold and silver sand adorn the south-east coast.

Carved into the western coast, away on the other side of the island, many glorious bays and lagoons form a distinctive and handsome contrast.

In the north stands the capital **Victoria** and all around it evidence of the great development, both civic and commercial, that has taken place during the last three decades.

But the southern lowlands remain largely unspoilt and untouched, despite the metal road that circles through **Quatre Bornes** and back to **Anse Royale**.

Some visitors fly straight off to **Praslin** in the belief Mahé should be bypassed to discover the real Seychelles.

Yet in many ways, Mahé is the most spectacular of all the islands. It has the highest peaks, covered in lush vegetation, where two of the granite islands' unique bird species find their only home.

Most of Seychelles' unique plants are found on Mahé, some of them nowhere else in the world, and there are beautiful beaches, mountain walks, marine parks, the most advanced facilities for watersports and diving, and much more.

The main island of Seychelles and by far the largest centre of business and commerce, it is home to the vast majority of the country's people. All imports and exports by sea pass through **Port Victoria** and all international flights arrive and depart from **Seychelles International Airport** at **Anse Dejeuner**. Wherever you come from, you will arrive at Mahé.

The island is well served by a network of good roads that circle and crisscross the island, although fortunately many areas are approached only by dirt trails or footpaths. It means you can discover Mahé either by car or on foot.

Most people visit Mahé for the beaches in particular but even beaches can pall and in between watersports and sunbathing you have the option of visiting unspoilt villages to meet the Seychellois in their own environment, study the distinctive architecture, plantations, churches, and local art and handicraft centres such as the pottery and the artists' ateliers among the palm trees.

There are many beaches — *anse* — small or large, deserted or crowded, highly visible or

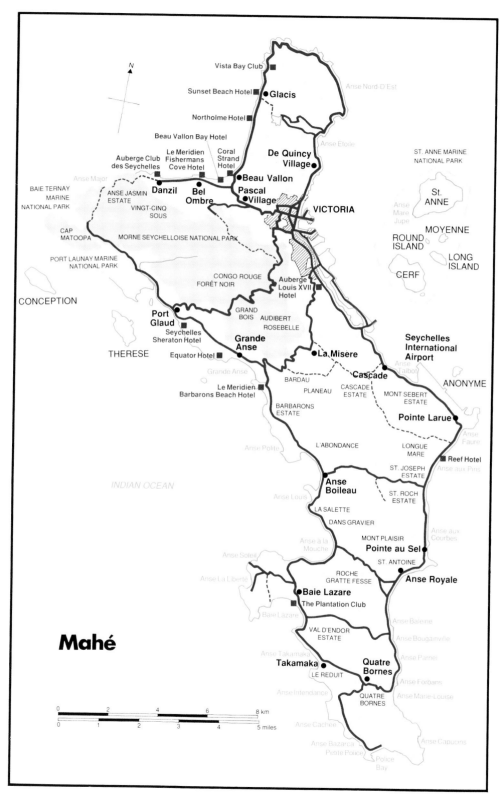

Mahé

Above: Youngsters frolic on a Mahé beach.
Opposite: Sun worshippers at Beau Vallon.

hidden away in some little-known part of the island.

Getting there

Mahé is served by air and sea. There are many regular scheduled flights from Europe, Africa, the Gulf, and Asia. There are no regular passenger services by sea but cruise liners occasionally visit Victoria, the capital, and many yachts and smaller mercantile craft make it a regular port of call. It may be possible to find passage on a freighter or trading vessel.

When to go

Mahé welcomes visitors all year-round. There is no winter or summer. The passage of the seasons is marked by the movement of the monsoon winds which radically affect the areas where diving is possible. But except for two or three months the sunkissed beaches remain . . . sunkissed.

Where to stay

Seychelles Sheraton (5-star), Meridien Fisherman's Cove (5-star), Coral Strand (4-star), Plantation Club (5-star), Northolme Hotel (5-star), Sunset Beach Hotel (5-star). There are many others of varying degrees of comfort and quality. See Listings for "Hotels".

Getting Around

To explore Mahé, you should rent a car for at least one day. Buses are inexpensive but, tied to local needs, timetables and routes do not allow you to explore some of the more remote areas.

Nor can you stop when you want to admire a view, savour the flora, spend time on a sun-drenched beach, or reach with ease the best way-marked paths.

Taxis, on the other hand, are good but fairly expensive. And tour operators offer a variety of tours which are an excellent introduction to the main island. For the independent visitor, however, or for those seeking to explore the true flavour of the island, you cannot beat self-drive.

Car Hire

Cars can be rented through hotels or guest houses, travel agents, or direct from the car

Above: Palms shade hotel pool on Mahé.
Opposite: Seychellois boy somersaults into the crystal-clear waters.

hire operators (see "Travel Brief", "Facts At Your Fingertips", and Listings). They can be delivered, and redelivered to or from almost any point on Mahé, such as your hotel, the airport, or **Victoria**.

Sightseeing

From Victoria, head north along the coast road, passing **Radio Seychelles** on the left. Just outside town you pass the **National Archives** (on the right) followed shortly by **Lobster Pot Restaurant**, an excellent place to return for lunch or dinner.

Lunchtime can be busy due to the proximity of Victoria, and the business community, but evenings are a good time to relax and enjoy fine Creole or continental cuisine with the lights of Port Victoria as a backdrop.

Continuing northward, you pass the **Far Eastern Broadcasting Association** — FEBA — where a "forest" of missionary aerials rises from the shallow waters beaming the Christian message to many Far Eastern countries.

A short distance beyond is **Anse Étoile**, the headquarters of a small British army contin-

gent during the Second World War. Their **lookout post**, a short distance to the north, still stands.

In the 1970s-80s it became an eyesore when rubbish was dumped to reclaim land from the sea. Now, although the rubbish tip has been bulldozed and the land is overgrown, many people still know it as "smelly corner".

Almost opposite **Manresa Guest House** at **Pointe Cèdre**, there is a signposted left turn to **La Gogue Reservoir**. Adventurous souls may wish to explore this route, although it means either missing the northern tip of the island and some spectacular scenery, or doubling back to take in this section.

Nevertheless, the road to the reservoir is extremely interesting as it winds its way through local houses to emerge at the dam wall. From the dam, a narrow road winds uphill, offering spectacular views of the **west coast** and **Silhouette Island** before descending steeply towards **Glacis**.

Returning to the main road at Pointe Cèdre, continue north, past the **Rehabilitation Centre** (on the left at **Anse Nord D'Est**) which was opened in June 1982 as a centre for the

73

Above: Traditional thatched home on Mahé.
Opposite: Anse Major — one of Mahé's many unspoilt beaches.

disabled. It provides physiotherapy, speech and occupational therapy, excellent modern facilities, and job training.

As the road rises, you pass **Carana Bay**, a beautiful, quiet, sandy cove, surrounded by giant granite boulders. There the road bends westward along the northern tip of the island before turning sharply to the south, opposite the tiny island of **L'Ilot** (or North Islet).

From this point to **Beau Vallon**, you drive past spectacular cliff-top scenery, descending occasionally to sea level. For those who wish to stop for a swim, or to go snorkeling, there are excellent sites at each of the three hotels along this section —.**Vista Bay Club**, **Sunset Beach**, and **Northolme**.

Beau Vallon

Beau Vallon is the main tourist beach, but controls on the quality and quantity of tourist development ensure the white sands are unpolluted and the beach uncrowded. It is pleasant to rest awhile and enjoy (or better still join in) the parasailing and other water-sports activities.

For diving enthusiasts, Beau Vallon is the headquarters of the **Seychelles Underwater Centre**. Situated on the corner of **Coral Strand Hotel**, Seychelles Underwater Centre offers a tremendous variety of dive sites; coral gardens, various granite boulder and cave dives (see "Exploring the Silent World Beneath the Waves", Part Three). Adventure dives to more distant sites such as **Shark Bank**, and the *Ennerdale* Wreck are also regular features.

If you simply want to relax and enjoy a bite to eat, you have also come to the right place. On the northern end of Beau Vallon beach is the **Baobab Pizzeria** and the **Beau Vallon Beach Pub**. Both serve snacks and main meals.

If you are more in the mood for a main meal away from the beach scene (but not too far) **La Perle Noir Restaurant** offers excellent cuisine; it is on the left shortly beyond the point where the road turns inland after the Seychelles Underwater Centre.

To Victoria

From Beau Vallon beach, follow the road

inland and turn right at the **Police Station**, continuing past **Beau Vallon Bay Hotel**, **Meridien**, **Fisherman's Cove**, and the **Le Corsaire Restaurant** (nouvelle cuisine).

A short distance beyond Le Corsaire are the workings of Seychelles' most famous treasure dig. Former Grenadier Guardsman Cruise-Wilkins put all his money, and a large part of his life, into the search for the fabulous treasure of the pirate le Vasseur, estimated to be worth £100 million back in the 1960s, when his search began.

The story has all the ingredients of a real pirate treasure story; codes, cryptograms, strange designs etched on the rocks, booby-trapped caves, and mysterious clues — even a pair of skeletons.

Sadly Cruise-Wilkins died without finding his treasure, but perhaps it is still there, waiting to be discovered by his sons, who have taken up the challenge (see "Pirates and Plunder", Part Three).

The road continues on to **La Scala Restaurant**, an excellent place for an evening out (it is essential to book in advance). The road ends just beyond there at **Auberge Club Des Seychelles**, and becomes a footpath.

This is the **Anse Major Nature Trail**, one of the few easy walks in Seychelles. If time permits, the two-kilometre (just over a mile) walk to **Anse Major** takes in picturesque cliff-top scenery before descending to a small sandy **cove**, which, if you are lucky, you may well have all to yourself.

From La Scala, turn around and drive back the same way, continuing on the same road to **Victoria**. Descending towards the capital, you pass **Marie-Antoinette Restaurant**, left, a beautiful example of a wooden colonial-style building. The proprietor, Mrs Fonseka, only serves authentic local cuisine. There is no choice and no menu. Instead, a variety of dishes, with — of course — the emphasis on fish, are served. The chilli sauce is a house speciality.

Sans Souci

About 400 metres (437 yards) beyond Marie-Antoinette Restaurant, turn right into **Bel Air Road**, immediately after the **wooden building** of **Vines Ltd.** To the left is the wall that surrounds Mahé's oldest **cemetery** where some of the first settlers are buried.

Among its interesting graves is that of the corsair, Jean François Hodoul, with the inscription *"Il fut Juste"*. The **Giant's Tomb** commemorates an early inhabitant who was more than 2.7 metres (almost nine feet) tall. According to legend he was poisoned because other settlers were afraid of his prodigious strength. He is said to haunt the cemetery — the most recent sighting was made by a tourist.

Top: Pure essence of wild vanilla.

Above: The flaming passion flower.

Opposite: Sandragon trees haunt the trail to Mahé's old hillside mission.

Overleaf: Glorious Intendance Bay, Mahé.

Above: Matronly tea picker at work on a Mahé plantation.

Another grave with an interesting inscription is that of a young British naval officer who died fighting a fire on board his ship.

Take care rounding the sharp hairpin bend, approximately another 400 metres (437 yards) along the road. Passing **Pension Bel Air** on your right, take the left turn into **Liberation Road**. After a short distance there is an excellent panoramic view of Victoria, including the **port**, **yacht basin**, **tuna fishing quay**, **Stadium** (Stade Populaire), and the main buildings of the capital.

It is fascinating to think that all the flat land you can see once belonged to the ocean. Successive land reclamation projects have extended the boundaries and greatly expanded the size of Victoria.

The tall trees in the foreground, smothered in greenery and the delicate blue flowers of the creeper, sky flower, make a pretty frame for photography.

Double back and turn left onto the **Sans Souci Road** (or continuation of Bel Air Road). The road climbs past several diplomatic residences, including that of the **American Embassy**, formerly the house to which Archbishop Makarios was exiled.

During his time in Seychelles, the Archbishop was noted for his eccentricities including his love for climbing — fully robed in black vestments — to the summits of the **Morne Seychellois** range, and sitting outside on the front lawn where he and fellow exiles would sing old Greek folk songs in the fading light of a Seychelles day.

Many Seychellois gathered in the valley to listen to the free concert. The house later passed to a British businessman, but the Archbishop remembered his place of exile with affection.

On one occasion, the businessman visited Cyprus and met the Archbishop. He asked him about the large collection of bottles he had found in the front garden of the Sans Souci house.

The Archbishop, with a smile, said that part of his agreement with the British Government over exile was that he received a generous supply of his favourite wines. "And now you know why we sang so well," he added with a twinkle in his eye.

The house, now called "1776", is a **national monument**, although private property.

A little way along the road is the **Forestry Station** of **Morne Seychellois National Park**. Take the narrow road immediately after the Forestry Station. On the right are some examples of **Wright's Gardenia**, which in the entire world only occurs in its natural state on **Aride Island** (see "Forests of Mist and Rain", Part Three).

After about 300 metres (330 yards), you come to a small **car park**, the starting point for the walk to the 699-metre-high (2,293-foot) summit of **Trois Frères**, the second-highest peak on Mahé, and the third-highest in all Seychelles. This pathway is an excellent introduction to the endemic flora including the insectivorous Seychelles pitcher plant, the beautiful Seychelles wild vanilla orchid, and a host of others.

You can either climb to the summit and return to the car park, or turn right shortly after leaving the summit onto a **pathway** to the **Le Niol Road**, at the northern edge of the national park.

Less adventurous souls can sit on the bonnets of their car, or the grassy verge, and admire one of the best views of the islands. It takes in twenty-two, more than half of all the granite islands and nearly one-fifth of all Seychelles' islands.

As you look from left to right, these are: **Aride** (on the horizon), tiny **Booby Island**, Praslin, **Cousin** and **Cousine** merging in the far north, only distinguishable on fine days. **La Digue** lies to the right of Praslin; the sisters — **Petite Soeur** and **Grande Soeur** — are visible through the gap between Praslin and La Digue, while **Marianne** is visible to the right of La Digue.

Frégate is seen on the horizon to the right, near the smaller islands of **Récife** (between Frégate and Mahé) and **Mamelles** (between Praslin and Mahé). In the foreground are the six islands of the **St. Anne Marine National Park**: **St. Anne**; **Round Island**; and **Moyenne** (blending into one island); **Cerf**; **Long** (visible just over the top of Cerf); and **Île Cachée**. **Beacon Island** (Île Seche) is also visible beyond the National Park.

To the right lying off Seychelles International Airport is **Anonyme** with **Rat Island** just beyond it. These only add up to twenty-one islands. Look around you — Mahé makes twenty-two.

Some plants around the car park are worth studying. Pluck a few pieces of the tall *citronelle* or lemon grass and rub it in your fingers; it gives off a pleasant lemon fragrance. A variety of this grass is the basis of the refreshing *citronelle* tea found on many Seychelles menus.

Touch the leaves of the **sensitive plant** in the shorter grass and see how fast the leaves close.

Framing the start of the Trois Frères walk are *kalis* trees on the left, *santol* on the right. *Kalis* yields one of the most popular decorative timbers in Seychelles, while *santol* bears orange-coloured fruits between mid-January to March, containing edible fleshy pulp.

Return along the same track and turn right onto the Sans Souci Road. You can enjoy another excellent view by taking the first turn left (about half a kilometre along the road) but this is not signposted and is easily missed. Park your car after a short distance and take the **steps** leading to the **viewing point** above **Rochon Dam**.

The trees to the left are *tangin* or ordeal plants which bear clusters of white flowers with a purplish centre. The poisonous sap from this plant was used for trial by ordeal — if you survived you were innocent, and if you were guilty, justice had been done (see "Forest of Rain and Mist", Part Three).

Turn around and continue along the Sans Souci Road. Near the highest point of the island is the house of the President, not visible from the road, marked by two **small cannons** at the entrance.

Another way-marked **path** that leads to the summit of 497-metre-high (1,630-foot) **Copolia** is signposted on the left-hand side of the road. This excellent walk enables you to see many endemic mountain plants.

After the President's house, the road descends a short distance towards the west coast to a point where a track leads off to the left marked by a green and yellow **signboard** announcing the **Salazie Tea Plantation**.

The dirt track soon deteriorates and it is easier to explore on foot than by car. Mahogany trees stand on both sides of the track. After about 150 metres (492 feet) the forest opens out on the tea plantation itself. It is possible to walk from here to **Fairview Estate** on **La Misère Road**, a fairly long (but relatively easy) walk.

The next point of interest is the **Mission Ruins**, signposted on the right-hand side of Sans Souci Road. Originally known as Venn's Town, it was established as a school for the children of the slaves liberated by the British Anti-Slavery patrol.

Raiding Arab dhows taking slaves up towards the Red Sea, this fleet tried to put an end to slave-trading on the East African coast. Africans freed south of the Equator were brought to Seychelles and the population soared.

At Venn's Town the children were given a basic education while the adults worked as labourers on the plantations below. The magnificent **avenue** of sandragon trees stands as a **monument** to their new-found freedom and the view of the west coast is remarkable.

On the Sans Souci Road you will see growing in the ditch, immediately to the right of the road, wild ginger and cardamom, and philodendron vines climbing the trees.

One more mountain path — the shortest of all, but in some ways the most dramatic — is marked on the right of the road, the **walk** to the **summit** of 667-metre-high (2,188-foot) **Morne Blanc**, where the cliff drops vertically some 250 metres (820 feet).

The next place of note along the main road is the **Seychelles Tea and Coffee Company**. Their **Tea Tavern** is a good place to stop for refreshment, before continuing down the mountain slopes, and to admire the most beautiful view of the west coast, including **Port Launay** and the islands of **Thérèse** and **Conception**.

Port Launay to Barbarons Beach

Arriving on the west coast road, turn right at **Port Glaud Police Station**. After about one kilometre (half a mile) you reach **Sundown Restaurant**, which serves very good Creole food.

A short distance beyond the restaurant is a **car park** and the departure point for the small **ferry** that carries passengers across to the tiny island of **L'Islette** which has another very good **restaurant** with the added bonus of a Robinson Crusoe-style atmosphere on one of the smallest of the granitic islands (See "Isles of Mahé").

Above: Takamaka trees shade the southern Mahé bay to which they give their name.

Opposite: Casuarina — among the most prolific of Mahé's trees.

Overleaf: Remains of a once flourishing coconut plantation. Until the 1980s copra was Seychelles' major export.

Above: For the art lover, a craft museum on Mahé.

It is only a short walk from the car park to a picturesque **waterfall** on the **L'Islette River**. Take the **path** immediately after the **church** on the right, keeping the **mangroves** on your left.

The path gradually narrows, but the sound of rushing water should point you in the right direction. The last section of the walk involves a scramble to the water's edge. The path goes through private land and you need permission to visit the fall.

Endemic plants, such as thief palm, adorn the riverside where the water cascades into a deep pool. If lucky, you may glimpse some other creatures unique to the islands, including several species of prawns (of the genus *Palaemon*) which have colonised the streams from the sea. One, *Macrobrachium*, reaches a length of twenty centimetres (eight inches).

Shrimps of the genus *Caradina*, an ancient race, occur alongside freshwater crabs, one species of which is particularly fascinating. *Dekenia allaudi* belongs to a group which only occurs in East Africa, another echo of that ancient link with Gondwanaland.

From L'Islette car park it is possible to drive another three kilometres (just under

two miles) along a narrow road to the shores of **Port Launay Marine National Park**, an enclosed sandy cove, with a fringing reef. The lagoon reaches a depth of twenty-five metres (80 feet).

Covering an area of one and a half square kilometres (just over half a square mile), the main features of this attractive park are its predominantly rocky shoreline interspersed with sandy beaches and mangrove forests against the steep, forested lower slopes of Morne Seychellois.

The deeper reefs fringing the rocky headlands are in very good condition with soft coral anchored on colonies of dead *Porites*. Green-backed herons haunt the mangrove forests.

Just by the park's north-west boundary, at **Anse Soullac**, the road reaches the **gates** of the **Baie Ternay National Youth Service Camp**. Beyond this, the extreme western tip of Mahé forms a sheltered bay and the boundary of **Baie Ternay Marine National Park**. Unfortunately you can only visit the park easily from the seaward side as the camp puts the shore off limits.

The northernmost part of the park, which

Above: Guest view of Île Thérèse, Sheraton Hotel's own resort island and beach.

lies outside the continuous fringing reef at the head of the bay, reaches depths of thirty-seven metres (120 feet).

Covering an area of eighty hectares (200 acres), the park's main feature is the reef which, grooved and cut by many surge channels, offers refuge to large numbers of reef fish.

Its **beach** is a breeding ground for the hawksbill turtle and the reef fish are prolific. Among the birds found on its shores are green-backed heron and some waders.

Since it is now impossible to approach from the land side, the only approach — easily accessible — is by sea from Beau Vallon. It is popular for swimming and snorkeling and glass bottom boats are available for hire.

From Port Glaud the coast road continues southward and, shortly after passing the Sans Souci turning, there is a picturesque view of **Petite Île**, not really an island as it is joined to the mainland by a jumble of granite rocks.

Immediately behind Petite Île is the superb **Seychelles Sheraton** where a spit of granite boulders has produced a sheltered sandy cove in which to enjoy safe swimming

all year. Excellent **restaurants** serve a variety of special dishes from Seychelles and around the world.

Climb the **hill** from the Sheraton and descend towards **Grande Anse** where a visit to **Equator Hotel**, another excellent hotel in a superb location, is well worthwhile.

Grande Anse itself is a huge sweep of white coral sand. Turn off the main road by **Grande Anse School**. Some are lucky enough to enjoy this wide beach all by themselves. At other times you may have to share it with perhaps half a dozen others.

But you should only swim there if the sea is really calm. There is a powerful undertow, and during the south-east monsoon in particular, when the sea builds up, huge waves pummel the beach creating a dangerous offshore current in places.

With a little common sense you should avoid being caught up in such a current. However, should the worst happen don't fight it. The offshore current runs in narrow channels and you should swim parallel to the shore to escape it. Drowning occurs when swimmers try to swim against the current — impossible — and soon become exhausted.

Above: Mahé's tiny Muslim population offers prayers at Victoria's Sheikh Mohamed bin Khalifa Mosque.

But in moderate conditions a swim there can be extremely stimulating.

The mountain that towers above Grande Anse is the stronghold of the **jellyfish tree**, one of the rarest in the world. To reach the site where the plants grow, you will need a guide as the path is hard to find and rarely used.

When you return to the main road continue southward. At this point both sides are occupied by many varieties of tropical fruits growing in experimental plots cultivated by the **Ministry of Agriculture Research Station**.

La Misère

At the south end of Grande Anse a **timber yard** stands on the left and the forest of aerials of the **BBC World Service Relay Station** on the right. There is also the turning into **La Misère Road**.

A short detour leads straight on to **Meridien Barbarons Beach Hotel**, on the right, and just beyond that, the **SMB orchid farm** on the left. Otherwise, turn left into La Misère Road.

La Misère is a shorter mountain pass than Sans Souci, but the views are equally good

and some of the bends equally challenging. About three-quarters of the way to the **summit** is the residential area of the **United States Tracking Station**, while immediately beyond the summit is the road leading to the two "golfballs" (as they are known locally) of the Tracking Station itself.

Each "golf ball" contains a satellite dish. It is enclosed in the sphere to maintain the air conditioning system that protects the sophisticated equipment which traces satellites and space shuttles.

One dish collects the data and sends it across to the other, which relays the information back into space to a geostationary satellite above the Atlantic. In turn this beams the data down to Washington. Finally, Washington transmits the information to a second geostationary satellite then back to earth to NASA headquarters at Cape Canaveral. In this way, Seychelles, one of the world's youngest and smallest nations, plays a role in mankind's great venture in space.

Halfway from the Tracking Station to the east coast is the **viewing point** of La Misère, marked by a lay-by on the right-hand side of the road. From there you can also see a great many of the granitic islands, and some of Mahé, from the most recently reclaimed land at Port Victoria to **Petit Paris** (a little to the north of the airport).

Between the **viewing point** and the east coast you will pass two good places for a meal. First is **La Moutia**, followed by **Auberge Louis XVII Guest House**, both to the right of the road.

East Coast to Intendance

On reaching the small roundabout at the end of the La Misère Road, turn right. After about one kilometre you reach, in quick succession, the **Seypot Factory Shop**, right, and the **Art Gallery** of Gerard Devoud, left.

The Seypot Factory cooperative produces a wide range of ceramics from local materials. Gerard Devoud, a Frenchman, vividly portrays Seychellois images with an emphasis on the luxuriant vegetation and typical Seychelles scenes (See "Arts and Crafts: A Heritage in the Making", Part Three).

A short distance beyond the art gallery lies the hulk of the old schooner *Isle of Farquhar,* which plied the outer islands, but now lies cut off from the sea by the land reclamation beyond its final resting place.

Two hundred metres (220 yards) further on, at the right, is one of the oldest surviving houses in Seychelles, the ex-**Chateau de Mamelles**, built in 1804. Once the home of the corsair Jean François Hodoul, it is now a **national monument**, and private property. Nearby, hidden from view, is the house of **La Rosarie**, where the King of Prempeh was once exiled.

If you continue towards the airport, about two kilometres (just over a mile) before you reach it stands the attractive white **Cascade Church**, another **national monument**.

Immediately south of the airport is the **Katiolo discotheque**, which also serves meals during the daytime. And after another one and a half kilometres (one mile) you come to the **Reef Hotel** and the only **golf course** for a radius of 1,600 kilometres (1,000 miles), albeit nine holes only (two more were planned in 1990 — an eighteen-hole course on Mahé, and a nine-hole course on Praslin), but with a plethora of palm trees adding to its charm and character.

The next mountain **pass** lies one kilometre (just over half a mile) south of the Reef Hotel. The stylish colonial building on the corner before this turning is **Maison St. Joseph**, now the headquarters of the **Kreol Institute**, and one of the most evocative buildings on Mahé.

Do not take this turn, but continue south along the east coast. After two kilometres (just over a mile) you reach the model boat centre, **La Marine,** where excellent scale models of old sailing vessels are produced. The old colonial building itself is a **national monument**.

Also worth noticing is the Chinese restaurant, **Ty Foo**, just before La Marine, which serves excellent Seychellois-style Chinese food.

As you continue south towards **Pointe au Sel**, the road undulates slowly to **Anse Royale**. The area close to **Île Souris** is excellent for both swimming and snorkeling but a fairly strong current runs parallel to the beach between the shore and the island. It is not dangerous, however, and it may be an interesting way to snorkel with the minimum of effort.

South of Anse Royale is a series of small beautiful bays: **Anse Balière**, **Anse Bougainville**, **Anse Parnel**, and **Anse Forbans** (Pirate Bay). At **Anse Marie-Louise** the road curves inland for about one kilometre (half a mile) to **Quatre Bornes** village, where you turn left onto the cement road opposite the Police Station (**Grande Police Road**).

After another kilometre (half a mile) bear right to **Anse Intendance**, one of the most beautiful bays in Seychelles although swimming is often dangerous, especially during the south-east monsoon.

It is possible to continue along the Grande Police Road beyond Intendance to **Anse Cachée** and **Anse Corail**, but not **Police Bay**, in the extreme south, which has been closed for military purposes.

South-west Mahé

Return to Quatre Bornes and turn left onto the **Quatre Bornes Road** to **Takamaka**, another beautiful bay where swimming is sometimes dangerous. In the south corner of the bay is an attractive Creole restaurant, **Chez Batista**.

From there the road swings north around Pointe Maravi to Baie Lazare, thought for a

long time to be the bay where Lazare Picault, leader of the first two French expeditions to Seychelles, landed.

He was sent by Mahé de Labourdonnais, then governor of Mauritius, to explore the islands and report on their potential to the French. The first expedition visited Mahé in 1742.

The largest hotel in Seychelles, the **Plantation Club**, stands on the northern edge of the bay.

After leaving Baie Lazare, past the attractive **church** on the right, the next turning is **Anse Soleil Road**, ideal for testing the strength of your car's suspension. Assuming you do not wish to discover how great an understatement the "uneven surface" signpost is, continue to **Anse aux Poules Bleus** and the home and gallery of Michael Adams, perhaps the most famous artist in Seychelles.

Anse à la Mouche, the next bay along the coast, is generally one of the calmest in Seychelles and its sheltered location makes it ideal for swimming, although you may need to walk out a considerable distance at low tide before the gently sloping sand gives enough depth.

The water is usually warmer than elsewhere. When the sea is calm and the skies clear, lounging in the shallows is like taking a hot bath.

There are several good **restaurants** in this area, notably the **Islander Restaurant** on the northern edge of Anse à la Mouche.

About three kilometres (two miles) north, the next major bay — **Anse Boileau** — is the true site of the landing by Lazare Picault's expedition.

Just beyond the **Montagne Posée Road** an excellent restaurant specialises in seafood, **Chez Plume**. If you are not dining, take the Montagne Posée Road to cross the island for the final time.

Near the summit, at **Bon Espoir**, is the Cable and Wireless **satellite dish** for international communications. It is also the centre for radio communications with ships and the outer islands of Seychelles.

If you plan a private trip to Aride, for example, you should contact Bon Espoir on 76733 to check arrangements and weather conditions. The excellent staff are always willing to help and pass on messages.

Bon Espoir is also the start of the **nature trail** to **La Reserve** and **Brulée**, Mahé's answer to the **Vallée de Mai** on Praslin. It is the best area of palm forest on Mahé with five of the six endemic palms present (all except the *coco de mer*, of course). It also includes excellent views of the west coast.

If you continue towards the east coast, you turn left on the coast road to Victoria.

Opposite: Palm trees frame one of Mahé's many Catholic churches reflecting the serenity of the islands.

Above: Fresh flowers decorate a Mahé religious grotto open to the Seychelles' sunlight.

Overleaf: Sundown frames traditional Seychelles' fishing boat, glowing tribute to one more memorable day.

Above: Island woman and her cow enjoy the shade on Mahé's North East Point.

Morne Seychellois National Park: Mist and Sunlight

The magic of the mountain mist forest is captured perfectly in the highlands of Mahé. There are pockets of original mountain forest on **Silhouette**, but these are extremely difficult to reach.

The **Vallée de Mai** on **Praslin** is green, but most hills on the island are totally denuded of mountain trees because of fire. Other islands do not reach that altitude where land merges with cloud, and where mist shrouds granitic cliffs and vegetation with a blanket of moisture.

When the sun shines on the shores of Mahé, a cloak of mist may still be lying on the summit of the island. As the tourists and islanders go about their daily activities, another world exists above their heads.

This is a world where ancient reptiles and amphibians move through the under-growth, where some of the world's rarest plants grow, and orchids cling to granite faces, and where unique birds fly through a canopy of trees found nowhere else on earth.

This other world is much the same now as it was before the peace of the world below was disturbed by the arrival of man. Luckily, although shaken, this strange upper world was not completely destroyed, as it was in so many other places.

Covering more than thirty square kilometres (11 square miles) the **Morne Seychellois National Park** occupies most of the west and central massif of Mahé and rises from sea level to 905 metres (2,969 feet).

Although largely invaded by exotics — many of them introduced — especially albizia, cinnamon, and *santol*, the park contains some fine areas of endemic trees.

The only visitor facilities are the **Mission viewing point** and well-marked **footpaths** to **Morne Blanc**, **Copolia**, and **Trois Frères**, all commencing from signboards at the side of the **Sans Souci Road**.

The park, in fact, protects a wealth of flora and fauna, much of which can be seen by driving over the Sans Souci Road and simply admiring the scenery. Still more can be seen, and a taste of the atmosphere of the

Above: Seychelles Sheraton with its own beach overlooking its own island.

rainforest savoured, by walking in the foothills of **Morne Seychellois**.

The Vegetation

The high slopes of Mahé did not escape the devastation wrought on the lowland forest by the arrival of man, with his need for timber to build ships.

However, steep mountain ridges and a climate that allows the rich proliferation of nature, have meant that some of the former majesty was saved. Few, if any, species have been lost. Nature has licked its wounds and gone about its business of restoring the natural order.

Today man is interfering again, this time with the wisdom of hindsight. The youth of Seychelles are being educated to love and respect their heritage.

Youth League members spend time in the natural classroom of Morne Seychellois National Park where they learn something of its riches and undertake projects to weed out the invading exotics, and protect the natural vegetation.

Around seventy-five species of plant are unique to the granitic islands, all but a handful

to be found within the park. They include five of the six palms (all except the *coco de mer*), all four screwpines, and some of the rarest trees and plants on earth.

One of these is the *bwa-d-fer (Vateria seychellarum)*, which was common when man first arrived. Growing tall and straight, it was ideal timber for shipbuilding.

One tree can be seen close to the **tea company factory**, amidst the tea — surrounded by a barbed wire fence to protect this endangered species. Most trees appear to have regenerated from cut stumps.

Bwa-d-fer has never been found on any other island and the Morne Seychellois National Park is vital to the species' survival, as it may well contain the entire world population of this rare tree.

Another tree is so unique it has its own genus, and so rare that until very recently it was thought to be confined to one hilltop within the park. This is the jellyfish tree, *Medusagyne oppositifolia*, or *bwa mediz*.

At one time it was feared that only six trees remained but a thorough search of the area revealed there could be as many as fifty. Its restricted range and low numbers makes

Above: Wheel of fortune in a Mahé casino.
Opposite: Windsurfing with best friend.

this curious plant one of the rarest on earth.

Perhaps the most beautiful of all the unique plants is the vanilla orchid, *Vanilla phalaenopsis*, or *Lovannir Maron*, seen at many points in the park, even by the roadside.

Look out for it as you descend from the tea company offices to **Port Glaud**. It only flowers after heavy rain, however, so you often only see the tangle of green, leafless stems entwined in small bushes.

Introduced species pose major threats to the endemic plants of the park. The rich valleys have been almost totally conquered by the albizia, while cinnamon is extremely common in the forests.

It is a feature of areas where cinnamon is dominant that the immediate undergrowth is virtually nonexistent. Chemicals in the leaves of cinnamon kill off competing plants.

There is no finer drive than the Sans Souci Road, but to really explore the mist forest, you must walk. A number of well-marked paths start from the roadside and lead up to **Copolia** 497 metres (1,631 feet), **Morne Blanc** 667 metres (2,188 feet), and **Trois Frères** 699 metres (2,293 feet). All these walks lead you to many more of the special plants — and spectacular views of Mahé.

You should also see some of the unique birds of Seychelles. It will be impossible to miss the Seychelles bulbul, and with luck, the Seychelles kestrel, sunbird, cave swiftlet, and blue pigeon will also be sighted. A little more luck will be needed to find the Seychelles white-eye and bare-legged scops owl.

However, there is always something about the eerie atmosphere of these high hills which makes you feel that almost *anything* could turn up, and that you could even stumble on the green parakeet, now thought to be extinct. It would not be the first "extinct" species of Seychelles to have been rediscovered in these remote mountains.

To reach the summit of Morne Seychellois, 905 metres (2,969 feet) high, is difficult as the path is badly marked and it is easy to get lost. However, with a guide, it is not too arduous for a reasonably fit person who does not mind getting a little muddy.

An excellent guide, Basil Beaudouin, conducts escorted walks in the hills, with trans-

Above: Sun-dappled forest glade in the Mahé mountains.

port, packed lunch, water, and first-aid (should it be needed) included in the cost. Well worth it to see some corners of the island virtually untouched by man and still rarely visited.

The best walk to see the mist forest is **Congo Rouz**. The route starts close to the Mission Viewpoint, passes through gnarled northea and *bwa rouz* trees dripping with damp moss and emerges on a ridge cloaked in tens of thousands of pitcher plants.

The path then descends to **Le Niol**, emerging close to the reservoir. However, this is another walk which *should not* be attempted without a guide.

For the lucky few who see the Congo Rouz, there is a glimpse of Seychelles as it used to be. The silence there is rarely broken except by the passing bulbuls, or the piping of frogs.

There are **tree ferns**, various species of *coco marron*, orchids, and unique trees. There are tiger chameleons, stick insects, leaf insects, mantids, nearly all the endemic amphibians, and an atmosphere quite unlike anywhere else in Seychelles.

Top: Mahé pitcher plant sets a lethal trap for insects.

Above: Endemic to the coast, Balfour's screwpine produces fruits that reach up to 25 centimetres in length.

Overleaf: Hobie Cat off Mahé at sundown.

Victoria: Home Town Capital

Victoria is one of the smallest capitals in the world, and the only town in Seychelles. It has always stood on its present site, overlooking a wonderful natural harbour, protected by the inner islands of **St. Anne** and **Île au Cerf**. In recent years, due to reclamation projects, it has expanded greatly as the town creeps seaward.

The first recorded visit to Victoria was made in 1609 by Captain Sharpeigh aboard an East Indiaman.

Lazare Picault anchored in the sheltered bay during his second expedition to explore the islands in 1744, and when Nicholas Morphey went to claim the islands for France in 1756, naturally he too used the same, excellent anchorage.

The **Possession Stone** was therefore laid in this area, which later also boasted the first Government House, built by Lieutenant de Romainville's small detachment of soldiers in the early 1770s.

In those days, the town was called L'Établissement de Roi. It was renamed Victoria, in honour of the British queen, in 1841. It is known now to most as simply "town", or even, affectionately, *toria*.

In those early days, the coast was thickly belted with mangrove swamp in which crocodiles flourished — difficult to imagine when you drive down towards Victoria today and see the town spread out before you, its patchwork of rusting roofs nestling against the green hillside.

With their quirky foundations and lop-sided charm, the quaint houses of the old town stand as contrast to the long straight roads and multi-storey buildings of new Victoria.

Whichever way you reach the town, from whatever direction, the **Clock Tower** is probably the best place to begin a tour of Victoria. Anyone will direct you there. Indeed, if a Seychellois wants to describe someone as a real idiot he will say, "he has not seen the 'orlage'".

If you drive into town yourself and need to park, find your way onto **Quincy Street** and the one-way system which skirts the town. Follow the road around noting first of all, at the left, the magnificent **Roman Catholic Priest's Residence** (a **national monument**), and the **Cathedral of the Immaculate Conception**, built in 1900.

On Sunday mornings women and children gather there in their finest clothes for mass. Often the cathedral is so full that worshippers cluster in the doorway to hear the service.

The turn right at the junction just after the cathedral leads along **Albert Street,** which is usually busy — parked cars, reversing lorries, and daydreamer pedestrians are among the hazards you may encounter.

Drive on past the **pedestrian crossing** and at the **Clock Tower** you can either go up **State House Avenue** (right at the roundabout) or straight on past the **Victoria Service Station**, just beyond which there is a left turn into the **Stadium Car Park**.

There are **car parks** on both the left and right at the top of State House Avenue but naturally, being so close to the centre, these tend to fill up quickly. The **car park** by the **National Library** is used by people "just popping in" to shops and offices who sometimes block other cars.

Should this area prove difficult, simply return down State House Avenue, around the roundabout to the Stadium Car Park, which is extremely large. There is always room during the day, and it is only a short walk back to the Clock Tower. All these car parks are free, with no time restrictions. If you can park in the shade, so much the better.

The Victoria Clock Tower does not chime twice, or indeed even once. It was meant to chime, in fact, but when the precious parts arrived from London, after many delays, the pendulum was dropped over the side of the ship during unloading and lost.

The engineer in charge of public works made a crude substitute, but because it was not exactly right, the clock could no longer chime.

The clock which does chime twice — just before the hour and on the hour — is in the **clock tower** of the Roman Catholic cathedral, built in 1898. This so fascinated author Alec Waugh that he wrote a book called *Where the Clock Chimes Twice*, which is no doubt why

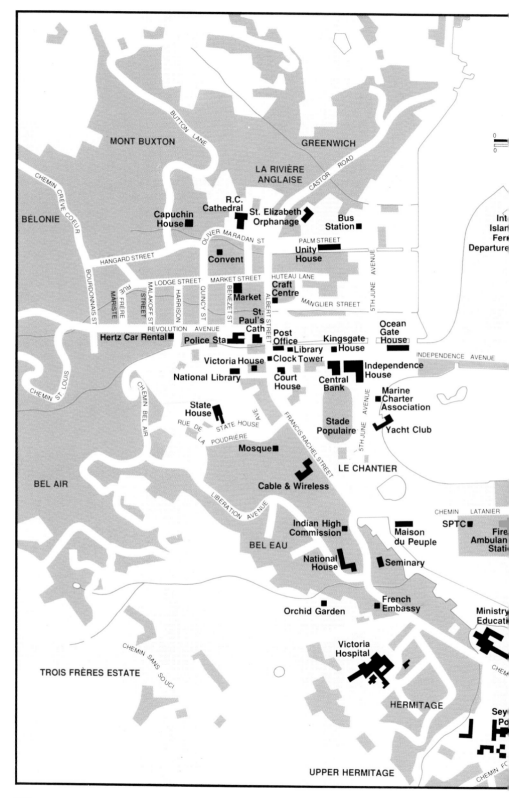

MONT BUXTON

GREENWICH

LA RIVIÈRE
ANGLAISE

BÉLONIE

R.C.
Cathedral

Capuchin
House

St. Elizabeth
Orphanage

Bus
Station

Int
Islan
Fer
Departure

OLIVER MARADAN ST

PALM STREET

Unity
House

Convent

HANGARD STREET

5TH JUNE AVENUE

CHEMIN CREVE COEUR

BUTTON LANE

CASTOR ROAD

LODGE STREET

MARKET STREET

HUTEAU LANE

Craft
Centre

BOURDONNAIS ST

RUE FRERE MARISTE

MALAKOFF ST

HARRISON STREET

QUINCY ST

BENEZET ST

Market

MANGLIER STREET

St.
Paul's
Cath

ALBERT STREET

REVOLUTION AVENUE

Post
Office

Kingsgate
House

Ocean
Gate
House

Hertz Car Rental

Police Sta

Library

INDEPENDENCE AVENUE

Victoria House

Clock Tower

National Library

Court
House

Central
Bank

Independence
House

CHEMIN ST LOUIS

CHEMIN BEL AIR

State
House

RUE DE LA POUDRIÈRE

STATE HOUSE AVE

FRANCIS RACHEL STREET

Stade
Populaire

5TH JUNE AVENUE

Marine
Charter
Association

Yacht Club

Mosque

LE CHANTIER

BEL AIR

Cable & Wireless

LIBERATION AVENUE

CHEMIN LATANIER

SPTC

Fire
Ambulan
Stati

Indian High
Commission

Maison
du Peuple

BEL EAU

National
House

Seminary

CHEMIN SANS SOUCI

Orchid Garden

French
Embassy

Ministry
Educati

TROIS FRÈRES ESTATE

Victoria
Hospital

CHEM

HERMITAGE

Sey
Po

UPPER HERMITAGE

CHEMIN FC

0
0

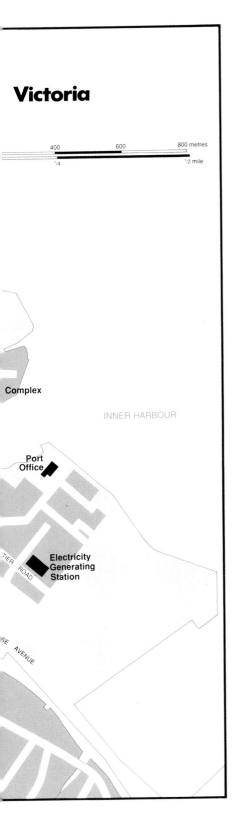

Victoria

400   600   800 metres

1/4   1/2 mile

Complex

INNER HARBOUR

Port
Office

Electricity
Generating
Station

TIER ROAD

SE AVENUE

this peculiarity has become so well known.

The Clock Tower itself is a replica of one which stands on London's Vauxhall Bridge Road, near Victoria Station. Paid for by public subscription, it was erected in 1903 as a tribute to Queen Victoria and to celebrate Seychelles' new status as a separate Crown Colony from Mauritius. It was also the wish of the governor of that time to make the town feel more "British" (See "The Coral and The Granite", Part One). Originally it was black in colour, not silver.

Along **Francis Rachel Street** (Francis Rachel died during the 1977 coup) one of the largest stores in Victoria, **Temooljee**, can be found along the right with the **shopping arcade** beside it.

The arcade has several boutiques and shops which sell tourist souvenirs. Some of the longest-established of Seychelles Indian shops are on the right, such as **Adam Moosa** and **Chaka Brothers**, owned by families who have lived on the island for generations.

Long ago this area contained one of Seychelles most famous hotels, run by a woman known, like the hotel, as "La Princess". Her establishment was more popular than respectable, particularly with the menfolk.

La Poudrière Lane runs between the shops and, as the name suggests, was the site of the colony's first ammunition store. The Possession Stone was probably first laid there, too, but there are doubts as to its exact location because at one point the stone was actually taken out of Seychelles.

It was well on its way to France when the authorities discovered the loss and demanded its return. It was replaced, but in a different location, and it is now safely housed in the **National Museum**.

On the left is the elegant **Law Courts** building where the impromptu **stalls** of the local craftsmen line the walls around the building. Just beyond these is the **bust** of **Pierre Poivre**, erected by the Seychelles Society in 1972 to remind Seychellois of their debt to this botanist-cum-statesman, governor of Mauritius, who had the idea of introducing spices to Seychelles in the early days of the colony. Cinnamon became a very important cash crop for the islands.

Close by is **Victoria Service Station**, by far the busiest on the island, and opposite is

Opposite left: Colourful customers at a street market in Victoria.

Opposite: Tropical fruits and vegetables for sale at Victoria's Selwyn Market.

Above: Sunday morning churchgoer on Mahé.

Opposite: Early 20th-century shop has survived for decades in Mahé's capital.

the restored building which houses the **SPUP Museum**. This was the headquarters of the Seychelles People's United Party (now the ruling party of Seychelles, the Seychelles People's Progressive Front), during the coup in 1977, and contains memorabilia relating the history of the party.

After the petrol station walk along the **Fiennes Esplanade**, once the Seychelles equivalent of the seaside "promenade", under shady trees.

Where now you see the **Stade Populaire** and its car park, sea once ebbed and flowed. The largest stadium in the country, it has hosted many varied events: football matches, Liberation Day parades, school sports days, music concerts, and a mass celebrated by Pope John Paul during his 1986 visit. Beyond the stadium is the site of the proposed new **library** and **archives building** which is being paid for by public subscription.

Across the road stands the striking, white **Cable and Wireless** building and, just behind it, a splendid old-style edifice (now a **national monument) Kenwyn House**, the residence of the Cable and Wireless manager.

The next roundabout is **Le Chantier**. As the French name suggests, this was once the boat-building and woodworking centre of Victoria. The monument in the centre of the roundabout, which portrays sailfish, symbolises unity. The fountains are floodlit at night. The monument was inaugurated in June 1989. The large trees on the left are sandragon, so named because of their crimson-red sap.

The road ahead leads on to the **Botanical Gardens** and the **airport**, along the old east coast road. The new road, **Bois de Rose Avenue** leading off to the south-east, is built on reclaimed land and shadows the old coast road.

You may see cattle egrets roosting in the trees like white paper bags. The local name for these birds is Madame Paton, though no one knows why — perhaps in memory of some former resident.

Latanier Road leads down to the **New Port**. The striking building on the corner, faced in red Praslin granite, is the **Maison du Peuple**, seat of Seychelles government, for which the foundations were laid in 1979.

If you turn down **5th June Avenue**

105

Opposite: Catholic priest's residence, Victoria — another cherished national monument.

Above: Praying before a statue of the Virgin Mary at Victoria.

(named in celebration of Liberation Day [5th June, 1977]), you pass pleasant **gardens**, left, and a large **children's playground**, which boasts many amenities, including a **boating lake**. It was completed in June 1989.

Also on the right is the entrance to the **Seychelles Yacht Club** and the **Yacht Basin**, with tiny **Hodoul Island** in the centre. On the left is the **Zomn Lib** monument which commemorates Liberation Day.

The next roundabout also has a **monument** in the centre. Officially called the **Bicentennial Monument**, it is known to everyone as **Twa Zwazo** and symbolizes the three elements of Seychellois ancestry: Europe, Africa, and Asia.

It was erected to celebrate 200 years of settlement on the islands. The road to the left leads down to the **Old Pier**, the **Fishing Port**, and **Schooner Quay**. The road ahead (a continuation of 5th June Avenue) leads along the coast towards **Anse Étoile**.

Turn left, however, passing **Independence House** on the corner. It accommodates many government offices and there is a **snack bar** in the cool shade beneath the building.

Independence Avenue lies ahead. To the left and right are shops, boutiques, craft shops, and others. **Studio Oceana,** the first shop in **Kingsgate House** on the left, sells tie-dyed beach and evening wear, batiks, carvings, and a wide range of T-shirts for all ages.

In the same block you can have photographs developed and printed within an hour at **Kim Koon**. On the left is **L'Amiral** patisserie and restaurant. **Photo Eden,** in the next block, also does sixty-minute photoprocessing and sells souvenirs and postcards as well as sports, diving, and camera equipment.

Beyond, left, is **Pirates Arms,** which used to be a hotel but is now a popular restaurant, cafe, and meeting place. There is also a small arcade with gift shops.

It looks out across the road at **Freedom Square**, formed during the 1862 avalanche from the mud and rubble which slid down onto the town from the hills of **St. Louis**. Seventy-five people died in the disaster.

The "square" — in fact a grassy area used for various sports — was originally named after General Gordon (he died later in Khartoum) who visited the island to report on the feasibility of defending them.

It was renamed **Freedom Square** because

early political rallies were held there. Beyond Freedom Square another grassy area was known as **Coronation Field**. The cost of this reclamation was met by the Post Office from the proceeds of the sale of the first King George VI issue of three stamps, which speculators bought in large numbers in the hope of making a swift profit (see "Collected All Over The World", Part Three).

Back on Independence Avenue, the **National Museum** is on the right, and the Post Office is just beyond, by the Clock Tower.

After Pirates Arms you will see **Barclays Bank**, then the **taxi rank**, left, in front of the **Boutique des Artisans** (Victoria's largest craft shop), and once again, the craft stalls.

The Clock Tower really is the hub of Victoria. If you now walk past the **Post Office**, over the **St. Louis River**, along **Albert Street** (named after Queen Victoria's consort), on the left you will pass the **main taxi rank**, shaded by flame trees.

This was always a spot where people gathered for a gossip and in the days before the motor age where they hired rickshaws. There is a **public toilet** and a new craft centre is being built next door.

Albert Street is usually bustling. On the right is Victoria's largest **supermarket, SMB** and, left, some of the town's older shops, including **Sham Peng Tong**'s two emporiums, where you never know what you might find.

Jivan Imports, on the left at the corner of Albert Street and **Market Street,** is as much an institution as a shop, and its proprietor, Kantilal Jivan Shah, one of Seychelles' most famous celebrities. He was made an MBE in the Queen of Britain's 1990 Birthday Honours. The branch of Barclays Bank across the road opens in the afternoons for foreign exchange only.

As you wander up busy Market Street, you will find yourself in old Victoria so watch out for deep storm drains and uneven pavement. If you have not seen the **Cathedral of the Immaculate Conception**, take the first turn left which brings you out on **Oliver Maradan Street** across from the cathedral, otherwise, keep straight on along Market Street. By the doorway of Kim Koon you may see old men selling local tobacco out of large tin boxes.

Opposite is the **Sir Selwyn Clarke Market**

Above: Patina-covered cannons guard the entrance of Seychelles' National Museum on Victoria's Independence Avenue.

Above: Les Mammelles, former home of the corsair Jean François Hodoul is now a national monument.

which you enter under the archway. The fish stalls, to the left, are always interesting. The stalls on the right sell some curious objects — coconut stools, mortar and pestles, spices, vanilla pods, bottles of locally-made vanilla essence, whisky bottles full of coconut milk, and smaller jars jammed full of fiery local chutney or pickled chillis.

Most of the vegetable stalls are in the centre. Deeper inside you pass several craft stalls and at the far end of the market are the meat stalls, patrolled by watchful cattle egrets.

Take the exit at the top right end of the market into **Benezet Street**, more of an alley-way than a street. The T-junction leads onto **Revolution Avenue**.

One of Victoria's oldest buildings, **Shipping House**, is on the left opposite the **Central Police Station**. To the right is **Mason's Travel**, to your left, **Kenya Airways**, and **Bunson Travel**.

Turn left into Revolution Avenue. Just beyond the Police Station is Victoria's Anglican cathedral, **St. Paul's**, built in 1857. Between the two buildings a **walled alleyway** beckons. Before entering it, look back across

the road and you can see Seychelles' largest cinema, the **Olian**, now disused. The only working cinema left in Victoria is Deepam's in Albert Street.

Follow the alley down beside the police station and over the **bridge** (again crossing the St. Louis River which teems with fish), an area used as a meeting place and unofficial car wash.

Walk past the State House car park to State House Avenue. To the right you will see the entrance to **State House** (closed to the public unless you have special permission to visit the grounds where several important figures from Seychelles history, including de Quincy, are buried).

Across the road is the attractive **old building** which houses the **National Library** at present. It was built with funds from the Carnegie Trust in 1907.

Victoria House, on the right-hand side of the road, houses a tour operator, **Travel Services (Seychelles)**, and the **USA** and **British diplomatic missions**.

The turn left into State House Avenue will bring you back to the Clock Tower.

Above: Victoria's colourful fishing port.
Opposite: Boats ring Hodoul Island in Victoria's bustling harbour.

Botanical gardens

To visit the **Botanical Gardens**, carry straight on at the Le Chantier roundabout along the Mont Fleuri Road. The turning, the first after Liberation Road, is on the left, and the car park is immediately left.

Small boys may offer to show you "the plant that catches flies" — not the **real** insectivorous pitcher plant, but a tour with them might be fun anyway if you take their "expert" information with a liberal pinch of salt.

The gardens, which cover about six hectares (fifteen acres), are pleasantly mature, having been laid out in 1901 by Rivaltz Dupont. Sadly few trees or shrubs are labelled, partly due to the ravages of vandals. However, it is planned to rehabilitate the gardens and hopefully specimens will be carefully labelled.

The **Sapin Restaurant and Snack Bar**, at the far right of the gardens, is in a beautiful spot beneath several towering Norfolk Island and Cook Island Pines. It is a popular lunch spot for people who work in Victoria, so either avoid the twelve to one spot, or arrive early if you want a meal at midday. At other times it is usually quiet as long as the fruit bats are not roosting in the large trees behind. The restaurant is closed on Sundays.

The **toilets** are located on the left, halfway up the main driveway. Note the interesting "Ladies" and "Gentlemen" signs on the doors.

It is difficult to identify many plant species without a guide, but some are notable. Flanking the driveway are several species of palm, including endemic lataniers and *coco de mer*.

On the right, in front of the building halfway up the drive, are several squat little palms. These are fully grown **Round Island bottle palms**, endemic to Round Island, Mauritius. Just beyond these, left, is the **Giant Land Tortoise Pen** with a *coco de mer* just in front of it.

A tree you will certainly notice if it is in fruit is the **elephant apple**, on the lawns to the right, a little further up the hill. The tree's large, hard, green, round fruits have a slightly rubbery smell.

Before you reach this, another tree you

Above: Inter-island launch powers through the sea off St. Anne Island in the Marine National Park.

cannot fail to spot when in flower is the **octopus tree,** which has a striking, large inflorescence that looks like the tentacles of an octopus.

Looking out over the lawns, left, is a disused **aviary** and some charming freshwater **pools** with pretty water lilies and the large-leaved taros, growing ankle deep in water.

In the area to the left of these you may find another strange seed with a long stalk, topped by a rounded ball of anthers; these have fallen from the drumstick tree — the reason for the name is obvious once you see these seeds.

The striking palms with a red collar just beneath the leaves are **sealing wax palms.** In the hollow to the right, look out for several species of **gingers** and **heliconias.**

If you cross the lawn and take the path beyond the pools you will see the Sapin restaurant. To the right of this there are **banyan trees** with their tangled roots forming natural steps and their aerial roots growing down, giving a very jungly feel to the area.

If you wander around through the trees in this vicinity you will probably notice the **cannonball tree** — an oddity that strikes almost every visitor, no matter what season of the year. It is the small boys' "plant that catches flies". It does not, in fact, but if you see the strange, rose-red, thick, waxy-petalled flowers you will understand why it could be mistaken for an insectivorous plant.

The flower looks like a clam, jaws ready to close on an unsuspecting insect. If you miss the flowers you will probably see the fruit. These are large, perfectly rounded, and grow on stalks which sprout, rather surprisingly, directly from the trunk of the tree, which takes its name from the shape of the fruit.

Returning downhill, either through the trees or along the Tarmac path, you will find a small **orchid garden** (turn left at the buildings, if you have taken the asphalt road down, along a wide track).

Plant lovers may well find a visit to the gardens frustrating because of the lack of a guide, or labels, but they are still a beautiful, quiet, and cooling place for a stroll.

Islands of Mahé: Satellites and Cohorts

By far the largest and most interesting islands close to Mahé are the group of six that forms the land area of **St. Anne Marine National Park**. St. Anne itself was the site of the first settlement in Seychelles. It also bears other marks of history, including an old **whaling station**, closed down in 1915 at the south end of the island, and a World War Two **gun battery** in the north-east.

Today it has an important **fuel storage depot** on its western coast and is the base for two **National Youth Service — NYS — camps** established in 1983 and 1985. It also has a **navigation light** atop its highest point as an aid to aircraft approaching Seychelles International Airport.

St. Anne, which covers more than two square kilometres (almost a square mile), is the most important nesting site for hawksbill turtles in the granitic islands, with a substantial number of females coming ashore at both **Anse Cabot** and **Grande Anse** in the north of the island. Unfortunately, however, St. Anne has been closed to visitors since 1983.

Another island in the group, **Long Island**, stretching more than three-quarters of a kilometre north-west to south-east and 300 metres (330 yards) across, covering an area of twenty-one hectares (51 acres) is also off limits to the general public. It houses a **prison** and **quarantine station**.

Moyenne, Round Island (Île Ronde), and **Île au Cerf** are all popular destinations for glass bottom boats, semi-submersibles, and other vessels which come to view the wonders of the marine national park.

Île Cachée, a tiny island just over two hectares (five acres) off the south-west corner of Île au Cerf, is another island where, as the name implies, treasure stories abound.

To the east of St. Anne Marine National Park is **Beacon Island** or Île Sèche, only one and a half hectares (three and a half acres) in size. It is a **nature reserve** where seabirds, especially noddies, breed. It is also a popular **dive site** when the north-west monsoon blows on the **Beau Vallon** side of the island, as it is sheltered from the wind (See "Exploring The Silent World Beneath The Waves", Part Three).

Just off the airport are two more islands: **Île Anonyme**, covering almost ten hectares (25 acres) and, **Île aux Rats** or Rat Island, a smidgen of rock less than one hectare (two acres) in size, which looks as if it was designed by an artist specialising in desert island cartoon strips.

Farther south along the east coast, **Île Souris**, under half an hectare (one acre) of land, is a tiny island easily reached by snorkelers from the northern end of **Anse Royale**.

On the west coast, **Chauve Souris** is little more than a rock off the west coast, between **Anse Soleil** and **Anse Aux Poules Bleues**.

Further north along the same coast lie the larger islands of **Conception** and **Thérèse**. As there is no beach, Conception, which covers an area of sixty hectares (150 acres), is extremely difficult to visit except in the calmest weather. But when this occurs there is excellent diving off the north-western shore. Game fishing in this area is also very good.

Île Thérèse, sometimes known as Sheraton Island, covers more than seventy hectares (one-quarter of a square mile) and offers beach barbecues. There are regular trips to this pretty island from the Sheraton Hotel.

About one and a half kilometres (almost one mile) off Grande Anse lies the relatively barren island of **Île Aux Vaches Marines**, which is under five hectares (12 acres) in size, where roseate terns once bred in good numbers. Now a **nature reserve**, perhaps one day this highly endangered seabird will return.

L'Islette, covering just over three hectares (seven acres) close to **Port Glaud** and easily visited by dinghy across the short stretch of calm water from Mahé, has a very good **restaurant**, well worth a visit.

L'Ilot, half an hectare (two acres), off the north-western tip of Mahé, offers excellent snorkeling and diving although the current is sometimes extremely strong.

Hardly an island at all, **Hodoul Island** —

Overleaf: Air Seychelles intercontinental 767 circles over the islands of St. Anne Marine National Park off the coast of Mahé.

113

in the **yacht basin** — has been enlarged by recent land reclamation and a new sixty-seat **restaurant**, offering both Creole and international cuisine, was scheduled to open there in late 1990 with berthing facilities for small boats alongside.

St. Anne Marine National Park

St. Anne Marine National Park, inaugurated in March 1973, includes the reef area surrounding six granite islands about five kilometres (three miles) east of Victoria. The park's deepest point is about 250 metres (820 feet) and it covers an area totalling more than fourteen square kilometres (five square miles).

The small, rugged granitic islands, their beaches, and offshore waters provide a number of marine and terrestrial environments — reefs, granite boulders, sand flats, sea-grass beds, intertidal rocks, and sandy beaches.

The sea-grass *Thalassia hemprichii* occurs between Round Island and Île au Cerf and

Above: Pot-like nest of Seychelles' indigenous mud dauber wasp, which preys on several species of spider.

Opposite top: Fascinating Moyenne Island abounds with legendary ghosts of pirates past.

Opposite: Tourists take a close look at a giant land tortoise in one of the reptile's last strongholds.

coconut palms predominate on the islands. The steep and rocky north-east side of St. Anne supports the native palm *Latainnyen fey* and Balfour's pandanus.

The marine life is exceptional, especially between Moyenne and St. Anne, with more than 150 species of reef fish, as well as crabs, sea urchins, marine worms, starfish, octopi, sea cucumbers, and a variety of underwater life.

It is also probably the main breeding site for hawksbill turtle in Seychelles. Among the birds are green-backed heron, various waders, and terns.

The reefs attract many tourists and there are several glass bottom boats for hire and semi-submersibles. Swimming, sailing, and diving are all allowed, but a national park entrance fee is payable and all marine life is protected. Viewing is only allowed in seven areas of delicate shallow coral and anchoring is prohibited.

The open islands

Île au Cerf, which is more than one and a half kilometres (one mile) long and almost one kilometre (half a mile) wide, reaches a height of 108 metres (354 feet), and lies five kilometres (three miles) east of Mahé.

Second only in size to St. Anne, Île au Cerf offers an excellent barbecue spread for day-trippers. The sheltered location of the island ensures enjoyable swimming all year-round off its sandy shores.

The island is named after the frigate, *Le Cerf*, which arrived at Port Victoria on 1 November, 1756. On board was Corneille Nicholas Morphey, leader of the French expedition which claimed the islands by laying a Stone of Possession, Seychelles oldest **monument**, now on display in the **National Museum, Victoria**.

Getting there

The boat trip from Port Victoria takes fifteen minutes.

Sightseeing

Covered with lush vegetation, Île au Cerf boasts a **jetty** and a **breakwater** by the **beach shed** on the main **north-east beach**.

From this point a **trail** leads across the island through a forest to the south-west coast.

Above: On Moyenne Island, an 18th-century pirate's grave has long inspired stories of buried treasure.

The trail branches to the north-west beach, where the offshore teems with marine life, and also continues round the southern headland back to the jetty. There is also a trail to the top of the forested hill.

The island has two tiny disused chapels, one Anglican, one Catholic. The **Beach Shed Bar and Restaurant** is an excellent **restaurant** which specialises in grilled fish, bonito, octopus, and shark curry with coconut chutney.

Moyenne

Covering nine hectares (22 acres) — just under half a kilometre long by quarter of a kilometre wide — **Moyenne** belongs to retired newspaper editor Brendon Grimshaw. It has long inspired tales of buried treasure and ghosts associated with the island, and contains some old **graves**.

The northern coastline offers the finest spectacle for underwater exploration. Among the fish most commonly seen are butterfly-fish and red soldierfish.

The interior is forested with a wealth of fruit trees: mangoes, oranges, and bananas. A **garden** separates the island's old **colonial residence** from the **Jolly Roger Bar**. There is also a superb **restaurant**, **Maison Moyenne**.

Round Island (Île Ronde)

Lying just a little way off Moyenne's south-west shores is **Round Island**, under two hectares (five acres) in size and less than 150 metres (500 feet) in diameter. But it is the **headquarters** of the marine national park.

There is a small sandy **cove** near the **restaurant**, **Chez Gaby**, where you can swim or snorkel. The best snorkeling area is between Moyenne and St. Anne.

Long ago Round Island was the home of a leper colony with a **house** for the nursing staff, **quarters** for the lepers, a **chapel**, and a small **prison**.

Today the chapel is the restaurant and the prison **cells** are used for **bar** and **kitchen** purposes. House specialities include skewered tuna fish with a local sauce, fried egg-plants, salads, fish and chicken curries, and lentils with different chutneys.

The Enchanted Isle

Nature strives to be protective of its wonders. And sometimes it succeeds, as the pristine beauty of **Silhouette** testifies. When it gave birth to this, the third-largest of the island archipelago, it also laid down the foundations for the barrier which has served to stem the tides of visitors and development that so often scars and destroys its creations.

Thus Silhouette, though it lies only nineteen kilometres (12 miles) north-west of **Mahé**, remains unchanged. Encircled by a continuous coral reef, for centuries it defied dilettante and entrepreneur, and served as a deterrent to all but the most determined sailor or settler.

Though its name perfectly describes its ethereal sundown image as seen from Mahé, it is in fact named after an eighteenth-century French minister.

Legend says that the famous French corsair Hodoul lived on Silhouette and local folklore is filled with stories of the treasure he is fondly believed to have buried somewhere in its craggy mountains or granite shores.

But the island may have been known to the Arabs before the Europeans: ancient tombs at **Anse Lascars** suggest Arab tradition and may predate the European era.

Rising from the submerged plateau of the **Seychelles Bank** to 740 metres (2,428 feet) above the sea, Silhouette is higher and more thickly forested than any Seychelles island except Mahé. It has one of the thickest virgin forests in the Indian Ocean. Circular in shape, roughly five kilometres (three miles) long by five kilometres (three miles) wide, its twenty square kilometres (eight square miles) of granite bedrock differs from those of the other granite islands. It is much more recently formed.

Just beyond the coastal littoral, the land rises sharply to a fairly level plateau some 500 metres (1,640 feet) above sea level: land ideal for the **coconut** and **cinnamon plantations** that now flourish there beneath the slopes of **Mount Dauban** — named after the family that first settled this island — and 621-metre (2,040-feet) high **Silhouette peak**. The island has a population of about 200 people.

Copra from the coconut plantations is processed at **Anse Mondon** to the north, **Anse Grande Barbe** to the west, and **Anse La Passe**

Above: Final resting place of Raymond Grimshaw, "father and friend" of Brendon Grimshaw, owner of Moyenne Island.

Overleaf: Magnificent Silhouette Island as seen from Beau Vallon beach, Mahé.

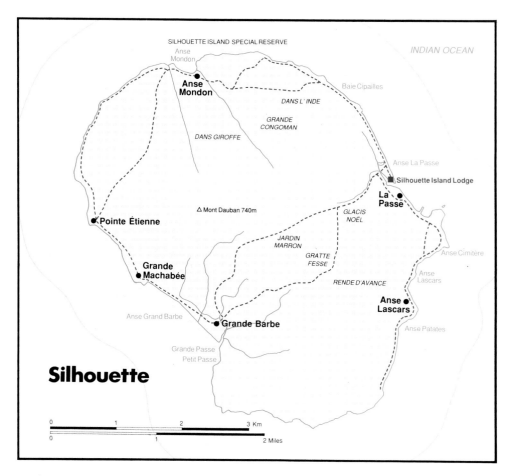

SILHOUETTE ISLAND SPECIAL RESERVE
Anse
Mondon
INDIAN OCEAN
Anse Mondon
Baie Cipailles
DANS L' INDE
GRANDE CONGOMAN
DANS GIROFFE
Anse La Passe
Silhouette Island Lodge
La Passe
△ Mont Dauban 740m
GLACIS NOËL
Pointe Étienne
JARDIN MARRON
GRATTE FESSE
Anse Cimitère
Grande Machabée
RENDE D'AVANCE
Anse Lascars
Anse Lascars
Anse Grand Barbe
Grande Barbe
Anse Patates
Grande Passe
Petit Passe

Silhouette

to the east. Avocados, cinnamon, tobacco, patchouli, and tangy *bigarads* — a small fruit similar to orange which gives its name to a sauce served with roast duckling and is used for making jam — are all cultivated.

Getting there

Because of the coral reef, boats were unable to put in to Silhouette. Now a newly-built jetty juts out into the sea, making landing easy. A rubber dinghy with an outboard motor ferries visitors from the boat to the pier at **La Passe**. Check with travel agents or the Marine Charter Association next to the **yacht basin** in **Victoria** for details of charters or ferries.

When to go

The island is open all year-round.

Where to stay

Silhouette Lodge is the only hotel on the island. It has twelve bungalows and is equip-

ped for watersports and trekking. Under Italian management, the restaurant food is excellent. Day visitors are discouraged.

Sightseeing

Silhouette is an island for nature lovers and walkers. With neither roads nor cars, post office nor police station, it is worlds apart from anything known to most visitors.

Shrouded in profligate trees and plants, the whole island is a sylvan reserve whose ambience reinvigorates even the most weary traveller. Chickens scuttle about the sandy **track** that leads out of the main "**square**" of Anse La Passe and poses as the village's "main" street. Even in this "urban" area the *takamaka* and breadfruit trees are so thick they cut out most of the direct heat of the sun and form a thick shade canopy.

It is in La Passe, near the jetty, that you can see an old, beautifully preserved colonial-style **planter's house,** built from indigenous

Above: North Island keeps watch over Silhouette from a scant five kilometres away.

woods that have since become rare. Close by is the island **hospital**.

From this unusual "capital" with its handful of houses, two paths lead up the mountains through the forest to link the east and west coast and La Passe with **Grande Barbe**.

Allow a full day to savour the beauty of this walk. The path is fairly steep in places but well worn by locals who "commute" regularly between Grande Barbe and La Passe.

To reach the summit of Mount Dauban and **Mont Pot à Eau** — where the finest rainforest survives — is difficult.

Bwa rouz, kapisen, bwa-d-nat, and other trees unique to Seychelles continue to dominate these steep cliffs, together with the Seychelles pitcher plant and many endemic orchids.

Bwa sandal is found only on Silhouette. In the past this was burnt for its fragrant incense and so this unique tree is now rare.

Another **two tracks** join the island from north to south and even on this twenty square kilometres (eight square miles) of rock with its 200 people you will feel as remote and as alone as you have ever felt. The scenery is totally wild and unspoilt, rugged cliffs giving way to long sandy beaches.

One of Silhouette's few churches is at Grande Barbe on the west coast, where the island's largest river, the **Séme**, feeds into the sea. The **church** overlooks a magnificent beach.

At **Pointe Ramasse Tout**, south of Anse La Passe on the east coast and above **Anse Cimitière**, shrouded in lush tropical growth, the impressive but neglected marble **mausoleum** of the Dauban family speaks of the isolated grandeur and wealth of the plantation aristocracy. Its marble pillars are strongly reflective of the French influence in America's deep south.

From the neighbouring beach of Anse Lascars there are marvellous views of cloud wreathed **Morne Seychellois** on Mahé. But Silhouette's real lure for holiday-makers is undoubtedly the swimming and snorkeling.

Five kilometres (three miles) north of the island stands its tiny satellite, **North Island** — a two-square kilometre (three-quarters of a square mile) chunk of granite rising out of the ocean.

The island's neglected fruit orchards testify to a time when it was a major agricultural centre.

A World All Its Own

Thirty-four kilometres (21 miles) east of **Mahé** stands postage-stamp size **Récife** a twenty-hectare (50-acre) uninhabited granite blob in the Indian Ocean. It serves as a marker on the sea voyage past the tiny rock of **L'Ilot Frégate** to **Frégate Island**, most isolated of all the granite islands, fifty-five kilometres (34 miles) from the main island.

Dominated by the 125-metre-high (410-foot) crest of **Mount Signal**, this island dreams on in lonely isolation — save for the **airstrip** that lures holiday-makers across the ocean from Mahé in fifteen minutes.

No more than twenty residents share the island's two square kilometres (three-quarters of a square mile) in the peaceful somnambulant style of the old, colonial days when each of these islands was literally a world of its own.

Because of its isolation from the rest of the group it is a favourite locale for the countless tales of buried treasure from the plunder of the eighteenth-century pirates who based themselves in the islands of the Indian Ocean (See "Pirates and Plunder", Part Three).

But whether any actually ever used Frégate as their secret hideaway from the naval ships sent in their pursuit nobody knows.

Fascinating ruined **walls** and **foundations**, including an old **well**, have always been associated with the pirates in folklore, but perhaps earlier Arab visitors left these relics, if not their tantalising legends.

With Mount Signal in the north and the slightly smaller 100 metres (330 feet) or so high **Au Salon** in the south, Frégate is under two kilometres (one mile) long and and little more than a kilometre (just over half a mile) wide.

Above: Unique giant tenebrionid beetle, found only on Frégate Island.

Although Frégate was once covered in lush vegetation, exotics such as breadfruit, banyan, and wild cashew have now largely replaced the original tall native trees. Sandragon is the dominant woodland tree.

The island is virtually denuded of all the natural vegetation that gave it its glory. Even the plantation has started to degenerate.

But its soils nourish crops like sweet potato, papaya, banana, and some vegetables for guests at the lodge. And time and man have done nothing to ravage its beaches, which are among

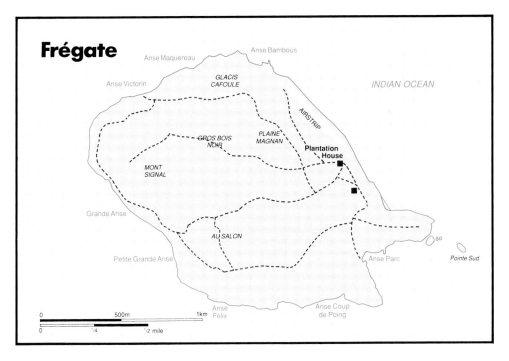

Frégate

Anse Maquereau
Anse Bambous
Anse Victorin
GLACIS CAFOULE
INDIAN OCEAN
AIRSTRIP
GROS BOIS NOIR
PLAINE MAGNAN
Plantation House
MONT SIGNAL
Grande Anse
AU SALON
Petite Grande Anse
Anse Parc
Pointe Sud
Anse Felix
Anse Coup de Poing

0   500m   1km
0   ¼   ½ mile

the finest in the archipelago.

Among the birds, the rare Seychelles **magpie robin** is also unique to the island although it was once common throughout the granitic islands. Its ground feeding habits made it easy prey to cats and now only a score or so of the birds cling to survival in this, their last refuge.

There is some hope. The last of Frégate's cats was eliminated in 1983 and a long-term study of the bird's needs is being carried out by the International Council for Bird Preservation in an endeavour to pluck one of the world's rarest birds from the brink of extinction.

Getting there

Air Seychelles operates daily flights to Frégate and you can charter yachts or boats at Victoria for the sea crossing.

When to go

The island is open all year-round.

Where to stay

Plantation House, the only hotel on the island, has twelve spacious rooms and specialises in Creole cooking. See Listings for "Hotels".

Sightseeing

A **coral reef** surrounds the island and the waters are full of shells such as cowries and cones.

Onshore there are many scorpions but they are nocturnal and provided you wear shoes when walking at night they are unlikely to cause you any trouble or pain.

Frégate also has a healthy population of caecilians: blind, legless amphibians difficult to observe on other islands. Giant land tortoises — introduced from **Aldabra** — roam the undergrowth where you may also see the usual plethora of green geckos and other lizards.

But perhaps the most extraordinary inhabitant of Frégate — indeed one of the most extraordinary residents of all Seychelles — is the **giant tenebrionid beetle**, *Pulposipes herculeanus*.

It is said that when the first specimens were sent to Europe entomologists refused to accept it as a new species. They claimed that it was a hoax — that the beetle was made up of several species stuck together.

The giant tenebrionid, unique to Frégate, is remarkable. Despite its knobbly wing-cases

it cannot fly and is usually seen clinging to the flanks of the sandragon trees. Its long legs are its other most distinctive feature.

But its Creole name, *bib arme*, which refers to a spider, suggests this weird and wonderful creature was initially wrongly identified.

Other bird species include the **Seychelles fody**, found only on Frégate, **Cousin,** and **Cousine,** together with the densest population of the **Seychelles blue pigeon.**

Sooty terns nest offshore on tiny L'Ilot Frégate, their only granite home apart from the huge colony on **Aride.**

Footpaths lead everywhere through the remnant woodlands and diminishing plantations. One from Plantation House leads up the slopes of Mount Signal to a point just four metres (13 feet) lower than the **summit** looking westward over the ocean to Mahé.

A longer **trail** leads across to the west coast and the sparkling beach of **Grande Anse** and, south, the adjoining **Petite Grande Anse.** Three northern beaches — **Anse Victorin,** **Anse Maquereau,** and **Anse Bambous** — have no protecting reef.

The only beach on the south coast is the tiny cove of **Anse Parc,** a short and pleasant stroll from Plantation House. The hotel is as romantic as the island and its legend-shrouded past.

You enter it through the **roots** of a giant **banyan tree** where, under the leafy shade, there is a **bird table** that draws dozens of clamouring birds each day to feed on the titbits left for them — or on the sugar-lined rim of the welcome drink handed to guests on their arrival at this beautiful island.

Above: Dream island in the Indian Ocean — Frégate — with its single landing strip on the beach in foreground.

Opposite left: Seychelles blue pigeon.

Opposite: Frégate is the last fragile claw-hold of the magpie robin, one of the world's rarest birds.

Overleaf top: One of Frégate's inviting sun-drenched beaches.

Overleaf below: Phantom-like forest of banyan trees with their aerial roots on Frégate Island.

Praslin — The Forgotten Eden

Apart from its glorious tropical beaches and fantastic marine life, **Praslin** is best known for **Vallée de Mai World Heritage Site**, one of only two places in the world where that botanical rarity, the *coco de mer*, grows wild.

These fantastic palm forests — there are five more rare endemic palms — earned the island first name, Îsle de Palme, from the French navigator Lazare Picault, who had to carve his way through the tangled undergrowth of the inland hills.

Stretching eleven kilometres (seven miles) from the north-west to the south-east, nowhere wider than five and a half kilometres (three and a half miles) across, Praslin is the second-largest island in Seychelles.

In 1768 Marion Dufresne led an expedition to the island and neighbouring Isle Rouge, renaming them Praslin and **Curieuse**. Dufresne placed a Deed of Possession in a bottle which he buried in the sands of a curving bay on the northern coast known as **Anse Possession**.

In 1810 the total population of the island amounted to ten families and it slumbered dreamily on through most of the century, the only noteworthy event being the arrival of General Charles Gordon in 1881.

The hero of Khartoum thought he had found the biblical Garden of Eden and pronounced that the *coco de mer* was the biblical tree of knowledge.

Covering a total of thirty-seven square kilometres (14.3 square miles), it lies forty-five kilometres (28 miles) from Mahé and reaches a height of 367 metres (1,204 feet). In 1990 it had a population of just over 5,000 people. Since independence the island has developed rapidly. In the cultural field the islanders have made great strides. Several artistic and music groups perform regularly at the island hotels and an art gallery was recently opened at **Côte D'Or**.

The development of Praslin's civic and tourist infrastructure has been even more dramatic. There are more than forty kilometres (25 miles) of road on the island and by 1991 seventy per cent of these will have been surfaced or resurfaced. An additional four kilometres (two and a half miles) of road at Anse Kerlan, where the sea washed away the existing access, and Côte D'Or, are planned.

Following the inauguration of public electricity in 1981, it now supplies neighbouring **La Digue** by submarine cable. Treated water is piped to most homes, and the island hospital was due to be rebuilt at the end of 1990.

A new **airport** at **Amitié**, opened in 1975, brought the island into the air age. The night landing equipment, installed in 1988, allows tourists to spend their entire holiday on Praslin, as they can now leave the island immediately before their scheduled international flights without having to spend a night at hotels on Mahé.

Many more developments are in hand to increase employment and diversify from traditional employment like plantation work, fishing, and quarrying. In this respect tourism is the leader, but a boatyard to build fishing boats has been opened at **Baie St. Anne**.

In fact tourism is the cornerstone of the island's economy. Indeed, in 1990 Praslin was experiencing an unprecedented boom with two new hotels (partly financed by foreign partners) being built at **Anse Bois de Rose** and **Anse La Farine**.

And planning approval has been given for an eighty-room complex at **Anse Kerlan,** which will be built by the Compagnie Seychelloise de Promotion Hotelière (COSPROH) together with a twenty-five room hotel at Côte D'Or.

Existing hotels are also constantly encouraged to upgrade their properties, refurbish and, in some instances, extend and expand their existing facilities.

Plans for new restaurants and the island's first **casino** are also in the planning pipeline and a private investor is developing a nine-hole **golf course** at **Anse Marie-Louise**. Watersports are well-developed and visitors have free access to non-motorised facilities.

These projects will take the hotel accommodation on the island close to the ceiling of 950 beds which the tourist authorities have set as the maximum.

Praslin's satellite islands — **Aride**, **Cousin** and **Curieuse** — are protected areas containing rare animals and plants. Praslin's north-western foreshore, the sea between, and all of Curieuse form a large marine national park containing the tiny islets of **Chauve Souris**,

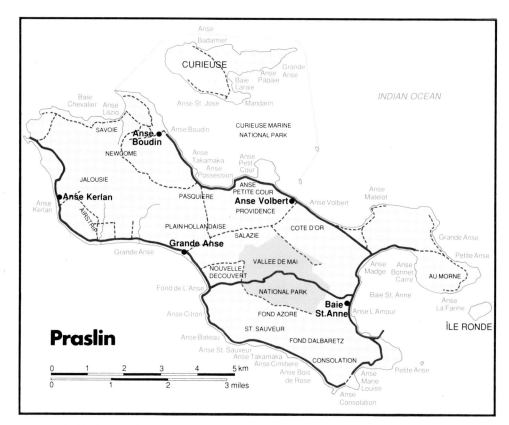

Praslin

```
0    1    2    3    4    5 km
0         1         2    3 miles
```

just over half a hectare (one and three-quarter acres), and **St. Pierre,** half a hectare (1.2 acres). Off the eastern coast **Île Ronde**, two square kilometres (three-quarters of a square mile), is an idyllic island retreat.

And Vallée de Mai is one of Seychelles' two UNESCO World Heritage Sites. It is also the home of one of the world's rarest birds, the black parrot. The Vallée de Mai is a living wonder, preserved by the Praslinois as one of the eternal treasures of Seychelles.

Getting there

There are scheduled daily air and sea services from Mahé. The flight takes fifteen minutes. The three daily ferry services by schooner take between two and a half and three hours.

When to go

Praslin is open all year-round and the weather is generally pleasant and warm.

Where to stay

There are some excellent 5- and 4-star hotels: Beach Villa, Grande Anse; Chauve Souris

Island Lodge, Anse Volbert; Flying Dutchman, Grande Anse; and Praslin Beach Hotel, Anse Volbert. There are many other hotels, beach resorts, and guesthouses of varying degrees of quality and service. See Listings for "Hotels".

Getting around

Praslin has six car rental firms providing jeeps, cars, and mini-mokes to visitors who prefer to drive around. There are fifteen taxis and the island has the archipelago's only woman taxi driver.

Sightseeing

From the main **landing stage** the island is well served by motor roads which extend along the entire northern coast and the south and south-western coast.

From early morning the waters of Baie St. Anne, the most scenic natural harbour in Seychelles, bustle with activity as the Praslin-owned schooners prepare to leave the inter-island quay before sunup for the journey to Mahé, where they arrive between 08.00 and 09.00 hours.

Above: Amitié, Praslin — with paved airstrip in background and sandy beach-strip in foreground.

Throughout the day the ferries to La Digue sail back and forth to and from this wide bay at the south-eastern end of the island, its waters well-sheltered by two prominent headlands and Île Ronde. Though the sea and the mastery of it runs in the veins of all the islanders, not everyone depends on it for a living.

Praslin has a large farming community in the fertile flat lands around Amitié in the north-west, tending crops of tomatoes, cabbages, beans, and other table produce that flourishes in the loamy fertile island soil.

At Côte D'Or a large state-owned farm also contributes to the nation's larder and both state and private farmers are expanding production. They all help make this island a greener place and where the land is not tilled **mahogany** trees now cover hectares of land razed years ago by fire and left exposed to the harsh sun.

One of Seychelles' most valuable timber resources, a rare, endemic tree, *bwa-d-nat*, renowned for the straightness of its limbs and trunk, is now part of a major reafforestation programme on Praslin.

Praslin's durable, red granite rocks, mined on private and State land, are much sought-after by the construction industry. Shipped to Mahé, it decorates the facades of many buildings. Ultimately, however, Praslin's real resources lie in its beautiful beaches. This truly heavenly island is surrounded entirely by one of the Indian Ocean's most outstanding coral reefs.

In the crystal-clear water a thousand marvels await the voyager by glass bottom boat, snorkeler, or scuba diver. Passes in the reef and majestic bays counterpose small, secluded coves and deserted beaches.

Anse Possession, where Dufresne landed in the natural harbour of **Baie Pasquière,** is one of four or five magnificent natural harbours. Baie St. Anne is the most outstanding and for anyone who makes the sea voyage from Mahé the breathtaking view that greets you as you sail into the bay leaves a lasting memory.

This is the island "capital" with **banks, shops, hospital, church,** and a curious **monument** to the *coco de mer.*

Praslin's main Tarmac road starts at the harbour **pier** and runs along the town seafront, past many smaller **jetties** and **moorings**

Above: Azure seas and skies offset Praslin's silver beaches.
Opposite: Cruising yacht rides anchor at Anse Lazio, one of Praslin's most popular destinations.

as far as the **causeway** where it turns west, past the hospital, and climbs the hills inland to run through the Vallée de Mai to **Fond de L'Anse**, the eastern headland of **Grande Anse**.

On the north-west coast the three-and-a-half-kilometre (two-mile) curve of gleaming silver sands looks out over Cousin Island. Although the beach is beautiful the monsoons bring in vast quantities of seaweed and the shallow water over the coral makes swimming impossible.

But this is still the island's most developed resort with a **village**, **church**, **school**, **police station**, **restaurants**, and **shops**.

Another magnificent beach lies on the opposite side of the island in the north. The four-kilometre (two-and-a-half-mile) curve of **Anse Volbert** on the Côte D'Or ranks as one of the loveliest beaches in the world, still yet barely touched by hotel development and fringed with casuarina.

Other favourite beaches, **Anse Bois de Rose** on the southern coast, **Anse Kerlan** on the west coast, and **Anse Boudin** on the northeast coast, are backed by incredible granite cliffs.

Anse Lazio at the north-west tip of the island, is one of the most famous beaches, excellent for swimming and snorkeling with views out to Aride. However, when you become bored of lying in the sun and watersports, remember that the many tiny secluded bays, forests, and other enchanting places make Praslin an ideal place to explore on foot.

The island is covered by a network of footpaths, but it is easy to get lost all the same.

Perhaps the most beautiful of all these walks is through the Vallée de Mai (See "The Forbidden Fruit"). The boundaries of the park touch **Fond Azore**, the island's highest peak, and its second-highest point, 319-metre-high (1,047-foot) **Takamaka**. But there are many other equally fascinating walks.

In the north-west a maze of footpaths leads from the main dirt road by the **church** at Anse Boudin and into the forests and headlands. If you keep on the main path you will arrive at Anse Lazio.

If you take the path north off the main path it will bring you to the northernmost point of the island, **Pointe Chevalier**. From

Above: Praslin woman preparing a fresh fish supper.

Above: Praslin fisherman brings home a fine day's catch of tasty *bourzwa*.

Anse Lazio a track leads south across the western end of the island to **Pointe St. Marie** and Anse Kerlan.

But the main walking itineraries tend to follow trails across the middle of the island.

About one-third of the way along, the path climbs out of Grande Anse close to the **church** and you will come to a fork. One is the **Pasquière Track** that leads up and over the central mountain ridge through lovely forest scenery and down to Anse Possession on Baie Pasquière.

The other fork leads north-east along the **Salazie Track**, through lush forests of palms and *takamaka*, to emerge at the magnificence of Anse Volbert close to the **jetty**.

You can then follow the coastal road past **Côte D'Or Lodge** where there is a turning north to **Anse Gouvernement,** the northern headlands, and **Anse Matelot**.

No trails are marked — but they do exist for you to continue on to **Pointe Joséphine**, **Grande Anse** (another of the same name), **Petite Anse,** and around **Pointe La Farine** to **Anse La Farine**.

You then backtrack around the slopes of Au Morne through the palm plantations of **Anse La Blague** to emerge at **Anse Takamaka**, the northernmost extremity of glorious Baie St. Anne, and from there on to **Anse Madge**, one of the bay's main beaches.

From Grande Anse a track also leads up to the summit of 213-metre (700 feet) high **Fond Diable**, if you should wish to explore this mysterious **summit**.

There are some attractive walks around the southernmost headlands, too. There are two options from Anse Marie-Louise, site of the proposed golf course. The first is to take the pathway cutting inland through leafy **Fond Ferdinand** to Baie St. Anne. The second is to take the small motor road from Anse Marie-Louise past **Pointe Consolation** to **Anse Consolation** along the south-west coast road.

Another enjoyable excursion is the boat ride to the tiny island of St. Pierre, opposite the long white strip of Anse Volbert, an ideal spot for snorkeling and picnics.

A boat leaves the beach opposite **Paradise Hotel** every hour from 09.00 until 17.00. Allow a whole day. St. Pierre boasts some of the finest snorkeling reefs in Seychelles.

Above: Timber-and-thatch house on Praslin. Overleaf: One end of Praslin's famous beach at Anse Kerlan.

Valley of the Forbidden Fruit

From the past, voices seem to call out reminding you that the eighteen hectares (45 acres) of the **Vallée de Mai** on Praslin is one of the most precious spots on earth.

"At last we ran in to the valley of the **coco de mer**: a valley as big as old Hastings, quite filled with the huge straight stems and golden shiny stars of the great palm; it seemed almost too good to believe that I had really reached it," (Marianne North, October 1883).

" ... I can conceive of no more antediluvian-looking place in the world than that ravine," (J. Horne, c.1870).

"There was an atmosphere of great antiquity about the place. The stream had been tinkling across the stones for centuries while the *coco de mer* trees grew silently inch by inch. How many thousands of years had it been like this?" (Athol Thomas, 1968).

"When no wind was blowing there was a still, cathedral-like atmosphere of silence. When the wind started, the enormous leaves clashed together like sheets of corrugated iron." (Rosemary Wise, 1985).

No one questions that the valley is a special place and no one comes away unmoved. Perhaps the church-like atmosphere makes the experience almost religious. Certainly you feel close to something extraordinary — God, or an inexpressibly distant past which seems imprisoned there, beneath the *coco de mer* palms.

Athol Thomas captured something of that unique atmosphere when he wrote in his book *Forgotten Eden*:

"A silence had dropped like a blanket over the valley as soon as he had switched off the ... engine. There was not a breath of wind and the leaves on the trees were perfectly still.

"Even the long, broken spears of a pandanus palm a few yards down the valley were quite motionless. I had never experienced such perfect stillness and such absolute silence.

"I had the feeling that, at this particular moment, the Vallée de Mai was the only place in the world to be completely at rest . . . I believed I was beginning to understand how Gordon felt about the valley. . . . "

General Charles George Gordon, of Khartoum fame, found *his* god in the Vallée de Mai. He was sent to the Seychelles in 1881 to report on the feasibility of fortifying the islands.

During his sojourn, he evolved a theory that the Garden of Eden was in Seychelles. He maintained that the archipelago was once a part of a magical continent, Lemuria, which joined India to the island of Madagascar.

Aden was Eden, and a river flowing from Seychelles became the four rivers of the Bible. The garden was part of the district of Eden, and it was somewhere in or near Seychelles. During the great flood, the garden was saved, nestling in the mountains of Seychelles, which Gordon thought were once between 2,438 and 3,050 metres (8-10,000 feet) high.

Excited, he warmed to his theory: "Thus far I think any requirement is fulfilled for deciding that the site of the district of Eden is near Seychelles."

Eyes alight with hope, he set off for Praslin in search of the "two mystical trees . . . that of the knowledge of good and evil, and of life". In the valley, he found them.

The *coco de mer* was Gordon's tree of knowledge: "a tree unique among trees; it is the Prince of Palms . . . a natural tree imbued for a time with a mystic property, or set apart sacred." His tree of life was the breadfruit, "a tree unique in its kind, an evergreen, a humble tree yet a life-supporting tree".

Such a dreamer as Gordon could not have failed to find his "two mystical trees", but he was fortunate to find a tree as special as the *coco de mer* to fulfil his fantasy. As he himself said, "if curiosity could be excited by any tree it could be by this".

Perhaps it was a little cruel of the writer, H. W. Estridge, at a later dinner party, to point out that Eve could not have bitten into this "forbidden fruit" with its ten-centimetre (four-inch) husk.

"I had never thought of that," Gordon said forlornly. Did his thoughts stray back to his Seychelles Garden of Eden during his last hours as the Mahdi swept into the city of Khartoum, just four years later?

That the valley has survived at all is a miracle. As early as the 1770s, "un anglais degradé" by the name of Charles Casulo was trading in *coco de mer* nuts, and when he found he had flooded his own market, he burned the palm forest to keep prices up.

Somehow the valley escaped. The true source of the fabulous *coco de mer* nut, which commanded prices as high as 4,000 gold florins each in the thirteenth century, was not discovered by Europeans until 1768 when a member of Dufresne's expedition found the *coco de mer* forest on the slopes of Praslin's hills.

Just a year later, one of the captains of the expedition's ships returned and took away so many *coco de mer* nuts that the market was ruined and the nuts became almost worthless.

As settlers moved in, the palm forests were ravaged by men in search of firewood and timber. The deep, dry leaf litter was always prone to fire, and fire was a useful tool for the colonists who needed to clear troublesome undergrowth quickly.

In the latter half of the nineteenth century, John Horne was worried that the nuts — then worth two to four shillings each — were "broken from the trees and sold before they are ripe", another threat to the unique palm forest that once flourished on the island.

By some quirk, the Vallée de Mai escaped again, and until the 1930s lay practically undisturbed.

Avoiding a "disgrace to civilization"

Plans were now afoot to "beautify" the valley, which is a sombre, eerie place, with mango and guava trees, sealing wax palms, and mother-in-law's tongue. The area was also thought suitable for coffee plantations.

Some dim echo of John Horne's impassioned pleas, however, reached the ears of the administration at last. "The destruction of the trees in that ravine," he had written, "would be an outrage on science and a disgrace to civilization."

Any visitor to the valley will agree with him, but it was a close run thing. The operation continued even after 1945 when the valley was acquired by the government.

But for some years now the aim has been to let the valley return to its original state. It will, however, take a long time before the exotic species disappear completely.

The valley is now at the heart of the **Praslin National Park**, and in 1983 it became Seychelles' second **World Heritage Site**. About 100 years earlier, Horne had asked that the government should purchase the *"coco de mer* ravine in Praslin"* to ensure its "conservation and preservation".

He can at last rest easy. The world has finally come to share his appreciation of this place where, according to John Procter (October 1973), you "may well acquire . . . a sublime sense of timelessness, in spite of the luxuriant, pulsating life. The noise of the huge leaves of the . . . *coco de mer* . . . clacking together in any stirring breeze, is awe-inspiring."

Getting there

By air or sea from Mahé; by car, bicycle, or on foot from Baie St. Anne, Praslin.

When to go

It can be visited between 08.00 and 16.30 daily. You can drive through it if you take the **asphalt road** from **Grande Anse** to **Baie St. Anne**.

Sightseeing

Praslin National Park, set in the central hills of Praslin, covers an area of more than three square kilometres (more than one square mile), including the whole of the World Heritage Site of Vallée de Mai, rising from twenty metres (65 feet) above sea level to 367 metres (1,204 feet).

There is a **shop** at the **park entrance** that sells souvenirs, refreshments, and a guidebook that gives route directions and brief descriptions of the plants and animals which live in the valley. The admission charge of twenty-five rupees goes to support Seychelles Islands Foundation.

The **nature trail** leads to all the interesting botanical species. The paths running through the valley are well looked after. At times the palm fronds form such a thick roof that the sun is obliterated and when the wind blows they make a noise like sheet iron rattling.

The valley is rich in tangible wonders: all six of Seychelles' endemic palms, twenty-eight of the endemic plant species, all four endemic screwpines, and fourteen endemic broadleaved trees, including *bwa rouz* and *bwa dur*.

Five endemic reptiles patrol the canopy or rustle in the leaf litter, and above that green-

Opposite: Catkin of the unique male *coco de mer* in Praslin's Vallée de Mai World Heritage Site inspired many legends and the fanciful theory that this was the Garden of Eden.

Opposite: The curiously shaped nut of the female *coco de mer* tree added sauce to the stories that claimed it was the forbidden fruit.

Opposite right: The long-lived *coco de mer* palm tree grows nowhere else on earth. The oldest specimen is more than 200 years in age.

139

vaulted ceiling five endemic birds live their lives, as it were, in the outside world.

This is a wonderful heritage. Again and again visitors are drawn back to the atmosphere of the place, its uncanny stillness beneath the tall trees, and above all, the sense that nothing has changed there since life on this planet began.

The Prince of Palms

It is difficult to say what gives rise to this feeling of timelessness. Perhaps it is the granite boulders, some 650 million years old, or perhaps it is the *coco de mer* trees themselves.

In fact, a quarter of all the trees in the valley are *coco de mer* (about 5,000) and fifty-nine per cent of the trees are palms. There are approximately equal numbers of male and female *coco de mer*, but despite an equal growth rate, the males are always taller, growing on average to 14.4 metres (47 feet) as compared to an average size of only 9.3 metres (30 feet) for a female.

This may be because the males live longer. A female tree, heavily laden with eighteen kilos (40 lbs) of *coco de mer* nuts is susceptible to a strong wind.

It might even be that the trees rely on a certain number of female palms being blown over to ensure a spread *up* the steep slopes on which they live, as well as *down* to the valley bottom. This theory is not proven. Some experts believe that the nuts do not roll downhill anyway, but remain trapped in the leaf litter around the mother tree.

Reports of longevity in these trees are sometimes exaggerated. In 1985-6, the tallest *coco de mer* was thirty-two metres (104 feet) tall and an estimated 215 years old. This is not as staggering as the 1,000 years often quoted as the age of some *coco de mer*, but it is worth reflecting this tree was alive when the first settlers established themselves on Mahé.

The ages of the *coco de mer* tell their own story of good times and bad in the valley. For whatever reasons, it is obvious that the *coco de mer* had a lean time in the late nineteenth century, and again in the late 1950s. Few trees took root at these times.

Palmis and *latannyen fey* also have long lives. The largest palmis palm is about 210 years old, and the oldest *latanyen fey* is a youngster of about 100 years.

Above: Seychelles pandanus, one of five species of screwpine found in Seychelles.

One way of dating the trees is to read the graffiti on the larger, older ones. Some use might as well be made of this tasteless defacement, but future visitors to the valley will hopefully remember the motto, "take only photographs, leave only footprints".

The *coco de mer* has the largest leaves in the world, and bears the largest nut, but it has as much mystery associated with it as fact.

Scientists are still baffled by its pollination. It seems unlikely, in that still world beneath the canopy, that wind is the agent of pollination, yet other candidates, the vivid green geckos or the large white slugs so often seen feeding on the sweet-smelling male flowers seem to eat more pollen than they carry away. The *coco de mer* may owe its survival to some as yet unsung insect go-between.

A Place of Legends

Those not preoccupied with such questions will relish the legends which, not surprisingly, have grown up in this place. The Seychellois do not need to know about the habits of strange slugs or insects.

They know that the roots of the *coco de mer* grow deep down through the bedrock of the island until they reach the sea, then the trees move, coming together to mate.

Others believe the trees only need a stormy night to awaken them, and trigger off their lovemaking. Given the suggestive shapes of the male catkin and female nut, you could not expect less.

Even General Gordon discreetly pointed out that "the heart is said by the scriptures to be the seat of desires and ... the fruit externally represents the heart, while the interior represents the thighs and belly ... which I consider as the true seat of carnal desires".

Naturally the nut has been used as an aphrodisiac, the dried kernel grated and sold as a love potion known as *nux medica.*

Sailors had their own ideas about the *coco de mer*. Until Dufresne's expedition discovered the true origin of the mysterious nuts which appeared (whether by natural process of sea and wind, or by the devious skills of Arab traders) in the Maldives and Sri Lanka, the tree which bore them was thought to grow beneath the ocean, in the navel of the world.

The trees grew so tall their branches peeped up through the waves and enormous vultures perched on them. Unwary sailors, seeing the greenery, drew their ships close in hope of finding land.

For their pains, the sailors were plucked off their ships and eaten by the vultures, or killed by the dragons which protected the trees.

Today, without any loss of life to giant vultures, some 3,000 nuts are taken annually to be polished and sold as souvenirs for considerably more than two to four shillings.

A Tinkling of Streams

The *coco de mer* palms perch on the drier slopes, but the valley is also a place of water. A **stream** runs by below where the local freshwater crayfish, or *camarins*, tiny shrimps, and freshwater crabs live.

Athol Thomas describes this pretty little river, the sound of which was "so pure that the water might have been trickling over stones made of silver". The stream leaves the reserve in spectacular fashion, tumbling out as a small **waterfall**.

Marianne North saw the same waterfall in 1883, dropping "fifty feet [15 metres] over a wall of rock hung with ferns into a pool among the boulders, half hidden by foam and steam". The rain which feeds the stream is gathered by the *coco de mer* palms with elegant efficiency.

The ridges of the huge leaves collect the water and channel it towards the trunk, depositing it in the soil around the base. The ground beneath the leaves themselves remains dry, however, and the trees offer good shelter in a heavy shower.

Birds of the Valley

Sharing this valley with the exciting flora are the birds, though you may hear rather than see them as they move about above the high canopy.

The Seychelles blue pigeon, bulbul, and sunbird live there, and the Seychelles cave swiftlet may breed in some secret cave in the reserve. The bird most associated with the valley is the **black parrot.**

It cannot, of course, feed on the *coco de mer nut,* and relies on the fleshier fruits of the other palms and the introduced trees. It nests in the hollow trunks of dead *coco de mer* and other dead trees.

The exact population is not known, the birds are very shy, but an estimate of eighty individuals is reasonable. They perhaps concentrated in the valley to escape the fires which have so often threatened the forests elsewhere on Praslin.

The birds breed between October and December, and one of the greatest threats to them are rats. In the long term, lack of suitable nesting sites could be a problem.

Within the valley, the only indication of their presence is usually their high-pitched whistles piercing the silence. It can sound as though some small boys are playing a game with you . . . and indeed many an excited birdwatcher has been disappointed to discover that his "parrot" is a tour guide doing a good imitation.

To see the birds, it is best to watch quietly at the margins of the park, waiting for them to fly in at dusk to roost, or find one of their favoured fruit trees, such as a guava or bilimbi, where several birds may gather, climbing about using beak and claw. They hold the fruit in one claw, daintily extracting the tastiest morsels with their curved bills.

The brightest of the endemic geckos lives there, as does the tiger chameleon, the Seychelles skink, the Seychelles wolf and house snakes, the Mascarene and endemic green tree frog, not to mention endemic caecilians and snails. You may also see the introduced tenrec busy searching for food in the undergrowth.

Whatever you are lucky enough to see there, you will come away with something of John Procter's "sublime sense", of Thomas's "perfect stillness and . . . absolute silence", and Gordon's Garden of Eden.

This is a place of legend, a place of mystery unlike anywhere else on earth, and the price of a ticket for this journey back in time is only twenty-five rupees.

The story is told of an English visitor who went there, excited by Gordon's theories about the valley. His guide was a young man who spoke good English with a French accent.

Sharing a picnic, the visitor asked the guide his name. "Adam, sir", was the reply, "as was the name of my father, my grandfather, my great-grandfather . . . . "

How the general's eyes would have sparkled to hear that.

Curious but Delightful

Lying just one kilometre (half a mile) from the northernmost point of **Praslin**, **Curieuse** is fifty-two kilometres (32 miles) from Mahé and covers three square kilometres (one square mile).

The island was originally called Île Rouge because of the exposed red earth which remains a feature of the island. But in 1768, following the expedition of Nicholas Marion Dufresne aboard the schooner La Curieuse — accompanied by the supply vessel La Digue — the name was changed.

Dufresne was struck by the verdant vegetation he saw, including the coco de mer, which grows naturally only there and on Praslin.

The magic did not last long. But once described as the "most degraded island in the Indian Ocean", where the fires that ravaged its forests laid bare the hillsides, Curieuse is beginning to bloom again thanks to a reafforestation programme. Now hopes are high that one day it will return to to its former glory.

Rising 172 metres (564 feet) high at **Curieuse Peak**, the island is three and a half kilometres (two miles) long and two and a half kilometres (one and a half miles) across at its widest point.

Curieuse and almost half the north-east foreshore of Praslin, along with the entire channel between Curieuse and **Anse Boudin,** form **Curieuse Marine National Park,** which reaches a depth of thirty metres (100 feet).

On Praslin the park stretches from the high-water mark along the coast between **Pointe Chevalier** and **Pointe Zanguilles,** including outlying **St. Pierre Islet**.

Altogether the park accounts for fourteen square kilometres (five and a half square miles) of marine and terrestrial environment. The marine section ranges from shallow water reefs to the deepest part, and includes mangrove swamp, rocky intertidal shore, and sandy beaches. Two areas have been set aside for swimming.

Today Curieuse is home to giant land tortoises brought from Aldabra some time ago in an attempt to establish a breeding colony on the granitic islands.

Previous page: View of Curieuse Island from Praslin
Above: Curieuse islanders making basket fish traps.

Initially it was hoped their numbers would double, but because of poaching there are now fewer than 100. In 1990 management of the island, however, was scheduled to come under the control of the Seychelles Islands Foundation, the country's principal conservation body. Among the planned amenities are a **conservation centre** and a renewed programme for captive breeding of giant land tortoises from **Aldabra**.

Curieuse has also been proposed as a potential site on which to introduce the Seychelles black paradise flycatcher now threatened by a growing population and tree felling on **La Digue**.

A leper colony was established on Curieuse in 1833 at **Anse St. Joseph**. One man-made causeway crosses the mouth of **Baie Laraie** creating a small lagoon known as **Turtle Pond**. Apart from seven families, one of whom is the warden and his family, the island is practically uninhabited.

Getting there

Reservations for trips to Curieuse, including a beach barbecue, may be made through hotels and travel agents on Praslin.

When to go

The island is open all year-round.

Where to stay

There is no accommodation on Curieuse but there are many first-class hotels on Praslin. See Listings for "Hotels".

Sightseeing

The long stone causeway across Laraie Baie protects the lagoon once reserved for captive turtles destined for export.

From the **landing stage** by the Turtle Pond, a **trail** cuts to the best of the beaches, **Anse St. José,** which is guarded by a coral reef.

It leads past the **ruins** of the old leper colony alongside the large **house** which was reserved for the doctor when he paid periodic visits from Praslin.

The **other trail** from the landing stage skirts the shores of the Turtle Pond and the **mango plantation** to cut across the island beneath the slopes of Curieuse Peak to **Anse Badamier** on the **north coast**.

The eastern headland is called **Rouge Point** because of its granite cliffs and just south of it is the tiny but delightful beach of **Grande Anse**.

Curieuse is one of only two islands where the *coco de mer* palm grows naturally. It is also noted for an endemic vine, and fine specimens of *kapisen* can be seen inland from Baie Laraie.

Curieuse, once covered with lush vegetation, is now badly degraded but some huge *takamaka* and casuarina trees overshadow beautiful beaches. Mangoes, bananas, oranges, mandarins, *kerdebef*, and jackfruit grow on the island, and the small crops help to sustain the island's inhabitants.

The beaches of Curieuse, however, remain exceptionally beautiful, especially in the south and east where the calm, sheltered waters offer one of the best **anchorages** in Seychelles and is popular with yachtsmen and even, occasionally, cruise ships.

In the wild between twenty and forty hawksbill turtles return each year to nest on the ancestral shores which have given life to them and their forbears through thousands of years.

Other marine life is abundant and varied and in the mangrove swamps you will see many land crabs. Corals, of which the most common are colonies of blue-tipped, mauve, or brown staghorn and pink *Pocillopora*, are healthy and prolific.

Fish include angelfish, grouper, and squirrelfish. There are many molluscs and scores of octopi.

Curieuse has some reptiles including Brahminy blind snake, geckos, and many lizards — including the Seychelles skink.

The bird species found on the island include Seychelles sunbird, Seychelles bulbul, and fairy tern. A number of black parrot have recently invaded Curieuse from Praslin and there are hopes that one day they may breed there, establishing a second Seychelles stronghold.

Below: Giant tortoise on Curieuse Island.

Above: One of Curieuse Island's idyllic bays.

Overleaf: Day's golden farewell to Curieuse Island.

145

Island of Sun and Shadow

In size the fourth-largest granite island of Seychelles, **La Digue** is third-largest in terms of population. It lies fifty kilometres (31 miles) from **Mahé** and four and a half kilometres (two and three-quarter miles) from Praslin.

With no natural harbour, protected on all but its south-east shores by a magnificent encircling coral reef, the island covers more than ten square kilometres (four square miles), retaining all the fascination of an untouched world.

Rising to a height of 333 metres (1,092 feet) **Nid D'Aigles** — Eagle's Nest — "mountain" covers almost the entire hinterland. The island's only lowland is in the west.

Between **Pointe Cap Barbi** in the northwest and **Pointe Source D'Argent** in the southwest, there is a magnificent three-kilometre (two-mile) long **beach** that steps down from tumbled heaps of giant granite rocks. These dramatic rocks, one heaped on top of the other, seem as though they might fall down at any moment. According to the angle of the sun, they appear either pink or grey.

La Digue's east coast is far wilder. Its remote beaches are hauntingly beautiful for the sand is tinged with a delicate pastel pink reflecting its affinity with the pink rock of the granite headlands.

Offshore dangerous currents threaten the swimmer. But the lagoons and shores, especially from **Anse Sévère** to **Anse Gaulëttes**, are rich in shells although, of course, their collection, dead or alive, is forbidden.

The island is also famous among ornithologists and bird-watchers for its unique flycatcher bird sanctuary.

The relaxed rhythm of local life and the beautiful, well-preserved colonial-style houses surrounded by palms and other tropical greenery, the air scented by the fragrance of brilliantly coloured blooms, tell of a more gracious and gentler age; one that can still be enjoyed on this island that time seems to have passed by.

Most of the people live and work on the coconut and vanilla plantations or earn their living fishing or boat building.

There are only six motor vehicles on the

Above: Copra drying on La Digue. Once Seychelles' major export, it was prized around the world for its quality.

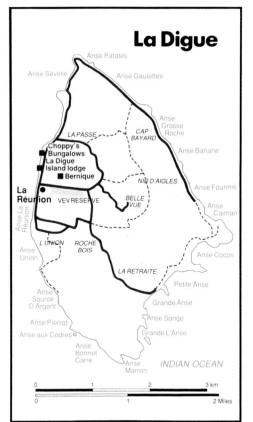

La Digue

Anse Patates
Anse Sévère
Anse Gaulettes
Anse Grosse Roche
LA PASSE
CAP BAYARD
Anse Banane
Choppy's Bungalows
La Digue Island lodge
■ Bernique
NID D'AIGLES
Anse Fourmis
La Réunion
VEV RESERVE
BELLE VUE
Anse Caiman
Anse La Réunion
L'UNION
ROCHE BOIS
Anse Cocos
Anse Union
LA RETRAITE
Petite Anse
Anse Source D'Argent
Grande Anse
Anse Pierrot
Anse Songe
Anse aux Cèdres
Grande L'Anse
Anse Bonnet Carré
Anse Marron
INDIAN OCEAN

0   1   2   3 km
0   1   2 Miles

island, all that are allowed. These are used to transport goods and building materials.

Getting there

By air or sea from Mahé to Praslin and then by local ferry or by the direct three-hour sea voyage from Mahé.

When to go

La Digue is open all year-round.

Where to stay

La Digue Island Lodge (minimum stay three nights) is the main hotel but there are also other hotels and guesthouses on the west coast. See Listings for "Hotels".

Sightseeing

Like the tourists, the 2,000 or so inhabitants use either oxcarts, bicycles, or the minibus service to get around. Riding in an oxcart or cycling along the shady roads, through the dense and leafy arches formed by the island's ancient giant trees, is an essay in light and shadow. Bicycles can be hired on the island but the best way to get around is on foot.

Walkers can reach any part of the island within an hour, and discover and observe so many wonders of this remarkable island.

Two minor roads circle the interior of the west coast and an extension of one crosses to three of the island's most splendid beaches on the south-east coast — **Grande Anse**, **Petite Anse**, and **Anse Cocos** in the lee of **Pointe Ma Flore**.

From there a footpath skirts the headland to **Anse Caiman**, another small beach, to pick up the road that circles the headland — north–south — to return to the island "capital" of **La Passe** on the west coast.

Many good tracks lead around the village areas like **L'Union** and there are many trails up into the hilly interior and across the island. One of them takes you through **La Digue Vev Special Reserve** where in the cool green woods you should see the small and rare Seychelles black paradise flycatcher.

Set on La Digue's **western plateau** ranging in height from sea level to 200 metres (656 feet), the reserve covers fifteen hectares (37 acres) and was originally established by the Royal Society for Nature Conservation — RSNC — in 1981 on land leased from Rene Payet.

When she died the government acquired the reserve which is jointly managed by RSNC and the Seychelles National Environment Commission.

Dominated by thick stands of *takamaka*, *badamnyen*, coconut, and casuarina, the north-western corner contains part of a large freshwater swamp which hosts the rare Seychelles terrapin.

Apart from five or six pairs of the rare and endangered Seychelles black paradise flycatcher, the reserve also contains Seychelles bulbul and Seychelles sunbird. The pathways are well-marked — for La Digue and the Seychelles paradise flycatcher are virtually synonymous and many bird lovers from around the world make the island their first port of call.

It is one of the few reserves in the world established to protect a single species, home to the only significant population of one of Seychelles rarest birds, undoubtedly the most beautiful of all the unique birds.

The reserve, which lies about one and a half kilometres (one mile) south of the La Passe **jetty**, is unable to support more than eight nesting pairs. But with a total island population of fewer than fifty pairs it is critical to the survival of the species although not enough to secure a future for it.

Paradise Flycatchers used to occur on many of the islands in the Praslin group, including **Praslin** itself, **Marianne**, **Félicité**, and **Aride**. Today, a few still survive on Praslin.

It has been suggested that a study should be made into the possibility of translocating a few pairs to Curieuse. In the meantime, the La Digue Flycatcher Reserve remains the best place to see this beautiful endemic bird.

The demand for timber and land for housing and farming on the La Digue plateau pose a continuing threat to the species on this island. In 1990, the reserve held perhaps no more than five pairs of flycatchers, all concentrated on the southern boundary, especially where the woodland meets marsh and tall *takamaka* and *badamnyen* trees grow by open, sunny pools of water.

Above: Drying vanilla on La Digue, another cash crop.

It is an ideal place to see the flycatchers as they flit through the canopy in search of food. The freshwater is a magnet for insects, and thus an important element in the success of the reserve.

The birds build their nests at the end of a branch right out in the open. Although this makes it vulnerable to bad weather, it is safer from predation by the Seychelles skink.

In fact, such a choice may also provide protection from introduced predators such as cats and rats, which have caused serious problems for other Seychelles land birds.

Other interesting creatures in the reserve are the terrapins. Two species are found in the reserve — the yellow-bellied terrapin and the star-bellied terrapin. Known as *torti soupap* in Creole, these extremely rare terrapins are protected under Seychelles law but are declining in most areas due to loss of habitat. **La Digue's Vev Reserve** is rare haven indeed — and not just for the birds.

If birds are not your scene, then you can enjoy many lovely walks around and across the island in solitude. Practically all end on a glorious beach which you may well have all to yourself.

The finest beach for snorkeling, scuba

diving, and windsurfing, of course, is the long western beach of **Anse Union** which faces the protective shadow of Praslin and is also guarded by a splendid coral reef. You should carry your equipment with you.

From **La Réunion** or La Passe you can follow the well-made coastal dirt road north to explore the beaches and bays at **Anse Sévère** and **Anse Patates**. The first section takes you past the busy little **harbour** and **police station** and across the back of **Cape Barbi** where you can detour to study the rocks and look out over the sea from the top of these rugged cliffs.

At the right of the road just beyond is the island's tiny **cemetery.** From there the road follows the graceful curve of glorious Anse Sévère around the island's northern cape to Anse Patates.

With no reef to guard it, great breakers curl over and smash themselves on the glittering silver sands. Great and ancient trees standing sentinel over this shore whisper in the warm breeze.

Another walk from La Passe takes you either along the seafront towards La Réunion and the turn east at La Digue Island Lodge into the interior or through the hills and forest around the back of **Allée Kersley.** From there

Top: Rusting rooftop on La Digue battles the elements.

Above: Clinging to life by a wing and a prayer — the Paradise Flycatcher is the world's most threatened species of bird.

Top: Main form of transport on sleepy La Digue is still the oxcart.

Above: Tourists explore the beauty of La Digue on bicycles.

Overleaf: Sculpted by wind, rain, and sun, nature's masterpiece adorns La Digue beach.

you can walk east on a well-made **footpath** to **Belle Vue** just beneath the **summit** of Nid D'Aigles.

The turnoff from the lodge leads past the walled gardens of a really grand old settler's house known to everybody as the **Chateau.** From there follow the **path** beyond a small cluster of thatched traditional island homes, on to the **mountain pathway** through lush and fascinating **forest**.

It takes roughly an hour to reach Belle Vue and from there it is a fairly vigorous scramble up a rough path to the actual island **summit** and fantastic views over the ocean east to **Marianne**, south-east to **Frégate**, south-west to Mahé, and north-west to Praslin.

Another path will bring you back down through the forest, past tumbled granite rocks and ravines, to the Chateau and the coast littoral.

South from La Passe and La Réunion, beyond the hotels and the **church**, the dirt road ends after half an hour's walking at the L'Union **coconut plantation**, where a trail leads on past an old **colonial house** to skirt the cliffs and some spectacular rock formations.

Many end their walk to sunbathe, swim, snorkel, or picnic at the idyllic cove of **Anse Source D'Argent**. But the trail leads on from

153

156

this beach, first to **Anse Pierrot**, and then **Anse aux Cèdres** and **Anse Bonnet Carré**.

It is sometimes possible at low tide to walk and scramble from this beach, around the foot of the rugged cliffs that mark **Pointe Jacques,** to **Anse Marron** and the mouth of the **Source Marron** stream which rises in the south-western forest to run two or three kilometres to the sea. You can also follow the trail over this headland if the tide is high.

An overgrown trail leads up the steep climb into the forest should you wish to explore the source of the stream and if you head east you will eventually come out on the dirt road that leads back to La Réunion and La Passe.

These southern cliffs and bays, and the hinterland, are wild and remote, overgrown with trees and shrubs and no clear paths, but you are never too far from home comfort. You also have the choice of continuing along the coastline, past **Point Camille** and **Grande Cap** to **Grande L'Anse**, another delightful beach from which a track leads to the motor road.

Just over **Pointe Canon**, to the east of the beach, however, is **Anse Songe** and the renowned beaches of Grande Anse, Petite Anse, and Anse Cocos.

These are at their best during the northwest monsoon between November and April. The beach has no protecting reef and the breakers and undertow are often powerful, although **Anse Cocos** is well sheltered by the headlands of **Pointe Turcy** and **Pointe Ma Flore**.

You can walk on from Anse Cocos to the long stretch of the eastern coast and the open beach of **Anse Caiman,** exposed to the powerful waves sweeping in across thousands of kilometres of ocean.

From there continue on to the reef-protected shores of **Anse Fourmis**, **Anse Banane**, **Anse Grosse Roche**, and the particularly long stretch of **Anse Gaulëttes**, all served by the island's main road, where on calm days wonderful expanses of sand and cliffs and boulders await picnickers and sunbathers.

Opposite top: La Digue fishermen repairing their boat.

Opposite: La Digue's hauntingly beautiful harbour.

Rent Your Own Island in the Sun

Dominated by an imposing summit that rises 231 metres (750 feet) above the Indian Ocean, tiny **Félicité Island's** two and a half square kilometres (one square mile) of granite is cloaked with a lush profusion of palms, and *takamaka.*

Its rocky shores, just over three kilometres (two miles) east of **La Digue** and fifty-five kilometres (34 miles) north-east of Mahé, boast only one real beach, guarded by a prolific coral reef that extends from western shore to northern headland.

Getting there

By sea or air from **Mahé** to **Praslin** and by boat from **Praslin** or **La Digue**.

When to go

Félicité is open all year-round.

Where to stay

Félicité Island Lodge is the only hotel and it stands on the only beach. It consists of two, two-bedroom, self-contained Seychelles-style houses with lounge, dining room, kitchen, and verandah. See Listings for "Hotels".

Sightseeing

The island has a permanent population of only twelve people who earn a living from the **coconut plantation**, smallholdings, and fishing.

The plantation-style lodge is basically for families or groups who rent it entirely — and therefore the island — and has all modern facilities and a full range of watersports equipment, including a motor cruiser for big game fishing.

Trails lead around the northern headland and to vantage points on the west coast. Two trails also lead through the forest up the hill to splendid views over the neighbouring islands and the ocean.

There are few birds to see, but the south of the island has some excellent stands of *takamaka* and dramatic granite cliffs.

Marianne

Some five kilometres (three miles) east of Félicité's southern tip is the deserted island of Marianne with coconut palms covering its almost one square kilometre (one-third of a square mile) of granite bedrock. It boasts two small **beaches**, one guarded by a coral reef.

This was once a marvellous island. Almost all the endemic birds of Seychelles were recorded there — Seychelles warbler, fody, black parrot, paradise flycatcher, and magpie robin.

These have all disappeared, as have the native forest, and the chestnut flanked white-eye, which in all the world was only ever recorded on **Marianne**.

Today the island is covered in coconut palms, but at the northern end of the island the native forest is beginning to regenerate.

Île Cocos

Half a kilometre (one-third of a mile) off Félicité's northern headland a coral reef encircles **Île Cocos**, a delightful two hectares (five acres) of interesting rock formations and verdant palms. And just beyond is a smaller island cohort, the half a hectare (1.2 acres) of **Île La Fouche**.

The island is a protected area and has been closed to visitors due to depletion of coral taken as souvenirs.

The sisters

These two tiny islets lie between Félicité and the two deserted islands of the Sisters, **Grande Soeur** and **Petite Soeur**, which stand two kilometres (just over a mile) to the north of Félicité.

Grande Soeur covers almost a square kilometre (one-third of a square mile) and has two coral-fringed **beaches** at its slender midriff, one on the east and one on the west. Petite Soeur, which has no beaches, covers only one-third of a square kilometre.

Zave

A tiny island between La Digue and Curieuse, **Zave** is one of the few islands without rats and as a result has five breeding species of seabirds.

Seabird Citadel of the Indian Ocean

Aride is the most important nature reserve of the granitic islands. Indeed, in some respects, it is of global importance. Seychelles boasts many extraordinary natural assets, but even among these Aride is beyond compare.

Nowhere else on earth will you find — together in one place — the beautiful, fragrant Wright's gardenia and a rocky hillside covered in nesting sooty terns, elegant roseate terns, and red-tailed tropicbirds.

Aride is home to the world's largest colony of at least one, and perhaps two, species of seabird. Even in the natural paradise of the world's only granitic ocean islands, there is nowhere quite like Aride.

It is the most northerly of the granite islands of Seychelles, lying fifty kilometres (31 miles) north-east of Mahé and sixteen kilometres (10 miles) north of Praslin. It is one and a half kilometres (one mile) long and just over half a kilometre (one-third of a mile) wide.

Discovered in 1756, its highest point, **Gros la Tête,** rises 134 metres (435 feet) above the sea from the submarine plateau of the Seychelles Bank. This verdant island, covered with lush tropical vegetation, is partially surrounded by a spectacular coral reef.

Until some years ago it was the least-known of the granitic islands but today this mostly rugged and precipitous island is rightly known as the seabird citadel of the Indian Ocean.

It was originally declared a private nature reserve in March 1970, by Guy St. Jorré, executor to the Chenard heirs (the island's original owners for nearly 100 years).

It was only to be sold on the condition set by the Chenards, that it remained a natural sanctuary. In 1973, Christopher Cadbury bought the island's sixty-eight hectares (167 acres) on behalf of the Royal Society for Nature Conservation — RSNC — and in June 1975 Aride was declared a Special Reserve under Seychelles law.

It not only enjoys its reputation as the

Opposite: Sooty terns take to the air above Aride.

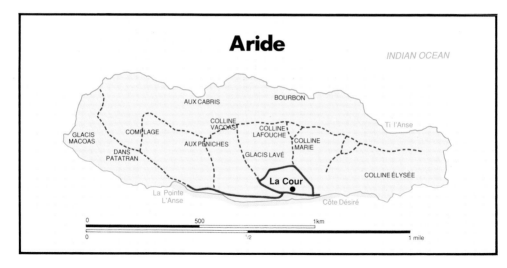

Aride

INDIAN OCEAN

AUX CABRIS
BOURBON
Ti l'Anse
COLLINE VACOAS
GLACIS MACOAS
COMPLAGE
COLLINE LAFOUCHE
AUX PÉNICHES
COLLINE MARIE
DANS PATATRAN
GLACIS LAVÉ
COLLINE ÉLYSÉE
La Cour
La Pointe L'Anse
Côte Désiré

0   500   1km
0   ½   1 mile

seabird citadel of the region but, along with Frégate Island, may have been another refuge and resort of the Indian Ocean pirates of the seventeenth and eighteenth centuries.

Ecologically, Aride is a key island in this region, its soils made up of red earths on the higher ground, with a deep blackish topsoil containing guano, deposited through the centuries by breeding seabirds, on the plateau.

It is probably the guano that has rendered Aride so fertile. Its vegetation is now the most natural of any of the smaller islands in the Seychelles' granitic group.

Most of the islands suffered wholesale clearance during the era of the copra industry, which replaced their native vegetation with a dense cover of coconut palms.

Seasonal monsoons are believed to create a slight up-welling of nutrient-enriched water at either end of the bank and around the Amirantes. These up-wellings increase the phytoplankton population which is significantly greater than those of similar reefs in the Pacific and Atlantic.

In fact, the reef complex of the Seychelles Bank, inhabited by a stunning variety of organisms, is one of the most productive natural ecosystems in the world, comparable to a tropical rainforest.

Aride has more varieties of breeding seabirds than any other Seychelles island except Aldabra. Of the ten breeding species found on Aride, six are terns.

Nowhere else in the world can you see such great numbers of **lesser noddy**. The roseate tern colony and the population of **white-tailed tropicbird** are also among the world's largest.

Fairy terns lay their single egg on bare branches throughout the island all year round, while the annual spectacle of the world's only hilltop **sooty tern** colony reaches its peak during the south-east monsoon.

Bridled tern and **common noddy** nest at variable times of the year, ensuring that there is always something of interest whenever you visit the island.

Two species of **shearwaters** — **wedgetail** and **Audobon's** — arrive in huge numbers towards dusk. During the daytime they travel long distances in search of food. Gliding on stiff wings, following the contours of the ocean realm, they catch small fish which they regurgitate for their young.

Shearwaters exhibit spectacular homing ability. In one experiment, birds transported to Boston in the United States of America returned to their burrows in Skokholm, Wales within thirteen days. Outside the breeding season, shearwaters wander the ocean on a global scale.

On land they are clumsy and have to scramble up rocks to gain height for take off, but once airborne they are aerial maestros.

Once Aride was home to a thriving population of the now endangered **Seychelles magpie robin**. A nineteenth-century list of the birds of Seychelles records drily that the magpie robin was "almost extinct" adding "specimens urgently needed".

Above: Bird's-eye view of Aride, seabird citadel of the Indian Ocean.

With this attitude among the natural historians of the day, it is amazing that the bird survived; in one day a Frenchman visiting Aride shot twenty-four birds, roughly equivalent to the present world population of the species.

Introduced cats and habitat destruction around the turn of the century sealed the magpie robin's fate on Aride, and today the species clings precariously to survival only on Frégate. Aride's cats were later eradicated, but too late to save the magpie robin.

An attempt to reintroduce the magpie robins to Aride in the 1970s failed for reasons unknown. One bird survived for ten years until dying a lonely death in April 1988.

The International Council for Bird Preservation is now carrying out a long-term intensive study of the species' requirements and a future translocation to Aride remains a possibility if it is considered desirable in order to save the species from extinction.

There are early records of **black parrots**, **paradise flycatchers**, and **Seychelles fody** on Aride, but all have now disappeared.

Yet, with the cessation of tree cutting and regeneration of the native forest, Aride could still become a home for many of Seychelles' endangered species, helping to reverse much of man's past destruction.

Aride is the last natural refuge for the endemic flowering shrub, **Wright's gardenia** (*Rothmannia annae*), or *bwa sitron*.

The plant may have also occurred on Mahé and Silhouette, but fell an early victim to habitat destruction as the trees around them were felled and the rich soils they required were washed away.

Wright's gardenia flowers several times every year. Flowering is triggered by torrential rain, the white flowers with purple spots appearing about ten days after. Flowering can occur at any time of year, but is most frequent during the wetter, north-west monsoon.

When the flowers die, inedible lemon-sized green fruits appear, giving the plant the local name *bwa sitron*. The shrub grows to the height of a small tree, about four metres (thirteen feet). When the gardenias flower, their fragrant perfume fills the air.

Today Aride ranks high among the world's most important nature reserves. Seychelles already possesses two sites designated as

Some of Aride's marvellous birds.

Left: The once endangered Seychelles warbler.

Left centre: Lesser noddy tern.

Top left: Baby fairy tern.

Top right: Mature fairy tern.

Above: Great frigatebird.

World Heritage Sites: **Aldabra atoll** and the **Vallée de Mai**. If a third site is proposed, then this must surely be it.

Aride represents one of the earth's most unique ecosystems — truly a world heritage. Egg and shell collecting are strictly prohibited, including dead shells on the sea-shore (a vital source of cheap housing for hermit crabs).

It is not permitted to start fires, except in an area set aside for barbecues next to the beach-side **visitors' shelter**. This is also the place to picnic and quench your thirst.

"This is where I want to build my home," said one awestruck writer, visiting Aride in 1986. A million or so ocean wanderers have been struck by the same idea.

Getting there

By boat from Mahé or Praslin. A nature reserve fee of seventy-five rupees is payable (sometimes included in the excursion cost) to help meet the costs of running this remarkable reserve. Visits can be arranged through travel agents or hotels on Mahé and Praslin.

When to go

Aride is normally open to visitors four days a week. Landing may be difficult during the south-east monsoon and the island is sometimes closed during this season. The warden keeps in daily touch with Seychelles Radio to advise on conditions during this period.

Be sure to put valuables in a waterproof bag for the landing and departure.

Where to stay

There is no overnight accommodation. The majority come to see the bird colonies, but bathing is permitted, and the snorkeling and diving are considered excellent. The shelter by the landing beach provides a place to picnic and escape the Equatorial sunshine.

The number of visitors is not restricted, but due to the location of Aride as the outpost of the granitic islands, parties are much smaller than elsewhere, and visitors number fewer than 1,000 a year (about one per cent of tourist arrivals in Seychelles).

Sightseeing

Because of the enormous number of ground nesting terns and tropicbirds, it is essential to stick to the **nature trails**.

You will be guided by the warden and his staff through the **plantation area** and the **coastal forest**, up the steep *mapou*-covered **hillside** to **viewing points** on the northern **cliffs**, where you can gaze out on a scene of unparalleled magnificence, little changed from a time when Seychelles was untouched by man.

It still remains one of those all too rare corners of the planet where nature rules supreme, undisturbed by modern day pressures, a place to fill the visitor with awe at the beauty, variety, and abundance of life it shelters in this tiny, self-contained world in the heart of the Indian Ocean.

A **nature trail** leads across the island to the **summit** of Gros la Tête and down along a **ridge** to a point above the **eastern cliffs**.

Some proper **footpaths** line its **one beach**, a half-kilometre-long stretch of sand fringing **La Cour**. The beach is protected by a glorious **reef**, as is the entire northern coast which has no beach, but the eastern and western shores face the open sea.

Among Aride's claims to fame is the world's largest colony of lesser noddy. With the protection of Aride, and the regrowth of trees, especially *bwa mapou* (a favourite nesting tree), the population of this Indian Ocean speciality has rocketed. In 1955, the population was estimated at about 20,000 pairs.

By 1973 this had increased to 90,000, and by 1988 the population exceeded 170,000. With the restoration of the plateau woodland, and as the hill woodland matures, the population could eventually reach an incredible 250,000 pairs.

The brown or common noddy is not as common as the lesser noddy, but there are still about 16,000 pairs on Aride. Both species nest during the south-east monsoon, but curiously the brown noddy has a secondary breeding season during the north-west monsoon, albeit in smaller numbers.

The elegant roseate tern once bred on several of the granitic islands. Alas it has apparently vanished from seven former breeding sites, including three outer islands.

Indeed, throughout the world the species is endangered. Populations almost everywhere have plummeted. The Aride population is therefore of vital conservation importance.

Uncontrolled egg collecting has wiped out

sooty terns on many islands, but protection on Aride arrived in time to preserve what is now the world's only hill-top colony of this species.

In 1973, when the RSNC took over the management of Aride there were perhaps 50,000 pairs. Today there are as many as 300,000 pairs making Aride an extremely noisy place from March onwards, as a rapid build-up of birds takes place, and preparations for the breeding season get underway.

The beautiful fairy tern, unlike the other terns, breeds all year round, and there are no prizes for guessing which island has the largest population in Seychelles. With up to 20,000 pairs, the answer is Aride Island.

The graceful white-tailed tropicbird also breeds all the year round, and like the fairy tern, Aride is home to the largest population of this species in the whole of Seychelles.

Even more importantly, Aride is the only breeding site in the granitic islands for the red-tailed tropicbird. Only a few pairs breed there, but a glimpse of this rarity can be the highlight of any bird-watcher's holiday.

As Aldabra is so remote, Aride will be the only opportunity most visitors have to see this species in what is thought to be its northernmost breeding site.

Up to 20,000 pairs of wedge-tailed shearwaters and twice as many Audobon's shearwaters make Aride their home, the latter certainly being the largest colony in the whole of Seychelles.

Bridled terns also breed in small numbers. This species is nowhere common in Seychelles and extremely little is known about it.

In total, ten species of seabird breed, more than the rest of the granitic Seychelles combined. Moreover, most of them have their Seychelles stronghold in this remarkable seabird citadel of the Indian Ocean.

The bird population is densest during the breeding months beginning with the first arrival of the sooty terns followed by the noddies and the roseate terns.

They occupy their established territories with hardly a dispute among them. Both sooty terns and roseate terns are of special interest to scientists — the sooties because this is their only large high-level nesting ground in the entire world (elsewhere they use the   flat sea-level sand cays); and the roseates because they are a distinct Western Indian Ocean race and this is one of the world's largest colonies.

During the south-east monsoon, the entire island from shore to summit of the hill teems with breeding birds and it is difficult to avoid stepping on the well-camouflaged chicks and eggs of sooty terns which cover the slopes in the thousands.

At this time seabirds are particularly vulnerable to predators, especially those species found mainly in the tropics with long incubation and fledging periods.

In the past, predation of shearwater chicks about to fledge was common. On their breeding islands of Aride, **Cousin**, **Cousine**, **Récife**, and **Desnoeufs**, they were indiscriminately killed and salted as a delicacy.

Once the chicks have fledged, the birds return to the vast expanse of the ocean for they are creatures of the open sea.

Where the Frigates Fly

Despite the staggering numbers and variety of breeding seabirds, perhaps the most spectacular sight on Aride is the hundreds of non-breeding frigatebirds which frequent the northern cliffs.

Visitors who climb from the plateau to the cliff-tops will be rewarded not only by the refreshing breeze at the summit, but a sight unique in Seychelles. Dramatic granite rocks stand majestically 122 metres (400 feet) above the turquoise seas.

There you may sit to recover your breath and perhaps be lucky enough to see a hawksbill turtle or a group of bottlenose dolphins swim past in the crystal clear waters below (See "Bats and Tenrecs, Whales and Dolphins", Part Three).

On the horizon, you can see the flat coral island of **Denis**. Above the waves, which crash onto the last solid rock before the Indian subcontinent, soar spectacular giants.

The vast majority of these are the great frigatebirds, with perhaps only one or two per cent being lesser frigatebirds.

This is a strange situation as both species use **Aldabra** as their nearest breeding site, where the lesser outnumber the great more than three-to-one. Great frigatebirds once bred on Aride, and with total protection it seems likely that they will return.

Above: Red-tailed tropicbird in flight.

Frigates are pirates of the air. They harry larger seabirds — especially tropicbirds — to make them disgorge their catch. It is truly amazing to watch these aerial acrobats twist and turn after their quarry, using their tails as rudders, then plummet seaward to snatch their reward even before it hits the surface.

Haven for rare land birds

Aride is perhaps the most unspoilt granitic island. At one time it was home to many rare endemics such as the magpie robin, paradise flycatcher, and black parrot. As the woodland matures, Aride may one day become a vital preserve for such rarities.

A model for an introduction programme could be the translocation of twenty-nine Seychelles warblers from **Cousin** to Aride, which took place in September 1988. All the birds transferred survived and quickly settled into an environment with six times the food supply of Cousin and far more territory.

It was not the breeding season, but this sudden windfall was not to be missed, and one pair built a nest within two days. In the first year the population doubled to fifty-eight and is now more than 100.

Thus snatched from the brink of extinction, the warbler is a great symbol of hope. If man can save this tiny bird then other species in Seychelles and, indeed, throughout the world can surely be saved by wise and careful conservation management.

Because of the success of the Aride programme, the Seychelles warbler has been removed from the Red Data list of endangered birds.

Unique flora

Aride's most precious plant is the beautiful Wright's gardenia. It is believed that at one time this plant occurred on other islands, but has vanished for reasons unknown.

On Aride there is a healthy population of about 1,300 of these small trees. Aride also boasts Seychelles' newest unique plant, a species of *peponium*, a type of cucumber.

No plant or animal lives out life in isolation. Perhaps one of the most fascinating inter-relationships between bird and plant is that of pisonia or *bwa mapou* and the seabirds which nest in its canopy. What other tree sets out to capture a bird with sticky seeds, thereby rendering it flightless?

The death of the birds marks the birth of a new tree — with a ready-made supply of fertilizer to start it out in life. Yet the trees are also vital to the birds as nesting sites.

Visitors are sometimes distressed to see an entangled bird quietly awaiting its fate, but this is nature's way, and the actual number lost is tiny — perhaps one per cent — while normal losses from egg failure or chick deaths can be about one-third of all eggs laid.

In return, lesser noddies obtain nesting sites and material (pisonia leaves being soft and malleable are ideal for the job) while sooty terns nest below its spreading branches where breeding success can be as high as seventy-five per cent compared to only twenty per cent in exposed sites.

All in all the birds have gained tremendously from wise management on Aride, where the old practice of cutting back pisonia — which has the effect of coppicing the trees — has been stopped and allows them to flourish and grow tall.

Other fauna

In 1986, after ninety-five minutes on Aride's reefs, Peter Scott recorded eighty-eight species of fish. No proper survey has taken place, but subsequent visitors and wardens have increased the number of recorded species to more than 150. Undoubtedly the final total will be much higher.

The striking **wedge-tailed blue tang,** with an electric blue and black body and a yellow triangle on the tail, is one fairly common species not encountered so often elsewhere.

The sea's greatest fish, the harmless **whale shark,** is sometimes seen offshore. It is well worth keeping your eyes peeled for this gentle giant when you cross the sea to Aride. **Dolphins** are commonly seen, and even **whales** have been sighted occasionally.

Hawksbill turtles nest on Aride's shoreline during the north-west monsoon, and even the rare green turtle — almost extinct in the granitic Seychelles — has come up on the beach a few times.

Two kinds of harmless snake—the endemic **Seychelles wolf snake** and the introduced **Brahminy blind snake**—also occur but visitors rarely see them.

By contrast, the number of **lizards** is among the greatest on earth, especially the

Wright's skink (found only on a few other islands) and the smaller **Seychelles skink.** The density has been measured at one skink to every 3.5 square metres (seven square yards), so watch where you put your feet. **Geckos** also abound, notably the large **bronze gecko** and the attractive **green gecko.**

Above: Aride's endemic peponium plant.

The Once and Future Island

Below: Fairy tern chick.

Above: Nesting white-tailed tropicbird.

One of the smallest granitic islands of Seychelles, **Cousin Island** is also one of the biggest conservation success stories of the Indian Ocean. Covering just over twenty-eight hectares (70 acres), Cousin's highest point is fifty-eight metres (189 feet) above sea level.

It lies forty-four kilometres (27 miles) north of Mahé and three kilometres (just under two miles) south-west of **Grande Anse** on **Praslin**.

This verdant ornithological sanctuary became a nature reserve in 1968, when with help from the World Wildlife Fund (WWF) and worldwide contributions, the International Council for Bird Preservation (ICBP) bought it as a haven for endangered species of land and sea birds. It was made a special reserve in 1975.

At a time when more and more species reach the edge of extinction, it is one place, no matter how small, where the process has been reversed. There, by careful conservation and management, an endangered species has been snatched from the brink.

In 1959 the number of Seychelles warblers left on earth was only twenty-six. They had been wiped out on **Marianne** because of habitat destruction, and possibly from the other islands even before their presence had been recorded.

The same inexorable road to extinction was being followed on Cousin where uncontrolled egg collecting had already eliminated the sooty tern. The original forest was almost gone. Introduced plants such as cotton and Rangoon creeper dominated wherever the coconut plantation left any space.

Hawksbill and green turtles had been collected for tortoiseshell and meat without regard for any limits, and the green turtle was eliminated as an exploitable resource. Wedge-tailed shearwaters or *fouke* were also taken for food, and the reefs denuded of shells. It was plunder on a massive scale.

It inspired the ICBP to launch an international appeal to save the island — and the Seychelles warbler — which is now managed by ICBP.

Under their protection the native woodland was encouraged to regenerate, resulting

167

Above: Cousin Island — sanctuary of the once-endangered Seychelles warbler.
Opposite: Cousine Island.

in a spectacular recovery of the Seychelles warbler population. By 1987 there were almost 400.

The Red Data Book recommended the establishment of a second population on another island as a long-term aim. So long as Cousin was its only home, the species would be considered to remain threatened.

Aride Island was chosen. The regeneration of Aride's woodland since its acquisition by RSNC had mirrored that on Cousin, and studies showed the island supported a greater density of the insects on which the warblers feed.

In 1990, following the success of the ICBP transfer project, the Seychelles warbler was taken off the Red Data list of threatened species — an all too rare example of man's actions *saving* a species.

Getting there

Cousin is open to visitors three mornings a week: Tuesday, Thursday, and Friday. Visits can be arranged through travel agents, and most Praslin hotels. Parties must obey certain rules and regulations as the island is a Special Nature Reserve. Admission is seventy-five rupees. The charge for commercial photography in 1990 was 400 rupees a day for still cameras and 1,500 rupees a day for film or video cameras, payable in advance. Flash photography is forbidden and so is the use of close-up lenses or tripods.

When to go

The best months for visiting are between April and September, when huge numbers of birds arrive for nesting.

Where to stay

There is no accommodation on the island. There are many first-class hotels on Praslin. See Listings for "Hotels".

Sightseeing

Six people live on the island, which is completely protected by an encircling reef. Swimming, shell collecting, smoking, and picnics are forbidden. Remember to stay with your guide, who speaks French and English, and never stray from the path.

The one **path** leads through the interior and around the north and west coasts of the island. The western beach is **Anse Vacoa**. There is a much bigger beach on the north and north-east shore and a delightful little cove, **Anse La Chaine** in the south-east.

Cousin is one of only three islands — the others are **Cousine** and **Frégate** — where fody or *tok tok* breeds. The bird has disappeared from the other islands and competition with the introduced Madagascar fody or cardinal was at one time suspected.

In fact, on Cousin the two can be seen side by side, each occupying its own ecological niche. The Seychelles species' diet is about three-quarters insects, while the Madagascar fody obtains more than eighty per cent of its diet from seeds, so there is little overlap between the food requirements.

The *tok tok* is an aggressive little bird, and a superior hunter to the cardinal. Moreover, the cardinal nests almost exclusively in coconut palms, and some pisonia sites, usually above six metres (20 feet), whereas the *tok tok* prefers low sites in bushy trees.

Also the cardinal breeds only once a year, during the north-west monsoon, whereas the *tok tok* appears to breed in relays throughout the year. Cardinals lay two eggs, however, and *tok toks* usually lay only one.

On Cousin, the two species appear quite happy to coexist and it is fascinating to watch their behavioural differences. Cardinal courtship behaviour is aggressive, but the *tok tok's* is not.

The *tok tok's* courtship involves an upright wing-beating display with the bill raised and tail depressed, while the cardinal's display is not erect, the bill points at the female, and the tail is straight. On this tiny island, two related species, one native and one introduced, appear to have come to terms with each other.

Cousin is also the best island on which to see the endemic subspecies, the Seychelles turtle dove. This bird has largely disappeared due to inbreeding with the closely related Malagasy turtle dove.

The latter was often carried by ships as a source of food, and deliberately or accidentally released in Seychelles. It is a little larger than the Seychelles turtle dove. Even on Cousin, there are many hybrids and the pure Seychelles race probably no longer exists.

Other endemic landbirds include Seychelles sunbirds and five pairs of Seychelles blue pigeons.

Seabird Spectacular

Rats and feral cats on most granitic islands have decimated the once rich seabird colonies. Amazingly, despite its accessibility and closeness to Praslin, Cousin escaped this onslaught. Cousin and Aride are the seabird centres of the granitic Seychelles.

Indeed, the wedge-tailed shearwater or *fouke* has its principal breeding site on Cousin with about 35,000 pairs breeding between October and March.

They are nocturnal birds and the adults are more often seen out at sea during the day. They return in the evening, when their eerie wails and cries fill the air. The chicks, which become very fat before fledging, were formerly eaten in large numbers. Today, their stronghold on Cousin is protected.

The Audobon's shearwater or *riga* breeds all the year round on Cousin. It is much less common than the *fouke*. It is also nocturnal and has a variety of bloodcurdling shrieks and calls.

The lovely fairy tern is common on Cousin, as is the ground-nesting, white-tailed tropicbird, which is found all over the island in great numbers. Both breed all year round.

The breeding colony of lesser noddy, with over 100,000 pairs, is second in size in the world only to Aride. Brown noddies nest in mid-year, in much smaller numbers with about 3,000 pairs, while a few hundred pairs of bridled terns nest in a unique eight-month cycle.

Frigatebirds roost in small numbers but return to **Aldabra** to breed. Your guide on Cousin will take you to a lookout point near the summit where these aerial giants can be seen soaring effortlessly above the island.

Vegetation

Although seventy-two introduced plants occur on Cousin, the most common trees are now well-established native varieties. These include the pisonia, *bwa mapou*, which is rarely found away from seabird islands because of the interrelationship between tree and birds.

Tortoise tree, or *bwa tortu*, is common on the plateau. Its fruits appear smelly and unappetising, but are a delight to the giant tortoises.

In addition, the flowers provide nectar for fodies and sunbirds, and the trees are a hunting ground for the warblers, which can be seen hopping from branch to branch feeding on insects.

The fruit bat tree or *bwa sousouri* is another indigenous tree which has associations with an endemic animal. The yellow fleshy fruit is sometimes eaten by fruit bats.

The endemic Balfour's pandanus is common on the hillside, while on the coast coconuts and casuarina dominate.

Introduced plants create their own interest. Cotton was once grown commercially on Cousin, and wild plants are common along the coastal trail.

Above: Brown bronze gecko, one of Cousin's many endemic species.

Castor-oil and pawpaw are also to be seen along the trail. The maternity plant is prolific in one area. This fascinating plant has thick, fleshy leaves which can grow roots and form new plants after they fall.

Other remnants of Cousin's days as a plantation include coffee, bamboo, chillies, lemon, jamalac, and mango.

Hawksbill Headquarters

The beaches of Cousin are among the main breeding grounds in the western part of the Indian Ocean for the endangered hawksbill turtle.

It is too late to save the green turtle as a

significant breeding species in this area, and until there is a change of attitude among ordinary people towards the conservation of turtles, there is no chance of the population recovering.

The hawksbill is another matter. With vigilant protection on Cousin, and a long-term study — perhaps the best in the world — of the species, there is hope for the future.

A tagging and monitoring programme which began on Cousin in 1973 has provided valuable long-term data of world importance, and various papers have been written under the auspices of ICBP.

Female hawksbills lay up to six times a season, at fourteen-day intervals. Tagged turtles return every two or three years.

Interestingly, no Cousin-tagged turtle has been recorded as nesting anywhere else. Clearly, if the hawksbill is to be saved, the few places where they are given complete protection, such as Cousin, are of vital importance.

The turtles nest in daylight from August to April. Older turtles appear to lay more clutches and they contain more eggs. After laying about 130 eggs in a shallow hole at the top of the beach, the females spend about half an hour carefully covering the eggs and disguising the site.

About sixty days later the young emerge, usually at night, when ghost crabs — their only predator on Cousin — are less of a danger.

The hatchlings, oriented towards the sea, scurry down the beach like little clockwork toys and head out into the ocean together, and into mystery. Next to nothing is known about their life until they return to breed.

Because of Cousin Island, and thanks largely to the ICBP, there is hope that hawksbill turtles will outlive the market for their tortoise-shell, and as tourists become increasingly conservation-minded, they will prefer the chance of seeing one of these creatures alive on a nesting beach, or gliding past underwater, to plastic-like trinkets produced from the shell of a dead animal which is clinging to the precipice of extinction.

Cousin is a good place to see Aldabran giant land tortoises roaming free, living as their extinct, endemic cousins once did on other granitic islands.

Cousine Island

Just two kilometres (1.2 miles) from Cousin lies the slightly smaller **Cousine Island** covering twenty-five hectares (61 acres). Lush with palms, encircled entirely by a glorious coral reef, two well-marked trails cut through the undergrowth from the long, golden beach of **Grande Anse** but you will need permission to visit this privately-owned island.

In 1990 several Seychelles warblers were transferred from Cousin in the hope of establishing a third home for this rarity.

Above: A brightly coloured cardinal with a sweet tooth.

Coral Jewel of the Indian Ocean

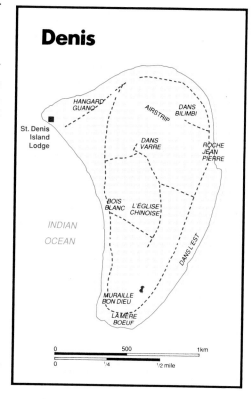

Denis

St. Denis Island Lodge

HANGARD GUANO

AIRSTRIP

DANS BILIMBI

DANS VARRE

ROCHE JEAN PIERRE

BOIS BLANC

L'ÉGLISE CHINOISE

INDIAN OCEAN

DANS L'EST

MURAILLE BON DIEU

LA MÈRE BOEUF

0   500   1km
0   1/4   1/2 mile

No doubt most people at some time have dreamed of ruling over their own tropical island paradise. Industrialist Pierre Burkhardt is one of the rare few who made the dream a reality.

Years ago, tired of the neurosis involved in running his cellulose manufacturing empire, he bought one and a half square kilometre (half a square mile) **Denis Island (Île Denis)**, which lies ninety-five kilometres (59 miles) north of **Mahé**, fifty-five kilometres (34 miles) from **Praslin**, and sixteen kilometres (10 miles) east of **Bird Island.**

The island is at the edge of the **Seychelles Bank** which plunges 2,000 metres (6,500 feet) down into the deep abyss of the sea.

It was named after Frenchman Denis de Trobriand, who landed there in 1773 from the French vessel *L'Étoile* to find it covered in a profusion of birds, giant tortoise, turtle, and dugongs — "sea cows".

Somewhere on the island he buried a bottle containing the Act of Possession, claiming it in the name of the King of France. This historical treasure still awaits discovery.

Guarded in the east, south, and south-west by a **coral reef**, creating an enormous and tranquil lagoon, encircled all around by an almost continuous, startlingly **white beach**, and no more than 1.8 kilometres (one mile) long and 1.3 kilometres (three quarters of a mile) wide, Denis Island is covered with deep deposits of guano formed through centuries of bird droppings and is extremely fertile.

However tiny the island, Mr. Burkhardt bought himself a large chunk of happiness. Thickly wooded **palm groves** cloak much of the island, making walking inland cool and shady.

After buying the island, which has a population of fifty people, the new owner built the small **landing strip, hotel,** and pioneered cultivation by developing a **farm** to work in tandem with the **coconut plantation** that produces copra.

One may well hope that he then lay back and enjoyed his own private paradise in the company of those exclusive guests lucky enough to check in there.

Mr. Burkhardt likes to stay ahead of the rest, nonetheless. The time on Denis Island is one hour ahead of the other 114 islands of Seychelles.

Getting there

Denis is one of five islands served by a daily Air Seychelles flight. The flight takes thirty-five minutes. You can also charter a yacht or schooner for the eight-hour sea voyage from **Victoria**. Day-trippers are not allowed and the minimum period you can stay is no less than three days. Mr. Burkhardt got it right.

When to go

The island is open all year-round.

Overleaf: Denis Island basks in its isolated solitude with clocks set one hour ahead of the rest of Seychelles.

Where to stay

There is only one hotel. Denis Island Lodge has twenty-four bungalows and, though hardly the place you can pop into on the off chance there might be a vacant table, is famous all over the Indian Ocean for its French and Creole cuisine. See Listings for "Hotels".

Sightseeing

A well-trod **footpath** circles the island with many trails leading inland where they intermingle. The tiny **village** is made up of about fifteen thatched houses and approximately fifty inhabitants. On the northern headland, close to the lodge manager's **house** is the **lighthouse** built in 1910.

There are two disused **prisons**, a **copra processing centre**, **farm** — and the only **ecumenical chapel** in the entire Seychelles Archipelago.

On the south-west coast some remarkable coral formations, known simply as **Caves**, are a popular spot for island visitors. It gives some indication of the forces and processes which go into the formation of a coral island.

There are watersports in plenty — swimming, windsurfing, snorkeling, scuba diving — and for strict landlubbers, tennis and golf.

Most of all, Denis has become a big game fisherman's Mecca whose waters are known — and coveted — by enthusiasts from around the world. At least five times these waters have yielded world record dog-tooth tuna.

If you want to write your name into the marlin record books, May, October, November, and December are notable months for opportunistic fishermen. If you are not that ambitious the year-round sport is still magnificent, even for marlin, and especially for barracuda, bonito, and sailfish (See "Fighting Fish of the Deep Ocean", Part Three). Move over, Hemingway.

Opposite: Bird Island as thousands of its avian residents see it.

Overleaf: Sooty terns breed in prolific numbers on aptly named Bird Island.

Following pages: The deserted beaches of Bird Island are shared only with the local winged inhabitants.

Strictly for the Birds

Anchored to the edge of the submerged plateau of the **Seychelles Bank** in the Indian Ocean, 105 kilometres (65 miles) north-west of **Mahé**, the one square kilometre (under half a square mile) of **Bird Island** boasts a feathered fantasia. From May to October it is the nesting site for up to one million sooty terns. Other species include lesser and common noddy, and crested fairy tern. You can hear the noise of the sooty terns as you approach the immense colony situated in the north-west corner of the island.

Only one and a half kilometres (one mile) long and just over half a kilometre wide, Bird Island's French name was endowed because of the now extinct dugongs — or "sea cows" — that the first French seamen to land there found in its waters 230 years ago. They called it Île aux Vaches.

Bird Island attracts many ornithologists in search of rarities. As the first landfall for Eurasian migrants, many unusual species have been recorded there: **broad-billed sandpiper**, **corncrake**, and **black** and **white cuckoo** to name a few. Regular visitors to the island include **sanderling**, **swallow**, **turnstone**, and **greater** and **lesser sandplover**. Guy Savy, the owner of Bird Island, declared it a wildlife sanctuary in 1986 and the sooty tern eggs, once heavily exploited, are no longer taken.

Getting there

There is a scheduled daily flight by Air Seychelles. Yachts or schooners can be chartered for the sea voyage at **Victoria**. Bird Island is eight hours cruising from Mahé by sea and thirty minutes by air.

When to go

The island is open all year-round.

Where to stay

The only hotel, Bird Island Lodge has twenty-five wood and thatch bungalows, each with its own verandah overlooking the ocean. It specialises in European and Creole cuisine. See Listings for "Hotels".

Sightseeing

The northern and southern tips of the island

are sometimes swept by strong currents. The lodge staff can tell you which beaches are safest for swimming and snorkeling. The one really safe **beach** is at **Bird Island Lodge**.

Inland, many pathways cut across the island and there are three **wells**, one small **reservoir**, and strangely enough, a **piggery**. The vegetables and fruit groves produce all the supplies for the lodge.The south-west coast from **Passe Cocos** to **Passe Endormi** is also safe inside the fringing reef.

The island's special pet is a giant tortoise, Esmeralda — a male, let it be said — which earned Bird Island immortality in the 1990 *Guinness Book of Records* as the largest and heaviest tortoise in the world. The 298-kilo (657-lb) creature is said to be 150 years old, although this is doubtful. Coconut palms line the cross runways of the **landing strip** and the lodge provides facilities for tennis and all watersports including deep-sea fishing for the same giants sought out by the boats from **Denis**. Coral reef protects the stunning south-west, south-east, and east beaches. If swimming, beware of the currents and the undertow outside the lagoon beaches.

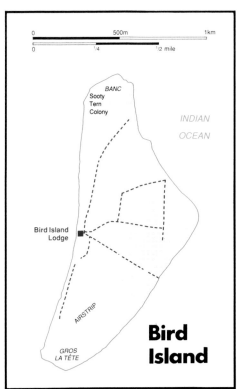

Two inbetween islands

Neither inner nor outer isles, **Plate Island** and **Coétivy** are very much the loners of Seychelles, both lying a considerable distance directly south of Mahé.

If anything, Plate Island is notable as a shipping hazard but Coétivy is the little-known, little-visited breadbasket of the Seychellois people, absolutely vital to the national wellbeing.

Half a square kilometre (0.2 square mile) of reef plate, 140 kilometres (90 miles) south of Mahé, Plate Island has little of special interest apart from its fabulous **coral reefs** and the **coconut plantation** run by the Island Development Company.

The reef has claimed at least two ships; the French corvette *La Perle* in 1863 and a lugger, the *Alice Adeline* in 1906.

Getting there

By air or sea charter. There is an airstrip and landing stage. There are no regular services.

When to go

As a non-tourist resort there is no season.

Where to stay

There is no tourist accommodation.

Coétivy

Named after the Frenchman who discovered it in 1771, the nine-square kilometre (3.7 square mile) island of Coétivy is 290 kilometres (180 miles) south of Mahé.

Getting there

By air or sea charter. There is an airstrip and a landing stage. There are no regular services.

When to go

As a non-tourist resort the island is a year-round terrestrial and marine agricultural centre.

Where to stay

There is no tourist accommodation.

Sightseeing

Relatively large by Seychelles standards, ten-kilometre (six-mile) long Coétivy — it is only one kilometre (half a mile) wide — boasts the longest unbroken shoreline in Seychelles.

With more natural flat land than Mahé, Coétivy is a vital breadbasket for the main centres of population and the island has long produced beef, pork, lamb, fish, copra, fruit, and vegetables.

Recently it has become a prawn breeding centre. Its unbroken shoreline makes it ideal for this new high investment project which involves breeding tiger prawns for the domestic and export market.

Although few visitors will reach this far-flung corner of Seychelles, at least many should have the opportunity to savour the magnificent prawns farmed there.

This prosperous little island, and the nearby submerged **Fortune Bank**, may hold the key in fact to the nation's future prosperity, the tantalising prospect of black gold.

Those privileged enough to have walked along its beaches may have seen the cloggy balls of oil regularly washed from the depths of the Indian Ocean, an almost sure sign of the mineral riches beneath the sea bed.

Major oil exploration was already planned in Coétivy's offshore region in 1991, drilling for a resource which could launch Seychelles — already a middle-income nation — into an era of unprecedented prosperity.

Seabirds and Sand, Sharks and Shipwrecks

When you climb to the highest point of Seychelles, the summit of dramatic **Morne Seychellois** on **Mahé**, and gaze westward you see an ocean stretching into infinity — an enormous, seemingly endless ocean. But it is not so empty as it seems.

Dotted here and there, green emeralds of land emerge from the depths to defy the ocean its solitude, a profusion of life clinging to the coral walls of their defences.

There are four groups in the outer islands of Seychelles — the **Amirantes, Alphonse, Farquhar,** and **Aldabra**, each group composed of many tiny islands and coral heads.

It was Captain Alexander Sharpeigh, leading the fourth voyage of the East India Company in 1609, who first recorded information about the Amirantes, noting nine uninhabited islands with huge flocks of doves. He also recorded, curiously, some stone walls which he estimated were at least a century old, perhaps built by pirates or Arab traders.

The bank on which the Amirantes stand was charted by the French in 1770 and the British in 1821-22. Captain Macleod of HMS *Alert* gave the first accurate survey of the limits of the Amirantes Bank.

Shallow lagoons, some of the most perfect beaches in the world, and a haven of peace and tranquillity await those who seek out these forgotten corners of the earth.

Many shipwrecks, both ancient and modern, are found there: the result of unwary seamen, lulled into a false sense of security by the endless blue horizon, failing to see the flat strip of green land, or hear the roar of breakers where the ocean meets the reef.

Today the tourist potential of these ultimate get-away-from-it-all islands has still to be exploited. Occasionally it is possible to reach them by joining a cruise. Some can be reached by air, but to charter a small plane can be costly.

For the moment these are the islands that time forgot — true treasure islands of absolute peace and beauty, the outer isles of Seychelles, jewels of the Indian Ocean.

Islands of The Admiral

Even before the granite islands of **Mahé** and **Praslin** and their cohorts were known to the outside world, Portuguese navigators had named the chain of coral islands which lies west south-west of Mahé the *Ilhas do Almirantes* — Islands of the Admiral. From the protected area of **African Banks** these stretch ninety-five kilometres (59 miles) south to **Desnoeufs**.

The Amirantes are closer to Mahé than the other three groups of the outer islands, the most northerly island, African Banks, being some 235 kilometres (146 miles) from **Victoria**. Desnouefs, the farthest flung, is some 330 kilometres (205 miles) from Mahé.

Of the twenty-five islands that make up the Amirantes Group, only four are inhabited: **D'Arros, Desroches, Marie Louise,** and **Poivre**. The first people believed to have set foot on these islands were the ninth-century AD Arab explorers and navigators who swept across the Indian Ocean carrying the flame of Islam.

But the islands received their name from the great Portuguese navigator, Vasco da Gama, who found the sea route from Europe to India at the end of the fifteenth-century.

During the second half of the last century, and throughout the twentieth, these flat coral islands prospered through their extensive coconut and timber plantations, most now managed by the government parastatal, Island Development Company. Otherwise life goes

Above: Barred ground dove.

on much as it always has with the boat to Mahé the essential lifeline for those who choose to live and work on the outer islands.

Only Desroches is served by air — although Marie Louise and D'Arros have landing strips — but every two or three months an inter-island vessel, on which people on business (workers, officials, and the like) have priority, calls on most of the others.

Most of the larger Amirantes islands are government-owned and many are totally uninhabited unless you count the millions of seabirds, hundreds of fish species, and the myriad, colourful life of the reef all existing in what must be one of the most exciting dive locations on earth.

Among the outer islands of the Amirantes the one-third square kilometre platform reef of African Banks is home to thousands of seabirds.

For decades it was a favoured breeding ground of the roseate tern but in recent years they have abandoned it — perhaps because of human predation of eggs or some other misfortune. Since it has been declared a protected area many ornithologists hope this rare and graceful bird will return to breed in safety.

Other islands include Île du Sud — South Island — covering 1.37 square kilometres (half a square kilometre) which is also a platform reef, and St. Joseph's Atoll, 250 kilometres (155 miles) from Mahé, which is made up of many little islets — St. Joseph; Fouquet; Resource; Petit Carcassaye; Grand Carcassaye; Benjamin; Banc Ferrari; Chien; Pelican; Vars; Île Paul; Banc de Sable; and Banc Cocos. These account for little more than one square kilometre (under half a square mile) of land.

A few of the islands are in private owner-ship and tourists should clear their visit with the respective owners.

Desroches

The most economically significant island of the Amirantes is **Desroches**, a platform reef that lies 230 kilometres (142 miles) south-west of **Mahé**.

The linear **surface rim** of a huge lagoon, the **island** is five kilometres (three miles) long and one kilometre (half a mile) wide — the rest of the rim is fully submerged.

Named after an eighteenth-century ad-ministrator of Mauritius, it is the only outer island with a regular air link to Mahé, and covers almost four square kilometres (one and a half square miles). It has been well developed with timber and coconut **planta-tions** and its copra is considered the best in the Indian Ocean.

Getting There

Air Seychelles flies Mahé-Desroches-Mahé three times a week — on Mondays, Wednes-days, and Saturdays. Flying time is sixty minutes each way. From the **landing strip** to the superb **lodge** is but a short walk. Trips can be arranged through Island Resorts (Seychelles) in Victoria or any travel agent. See Listings.

When to go

The island is open all year-round. Diving from the lagoon edge is best during the north-west monsoon from October to April.

Where to Stay

There is only one hotel. Desroches Island

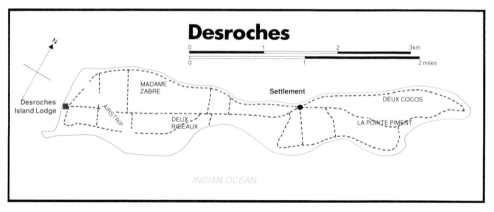

Above: Sooty tern nesting season on Desnoeufs.

Lodge has twenty twin-bed chalets and guests need sacrifice none of the comforts of the outside world or its contacts in order to escape its pressures. Spacious rooms with hot and cold running water lie a few steps from a beautiful sandy beach. And satellite links provide telephone, telex, and telefax facilities for those who cannot bear to sever their ties altogether.

Sightseeing

The island is so remote that in many ways landing on Desroches is almost like landing on another planet. But it is rich in both its terrestrial and marine attractions and a maze of footpaths lead along — and across — this idyllic island.

One pleasant **woodland walk**, with refreshing shade, runs parallel to **the beach.** You can branch off on to the beach for underwater exploration at any of the well-marked snorkeling points between the lodge and the **village**, which lies about two kilometres (one mile) from the hotel.

One of the more densely populated outer islands and home to about forty plantation workers, Desroches makes a substantial contribution to the copra and timber supply of the islands.

If you are lucky you may glimpse a grey francolin in the undergrowth, a small, plump game bird introduced to a few islands for sport some years ago but now found only on Desroches and remote **Coétivy**.

Another surprise is the number of house sparrows which have made their home on this isolated island. They probably arrived by ship, but why they settled in the Amirantes and not the granitic islands remains an enigma.

Watersports to be enjoyed include windsurfing, canoeing, snorkeling, scuba diving, and big game fishing. The well-equipped diving centre has a qualified instructor who takes diving trips to sea twice a day.

The best season for diving is during the north-west monsoon when calm seas allow visits to the fantastic submerged **outer rim** of the **lagoon** where the wall of coral plummets precipitously thousands of metres into the depths of the Indian Ocean. The wall is alive with corals and marine life, truly an underwater paradise.

Occasionally it is also possible to visit the wall during calm periods in the south-east

185

monsoon but even when it is off-limits there is still plenty to see for visiting divers.

The shallows of the well-sheltered north-western lagoon offer an incredible display of myriad fish life, including Madras snapper, moray eels, groupers, butterflyfish, and countless other species.

From Desroches you can explore many of the other islands of the Amirantes group, including D'Arros, either on a day trip or an extended cruise.

Moving southward through the Amirantes chain you come across a number of tiny, delightful evocatively-named islands — **Île Rémire** (referred to as Eagle Island on early charts), a smidgen of a platform reef 245 kilometres (152 miles) from Mahé, which covers less than a quarter of a square kilometre (0.1 square miles).

It is large by comparison with **Boudeuse**, which is little more than a rock covering one and a half hectares (three and a half acres) and lying 330 kilometres (205 miles) from Mahé — exactly the same size as **Étoile,** which is twenty-five kilometres (15 miles) nearer to the capital island. Both Boudeuse and Étoile are protected **bird reserves.**

You may wonder, too, about the romance of the half a square kilometre of nearby **Marie-Louise** and why this lonely platform reef was so named — after ship, wife, mistress, or noble lady?

Yet of all these tiny, magic isles and islets glistening in the turquoise water of the Indian Ocean, **Desnoeufs** is perhaps the most interesting. It lies 325 kilometres (201 miles) from Mahé but it is ever close to the hearts and minds — and tongues — of the citizens of the island capital.

For Desnoeufs, which covers an area of thirty-five hectares (86 acres), is home to the largest sooty tern colony in Seychelles — more than three times the number that breed on more famous **Bird Island** — and between May and July this platform reef, heaving and palpitating under the tropical sun, seems to be alive, a mass of fluttering feathers.

This is the time when government collectors step ashore and gather vast quantities of eggs, which are regarded on Mahé with the rever-ence that gourmets normally reserve only for the rarest of dishes.

When the first batch of eggs arrives queues quickly form. Non *aficionados,* however, may well wonder what all the fuss is about. To the indiscriminate tongue the taste is remarkably like that of an ordinary chicken's egg.

It seems a shame to sweep up such large numbers of future generations of this remarkable bird simply to satisfy a food fad and Seychelles' conservation authorities have now set aside part of the island as a protected **breeding reserve** — a measure that hopefully will ensure that the sooty tern continues to breed with profligate abandon.

Finally, guests can enjoy a pleasant day's cruise by motor launch to the nearby privately-owned island of **D'Arros**, covering one and a half square kilometres (half a square mile) of ocean some forty-five kilometres (27 miles) west of Desroches.

D'Arros, which lies 255 kilometres (158 miles) from Mahé, was formed in similar fashion to Desroches but also boasts its own satellites, for close by is a ring of islands known collectively as **St. Joseph's Atoll** that you pass on your way to the island. D'Arros has its own **landing strip**.

It was discovered on a voyage of explo-ration in 1771 and named after Baron D'Arros, naval commander of Île de France (Mauritius).

Day trips from Desroches can also be arranged to **Poivre**, which is roughly the same distance away but due south-west.

Spice island

Lying 270 kilometres (167 miles) south-west of Mahé, Poivre is the most important atoll in the Amirantes — made up of three islands, Poivre, **South Island**, and **Florentine**. These are surrounded by a **coral reef** which is only covered sufficiently for a boat to cross at high tide, the only time it is possible to reach these two islands.

Covering just over one square kilometre (just under half a square mile), Poivre takes its name from the Intendant who governed Mauritius in the name of France between 1763 and 1772. Pierre Poivre was the man behind the introduction of spices to Mahé.

Opposite: Chartered catamaran cruising in the Outer Islands.

Getting there

By sea only. The boat transfer from Desroches **landing strip** takes two hours. But some may prefer to make the eighteen-hour journey by charter boat from Mahé.

When to go

The island is open all year-round.

Where to stay

There are thatched huts for people who wish to spend a night on the island, but little else.

Sightseeing

The island is lush with vegetation. It is split in two halves. At low tide these are joined by a natural **causeway**.

Poivre island's proudest boast is that the largest marlin ever boated in Seychelles, more than 400 kilos (880 lbs), was caught just a few minutes cruise from **the lagoon**.

The island is one of the top cruise destinations of the archipelago. Chartering one of the traditional two-masted *takamaka* Seychellois schooners, with four double-berth cabins with shower, eight people can enjoy a ten-day stay at Poivre, including the return voyage from Mahé, complete with use of launch and snorkeling, scuba diving, and windsurfing equipment, for little more than the cost of staying in an ordinary hotel. For bookings see Listings.

Magic Lagoons, Lonely Horizons

The three islands of the **Alphonse Group** lie ninety kilometres (56 miles) directly south of the last island of the **Amirantes**, **Desnoeufs**, and 400 kilometres (250 miles) south-west of **Mahé**.

Getting there

By chartered yacht or schooner. There are no passenger services and there is no landing strip on any of the islands.

When to go

The islands do not cater for tourists and are not subject to any seasons.

Where to stay

There is no accommodation and no permanent residents. You can only anchor and sleep aboard your charter vessel.

Sightseeing

Of all the 115 islands of Seychelles, **Alphonse** almost certainly ranks among the most beautiful. Its circular **lagoon** makes it possible to enjoy scuba diving all year round, no matter what the season.

Covering almost two square kilometres (more than half a square mile), this deserted island is an ideal away-from-it-all retreat.

Spread out on each side of it is a wing of the lagoon rim. One is named **Dot**, the other **Tamatave**. The names commemorate the ships these lovely but treacherous reefs lured to their doom.

A French coal steamer, *Dot*, was on a voyage to Réunion when she sank in November, 1873. Even at high tide her funnel remained visible for more than half a century, acting as a warning beacon to other vessels that might have otherwise shared her fate. The remainder of the wreck is still on the reef and can be explored at low tide.

Thirty years later, in 1903, the reef on the other side of the island claimed the *Tamatave*.

Once Alphonse was renowned as a home of the endangered magpie robin, now found only on **Frégate,** which were introduced in 1895. They flourished until cats were landed on the island in the 1950s and within years they were wiped out.

Five kilometres (three miles) from its shores stands another smidgen of reef, **Bijoutier**, yet to be surveyed and scarcely big enough to swing one of the proverbial cats from its larger neighbour, but still a round jewel in the ocean.

Five kilometres (three miles) beyond Bijoutier stands the minuscule seventeen hectares (41 acres) of **St. François** — the last pinprick of land before the **Farquhar Group,** 300 kilometres (186 miles) to the south-west.

Sail a short distance from St. François and four kilometres (2.5 miles) of ocean depth sound beneath your keel as you cruise on to the next setting of island jewels in the necklace of Seychelles.

Beautiful But Deadly

Separated from each other by the **Farquhar Ridge**, more than 100 kilometres (60 miles) lies between **Providence,** the northernmost island of the **Farquhar Group**, and **Farquhar,** the southernmost point located 770 kilometres (478 miles) south-west of Mahé.

As remote as any islands in the world, you gather some idea of the immensity of the ocean and their isolation when you venture beyond the **Amirantes**.

Reaching them is difficult enough. Travel beyond is virtually out of the question for all but those who own a yacht or schooner or charter one.

Farquhar was discovered in 1504 by the Portuguese navigator, Jaoa da Nova. The main islands of the group are Farquhar, **Île au Cerf**, **St. Pierre**, and Providence. Few live, or ever have lived, in these lost worlds although many have seen their beauty and experienced their danger.

In the nineteenth century Edward Ross, a young cadet, was one. He was shipwrecked during a stormy June night in 1854, when the *St. Abbs*, bound for Bombay out of London, struck the reef and sank.

Almost all on board died — either by drowning or victim of the sharks that swarmed around the dying vessel when the desperate sailors hurled rations and stores overboard to lighten ship. Only six survived — lonely castaways on this deserted island.

"... had I known that besides the danger of the surf and breakers, there was a still more appalling one to run," Ross later recalled, "I know not if I should have had the courage to face it. For afterwards I discovered that the surf swarmed with sharks.

"As soon as Bell and I reached the water, a heavy roller overtook us, and parted us for ever. I was told afterwards that, while apparently swimming through the surf, he was seen by those on the wreck to throw up his arms and suddenly disappear, and I fear he must have been dragged under by a shark."

The six survived by killing and eating — raw — seabirds and turtles and drinking the foul water they found in muddy, brackish pools. It was five weeks before they were rescued by a passing ship.

Ross, who landed in India and served during the Indian Mutiny, eventually became Britain's Consul-General in the Persian Gulf. Knighted in 1892 for his services to the empire, he died in 1913, fifty-nine years after he was shipwrecked.

Farquhar is not alone in its innocent treachery. Its cohort to the north, Providence and its **atoll**, 710 kilometres (440 miles) south-west of Mahé, has probably claimed more ships than any other island in the archipelago. At least eight vessels have foundered there in the last 250 years.

In 1763, carrying a load of treasure, the French frigate *Heureuse* was wrecked and in 1836 the British brig *Aure* went down, followed more than half a century later by the French barque *Federation* in 1894.

In this century, its tranquil-looking reefs have claimed the schooner *Maggie Low*, the *Endeavour*, the *Jorgen Bank*, and the SS *Syria*.

Getting there

Farquhar has an **airstrip**, but at 710 kilometres, (440 miles) from Mahé, it is beyond the reach of Air Seychelles' smaller planes. Sea is the only reliable way to travel to this group.

When to go

There are no tourist facilities. The group is the most southerly of the islands of Seychelles and is occasionally hit by cyclones, especially between December and February.

Where to stay

There is no tourist accommodation on any of the islands but you can anchor and sleep aboard your charter vessel.

Sightseeing

More than one and a half square kilometres (more than half a square mile) in size, the **reef platform** of Providence is the first landfall after **St. François** in the **Alphonse Group**.

The slightly larger raised limestone of **St. Pierre** lies some forty kilometres (25 miles) to its west and a similar distance south you strike the waving palms of **Banc Providence** and its seventy-one hectares (175 acres) of tropical island and beaches.

Across the Farquhar Ridge the sylvan island and islets of the Farquhar Atoll, totalling altogether eight square kilometres (three square miles), beckon. These include: **Île du Nord**; **Île du Sud**; **Manaha Nord**; **Manaha Milieu**; **Manaha Sud**; **Goëlettes**; **Lapin**; **Île du Milieu**; **Depose**; **Bancs de Sable**; and **Farquhar**.

Shaped like a hook, Farquhar guards what must surely rank as one of the Indian Ocean's most beautiful **lagoons**, a safe haven for the many ships who seek anchorage within its always tranquil waters.

The island's economy is based on copra production and fishing. Covered with thick groves of coconut palms and graceful casuarina woods, the shores of the verdant atoll islands also have a splendour all their own, including the smooth one and a half kilometre (one mile) stretch of **Twenty-Five Franc,** a fine-grained topaz beach sloping gently down to the warm and shallow waters of the sparkling lagoon.

Goëlettes, the main island in the southernmost atoll, has long been an important transmigratory haven for many species of birds, especially terns. The **airstrip**, built many years ago, is on the **main island** of the **northern atoll**.

Aldabracadabra — Magic in the Ocean

Lying 1,150 kilometres (715 miles) southwest of Mahé, three magnificent atolls and one platform reef form the islands of the **Aldabra Group**.

Aldabra is arguably the least touched by man of any of the Indian Ocean islands — an atoll so huge that you cannot see one side from the other. Indeed, Mahé would fit neatly inside the lagoon.

It has a magic that distinguishes it from almost all the other islands of the world save, perhaps, the Galápagos. "Aldabra", wrote Sir Julian Huxley in 1970, "is one of nature's treasures and should belong to the whole world."

A probable basaltic basement less than one kilometre below the surface betrays the volcanic origins of Aldabra. As if from nowhere, the whole atoll rises suddenly out of the depths of the Indian Ocean.

Made up of a chain of more than a dozen islands — **Grande Terre; Picard; Polymnie; Malabar; Île au Cèdres; Île Michel; Île Esprit; Île Moustiques; Îlot Parc; Îlot Emile; Îlot Yangue; Îlot Dubois; Îlot Magnan;** and **Îlot Lanier** — Aldabra covers 154 square kilometres (59 square miles), a good third of Seychelles' total terrestrial territory. The greater part of these land surfaces are made up of mushroom-shaped coral banks worn by erosion.

Mecca of the green turtle, world headquarters of the giant land tortoise, Aldabra is the island that time — and man — forgot, 640 kilometres (400 miles) east of the African mainland and 400 kilometres (250 miles) northwest of Madagascar. It is home to 273 species of flowering plant and fern, of which nineteen are endemic and twenty-two shared only with neighbouring islands.

Aldabra appears on a Portuguese map of 1509 — a century before Captain Sharpeigh made the first recorded landing in the granitic Seychelles — but the forbidding coastline, the mushroom-shaped pinnacles of rock, the lack of fresh ground water or good timber for shipbuilding, and its distance from the main shipping routes and bases were the salvation of Aldabra.

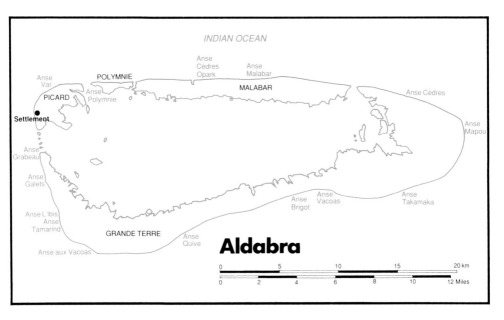

The map shows various place names including: INDIAN OCEAN, Anse Cèdres Opark, Anse Malabar, POLYMNIE, Anse Var, MALABAR, Anse Polymnie, PICARD, Anse Cèdres, Settlement, Anse Mapou, Anse Grabeau, Anse Galets, Anse Vacoas, Anse Takamaka, Anse Brigot, Anse L'Ibis, Anse Tamarind, GRANDE TERRE, Anse Quive, Anse aux Vacoas, **Aldabra**

0 5 10 15 20 km
0 2 4 6 8 10 12 Miles

Even the name has a mysterious sound to it. Possibly it is a corruption of *Al-Khadra*, Arabic for *the green*. Certainly Arab sailors trading between Zanzibar and the Comoros since the Middle Ages must have known of this limestone atoll which rises eight metres (26 feet) above sea level.

Galápagos of the Indian Ocean

Charles Darwin made the Galápagos Tortoise famous, and also played a role in the early conservation of the tortoise in the Indian Ocean. In a letter to the Governor of Mauritius in 1874, Darwin and others wrote:

"The rescue and protection of these animals is recommended less on account of their utility . . . than on account of the great scientific interest attached to them."

In the days before fridges and freezers, a giant land tortoise was a giant convenience food as far as seamen were concerned. They were large, hardy, remained alive for long periods without attention, and provided an excellent source of fresh meat on long voyages.

Despite the appeal of Darwin and his friends, few steps were taken by the Mauritian Government, and while they hunted their own tortoises to extinction, Aldabra was leased to Jules Cauvin of Mahé in 1888 at a peppercorn rent, for commercial exploitation.

In 1891, Cauvin's successor, James Spurs, banned the taking of tortoises. He even tried to repopulate **Picard**, "West Island", and slowly, the giants returned.

Mecca of the Green Turtle

James Spurs' love of tortoises unfortunately did not extend to turtles. He proposed "limiting" his catch to 12,000 a year (about six times the present population).

In 1900 the lease passed to a commercial company which concentrated on fishing, but in 1904 a new lessor, D'Emmerez de Charmoy, together with James Spurs who was his manager, almost wiped out the great **green turtle** colony of Aldabra. The slaughter continued uncontrolled until 1945. Somehow the turtles survived and the level of exploitation fell.

In 1964 Great Britain and the United States planned to establish a military base on Aldabra together with other bases on **Desroches**, **Farquhar**, and **Diego Garcia**.

The manoeuvre was counteracted by English ecologists and Seychellois working through the Organisation of African Unity. In the end only Diego Garcia was turned into an airbase.

Tony Beamish in *Aldabra Alone* tells how he arrived at Aldabra in 1967 with Harold Hirth, a green turtle expert. "I should really bow three times to Aldabra", said Hirth. "Mecca of the green turtle, I never thought I'd have the chance to see it."

Above: A mushroom island in magical Aldabra atoll.

at the turn of the century. But there are signs that numbers are increasing.

The Aldabran population is perhaps as much as fifty per cent of the total Seychelles' population. With careful management by the Seychelles Islands Foundation, perhaps Aldabra will once again become a world centre for these creatures.

The United Nations proclaimed Aldabra a **World Heritage Site**, protected by the SIF.

Getting there

An airstrip was completed on **Assumption** in mid-1990. But the range is too great for Air Seychelles' domestic fleet.

The sea is still the only reliable means of approach. But it is impossible to anchor a short distance offshore and ships that approach too close are in danger of running into Aldabra's first line of defence — the **coral reef**.

When to go

The atoll is not developed yet as a tourist resort and there are no seasons as such.

Where to stay

The atoll is virtually off limits because of its unique and fragile ecosystem and special permission is required if you wish to land there. The only inhabitants are about a dozen people. There are no visitor facilities. Any visitors must anchor their yacht and sleep aboard.

Sightseeing

Aldabra's four main islands are Picard, on which there is a **research station**, Polymnie, Malabar, and Grande Terre. The four **entrances** to the **lagoon** they surround act like the sluicegates of a lock. The huge lagoon empties almost completely when the tide goes out, and fills with the incoming tide to a depth of about three metres (10 feet).

This titanic action which takes place twice a day populates the lagoon with multitudes of fish, including **barracudas** and **sharks**.

The island limestone probably dates from about 125,000 years ago, or about the time of the last interglacial period. There are two distinct terraces, one at four metres the other at eight metres, formed as sea levels fell.

The mushroom-shaped surfaces — elabor-

Giant land tortoises belong to one of the most ancient groups of animals alive today, and have survived unchanged for perhaps 200 million years.

They were formerly found throughout the Pacific and Indian oceans, but today are confined in their natural state to Seychelles and Galápagos. Aldabra, with over 150,000 tortoises, boasts far and away the world's largest population.

They can live for up to a century, and go weeks without food. These giant chelonians are also good swimmers and perhaps this enabled them to invade Aldabra several times in its history through a succession of appearances and disappearances.

In the granitic islands and **Amirantes**, the **green turtle** is finished as an exploitable resource, and the few that choose to nest there place themselves in grave danger, especially in the granitics.

CITES, the Convention on International Trade in Endangered Species, lists all marine turtles as endangered. The world over populations have been decimated, and even in Aldabra there are perhaps fewer than 2,000 individuals: a fraction of the figure that existed

Above: Constant tidal erosion creates Aldabra's strangely-shaped islets.

ate honeycombed pinnacles of limestone — make walking a difficult and potentially dangerous exercise.

This craggy landscape has been formed by the dissolution of limestone by rainwater. Even the giant land tortoises are sometimes caught out and carapaces can be found in hollows, marking the grave of unlucky adventurers.

The bases of the limestone tables are often undercut by marine erosion, producing the strange **mushroom islets**, and in places an almost impenetrable shoreline.

Unique Avifauna

Thirty species and subspecies of birds are confined to Seychelles. Twelve of these are to be found on Aldabra; that is three more than Mahé, and indeed only three fewer than the whole granitic group combined.

Only two of these are full species, but that includes one of the most remarkable birds in the Indian Ocean: the flightless **white-throated rail.**

On Mauritius, with the aid of the feral dogs, pigs, cats, rats and monkeys he brought with him, man hunted the dodo to

extinction by 1680. The elephant bird of Madagascar — the largest bird ever to roam the earth — was wiped out at around the same date.

The Rodrigues solitaire, the Réunion Solitaire, and the white dodo of Réunion followed within the next century. The Mauritian red rail and Leguat's rail (again on Rodrigues) were likewise exterminated by about 1700. There were rails on Assumption, **Astove**, and **Cosmoledo** at one time, but in the Indian Ocean only on Aldabra has flightlessness survived.

The other full species is the **Aldabra drongo.** This jet-black bird has an unusually large bill for a drongo — a product of island specialisation. A third full species — the **Aldabran brush warbler** — was only discovered in 1968. Despite intensive searches, however, it has not been seen since 1983.

It may survive within the inner reaches of the dense pemphis scrub, but as time passes and successive wardens and expeditions fail to locate the bird, this looks increasingly doubtful.

Subspecies abound on Aldabra, evolutionary stepping stones between the arrival of a

193

Above: Giant land tortoise in their last stronghold on Aldabra seek shade from the broiling sun.

continental species and the emergence of a fully distinct island race. The sacred ibis and green-backed heron on the shorelines have evolved into island forms.

The unusual-shaped **coral banks** are teeming with terns and frigates and in the interior one can find races of **fody, sunbird, white-eye, bulbul, nightjar, coucal, pigeon,** and **turtle dove,** all sufficiently different from their ancestral races to merit separate treatment.

Apart from the endemics, Aldabra is a fascinating place for bird-watchers. It is much closer to the African mainland than the granitic islands, and a wide variety of Eurasian migrants could turn up. The **red-tailed tropicbird**, present in central Seychelles only on **Aride**, is fairly common.

Various terns, including **Caspian, black-naped**, and **Saunders**, fish the rich Aldabran waters. The beautiful **greater flamingo** can also be seen regularly in Seychelles only on Aldabra. The same applies to the **Malagasy kestrel**, which is probably a recent colonist.

Most spectacular of all are the frigate colonies. Two of the world's five species, **lesser** and **great frigatebirds** breed in immense numbers. The breeding males show off by inflating their red throat pouches like balloons, flying apparently unhindered by this ludicrous undercarriage.

The sight of these birds wheeling and soaring, with their slim bodies, hooked bills, and disproportionately long scimitar wings, is breathtaking.

Curiously, **boobies** nest alongside the frigates, the two groups apparently getting along as good friends and neighbours.

Yet the frigatebirds are marauding pirates which will "buzz" the boobies, forcing them to drop their catches of fish, providing the frigates with an easy meal.

Another species of note is the pied crow. They are strong flyers and may have arrived naturally, but could also have hitched a ride on a ship.

Mammals

The **Aldabra fruit bat** is related to the Seychelles fruit bat, but again has evolved a unique island form, with a whitish face, unlike its cousins on the granitic islands.

Three other species of bat occur on Aldabra, and although these are not unique to the island, none of them are found in central Seychelles or the Amirantes.

In the deep waters offshore, **spinner dolphins** and other cetaceans can be seen far more regularly than in the shallower waters around Mahé. **Dugongs** — large herbivorous marine mammals — have occasionally been seen off Aldabra.

Three unwelcome, introduced mammals also survive: cats, rats, and goats. The goats compete with tortoises for vegetation. Attempts to control their numbers have been made, but these wily animals stubbornly cling to survival.

An Ancient Flora

Unlike almost every other tropical island the world over, Aldabra has not been invaded by introduced plants. Only two species have spread widely throughout the atoll, and natural flora covers most of the island.

That is not to say the flora is spectacular, for island forms are not generally large or colourful. Nevertheless, it includes a number of fascinating varieties such as the remarkable **Aldabra lily** (*Lomatophyllum aldabrense*), which has fleshy, thorny leaves, and a spike of orange-red flowers.

Other attractive flowers of the atoll include **Aldabra jasmine** (*Jasminum elegans*), which has highly perfumed white flowers, and **bwa zangwet** (*Capparis cartilaginea*), with white, many-stamened flowers. The **Aldabra screwpine** (*Pandanus aldabrensis*) is another unique species.

Mangroves cover a wide area around the lagoon. The species are the same as on the granitic islands, but the huge stands of these trees are far more dramatic.

Underwater Paradise

The steep walls on which the raised limestone islets of Aldabra are perched are rich in marine life, including sharks, which are also common in the lagoon. At low tide, they will swim in water barely deep enough to cover their bodies.

Strictly speaking the **robber crab** is not an *underwater* species. It is common on land, where it is an unnerving sight. Full-grown specimens measure up to sixty centimetres (two feet) or more across, and they have powerful pincers and a firm grip to match. Some are blue-green, others red, depending on the stage of the moult.

Below: The china-blue eyes of the Aldabra sacred ibis makes this Seychelles resident a separate sub-species, distinct from its African cousin.

Above: A bright orange flash of beak is the signature mark of the Malagasy bulbul.

They can easily embrace coconut trees, which they climb to cut down unripe green nuts. They then nip these open with their formidable claws and feed on the soft flesh within.

With special pouches in their shells which enable them to breathe on land, these crabs only return to the sea to breed and spawn. Their larvae will travel on the ocean currents, perhaps to reach some other remote corner of the world where they can find a niche.

Inevitably, because this **World Heritage Site** is unique and so unspoilt, the spotlight in this area of the Indian Ocean falls on Aldabra and the rest of the group tends to slumber on in almost unnoticed obscurity. Yet they, too, have their own fascination and distinctive character.

Assumption

Some twenty-seven kilometres (17 miles) south of Aldabra is **Assumption**; 1,140 kilometres (709 miles) from Mahé and eleven square kilometres (four and a half square miles) of raised limestone **platform reef**.

Once the only one of two places on earth where the **Abbot's booby** lived, it must have been a marvellous island. For beside the booby there were flightless rails, and a whole host of rare birds and plants.

Rich in guano, Assumption sadly attracted the interest of entrepreneurs interested only in exploiting its wealth. The island was destroyed with a ruthlessness that, by good fortune if not intent, was somehow avoided in the rest of Seychelles.

To exploit the guano the vegetation had to be destroyed. To destroy the vegetation was to destroy the goose that laid the golden guano (as it were).

For good measure, the same exploiters also hunted the **green turtles**, which had bred there for millenniums, to the brink of extinction. One director of Agriculture in Seychelles who visited Assumption in 1929 was appalled.

"Assumption also abounds in other sea resources, but as soon as guano was started, all of the land and seabirds were destroyed by labourers.

"It is wonderful, however, to think that after nineteen years of constant fishing the resources in turtle have not been depleted

except to a slight extent." They were still able to take 1,000 a year.

The *wonder* did not last. Because turtles are so long-lived, it was possible to exploit several generations, but as fewer and fewer eggs were laid, the species approached the abyss of oblivion where it still clings precariously to a last tenuous toehold on life. Today, only about 200 of these creatures return each year to breed.

Now bereft of all its natural wealth, two introduced birds, the **red-whiskered bulbul** and **Mozambique serin**, threaten Aldabra's unique avifauna only twenty-seven kilometres (17 miles) to the north-west and Assumption is a sad sight.

But there is hope. In mid-1990 a new **airstrip** was being built and it is planned to open Assumption to a small number of privileged visitors who will fly to the doorstep of the wonderland of Aldabra.

The benign exploitation of Seychelles' natural assets as a tourist attraction will hopefully lead to the elimination of the introduced species which threaten Aldabra and also restore some of the wonders of Assumption.

Cosmoledo

Lying 110 kilometres (70 miles) east of Assumption, and 1,045 kilometres (650 miles) from Mahé, **Cosmoledo Atoll** is a huge ring of **twelve islands**, many of them unsurveyed, around a roughly circular **lagoon**. The islands include the two and a half square kilometres (one square mile) of **Menai**; the twenty-one hectare (52-acre) **Île du Nord**; unsurveyed **Île Nord-Est**; the half-hectare (1.2-acre) **Île du Trou**; the three-hectare (seven-acre) **Goëlettes**; and **Grand Île — Wizard Island** — which covers almost two square kilometres (three-quarters of a square mile).

Others, all unsurveyed, are **Grand Polyte**; **Petit Polyte**; **Pagode**; **Île Sud-Ouest**; **Île Moustiques**; **Île Baleine**; and **Île Chauve Souris**.

Malagasy grass warblers, possibly an extremely recent natural invader as there are no records of it before 1940, are common in the undergrowth. **Boobies** and **terns** breed on several islands in the group, as do **red-tailed tropicbird**, so rare in the granitic islands.

Both Assumption and Cosmoledo have

their own subspecies of the **souimanga sun-bird**, which is also to be found on Aldabra. It is fascinating how three distinct varieties of bird, fairly close to each other, have developed from a single invading species.

Astove

The six and a half square kilometre (two and a half square mile) atoll of **Astove**, which is the same distance from Mahé as Cosmoledo, lies sixty kilometres (37 miles) directly south of the Aldabra atoll.

The island's name is synonymous with stories of lost treasure. Legend says that when the Portuguese frigate, *Dom Royal*, laden with cargo and slaves, went aground there in 1760, the captain and crew abandoned the slaves and attempted to reach East Africa by longboat — never to be seen again.

Word reached Mauritius — or Île de France as it was then — that a rich cargo of slaves was there for the taking, and two French ships set sail.

Both vessels were wrecked in mysterious circumstances on the same reef. The liberated slaves, meanwhile, set up their own miniature republic.

Twenty years later, another ship which called there reported that on their approach they "set up wild shouts of defiance and placed themselves in an attitude of defence".

The vessel left empty-handed and reported the incident to the authorities at Bourbon, (now Réunion). Another vessel set out, and again, was lost.

In 1796 a British ship left Mahé and attempted to take the slaves by force. Many were killed in the subsequent clash. Another ship was despatched, and embarked about 100 slaves. It was wrecked as it tried to find a passage through the reef, back to the open sea, and all on board were lost to the waters and the sharks.

Later, all the castaways were picked up and taken to Mahé, leaving just one man behind, but he too vanished for reasons unknown, for the next ship to visit Astove, in 1799, reported that the island was deserted.

Astove has an **airstrip** but is well beyond the range of Air Seychelles' domestic fleet.

Above: Large robber crab on Aldabra. The species lives on coconuts and returns to the water only to breed and spawn.

Overleaf: Schooner at sunset.

PART THREE:
SPECIAL FEATURES

Above: Free-form parasailer communes with the clouds over Mahé.

A Time Forgotten World in Miniature

Ocean covers most of the world. Within these vast stretches of blue water are set tiny fragments of land — some the tips of underwater volcanoes, some mere rings or cays of coral, some raised limestone atolls.

But in one special corner of the planet, the western Indian Ocean, there is an area with all these features, and more: the earth's only ocean islands of solid granite.

These enclosed miniature worlds, microcosms where unique plants and animals evolved in extraordinary ways, form Seychelles, a place where some of the world's rarest birds find haven amidst rich and exotic tropical flora.

Where primaeval giant land tortoises browse on sun-drenched scraps of land set in a turquoise sea.

And where beneath that sea, nature's profusion knows no bounds, with a variety of colours and patterns that dazzle the eye.

The forces that split Gondwanaland isolated Seychelles at a time when the reptiles were kings so that many millenniums later, when the first mammals evolved, none could cross the ocean to challenge their supremacy.

A few bats and birds did make it and stayed on to evolve into completely separate species. The birds may also have brought seeds in their feathers, while other seeds were carried ashore on the ocean currents.

Thus the unique birds and plants of Seychelles reflected both Asian and African characteristics and, protected within their isolated islands, remote and undisturbed, species found nowhere else on earth flourished.

With man came the familiar story of destruction. Predators, notably rats, cats, goats, and (much later) Barn Owls, found the native fauna unprepared for their onslaught.

Vigorous, introduced exotic plants spread and the tall forests were felled to supply, repair, and build ships. Tortoises and turtles provided a ready supply of easy meat.

Yet few species disappeared altogether, and Seychelles fared much better than most other island states.

Today, with the backing of a wide variety of conservation laws and an increasing awareness of the importance of the environment, there is much to be optimistic about.

Nature is making a comeback and the natural heritage of Seychelles, its richest asset, is being nurtured for the benefit of the Seychellois, the tourist, and the future.

Birdlife: A Rare And Feathered Magic

The vast majority of all bird extinctions during the last 300 years have been island forms, and today more than seventy per cent of endangered species are confined to islands.

No recent avian extinction has been documented for the African mainland (although one species has not been seen for more than 100 years), while by contrast twenty-nine endangered species are found only on Indian Ocean islands. Eight of these species are unique to Seychelles.

Thirteen endemic species (eleven of them in the granitic islands) and a further seventeen endemic subspecies (four of them in the granitics) are also found in Seychelles.

Despite their rarity, all except those confined to the outer islands can be seen in a relatively short time by the determined birdwatcher.

In addition Seychelles boasts some of the world's finest seabird colonies, especially those on Aride, Cousin, and Aldabra.

Aride is home to the world's largest colony of lesser noddy — a speciality of the Indian Ocean — and one of the world's largest colonies of roseate terns, a species in decline throughout its range. The frigate colonies on Aldabra are also of global importance.

The location of Seychelles at the crossroads of the migratory routes between Africa and Eurasia makes bird-watching fascinating. Species breeding within the Arctic Circle migrate to Seychelles, the same bird returning each year to the same tropical beach to escape the long harsh winter.

Birds rarely seen in Europe are regulars. Almost any Eurasian migrant can turn up. Indeed the vast majority of the species recorded in Seychelles do not breed there.

Man has brought a number of species to Seychelles from other corners of the globe. Not all survived, but some are well-established and integrated into the avifauna of these fascinating islands.

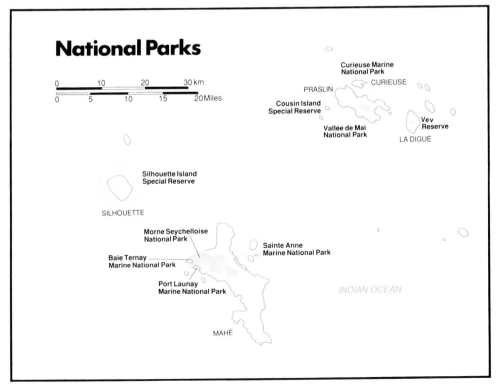

Above: The Seychelles bare-legged scops owl, a bird so rare that no nest has ever been found.

Unique: Birds Found Nowhere Else

Eleven species of land birds, most of them confined to no more than three islands, are unique to the granitic islands of Seychelles. Two, the **Seychelles grey white-eye** and the **Seychelles scops owl**, are confined solely to the mountains of **Mahé**.

For much of this century both species were thought to be extinct. But in 1959 the scops owl, and then in 1962, the white-eye, were rediscovered by Philippe Lousteau-Lalanne, a local ornithologist.

The white-eye is a tiny, grey-brown bird with a white circle around the eye. As small groups or family parties move through the trees hunting for insects, their soft, whispering calls — unlike the harsher calls of similar-sized birds — betray their presence.

The scops owl, a small, dark-brown bird, is more often heard than seen. Its strange, low rasping call gave it the Creole name of *syer* — meaning woodcutter. Despite their location on the most populous and developed

island, these are two of the most difficult land birds to locate.

But Mahé is the island on which you are most likely to see the **Seychelles kestrel**, a tiny bird of prey known locally as *"katiti"* from its flight call, a continuous "ti-ti-ti-ti". Some Seychellois who regard the bird as an omen of death, kill them when they approach too close to their houses.

Church rooftops, telegraph poles, and even lampposts and buildings in the centre of **Victoria** are good places to see this attractive bird as kestrels perch on vantage points to scan the ground for lizards and large insects. On occasion they may also take small birds.

The **Seychelles blue pigeon** is especially attractive. The adult has a red cap and wattle, a white bib, and a blue back and lower body. The colour pattern, which resembles the Dutch flag, gives it the local name of *Pizon Olonde* — Dutch Pigeon.

Unlike other pigeons, blue pigeons belong to a subfamily which have muscular gizzards capable of breaking down and digesting seeds and so do not spread their food plants since their droppings contain no viable seeds. As a result, the birds depend far more on the conservation of their habitat for their survival.

The **Seychelles sunbird** is the most common of Seychelles' unique species, found on all but the tiniest granitic islands from sea level to the forested hills.

They are as much at home feeding on the nectar of introduced plants such as hibiscus and banana flowers as they are feeding on natural vegetation. Indeed, they are probably the only species to have benefited from the arrival of man.

Easily recognized by their small size, down-curved bill, and frantic activity, they call loudly to each other as they move through the flowering shrubs.

The male has a repetitive trilling call, and both sexes have flight and alarm calls. Mostly dark in coloration, the breeding male has a metallic blue throat and a flash of orange or yellow around its "armpits".

They build elongated hanging nests, with a porch-like projection over the side entrance, bound together by spider webs. The birds appear to dice with death as they hover in front of webs to collect the sticky threads.

The unmistakable **Seychelles cave swiftlet**, which resembles a smaller version of the European swift, is the only bird of its type in Seychelles.

There are thought to be about 1,000 pairs on Mahé, **Praslin**, and **La Digue**, where they can be seen wheeling through the sky feeding on small insects taken on the wing.

They have extraordinary powers of echo location and skilfully manoeuvre in their nesting caves by use of an electronic sounding low-pitched call.

Above: Seychelles' cattle egret can be found along the shoreline and further inland.

Overleaf: Lesser noddy gather on a tree roost.

The noisy **Seychelles bulbul**, which does not seem to have suffered from man's arrival, is fairly common in the hills of Mahé and Praslin. They have raucous calls and can often be seen chasing each other through the trees, accompanied by a great deal of noise.

The adults have a bright orange beak and a scruffy crest. They are excellent mimics. But when they imitate mynah birds, the mynah birds in turn can be heard imitating the bulbuls.

By contrast, the **Seychelles magpie robin**, one of the rarest birds on earth, is confined solely to tiny **Frégate Island**. Once common throughout the granitic islands, its tame nature led to its downfall.

Only about twenty-five birds remain, but

Above: Spending most of its life over the open seas, the sooty tern returns to shore to lay its single egg.

plans are afoot to improve their habitat on Frégate and possibly introduce them to another island to establish a second population.

The **Seychelles warbler** could be the model for the future conservation of the magpie robin. Its world population once stood at just twenty-six — confined to **Cousin**.

The establishment of the Cousin Island Nature Reserve, and the acquisition of the island by the International Council for Bird Preservation helped the bird to multiply to about 400 individuals.

In September 1988, twenty-nine birds were transferred to Aride Island, where they quickly established themselves. Now the population there is more than 100, with every possibility that it will surpass that of Cousin due to the greater size and richer habitat on Aride.

The **Seychelles fody** also has a stronghold on Cousin as well as Frégate and **Cousine**. The breeding male has a yellow throat and forehead, while the female is dull brown and sparrow-like with a pale chest.

It is difficult to say why the Seychelles fody has such a restricted range compared to its introduced Madagascan cousin. They appear to be hardy, aggressive little birds, quite capable of standing up to competition.

Possibly the most spectacular of the endemic land birds is the **Seychelles black paradise flycatcher**, almost entirely confined to La Digue, with a few individuals on Praslin.

It has been seen on other islands in the Praslin group in the past. Perhaps one day, given careful protection and management, it may return to some of its old haunts. The male is blue-black with an enormous tail plume. The female is smaller, chestnut on the back and wings, white below, with a blue-black head.

The black coloration of the male gives it its Creole name, *vev* or widow. The female builds a nest on a hanging branch, often over water. In the entire world only about eighty of these beautiful birds survive.

To complete the list of endemic species you must turn to the remote **Aldabra atoll**. The **Aldabra drongo**, with its nearest relative in Madagascar, has evolved as a completely separate species. It is a slim, shiny-black bird with a distinctive deeply-forked tail.

The atoll's other full endemic species is the **white-throated rail** — the last remaining flightless bird of the Indian Ocean following

205

the extinction of the dodos, solitaires, and flightless rails of Mauritius, Réunion, and Rodrigues.

A third unique species was discovered on Aldabra in 1967, the **Aldabran brush warbler**. But very few birds were ever found, and sadly it has not been seen since 1983 — despite intensive searches of the tiny area it was known to occupy — and it is probably now extinct, maybe due to introduced cats or rats, although this could possibly be a rare example of a natural extinction.

The only other documented extinction of a full species is the **Seychelles green parakeet,** which was shot by early settlers who regarded it as a pest.

Two other species, not unique to Seychelles, deserve mention. The **moorhen**, familiar throughout much of the world, occurs naturally in Seychelles. It appears a poor flyer yet, amazingly, has found its way to many ocean islands.

In Seychelles it has adapted to eating the local snails, lizards, insects, and even crops such as sweet potatoes and bananas.

Unknown outside Asia and its adjacent islands, other than in Seychelles, the **Chinese bittern** is probably a recent coloniser as there is no apparent difference from its Asian cousins.

It is a shy, streaky, yellow-brown bird, which freezes when alarmed, with its bill pointing upwards. This response makes it almost invisible among the reeds of the marshes which it frequents.

Below: Audobon's shearwater.

Above: Rare Malagasy kestrel.

Birds in a World of Their Own

Isolated birds on remote islands cannot turn into new species overnight. As subspecies form a bridge between ancestral stock and new forms, evolution is slow. But Seychelles has many bridges along the road of evolution.

Of these, perhaps the most interesting is the **Seychelles black parrot** — subspecies: *barklyi* — the only parrot of the islands (and the national bird of Seychelles). You will hear its high-pitched whistle where it breeds — in the **Vallée de Mai** and other places on **Praslin**.

It is also encountered around the edges of

Above: Common noddy tern with chick.

the Vallée de Mai and in the lowlands, especially when *bilimbi* and guava fruits lure it out into the open. Recently, it invaded **Curieuse** and it may formerly have occurred on other islands in the Praslin group.

The **Seychelles turtle dove** — subspecies: *rostrata* — almost disappeared due to interbreeding with its introduced Malagasy relative. Only on **Cousin** and **Cousine** will you see the true Seychelles bird, somewhat smaller and distinguished from its grey-headed cousin by a purplish-red head.

On the shoreline the **green-backed heron** — subspecies: *degens* — is often seen standing motionless as it scans the water for its prey. Curiously this small, brownish, hunchbacked heron is thought to be most closely related to the African race, while a separate subspecies occurring on Aldabra is considered to be of Asian origin — a strange overlap that is yet another reminder of Seychelles' birthplace at the parting point of two continents.

The **cattle egret** — subspecies: *seychellarum* — may also be seen on the shoreline, but will be more often encountered inland.

With few bovines or pachyderms for the bird to follow in Seychelles, rubbish dumps and fish markets make perfectly acceptable substitutes in the search for insects. There is a large roost near the **Le Chantier** roundabout at the edge of **Victoria**.

On the outer islands you will see another race of the **green-backed heron** — *crawfordi* — found from the **Amirantes** to **Aldabra**. The Creole name for the green-backed heron is *manik* or *makak* — a good phonetic description of its call.

The **Malagasy turtle dove** is recorded both in the **Amirantes** — *aldabrana*, a misnomer — and **Aldabra** — *coppingeri* — but it has not interbred with the Malagasy *picturata* stock.

Aldabra, in fact, boasts more unique subspecies than any other Indian Ocean island, of which one of the most endearing must be the **Aldabra sacred ibis** — *abbotti*.

China-blue eyes distinguish this unmistakable bird from its African relative, both having black and white plumage, bald head and neck, and long decurved bill.

In the Aldabran interior you may encounter the **Comoro blue pigeon** — *minor* — with its silver-white head, blue wings and tail, and a red circle around the eye. Skulking in the pemphis scrub, you may glimpse the **Malagasy**

Above: Crested terns explore a wind-swept beach.

coucal — *insularis* — which builds an unusual large, barrel-shaped nest, with an entrance at one end.

Another land subspecies of Madagascan origin is the **red-headed forest fody** — *aldabrana* — common throughout most of the atoll. It is more insectivorous than the other fodies, a sign of its adaptation to island life.

Three subspecies of the **Souimanga sunbird,** the brightest sunbird of the Indian Ocean islands, occur in the Aldabra group, — *aldabrensis*; **Cosmoledo**, *buchenorum*; and **Assumption**, *abbotti*.

The colour of the underparts is the primary difference. They probably evolved distinctly from one another as these tiny birds rarely fly from one island to another.

The **Malagasy white-eye** — *aldabrensis* — and the **Malagasy bulbul** — *rostratus* — replace the Seychelles species. The **Malagasy nightjar** — *aldabrensis* — completes the list of subspecies from this remarkable World Heritage Site.

At one time the **Malagasy kestrel**, also found on Aldabra, was also given the sub-specific name *aldabrensis*. It is now regarded, however, as just a local race.

One subspecies, the **chestnut flanked white-eye** — *semiflava* — formerly recorded from **Marianne**, became extinct around 1900, at about the same time as the Seychelles green parakeet. But, unlike the parakeet, its demise was probably due to the destruction of its habitat rather than persecution.

It is likely that other subspecies have disappeared from the outer islands, especially **Assumption**, which suffered severely from the mining of guano, and the subsequent loss of natural vegetation.

Nevertheless much remains to excite and intrigue visitors to these enchanted islands.

Feathered Aliens Which Feel at Home

All over the world, man has introduced birds to oceanic islands — for pest control, for sport, for aesthetic reasons, as cage bird escapes, or as ship-borne migrants.

All are the means by which introduced species, so very much a part of the avian scene, arrived in Seychelles.

Among the most striking of these introductions is the **Madagascar fody**. According to local legend, a rice grower introduced the birds to his neighbour's land to sabotage his rival's rice crop as revenge over a land dispute.

From September to April, the male is brilliant scarlet, while the female and juveniles are sparrow-like. Adult males are often seen during the breeding season chasing each other around the vegetation.

Proud of their magnificent livery, they often perch next to car wing mirrors to gaze in admiration at themselves. Large flocks can sometimes be seen around houses or shops where the owners put out rice for them.

No visitor can fail to notice the common and widespread noisy **Indian mynah**, introduced from India to Mauritius in order to control locusts—and from there to Seychelles. As there are no locusts in Seychelles, it may initially have arrived after escaping from a cage.

Extremely successful, these birds appear able to exploit every niche — from the high hills of **Mahé** to the shoreline itself.

Occasionally, a mutant form with a bald yellow head, called a "king mynah", can be seen. Local belief says that the bald yellow head results from overeating ripe mangoes.

They are superb mimics: their repertoire includes the raucous chorus of roosting birds and a delightful courtship call, which roughly translates as "keek-keek-keek-kok-kok-kok-churr-churr-churr", accompanied by much bowing of the head, and fluffing of the feathers.

Aesthetic reasons alone account for the introduction of the **barred ground dove**, a delightfully tame creature often seen in hotels wandering between the tables searching for crumbs. The breast is a light terra cotta with black barring on its wing, back, and sides.

The base of the bill, and the skin around the eye, is pale blue. Males attempt to impress females by bowing, fanning out their long tails, and cooing.

Less common, despite the name, is the **common waxbill**, found in grassy areas on Mahé and **La Digue** where it feeds on seeds. Of African origin, it was probably the first bird introduced to Seychelles when it arrived in 1786 as a cage bird.

The **barn owl** was introduced in 1951, supposedly to control rats, despite the complete failure of a pilot scheme on **Plate Island** where amid a plague of rats the birds failed to survive.

But on Mahé the owl found the local birds easier targets. Now there is a bounty on their head, but the birds are well established on most of the large granitic islands.

Perhaps the most ominous introduction of all was the **Indian house crow** which probably arrived by ship. These birds have caused havoc along the Red Sea and East African coasts, driving away much of the local avifauna.

Fears that they may stage a similar take-over in Seychelles have led to attempts to eradicate them and their numbers have declined. But these wily birds are not easy to eliminate, and still pose a threat to the islands' fragile birdlife.

Grey francolin, which were introduced as sporting birds to some islands, still survive on **Desroches**, where they are seen around sunrise at the edge of the airstrip. During the daytime they lie low in the coconut plantation and are extremely difficult to find.

The Indian race of the **house sparrow** has also found a niche on Desroches, and other islands in the **Amirantes**. It probably arrived by ship, but it seems strange that this species has yet to find its way to the most populated islands of the granitic group.

Migrants: A Mesmerising Mystery

Nobody has yet fully understood the mystery of migration, the seemingly miraculous mechanism that enables a tiny bird to fly from its breeding ground on the Arctic tundra, across the length of Asia, and a huge expanse of featureless ocean, to pinpoint, year after year, the same beach, on the same scrap of land, in that same vast ocean — a feat commonly performed by many waders seen in Seychelles.

Indeed, the vast majority of migrant birds move between Eurasia and Africa. For many Seychelles is an essential landfall on their long journeys.

It means almost any Eurasian migrant

Above: Fairy terns, with their bright blue bills, are now commonly found on both Cousin and Aride islands.

may turn up and visitors from Europe need not be surprised to see a number of familiar species, such as **turnstone**, **whimbrel**, **bartailed godwit**, and **grey plover**.

Other species, rarely seen in Western Europe except as vagrants, are also fairly common during the northern winter, including **Terek sandpipers** which dart across the mud flats like clockwork toys as they search for food. **Curlew sandpipers** turn up in large numbers and can sometimes be seen even in grassy areas around **Victoria**.

It is not just the waders that take a winter break in Seychelles. The **European hobby**, one of the few birds of prey to migrate to and from Europe each year, turns up every northern winter. This most aerial of predators is capable of catching even the speedy **Seychelles cave swiftlet**.

One of the world's most extraordinary migrants is **Eleanora's falcon**, a bird of prey that breeds on Mediterranean cliff-tops. Each winter they migrate south to Madagascar in an arc via the Red Sea and Horn of Africa.

Inevitably, some turn up in Seychelles and are probably frequent visitors to the outer islands.

Even passerines are sometimes seen. **Swallow**, **tree pipit**, and **wheatear** are regular visitors. Tiny warblers such as **blackcap** and **willow warbler** challenge the might of the Indian Ocean to winter in a land very different from their country of birth.

Many of these avian visitors are windblown vagrants. After strong northerly winds and heavy rain during the north-west monsoon, birdwatching can be particularly exciting.

Perhaps Seychelles is one of the few places on earth where the careful tourist stands a real chance of recording birds never previously seen in the country. There is as yet no official records committee, but plans are in the pipeline.

Birdwatchers are requested to send any interesting records and notes to: *Adrian Skerrett, RSNC Executive Officer, Mahé Shipping Co. Ltd., Shipping House, PO Box 336, Victoria, Seychelles.*

Where Seabirds are thick on the Ground

Seychelles is home to some of the most spectacular seabird colonies on earth. Scenes reminiscent of Alfred Hitchcock's film, *The Birds*, remind visitors to whom these islands *really* belong.

The human population of **Aride**, for example, is five: its seabird population is often well over one million.

The **sooty tern** breeds in immense colonies on **Desnoeufs**, **Bird**, and Aride. From April to September the sky above these islands can be filled with huge numbers of excited birds calling "wideawake" to each other. This gives it its other name **wideawake tern**.

At one time there were many more, but uncontrolled egg-collecting wiped them out on all but a few islands. In 1931, 70,000 eggs were collected on **Cousin** and by 1955 the bird was wiped out as a breeding species on the island.

The same story was repeated on **Récife**, **Mamelles**, and other colonies. With careful management and protection on Aride and Bird, and controlled collecting on Desnoeufs, this decline has been arrested.

The sooty tern is a seabird *par excellence*. Indeed, if it could lay its egg at sea it would never come to land. Once chicks fledge they head for the open ocean where they wander the world, hundreds of kilometres from land, eating and sleeping on the wing until they return to breed about seven years later.

The **bridled tern** is extremely similar, but is brownish-grey, not black, on the wings and mantle. Unique among the seabirds of Seychelles it breeds synchronously in an eight-month cycle.

As an exclusively tropical species, the actual month of breeding is not critical. It may be that by choosing different times of year between one year and the next, the species is able to hedge its bets in the event that one season is unusually difficult for breeding.

The **roseate tern** is found the world over, but sadly it is becoming very scarce. Taxonomy is difficult, but Aride is the locality of what may be a separate Western Indian Ocean race — *arideensis* — breeding in Seychelles,

Mauritius, and Caragados Carajos. The breeding birds have bright-red bills and legs and underparts tinged a delicate pink.

The **lesser noddy** is a speciality of the Indian Ocean, although in truth it may be the same species, or closely related to the **black noddy** of the tropical Pacific and Atlantic oceans. The world headquarters of the lesser noddy is Aride Island, and to a smaller extent Cousin.

Numbers are increasing on both islands as, with careful management, the **pisonia** trees, in which the birds nest and from which they obtain nesting material, flourish.

Formerly, the pisonia was cut, and the coppicing may have led to a huge increase in the sticky seeds which tangle feathers and kill the seabirds.

The larger, more heavily built **brown noddy** is much less common, but breeds in good numbers on many islands throughout Seychelles. Brown noddies nest mostly during the south-east monsoon, but have a secondary breeding season during the north-west. Like the bridled tern, this may be another case of not putting all your eggs in one monsoon.

For good reasons — this pure white bird is a symbol of beauty, elegance, and gentleness — Air Seychelles chose the **fairy tern** as its logo. It breeds all year throughout Seychelles. Remarkably, it lays its single, somewhat spherical egg on a bare branch.

The newly-hatched chick has huge feet in relation to its size, giving it a comical appearance. The base of the bill is a beautiful midnight blue. Unlike other terns it feeds close inshore much of the time and is rarely seen far out at sea. They are now rare on **Praslin** and **Mahé** due to the introduced barn owls.

White-tailed tropicbirds, with their long graceful tail streamers, also breed throughout the year. Their courtship display, in which stiff-winged pairs trace complex patterns across the sky, takes your breath away.

Chicks can weigh a quarter as much again as their parents. As chicks grow older parental visits become shorter until after about twenty-five days they are only fed once a day. Eventually the hungry chick is forced to go out and find its own meals.

In the granitics, **red-tailed tropicbirds** breed only on Aride, the northernmost outpost of this species. They are much more common in the Aldabra region. Sailors named tropicbirds "bosun birds" as their long tails resembled a bosun's spike.

At night, on Cousin and Aride, strange sounds betray the presence of shearwaters, or "mutton birds". Two species, **Audobon's shearwater** and **wedge-tailed shearwater**, breed.

In the past, the latter, known locally as *fouke*, was eaten in great numbers but happily its main breeding sites are now protected. Shearwaters are often encountered at sea, where they glide on stiff wings, just above the waters, flowing over the contours of the waves.

The **great frigatebird** and **lesser frigatebird**, which breed only on **Aldabra** in Seychelles, are frequently encountered as non-breeding birds in the granitics, especially on Aride.

Frigates are pirates of the air, harrying large seabirds and forcing them to drop or regurgitate their catches.

They dive and twist acrobatically, using their tails as rudders as they attack their quarry. The breeding male has a red throat patch, which inflates like an enormous balloon to impress its mate.

Some seabirds do not breed in Seychelles but as the ocean is their home they inevitably turn up on occasion. During the southern winter from June to August the large, powerful **Antarctic skua** is often seen.

From the other end of the globe, during the northern winter, come gulls from Eurasia, such as the **lesser black-backed gull** and **brown-headed gull**.

Boobies are rare sights in the granitic islands, but breed in large numbers especially in the Aldabra region where the **red-footed booby** breeds alongside frigatebirds despite the fact it is persecuted mercilessly by these birds. **Masked booby** and **brown booby** are also seen, though less commonly.

Once **Abbot's booby** bred in mangroves on **Assumption Island**. Sadly it was wiped out and in the entire world now only occurs on Christmas Island.

Below: The diminutive Malagasy white-eye.

Above: Brown noddy tern.

Discovering the Marine World

Many people become entranced by the warm clear waters and the spectacle of the reefs around the islands of Seychelles. The calm waters provide ideal conditions to view first-hand the abundant marine life. Most are surprised to learn that the reefs themselves are vital living organisms with well-structured societies.

The coral reef is an amazingly complex, physical structure: in many ways an ocean's version of tropical jungle. The different coral formations provide an enormous variety of habitats, which are colonized in turn by a multitude of marine creatures.

Each coral head is made up of hundreds of living polyps — tiny animals that secrete an external skeleton of limestone. The reef grows on the amassed remains of millions of tiny individual coral skeletons, compacted and built upon by successive colonies over the centuries.

Although the base may be a strong, rock-like structure, the living surface is fragile and easily damaged.

The polyp is an animal that requires fairly specific conditions for growth and reproduction. They need clean, well oxygenated sea water between 18° and 30°C (64°–86°F). They will not survive above or below this temperature range.

They feed by ensnaring tiny prey with the aid of a ring of tentacles armed with a formidable arsenal of stinging cells.

Like building the walls of a house, they secrete their limestone skeletons onto a foundation made of the remains of previous coral skeletons. Thus they are immobile and need a constant flow of food-laden water passing over them to feed from.

The tissue of their sack-like bodies contains microscopic, single-cell organisms, *Zooxanthellae*, which assist corals by giving them the plant-like ability to produce energy by photosynthesis.

Therefore corals thrive in warm, clear waters down as far as the sunlight reaches but growing best of all in the brightest areas — closest to the surface.

The size of the colony increases as the corals reproduce by literally "budding-off" baby polyps from their own tissues. They also produce larvae by sexual reproduction. These free swimming offspring are carried as plankton on the ocean currents.

Ultimately, surviving larvae settle on the sea-bed. If the surface they land on is suitable, they develop into a new polyp and start a new coral colony which, normally, is similar in appearance to the parent colony although they assume differing shapes according to the volume and strength of water movement they experience.

Slow-growing organisms, the coral reef systems of Seychelles may have taken as long as 10,000 years to reach their present size. Thus, as the numbers of visitors to the reefs increases, it is vital that all ensure their activities do not damage the corals — either intentionally or accidentally.

Reef types

The coral reef forms around the **Inner Islands** are either fringing reefs, which grow from the main landmass, or patchwork reefs on shallow sandbanks or granite outcrops in protected bays.

The **Outer Islands** include good examples of coral atolls, the ultimate result of reef development. There are no examples of the barrier reef formation in Seychelles.

Fringing reefs provide a number of distinctive habitats, which are far less distinguished in the patchwork reef. Each has animals and fish that are specific to them, but they also support many wandering species.

These reefs, the object of continuing study, provide hours of entertainment for reef and fish watchers who quickly learn to identify the regular inhabitants of an area.

The coral atolls of the Outer Islands present a similar variety of species depending on the continuity of the outer reef formation. In some the only visible remnant of the reef formation is an island, such as **Plate Island**. Others are typically a large lagoon ringed by islands such as **Aldabra**. This formation is known as an atoll.

Above: Guinea fowl moray eel in a Seychelles' coral garden.

Inside these well-formed inner lagoons, there is usually a relatively uniform sand bottom with occasional coral heads. How much coral forms depends on the flow of clean water through the reef. Generally the growth is more prolific around the channels through which the reef fills and drains with the tide's ebb and flow.

In lagoons which are particularly silty, coral growth may be inhibited as corals soon die if they become covered with sediment.

On the slopes of the ocean-facing reefs of the outer islands, such as the Amirantes, the coral formations are dramatic — with awesome wall-like drop-offs. Others have steep, bare slopes which are constantly eroded by the continual action of strong currents and destructive wave action, prohibiting all but the hardiest of coral formations.

Granite reefs

Besides the coral reefs there are also a large number of granite reefs around the Inner Islands. Essentially, these are the remains of what were once mountains and can often be traced as a continuation of the existing land ranges.

Although made of granite, they are far from just dead rock. To the contrary, they are generally covered in an amazing array of encrusting sponges and corals of many varieties and colours.

They also offer a much greater range of vertical surfaces and crevices between their slabs and boulders. In turn, these make ideal sanctuaries for many different kinds of fish.

Thus the granite reefs are often just as interesting to the budding marine enthusiast as the coral reefs.

Conservation

Seychelles has established a network of marine parks which grows larger every year. In these parks, strict rules forbid the taking of shells and the damage or removal of any coral, whether alive or dead.

Please observe these rules not only in the designated parks but also in any reef system: your efforts will allow those who follow you to observe one of the real treasures of the islands and help to conserve the Seychelles reefs for generations to come.

There are many opportunities to discover and explore the marine environment. The only limits are time and your own enthusiasm. The abundance of fish life and the sheer variety of reefs means that there will always be more to see and thus a reason to return.

Glass bottom boats

For those who want the best of both worlds, to see the magnificent reefs and to stay dry, there are glass bottom boats and semi-submersibles with underwater viewing cabins.

These and the larger glass bottom boats operate in **St. Anne Marine National Park**, reached from the **Victoria Yacht Basin**.

Excursions are usually for half a day or full-day with lunch at one of the rather special restaurants on the various islands in the park. The restaurants have a reputation for the best of Creole food and lots of it, so do not plan on doing too much in the afternoon except sunbathing. Bookings can be made through any tour operator or through their representatives at the hotels.

If you do not fancy a big group, or would prefer to visit different areas, you will find that individual operators run several smaller glass bottom boats. You can ask at your hotel or on the beach or through the **Marine Charter Association** in **Victoria**.

Many specialise in personal service and will take you to almost any area that you wish to visit, either on a half- or full-day basis. Full-day excursions normally include a beach barbecue in some deserted cove that can be reached only by boat.

These trips are extremely popular around north-west Mahé where you sail into the **Baie Ternay Marine National Park**, perhaps the most spectacular shallow reef of the inner islands.

Individual operators on **Praslin** and **La Digue** offer similar services, most of which are advertised in the hotels from which they operate.

The Seasons and The Ocean

The widespread distribution of fish and marine life species throughout the Indian Ocean is mainly due to the prevailing winds that drive the ocean currents. Sea and wind are extremely important to all waterborne activities.

The most dynamic force in the Indian Ocean is the South Equatorial Current, which pulls in water from the Pacific Ocean. Flowing from east to west throughout the year, it ricochets off the coast of Africa to become the East African Coastal Current, which flows around Seychelles.

When the south-east monsoon trade wind blows between April and October it brings cool, generally dry weather to the islands and helps the northward flow of the main current along the coast of Kenya and Somalia — and around and over the Seychelles bank.

Often the winds are strong resulting in rough seas offshore and heavy surf on all but north and west facing beaches when such bays as **Beau Vallon** become relatively calm with offshore winds.

These continuous winds cause an upwelling of colder water to flow over the marine plateau, cooling the surface temperature to 25° C (77°F) in August. At the same time, the sea becomes much murkier because of the plankton-rich water and inshore visibility will be down to between ten and fifteen metres (30 to 50 feet).

Then, during October, as the south-east trade wind blows itself out, the seas become calmer and warmer. The plankton-laden water sinks down into the ocean depths leaving the sea above warm and clear.

It is one of the prime times for diving over the offshore areas and **Outer Islands** and undoubtedly the best time to go cruising between the islands — but not so good for windsurfers or Hobie Cat enthusiasts.

In December, the north-west monsoon is neither as strong nor as consistent as the south-east bringing moist, humid air and short but heavy tropical downpours.

Even so the sea continues to warm up and the water remains clear except during spells of rough weather which churn up sediments over the inshore sites on the plateau.

This is the time when the north and west facing beaches experience heavy seas and diving activities move over to the **Victoria** side of the island where it is calmer.

These north-west winds drive the southward flowing current off the coast of Somalia to meet the northward flowing East African Coastal Current. Together they swing due east and become the Equatorial Counter Current, that flows over and around the reefs

Above: Red-spotted coral fish.

of the Outer Islands, with an eastward current moving over the plateau.

When the north-west monsoon subsides during March the sea temperature rises as high as 29°C (84°F) and there is a brief lull before the south-east returns, normally towards the end of April and into May, to start the cycle all over again.

This brief period of exceptional calm is a prime time to visit the offshore diving spots and for island cruising as the windsurfers polish their boards and stretch sails in anticipation of the coming south-east monsoon.

By studying the expected conditions at any given time of the year you should be able to arrange your vacation to give you the best chance to make the most of your chosen watersports activities in Seychelles.

Marine Fish: Colourful World of the Inner Universe

Nowhere is the rich diversity of nature displayed to such spectacular effect as on the coral reef. Swim out over the edge of the reef and slip down into the warm turquoise waters to enter a fantasy world filled with an astounding variety of colour, shape, and form.

Most beautiful of all, perhaps, is the kaleidoscopic range of marine fishes which fall into two major classes: the bony fish, *Osteichthyes*, and the sharks and rays, *Chondrichthyes*.

The vast majority of fish numbers and species are bony fish, and there are many striking varieties on the coral reefs of Seychelles. Almost 1,000 species have been noted.

More than 200 species have been found on the reefs of tiny **Cousin Island**. On **Aldabra**, 185 species were recorded in one study from a single three-square-kilometre (one-square-mile) section of reef.

About three-quarters of all species in Seychelles are found throughout the Indo-Pacific, of which perhaps four per cent have their western limit in Seychelles.

Approximately 17.5 per cent are Indian Ocean forms, and fifteen per cent may be confined to the Western Indian Ocean. Less than four per cent are endemic forms.

Much still remains to be discovered but what is known is fascinating.

Moray eels look menacing, but are harmless if left alone. On **Desroches** the divemaster will sometimes entice a moray out to feed from his hand, but this is not recommended for beginners. Several species are commonly encountered, including the **zebra moray**, the **geometric moray,** and the **leopard moray**.

The **crocodile needlefish** have extremely slender streamlined bodies and elongated, pointed jaws. Gliding through the water just below the surface, they occasionally leap from the surface — flying through the air like a living harpoon. They have been known to injure people, but this is rare.

The **tropical two-wing flying fish** is more likely to be seen when you are above the surface as it takes off from the water to escape predators and glides for a considerable distance. Look out for these aerial maestros on sea crossings, especially in calm weather.

By contrast, the **squirrelfish** will usually be found skulking in caves and crevices by day. As their large eyes suggest, they are nocturnal predators. Some have strong, moderately venomous spines.

The **trumpetfish** can be bright yellow or brown. It is an elongated fish that sometimes hides among corals or alongside larger fish to get closer to the smaller fish and shrimps on which it preys.

The **flutemouth** is similar, but has the ability to change colour, displaying sequences of blue or brown bands. The tubular snout is used to suck in small fish, which it moves in on stealthily, relying on camouflage.

Seahorses are rare, but the closely related **pipefishes** are common. Apart from their beauty, these creatures are remarkable because it is the male which becomes "pregnant", rearing the eggs in a ventral brood area or pouch.

Razorfish have the curious habit of swimming in shoals head down. This enables them to pluck crustaceans from between the coral branches using their long snouts.

The **lionfish** (or **turkeyfish** or **firefish**) are among the most spectacular of fish. They move as though in slow motion, with pectoral fins spread like the wings of a butterfly and long dorsal rays extended. Most common are the **red firefish** and the smaller **long-spined** or **radial firefish**.

The **scorpionfish** is a master of disguise which lies in wait for fish or crustaceans to make the mistake of venturing too close. They are so called because of the row of venomous spines along their dorsal fin.

Stonefish have thick, warty skin, and no scales. They match their background almost perfectly. They are perhaps the most feared venomous fish of all, and wounds can be extremely painful. Fatalities have been reported elsewhere.

Always wear flippers or at least plastic shoes when you venture over the reef edge, and take care where you put your hands and feet.

You will need to be keen-eyed to spot the **frogfish**, an odd-looking globular-shaped fish covered in fleshy warts and appendages, matching the colour of its surroundings.

It fishes using a lure which it waves above its mouth. It also slowly stalks its prey, however, and can engulf fish or crustaceans larger than itself by expanding its abdomen.

The **sea goldie** gathers in small groups around coral heads. The females resemble goldfish, while the male is darker orange with purple markings. Females greatly outnumber males. All sea goldies start life as females, and if a male is removed from a group, a female will change sex to take its place.

Groupers or **rockcods** (known in Creole as *vye*) are common and varied reef fishes. They are carnivorous, feeding on fish and crustaceans, and in turn some species are important commercial fish in Seychelles.

More species occur in deep water than

Overleaf: The largest fish in the seas — whale shark with watching diver.

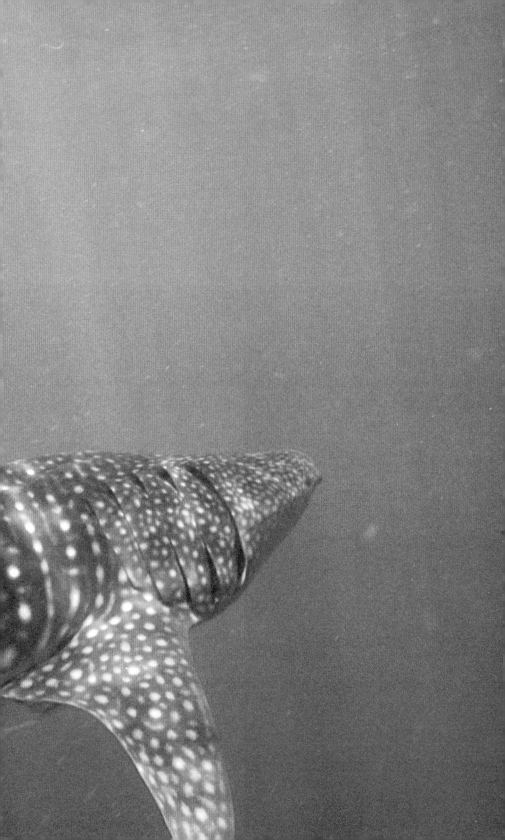

shallow water, but many can be seen on shallow reefs. The **slender rockcod** is an elegant fish of silver brown, covered in bright orange spots. It rejoices in the Creole name of *sevalye dibwa* or "knight of the wood".

Peacock rockcod is a colourful common variety. They have a brown-banded body covered in turquoise blue spots.

Sweetlips are another vivid group. They are also known as *grunts* due to their ability to emit sound by grinding their teeth, a sound that is amplified by their gas bladder.

Some species undergo dramatic colour changes as they mature, such as the **black spotted sweetlips** or *matongo*. Juveniles have horizontal black and yellow bands: with age the body turns to silver and the fins become yellow with black spots, which continue along the body, decreasing in size from the dorsal area to the plain underside.

Many species of **snapper** occur in Seychelles, mostly in deep water, but some also on the shallow reefs. They are popular commercial fish, and your first introduction to **red snapper,** *bourzwa*, one of the largest and tastiest, is likely to be on a restaurant menu.

One of the most elegant snappers is **black beauty**. The juvenile form is pure white with black patches over the eyes, back, and around the base of the fins. The patches gradually spread as the fish matures, leaving a horizontal white stripe and a few white spots on the back. Eventually these too disappear and the black beauty becomes totally black.

A common reef fish is the **blue-banded snapper** which is particularly colourful with a yellow body displaying four horizontal blue bands. It is sometimes found in huge shoals.

Fusiliers are common tropical plankton feeders related to snappers. Most beautiful of all is the **rainbow fusilier** or **rainbow flasher.** Large, fast-moving shoals of these colourful fish occur at certain times of year. Approximately the shape of a mackerel, they have yellow backs above a band of blue, and silver-pink bellies.

The **gold striped fusiliers**, with a light blue body marked by a golden streak, are perhaps the most common of all.

The **yellowstripe spinecheek** is one of the first fish you may encounter in shallow water. Spinecheeks are characterised by a

sharp pointed spine immediately under the eye and a series of shorter spines below. This streamlined silver fish with prominent blue and brown horizontal stripes is normally solitary, but occasionally seen in small shoals.

Batfish are extremely distinctive with their compressed, almost circular bodies. Of seven genera, only *platax*, which includes the **orbicular batfish** and the **longfin batfish**, are associated with coral reefs. Batfish sometimes gather in huge mid-water shoals over reefs or granite rocks.

The **diamond fish**, silver in colour, is common in shallow waters. It is small and diamond-shaped. They are also sometimes known as moonies, again because of their flattened shape and silver colour.

Goatfish are distinguished by a pair of long barbels on the chin, with which they probe the sea bed in search of worms and crustaceans. In some parts of the world the flesh is reputed to be poisonous, causing hallucinations, vivid nightmares, and bizarre dreams. In Seychelles, however, they are excellent eating.

Angelfish have deeply compressed bodies and a long spine on the edge of the gill. They are among the most colourful reef fish, sometimes undergoing great changes in pattern and colour as they mature.

The **emperor angelfish**, for example, has a dramatic black, blue, and white concentric pattern in the juvenile form. The adult has blue and yellow horizontal stripes on the body and a blue-black pattern around the head.

The **royal angelfish** is one of the most spectacular of all, with a golden body, crossed by blue and black-edged white stripes, a golden tail, and a golden and blue-banded fin.

Butterflyfish, closely related to angelfish, lack the gill spine. One of the greatest pleasures of fish-watching can be identifying the many colourful members of this family.

What can you say about a fish that rejoices in the name of **gorgeous gussy**, except that it has many rivals in the underwater beauty contest, including the **threadfin**, **purple**, **yellowhead**, and the exquisite **longnose butterflyfish**?

The **trevally** or **jack** family are strong-swimming, open-water fish. These carnivores

Above: Blue-barred parrotfish.

are often seen hunting over the reef. Indeed, the small, juvenile **golden trevally** will sometimes "pilot" a snorkeler, staying close to the mask as you swim along. Known locally as *karang*, these are popular eating fish.

The **bluefin trevally** will use the topography of the reef to approach unaware prey, or sometimes follow other predators to take advantage of their feeding activity. Sometimes a group of bluefin trevally will rush a shoal of prey to disperse them and pick off victims.

The **remoras** are unique in possessing a suction disc above the forehead with which they attach themselves to a variety of hosts including turtles, sharks, and rays. The **sharksucker** may even try its luck with a diver's scuba tank. They are not parasitic, but merely hitchhike in search of a free lunch from the scraps left by the host.

Hawkfish, by contrast, are sedentary, lying in wait for their prey. The **freckled hawkfish**, looking like a miserable youth with a serious case of acne, is a common sight, sitting on reef heads, while the smaller **spotted** or **pixy hawkfish** lie within coral heads for protection against larger predators.

The **damsels** are a huge family of small, attractive reef fish. Many are zooplankton feeders, which gather in huge aggregations above coral heads, such as the **sergeant major** and the similar **scissortail sergeant**, distinguished by a black scissor-like line on each half of the tail fin. Several species of **chromis** are also commonly seen in large numbers in mid-water, especially **blue chromis** and **golden chromis**.

Around the coral heads, smaller groups of damsels can be found, such as the appropriately named **chocolate dip** with a chocolate brown front half and white rear half. The **zebra humbug** and **two-bar humbug** are also common in and around coral branches.

Two of the most colourful damsels come from the genus *Pomacentrus*. The **sulphur damsel** is a striking bright yellow with a small black pectoral spot.

One of the most beautiful members of this family is the **blue pete**. This small, exquisite, bright blue damsel with yellow tail and belly is extremely common in Seychelles.

The **skunk clownfish**, a pinkish damsel with a white line on its back from nose to tail, is found within long-tentacled anemones. Each anemone harbours a large, dominant female and a smaller male, and possibly a few juveniles.

Like other reef fish, it can change its sex, but it is the male which changes to a female if the latter is removed. The clownfish rely on the anemones for protection, sliding restlessly among the tentacles, immune to their venom.

Less common is the largest of the local clownfish, the **Seychelles three-barred clownfish**, which has a similar lifestyle.

The wrasses form another huge family with many representatives on a typical Seychelles reef. They are the most diverse family of all, ranging in size from tiny fish to the enormous **humphead wrasse** which grows to two metres (six to seven feet) long.

The **slingjaw** has the astonishing habit of projecting and retracting its trunk-like mouth to suck in prey.

The **bird wrasse** uses a different technique. This distinctive fish has an elongated, tubular snout used for working out its prey.

The **bluestreak cleaner wrasse** is another gender bender. Females can change to males within four days. Each male controls a harem of about six females. They set up a cleaner station patronised by larger fish which attend the station to have ectoparasites picked off them.

The cleaner and host fish go through a series of behavioural responses to advise each other of their intentions. Individual cleaners can work through 150 to 200 hosts an hour. The cleaners also endeavour to chase off the **mimic blenny**, which have a comparable colour, but feed on the fins of unsuspecting hosts. Some wrasse have distinctive colour forms for juveniles and adults.

The **queen coris** also has different male and female forms. They feed mainly on molluscs, crabs, and hermit crabs, and will turn over rocks in search of prey. They are equally content to follow divers who provide the same service for them.

Parrotfish are well-named both for their bright colours and their fused, beak-like dental plates which they use to browse on the

Opposite: Striped batfish in a coral garden.

algae growing on limestone corals.

This manner of feeding makes them the most important fish for sand production . . . a strange thought when you lie on the pure white coral sands. Like some wrasses, they undergo marked colour changes from juvenile to adult, and are capable of sex reversals.

The initial phase is usually drab. Colourful males may develop from the sex change of a parrotfish that has risen through the pecking order. The initial phase of most species may be male or female, but primary males can also

Top: Spiny crayfish.

Above: Juvenile lionfish.

change colour to the terminal phase.

Common species include the **blue-barred, dusky,** and **bullethead parrotfish**. The aptly named **humphead parrotfish** is particularly huge, reaching 1.2 metres (four feet), and often occurring in large numbers.

The **pickhandle barracuda** is a favourite eating fish. This carnivore normally occurs in shoals, whereas the **great barracuda** is generally solitary. Barracuda may look fearsome, but the fish watcher in clear waters has little to fear from this streamlined predator of the reef.

Along the shoreline, on the granite boulders or in the mangrove creeks, you may see the strange **rockskipper** or **mudskipper**. There are several different species, each with its own habitat preferences.

These gobies frequently leave the water, and using their pelvic sucker to stay in place when the waters rush over them, patrol the intertidal zone using their pectoral fins as legs.

Their high, bulging eyes give good all-round vision, making them very alert to predators. At the least sign of danger, they return to the water, skipping across the surface with rapid strokes of their tails.

The sand-dwelling gobies form a fascinating symbiotic relationship with alpheid prawns. In Baie Ternay Marine National Park, twelve species of goby have been found living with seven species of prawn. The prawn's burrow is a valuable hideout.

The goby stands alert to danger while the prawn concentrates on housekeeping. The goby communicates the least sign of danger to the prawn, and both creatures seek refuge in the burrow.

Another type of symbiosis can be seen between **surgeonfish**, notably the **blue-banded** but also the **powder blue surgeon**, and the **dark damsel**. On Aldabra, the damsel is largely confined to surgeon territories. Both compete for limited food, but while the surgeon defends the territory against larger fish, the damsel may perform the same defensive task against smaller competitors.

Surgeonfish are so called because of a sharp, blade-like spine at the base of the tail with which they can slash other fish — and careless humans — with a side sweep of the tail, thereby establishing their dominance.

The two species already mentioned are especially colourful, but most bizarre of all surgeons may be the **unicorns**. The dorsal snout of the **spotted unicorn** is especially large and gets longer with age.

The **moorish idol** is so named because it is held in great respect by some Oriental races, and is believed to be endowed with mystical powers. It resembles a butterflyfish with a trailing feathery dorsal filament, but comes from a completely separate family.

Rabbitfish, a popular eating fish in Seychelles, has a small, rabbit-like mouth and nose. The spines are sharp and venomous, and while they do not have as nasty a poison as scorpionfish, they should be handled with great care.

The **kingfish** is a powerful, streamlined game fish. It is brilliant dark-blue above, silver below. Kingfish steaks are a common feature of a Seychelles menu or barbecue.

Tuna need no introduction. The **yellowfin tuna** is particularly prized, while **the eastern little tuna** or **bonito** is perhaps the most common catch on the game fishing boats.

The **sailfish** is probably the greatest prize for the game fisherman. This fast-growing predator reaches almost two metres (six feet) in only one year. The sight of the blue, sail-like fin breaking the surface is breathtaking.

The **Picasso triggerfish**, like other trigger-fish, has a deeply compressed body with eyes set high on the head and a long but not protruding snout. The first dorsal is very strong, and can be locked into an erect position with the small, second spine. They are usually solitary and fairly shy.

Harlequin fish, closely related to trigger-fish, are considerably smaller. They are secretive and often hide among coral branches.

Boxfish are named because of their box-like, hard, external carapace, made up of bony, hexagonal plates. They are slow-swimming bottom-dwellers, propelling themselves along with a sculling motion of the dorsal and anal fins.

They are often seen on sale as novelty money boxes, but these are a poor substitute for viewing the colourful live specimens swimming around the reefs.

The **model toby** — like an underwater wind-up toy — is a kind of puffer. Puffers are well-known for harbouring toxin, and serious illness or death can result from eating their flesh. The larger species, such as **black-spotted puffer**, are sometimes eaten as **fugu** in Japan in a gastronomic version of Russian roulette.

If a tiny morsel of the ovaries, intestines, or liver is left in the flesh, a painful death can result within minutes. Hundreds of times more deadly than cyanide, it claims about twenty lives a year in Japan. There is no known antidote.

The **porcupinefish**, closely related to the puffers, have much larger spines. They can inflate their bodies for protection, wedging themselves in holes or turning themselves into unmanageable spiney footballs.

Rays, together with the sharks, make up the cartilaginous class of fishes, characterized by five to seven gill slits each side, no gas bladder, a spiral valve intestine, and internal fertilization.

Most species originated during the Cretaceous period 135 million years ago. One of the largest of the stingrays is the **round ribbontail ray**, a huge, majestic, plate-shaped fish with a sharp, poisonous, barbed spine — to be avoided.

The **spotted eagle ray** is smaller, with large blue spots, but the king of them all is the breathtaking **manta ray** sometimes encountered on deeper dive sites, such as **Shark Bank**.

Sharks are not often seen in the shallow waters around the granitics, even though there are more species of shark than any other fish family. The **white tip shark**, a harmless species, is the most common, while almost every fish-watcher's dream, to have a close encounter with the biggest fish in the ocean, the plankton-feeding **whale shark,** is also possible in this area.

In deeper waters, sharks become far more common. On the outer edge of the Seychelles plateau and on the Amirantes Bank, sharks make up about twenty per cent of the fish caught on handlines.

The first few experiences of life on the coral reef will leave you breathless with amazement and excitement, but it may take a great deal of time and patience to come to grips with fish identification. The effort is worth it — the first step to understanding a little of the remarkable world that lies literally within a stone's throw of the world we know.

The Rare and Endangered Marine Turtle

Today all marine turtles are classed among the most endangered animals under the Convention on International Trade and Endangered Species (CITES).

Seychelles prohibits the export of whole Turtle carapaces, but allows the sale of curios fashioned from "tortoiseshell". Before purchasing these curios, the tourist should bear in mind that it may be illegal to import them when they return home, if their country is a signatory to CITES, and should ask themselves, "do I really want to buy a product that could contribute to the extinction of a species?"

Of the world's eight species of marine turtle, four occur in Seychelles. The **green turtle** (*Chelonia mydas*) has almost been wiped out from the granitic islands and most years fewer than ten females nest. Its edible meat was its downfall.

Aldabra remains the Mecca of this species, however, and several thousand still nest each year in the southern islands of Seychelles. Thanks to protection on Aldabra, numbers are beginning to rise. The population is still only one-third of what it was at the turn of the century, but it appears the corner has been turned.

The **hawksbill turtle** (*Eretmochelys imbricata*), by contrast, is not exploited for its meat. The flesh can be poisonous, often fatally so.

This fact has not prevented its exploitation by man, however, the attraction being the carapace or "tortoiseshell" as it is known. This is fashioned into ornamental butterflies, picture frames, spoons, combs, keyrings, and the like.

Hawksbill are hunted intensively and females are often captured on the beach even before they can lay their eggs. The granitic Seychelles islands are still home to the greatest concentration of hawksbills in Seychelles, but few survive today to nest on the heavily populated islands of **Mahé**, **Praslin**, and **La Digue**.

On the positive side, about 200 hawksbill turtles nest each year in the nature reserves and while, even there, survival is not guaranteed, there is some hope that these protected areas will ensure the future of the species in Seychelles.

On land, turtles appear heavy and ungainly, but if you are lucky enough to encounter one in the sea, you will witness the true grace of these creatures in their natural environment, as they glide effortlessly by. Hawksbill can swim at fifty kilometres (31miles) an hour.

The giant **leatherback turtle** (*Dermochelys coriacea*) rarely nests in Seychelles, but is sometimes encountered in local waters. It is the largest, living chelonian. Adults measure up to two metres (six-seven feet) across the front flippers and weigh up to 450 kilos (1,000 lbs). The greatest reliably recorded weight is 865 kilos (1,980 lbs). Leatherback are said to swim at more than seventy kilometres (43 miles) an hour.

They feed on jellyfish, and their local name, *torti karanbol*, is due to their resemblance to the *karanbol* fruit with its distinctive ridges.

The **loggerhead turtle** (*Caretta caretta*) is also seen on occasion. Although it breeds in South Africa and along the Arabian coast, it does not breed in Seychelles and is known locally as *nam cogo* because of the belief that it is part green turtle and part hawksbill.

Opposite top: Endangered hawksbill turtle nesting on Cousin Island.

Opposite: Green turtle, another endangered species. Only about ten return to breed in the granitic islands, but Aldabra is their Mecca, home for about 2,000 nesting females.

Reef Life: Fire and Leather, Staghorn and Brain

Corals are animals. True, not the sort you keep as pets and walk every evening, but animals they are — complex, colonial animals which have created massive and wonderfully balanced ecosystems throughout the tropical undersea world of Seychelles.

On some islands they form the substrata of the whole island. For example, **Bird Island** is a coral cay — pronounced key — as are **Denis Island**, **Desroches Island**, and, in fact, all the southern group of **Aldabra**, **Astove**, and **Farquhar**.

These islands were formed from the calcareous skeletons of millions and millions of dead coral colonies — the stony, or "reef building" corals — and these huge colonies are the main basis for most of the extensive coral gardens found throughout Seychelles coastal waters.

As colonial animals, corals are extremely susceptible to changes of environment, pollution, or physical damage, and are quickly wiped out. To flourish, corals require specific conditions: the sea temperature must never be below 18°C (64°F) and — for optimum growth and vigour — never above 30°C (86°F); salinity should be between thirty-three and thirty-six per cent and the water must be clear enough to allow good penetration of daylight, essential to stony corals.

Individual coral colonies are complex units. They have myriad small polyps which feed by waving their slightly sticky tentacles in the water to capture tiny planktonic food items and transport it to the mouth, where it is absorbed for the good of the whole colony.

To improve the whole system, stony corals have living within them symbiotic algae (*zooxanthellae*) which help — in a way not yet fully understood — to create the optimum conditions for growth.

The symbiotic algae are dependent upon clear water since, like land plants, they require sunlight for photosynthesis. This, then, limits the depth for the maximum growth in coral which is why, generally, corals are found in shallow water.

The common stony corals of Seychelles are the **brain corals** (*Lobophyllia sp*), the **staghorn** type corals (*Acropora sp*), and the **bommies** (*Favia sp*). With a number of others, these are the reef builders.

They all lay down calcareous skeletons, known as *corallum*, which are secreted at the basal areas of each polyp.

Thus the corallum becomes the "concrete" that forms the basis of the reefs. Chemically, as the coral breaks up and sand fills in the spaces, the corallum acts as cement and consolidates the whole mass. In turn, this allows further colonisation by other corals in the continuous chain of reef building.

Stony corals are most important for reef building, but they are not the only corals found on the reefs. More beautiful by far are the **soft corals**, **fan corals**, and **leather corals**. To believe that a fully expanded and feeding soft coral (*Dendronephthya klunzingeri*) is an animal is a real test of the imagination.

These colonies are the most colourful of all the corals, if not the most spectacular (this accolade goes to the **gorgonian fan corals**).

Fan corals are an extremely diverse grouping with representative species living both in the coral sea shallows and down to extremely great depths elsewhere.

Around Seychelles the most common of the gorgonian fans is the **white gorgonian** (*Eunicella verrucosa*) which forms stunning displays when all the polyps are feeding. These fans always grow at an angle of ninety degrees to exploit the potential for maximum feeding from the prevailing currents.

Leather corals, the least impressive of the non-stony corals, are represented in Seychelles' waters by a number of different species.

The most common are probably the **leather ear coral** (*Sarcophyton trocheliophorum*), and the **leather finger coral** (*Heliopora coerulea*), which can be found just about anywhere in the coastal waters.

Other beautiful, commonly found corals are the **cup corals** (*Balanophyllia sp*) and the **fire corals** (*Millepora sp*). Normally cup corals are nocturnal and therefore are not often seen

Opposite: Scuba diver examines cushion starfish and its gloriously coloured coral hosts.

Above: Leather coral reaches for the sunlight in a Seychelles' marine garden.

in their most attractive condition — feeding with their glorious, bright-orange tentacles fully extended.

On the other hand, fire coral is ginger-coloured plate, or ginger-like coral, with creamy-white tips and is not a true coral. It is, in fact, a *hydrozoan*. But because it is stony it still is part of the reef proper.

For the diver the main consideration must be the fact that it stings, causing symptoms ranging from a mild nettle sting to a full-blown allergic reaction. If stung, a mild vinegar solution helps alleviate these symptoms, although antihistamine is recommended for severe cases.

Because of their finely balanced ecosystems, coral reefs and coral gardens can be used to measure the state of the seas in and around the tropics.

Healthy and flourishing coral shows all is well. But if the coral is patchy or dying back, there is a possible problem. And if the coral is dead and broken — or down to just one or two species — there is a real problem, possibly pollution, maybe dredging.

Dying coral reefs are usually caused by human activity. Remarkably the corals all around the islands of Seychelles at this time are mostly healthy — with only small areas of local damage, or small areas that are recovering from earlier dredging.

Shell Life: Seashells of Seychelles

The granitic islands of Seychelles, the summits of an undersea mountain range, are surrounded by an underwater plateau and its offshore waters are reasonably shallow as well as tropical.

Combined with a fairly low, controlled level of tourism and no noticeable pollution, the unspoilt coastlines mean that marine life in the coastal waters around Seychelles is both prolific and varied — none more so than the seashells.

Like the turtles and fishes, these are part of the true wealth and heritage of Seychelles.

Seashells are molluscs. Their outer coverings protect the soft invertebrate animal inside. Occasionally the shell is internal, as in *Dolabella auricularis*, the sea hare.

Seashells have enormous variations of form, but two classes are most commonly seen — *gastropoda* and *bivalvia*. *Gastropoda* form approximately eighty per cent of all living molluscs with possibly fifty-five per cent of these being marine. Both classes are well represented in the waters around Seychelles.

Seychelles also has a number of other mollusc classes less widely realised. For instance, *cephalopoda*, which includes octopus, squid, and cuttlefish (with no external shells) and *polyplacophora*, the **chiton** or **coat of mail** shells (seen clamped to rocks all around the tidemark throughout the islands).

Tropical seashells are probably the most beautiful and varied in the world and their colours and patterns are a constant source of wonder and pleasure.

Throughout the ages, seashells have been used by humans — as ornaments, money, trumpets, aphrodisiacs, jewellery, buttons, and food. The major worry is over exploitation. Without protection it would be too easy to denude the tropical coastlines of the world.

In Seychelles there are a number of marine parks where nothing may be taken from the sea. The **triton trumpet shell** (*Charonia tritonis*) is fully protected and it is illegal to sell or buy it.

Although seashells are mostly thought of as souvenirs, the living animals inside them are often quite stunning. It is certainly well worth snorkeling or diving to see them in their natural habitat.

Some of the most commonly seen shells are the **tiger cowrie** (*Cypraea tigris*) — a glossy, spotted cowrie of large size; the **Arabian cowrie** (*Cypraea arabica*) — a lustrous, open-patterned small- to medium-size cowrie; and the **pink-lipped murex** (*Murex virgineus*) — a large white murex with a tinge of pink around the aperture, used as food in a number of Creole recipes.

The **harp shell** (*Harpa major*) is a glossy, sand-living shell usually found in shallow water, with beautiful zigzag markings over the ribbed shell, and small to medium in size; while the **geography cone** (*Conus geographus*) is a medium-sized lightweight cone with tented marks and lines.

Many cone species are found in the waters of Seychelles. A word of warning, however, for many live cone shells are extremely venomous. Of these, the worst is the geography cone which in some parts of the world, though fortunately not in Seychelles, has killed people.

Generally, cones have developed systems for both offence and defence — basically a venom sac powered by continuously replaced harpoons.

Although quite small, these harpoons are well able to deliver their venom — even through human flesh. In the majority of cone species the venom is harmless to humans, except for one or two deadly instances.

So for obvious reasons follow the general rule — never handle live cones, and certainly never carry them close to the body.

If cones are the villains of the seashell world, then surely cowries are the sweethearts — highly glossed, beautifully patterned, highly desirable, and sometimes expensive.

Alive, they have a modified mantle which wraps around the shell dorsum and secretes the deposits which keep the shell polished and repaired.

It forms the very distinctive patterns that distinguish the different cowries and camouflages the shell by breaking up the outline. In their firm substrata, rock, or coral home, the shell is often hard to spot. Cowries are highly susceptible to collectors. They could easily become endangered.

Above: Some of the many beautiful shells found in the waters and on the shores of Seychelles.

Harps, olives, and moon shells have a large modified foot which is varied and colourful. It is adapted to propel the animal through the sand, usually just below the surface, leaving a distinctive trail.

Murex and Bursas, found in many diverse colours and sizes, are often highly camouflaged. The most sought-after shells are becoming ever rarer, and trade in these creatures already causes concern.

Within the same class as seashells are *opisthobranchia*, seashell-like animals without the shell. Within this subclass are the *nudibranchia* or **sea slugs**, a misnomer, for *nudibranchia* are amongst the most brightly coloured of all sea creatures. In many ways, they have strange biologies, fully functional hermaphrodites, with male and female reproductive organs.

Theoretically they are capable of self-fertilization, although this rarely happens. Cross-fertilization is the norm. Both then lay eggs for the next generation — in jelly-like ribbons or strings as colourful as the creatures which laid them.

Although *nudibranchia* are gaudily coloured, they are rarely eaten by predators. The reason

seems to be that they are distasteful in the extreme. This protection has inspired a number of creatures to mimic the most distasteful of the species. One family within the group is *aelodiidae*, which cover their bodies with fleshy lobes called cerata to protect them against predators. *Aeoliidae* eat hydroids and stinging corals, and these stinging cells (nematocysts) are then passed undischarged via the gut into each of the cerata, from which they are fired should any predator attack.

In turn, this remarkable defence mechanism has also inspired a number of mimics which look like *aelodiidae* but, in fact, are defenceless.

Seychelles has a huge variety of *nudibranchia*, many of them easily found by snorkeling.

Crabs and Shrimps, Sponges and Oysters

The marine invertebrates of Seychelles are abundant in the extreme. From coral, jellyfish, sponges, and hydroids to crabs and crayfish, Seychelles is home to a concentration of sea life from the whole of the Indian Ocean. It is a microcosm of marine invertebrates almost without equal.

Among the most prolific invertebrates, sponges form a large grouping. That sponges are also animals is not always understood. Recent research has shown a number of species contain substances with chemical properties which may be useful medically but much research is still needed.

Seychelles is also well-endowed with shrimps, crabs, and lobsters. Beautiful, brightly coloured coral crabs are found everywhere around the coasts.

When snorkeling look carefully into the branches of the *acropora* corals: at almost every base the little crabs are in hiding, many different types, almost all small and pretty.

Do not try to remove them, as it is too easy to break the coral and the crabs, a favourite food of wrasses, are instantly attacked and eaten.

Watch out for anemones, the favoured home of a number of different **harlequin shrimps**. Even very small anemones can support four or five little shrimps. Other shrimps to look for are the **cleaner shrimps** or **banded shrimps**, found under overhangs of coral or rock and easily spotted by their long white whiskers.

The translucent shrimp, with its orange-red bands and two long pincer claws, is often seen moving over the body or gills of large fish, cleaning it of parasites.

Crabs and shrimps are found in the shallowest water, along with many other species. This profusion right into the shallows is common throughout the islands; perhaps because they are outside the cyclone belt, with only a limited tidal range, that allows long periods of calm, undisturbed conditions. The warm clear waters also appear to encourage this proliferation of invertebrate life.

When snorkeling, look for two bivalve shells which grow quite large. Firstly the clam (not the giant clam of Australia, though), partly open with its many-coloured mantle showing, is a superb sight. The other common bivalve is a variety of **leaf** or **cockscomb oyster**.

Its distinctive shell, with a zigzag opening between its bivalve shells, weighs up to 4.5 kilos (10 lbs) or more and can be found attached by its base to the coral or rock substrata. Although somewhat ugly, it is important to the overall building of the coral reefs. Both bivalves are edible, although rarely, if ever, collected for food.

Another invertebrate animal found in almost the same conditions but living in holes or hollows is the octopus *(cephalopod)*. Truly masters of disguise, they change shape and colour faster than the eye can perceive.

Although this may be enough to save them in a world without humans, the Seychellois have been catching and eating octopus for a long, long time and are experts. Octopus is used throughout Seychelles for a number of classic recipes — and is well worth trying (See "Tastes of Seychelles", Part Three).

Away from the close inshore waters, another species is often seen swimming or hovering in small shoals. This is the **squid** — a close relative of the octopus — which has great mobility.

For speed they use their syphon-like hydro-jet and race off backwards in a series of jerky movements. For a slower "hunting" method of swimming, however, they use fins on each side of the body, angling the syphon to a very fine degree.

Unlike the octopus, which has eight legs, the squid has ten — eight short ones which are used to hold their prey (usually small fish), and two long tentacles with pads on the end covered with suckers that shoot out very quickly to grab the prey and return it to the many-suckered arms surrounding the mouth.

Found in the centre of these tentacles, the cephalopod mouth takes the form of a parrot-like beak. In some instances it may have a venom which can be administered to quell an active prey, or used in defence.

Care should always be taken, however, if handling a live cephalopod of any sort, since — with or without venom — a nip from its beak can be extremely painful.

Underwater Seychelles is a kaleidoscope of shapes and colours of invertebrate life — corals, shells, hydroids, jellyfish, comb jellies, . . . the endless list is a profusion of beauty which, together with the vertebrate fish, form a marine ecosystem that has few rivals.

Wildlife: Bats and Tenrecs, Whales and Dolphins

Many an unsuspecting tourist, watching the sun go down on their first day in Seychelles, has been surprised by the appearance of some strange, enormous dark creatures swooping in to land in the trees, their noisy squeals breaking the silence of the night.

These are **Seychelles fruit bats**. Apart from their excellent eyesight and the fact that they live on fruit, not insects, fruit bats differ from ordinary bats in several other important ways. The males have distinctive pouches in their cheeks which act as very effective resonance chambers to enhance their calls.

Sometimes known as flying foxes, fruit bats lack the ability to echo locate, and neurological and morphological studies show a closer affinity to primates than true bats. They may have developed flight entirely independently, a fourth example of the evolution of this ability, the others being birds, insects, and true bats.

Fruit bats play a crucial role in plant reproduction by spreading seeds and this is one species which may have benefited from man's arrival through the proliferation of fruit trees. In Seychelles, fruit bats are popular as food, often served in curries. The taste is reminiscent of beef with fish bones.

Another, much rarer bat is also found only in Seychelles. The **Seychelles sheath-tailed bat,** a small, insectivorous, cave-roosting species once common on **Mahé** and also on **Praslin**, is now extremely rare for reasons unknown.

Smaller still, the **Silhouette sheath-tailed bat** was once regarded as a separate species but has now been assigned to the rank of subspecies.

Ancient

Tenrecs are strange, ancient mammals, introduced to Seychelles for food (from Madagascar via Réunion) around 1880, and now fairly common.

The first mammals on earth had one thing going for them in a world dominated by the reptiles — endothermy. In other words, they could raise their body temperature.

This enabled them to forage at night, so the first mammals became nocturnal insectivores. They could also breed prolifically. The tenrec is no exception.

One tenrec can produce litters of twenty or more young. The record is thirty-two. Not surprisingly, they also hold the world record for the number of nipples — twenty-four. These creatures look like hedgehogs, with long snouts which they use to detect their prey, which includes invertebrates, and even lizards, snakes, and caecilians.

The **Indian hare** is a shy, nocturnal species found on **Cousin**. **Rabbits** are present on some islands, while feral **cats** and **dogs** can be seen along roadsides of **Mahé** and **Praslin**, especially at night.

Marine Mammals

At the 1979 meeting of the International Whaling Commission, a proposal to create the huge Indian Ocean Whale Sanctuary was adopted. The proposal to save the largest creatures on earth was put forward by one of the earth's smallest nations: Seychelles.

Forty-three species of cetaceans — whales and dolphins — are known to exist in the Indian Ocean Sanctuary, many of which turn up on occasion in the territorial waters of Seychelles.

Sperm whales are frequently encountered, usually as single individuals, but occasionally in groups. They are most frequently seen in the deeper waters from the **Amirantes** to **Aldabra**, but they also swim and sound around the granitic islands.

The cetacean most likely to be seen by the visitor is the **bottlenose dolphin**, particularly during sea passages between Mahé and Praslin, while the northern cliff-tops of **Aride** make a good viewpoint to look for these graceful, gentle creatures. In calm weather they can sometimes even be seen from the Mahé coast.

Shortfin pilot whales prefer deep waters and are often seen off Denis Island where the **Seychelles Bank** drops away for the last time.

Opposite: Roosting fruit bats on Mahé — considered a culinary treat by islanders.

Unless you are cruising Seychelles waters, sightings of cetaceans can be rare, but it is always worth keeping your eyes peeled during any sea passage.

Whales must have been much more common at one time and were noted in John Jordain's 1609 log during the first recorded call at Seychelles. In the nineteenth century, Yankee whalers operated all year from their Seychelles base, but closed down around 1865.

In 1913, a land-based whaling station served by three vessels was opened on St. Anne. During its brief operation the station took about 450 sperm whales, mostly off **Denis Island** and **Bird Island**.

Dugongs

Dugongs, which are large, herbivorous animals found along the East African coast, were recorded in Seychelles during some early voyages of exploration.

Also known as "sea cows", they have now vanished from the waters of Seychelles but are commemorated in the island names of **Île aux Vaches Marines** (off West Mahé) and **Île aux Vaches**, better known as Bird Island.

Stray individuals are occasionally seen off Aldabra and possibly the Amirantes, giving a glimmer of hope that one day this rare, gentle marine herbivore may return to browse in the sea meadows around Seychelles.

Above: Ancient survivor from the early mammals, the tenrec was introduced to Seychelles as recently as the 19th-century and is now firmly established.

In a World of their Own

Before man arrived, Seychelles belonged solely to the reptiles. Several species of giant land tortoise, including **Marion's tortoise** (*Dipsochelys holoissa*) and **Arnold's tortoise** (*Dipsochelys arnoldi*) roamed the granitic islands, while crocodile inhabited the creeks and rivers.

But with the arrival of man the reign of the reptiles, which had lasted unchallenged for more than 100 million years, was over. The unique species of the granitic islands, such as Arnold's tortoise and Marion's tortoise, were hunted to extinction.

And the days of the **Nile crocodile** (*Crocodylus niloticus*) were numbered. John Jordain tells us that the "allagartes" were the only creature to fear in Seychelles. In truth, the "allagartes" had more to fear of man, and they too were exterminated without mercy.

It is a sad story. William Revett, a sailor aboard the British ship *Ascension*, which made the first recorded visit to Seychelles, noted "land turtles of so huge a bigness which men will think incredible; of which our company had small luste to eate of, being such huge defourmed creatures and footed with five clawes lyke a beare".

John Jordain, chief factor of the *Ascension,* also noted the giant land tortoises.

"Soe the boate retourned and brought soe many land tortells as they could well carrie. Soe wee stoode along towards the other ilands. The tortells were good meate, as good as fresh beefe, but after two or three meales our men would not eate them, because they did looke soe uglie before they weare boyled; and soe great that eight of them did almost lade our skiffe."

Ugly or not, there was to be no respite for the tortoises. With the coming of human settlement, the land tortoises were exploited in huge numbers. Their size and longevity meant they were ideal for ships' provisions. Inevitably, demand outstripped supply.

In 1787, de Malavois, commandant of the Seychelles colony, wrote that in the previous four years 13,000 land tortoises had been removed from Seychelles both legally and illegally. He calculated that it would be extremely difficult to find 6,000 to 8,000 individuals remaining.

Alarmed by this depletion, de Malavois established reserves on **St. Anne** and **Île au Cerf**, and transferred tortoises to these islands, until they reached a combined population of about 7,000.

De Malavois also made an impassioned plea to conserve the marine turtles, but, alas, he was a man ahead of his time. In 1790 he resigned due to pressure to create an administrative committee independent of Mauritius, directly responsible to France.

Nevertheless, much survives to remind us of the importance of reptiles to the natural history of the Indian Ocean.

Giant Land Tortoises

The **Aldabra giant land tortoise** (*Geochelonia gigantea*), due to the remote location of its home and its protection within the hostile environment of Aldabra, survived the onslaught.

Similar giants were once common on many Pacific and Indian ocean islands, but today only the Galápagos and Aldabran races bear witness to their former dominance.

Today Aldabra has the world's largest population of these unique chelonians — an estimated population of more than 150,000 individuals. Yet even there, survival was a close-run thing.

At the beginning of the nineteenth century they were reported to be abundant, but in 1878 it took one visitor three days to find a single animal. In 1891, James Spurs, lessee of the island, prohibited their killing and slowly the tortoises made a comeback.

An average giant land tortoise weighs about fifty kilos (110 lbs) and lives between sixty-five and ninety years. Despite all the legends, there are few instances of tortoises surviving longer than 100 years.

The greatest authenticated age for any tortoise is 152 years for a male Marion's tortoise, which was taken from Seychelles to Mauritius in 1776 by Charle Fresne, who presented it to the Port Louis army garrison. It became blind in 1908 and died in an accident ten years later.

A tortoise younger than twenty-five years shows its age by the number of "growth rings" on its scales. Each year a new ring of shell is added to the outside of each scale.

Their diet consists mostly of plants which grow close to the ground, but they also take leaves if they can reach the lower branches of the trees.

Since Aldabra is grudging with its food supplies, they are also scavengers eating the meat of dead animals, including tortoises, and any food careless visitors may leave lying around.

A high priority for the creatures is to stop themselves from getting too hot and literally "cooking" inside their own shell — a nasty fate. Aldabran tortoises orientate their bodies away from the sun to reduce the exposure of their skin to direct sunlight.

The shadow cast by their huge carapace also helps them to keep cool. They sleep in the shade during the heat of midday.

Due to the scarcity of ground water on Aldabra, the giant tortoise has developed the ability to drink through its nose, enabling it to exploit shallow puddles and water-filled cavities.

Mating is a noisy affair. Indeed, the groans and grunts of the rutting male Aldabran giant land tortoise has been described as the loudest noise in the reptile kingdom.

Despite this, however, the success ratio of matings is as low as one to two per cent, so whether the noise results from satisfaction or frustration is open to debate.

Should the mating go well, the female tortoise scrapes a hole in soft soil in which to lay her eggs, using her back feet to remove the unwanted earth.

She urinates during nest building to soften the soil and make it easier to dig. The whole process of digging and egg laying may take up to eleven hours, an exhausting marathon.

Now the copious urine (up to a gallon [almost four litres]) which the mother excreted in the soil fulfils its second function. As it dries, it hardens the soil around the eggs to prevent other animals and predators from digging them up.

She lays between four and sixteen eggs at a time. They have hard shells, and are about the size of a passion fruit. Three to six months later, the baby tortoises begin to hatch, usually at the start of the rainy season when the soil is softer and food is in good supply.

You do not need to travel to Aldabra to see

these leviathans. They now make their home on **Frégate, Cousin**, and **Curieuse**. Many Seychellois keep tortoises as pets, and they can also be seen in an enclosure within the **Botanical Gardens**.

To see the world's heaviest tortoise, however, you must travel to **Bird Island** where Esmeralda — a male tortoise — browses happily amid the tourist chalets (See "Strictly for the Birds", Part Two).

Geckos

Arriving in Seychelles after a long flight, you will most probably check into your hotel or guesthouse, go to your room, lie back, and close your eyes for a few moments. Then you may well hear a "dirty laugh" from behind the curtains — and you know you have a resident **gecko**.

Common throughout Seychelles, you see them wherever you go. They are completely harmless, and very engaging members of a family many people dislike.

Much as the local housewife might bemoan their droppings on the walls, or their eggs laid carelessly in odd corners of the house, they are in fact an ally in the home.

Most geckos are nocturnal, hunting for insects around a favourite light, and fiercely defending their patch of wall against other geckos. Picture frames are a common refuge indoors. Geckos apparently achieve the impossible, walking up walls, and even windows.

They can do this because they have stiff hairs on the soles of their feet which cling to the imperfections that exist even on the surface of plate glass. These night-time hunters, usually pinkish-brown or grey, are semi-transparent. With the light behind them, you can see their heart beating.

They change colour, going extremely dark when frightened. Some geckos have a sweet tooth, and enjoy cake crumbs and sugar. For this reason, one local name for them is **sugar lizard**.

Day geckos are very attractive. There are many species, but most of them are vivid green with red spots on the back. They have round, black eyes that seem to stare constantly at you because, in fact, their eyelids are fused shut, and they are peering at you through a window in the lower eyelid. They often clean this window by licking it with their pink tongues.

Day geckos are seen on the trunks of trees, in the bushes, in fact almost anywhere outdoors — even, at times, clinging desperately to a car windscreen as it drives off. They also come into houses to patrol the lights, but most are active during daylight.

Geckos are quite vocal, communicating with throaty chuckles. If they are in danger from a predator, they have the surprising ability to shed their tail, which thrashes about for several minutes, distracting the predator and hopefully enabling the gecko to escape unnoticed.

Mynah birds deliberately "dive-bomb" geckos to make them do this, then make a meal of the tail. It is not unusual to see a gecko with many "tails", which must be caused by some hitch in the system.

They lay round, white eggs which look like mint imperials (an English sweet). They are usually found in batches of two, and turn up in the most unlikely places, such as behind books on bookcases, in storage boxes, or the folds of curtains. More naturally they are found in niches in trees, or in some cases, sticking to the trunk itself.

About ten species are unique to the Seychelles. As you island-hop you will notice the slight variations in colour and even voice. Many of these do not have English names in common use, but descriptive names are suggested here as an aid to identification (with apologies to scientific purists.)

Every visitor to the Vallée de Mai will notice how exceptionally bright is the colour of the **Praslin green gecko** (*Phelsuma dunbergli*), compared to that of the **Mahé stripeless green gecko** (*Phelsuma astriata astriata*), or the **Mahé bar-tailed green gecko** (*Phelsuma longinsulae pulchra*).

Of course, they are closely related, but even a few kilometres of ocean has been a sufficient barrier to ensure that different characteristics developed in different races.

The **bronze gecko** (*Ailuronyx seychellensis*) is the largest gecko in Seychelles, growing up

Opposite: Bird Island's Esmeralda earned the island fame as the world's heaviest tortoise in the 1990 edition of the *Guinness Book of Records*.

to a maximum length of about twenty centimetres (eight inches). They are nocturnal, have a vertical pupil, and a golden eye.

Basically bronze in colour, they have many spots and bars. You may see them on the trunks of trees in the **Vallée de Mai**, and in houses on **Aride** and **Cousin** and **Frégate**, but they do not seem as fond of human company as those found elsewhere.

They eat insects, but also lap nectar and pollen, and feed on seabird eggs. As a defence against predators, they easily shed almost their entire skin when seized. Again, this enables the gecko to escape, leaving the confused predator with the discarded skin.

Skinks

Skinks are much more streamlined and "lizard-like" than geckos, having shinier skins. Six species are found in Seychelles. The visitor is most likely to see the **mangouya**, or **Seychelles skink** (*Mabuya sechellensis*).

This handsome lizard is the colour of bronze and copper, with a cream stripe down each side of its body. They have long thin tails, which they can shed as geckos do, and which sometimes "branch" in a similar way.

They occur on nearly all the granitic and coral islands, and in great densities on seabird islands such as Cousin and Aride. They prosper there because of the abundance of extra food sources, such as eggs and fish dropped by birds.

These opportunists will take any discarded food. In the picnic shelter on Aride, they swiftly move in to clear the dirty plates after a meal, and happily investigate the contents of shopping bags or camera cases.

They live outdoors, feeding among other things, on insects. They breed throughout the year, burying their eggs in soil, or under piles of coconut husks and stones.

The **Wright's skink** (*Mabuya wrightii*) is a larger version of the Seychelles skink, usually only found on islands which have colonies of breeding seabirds.

The relationship between these skinks and the seabird colonies is unclear. The extra food the birds inadvertently provide is an obvious factor — it could also be important that sea-bird islands have no rats, and the Wright's skink is vulnerable to rat predation elsewhere.

The leaf litter on these islands sometimes seems to erupt with skinks as they rummage about in search of food. They will even take dead chicks which have fallen from the trees.

It will not surprise the visitor to Aride or Cousin to learn that these skinks reach incredible population densities — in fact, one of the highest densities of lizard on earth — more than 4,000 skinks to the hectare, or an amazing 184 kilos (406 lbs) of lizards to the hectare.

More difficult to see, but truly fascinating is the **snake-eyed fishing skink** (*Cryptoblepharus boutonii*), found on many of the outer islands.

This is one of the few lizards which lives happily in the intertidal zone. It feeds on crustaceans and small fish, and has the astonishing habit of diving into rock pools if disturbed.

Chameleons

The **tiger chameleon** (*Chamaeleo tigris*), Seychelles' only representative of the chameleon family, is a creature at the centre of much local superstition and fear.

They make their way slowly through the trees in which they live, clasping the twigs with their grasping feet, looking like old men with their jerky, deliberate movements.

They have eyes set in large orbs which swivel independently, so that a chameleon can watch the branch ahead and the branch behind at the same time. It has an extremely long tongue which shoots out to catch insects on the sticky tip and drag them back into the mouth.

The tiger chameleon is normally grey or pale yellow, but goes bright yellow or black if frightened, no matter what colour its background. They grow to a length of about sixteen centimetres (six inches).

They occur on Mahé, **Silhouette**, and Praslin, and can sometimes be seen making a very stately — and therefore risky — road crossing. Cinnamon, mango, and citrus trees seem to be their favoured habitat.

Snakes

Most visitors will not want to see a snake and can rest assured they are unlikely to do so. Even if they do, it will probably disappear as fast as possible in the opposite direction. Seychelles' land snakes are not venomous.

Two species are unique to the islands. The first is the **Seychelles house snake** (*Lamprophis geometricus*), a small nocturnal constrictor that strangles lizards, mice, and even young chickens and cats, although it only grows to just under a metre (three feet) in length.

There is a Seychellois superstition that they enter houses to suck the milk of young mothers while they sleep.

The second unique species is the **Seychelles wolf snake** (*Lycognathopis seychellensis*), which grows to about 1.2 metres (four feet). They eat lizards and frogs but are harmless to man. This is the most frequently observed snake, sometimes seen by those who go walking in the mountains.

The **brahminy blind snake** (*Ramphotyphlops braminus*), which looks more like an earthworm than a snake, is only about seventeen centimetres (seven inches) long.

A shy, burrowing creature, brought in accidentally in the soil of introduced plants, it is an all-female species, producing eggs without male fertilization.

When handled they release a foul-smelling substance so, although harmless, they are best left in peace. They eat termites and other small invertebrates.

The highly venomous **yellow-bellied sea snake** (*Pelamis platurus*) occurs throughout the Indo-Pacific. Truly a pelagic animal of the open ocean that only comes inshore by misfortune, they have on rare occasions been seen by fishermen in Seychelles, or found dead on beaches. The chances of a visitor encountering one, however, are virtually nil.

Terrapins

Extremely little is known about terrapins in general, and the Seychelles species in particular. In fact, no one is sure exactly how many species there are because there is a great deal of confusion about their taxonomy.

It seems most likely that there are three species, one of which is endemic, the other two also occurring in Africa and Madagascar. Even these, however, seem to have evolved racial differences during their isolation in the islands.

They were thought to have been introduced by man as a food source (they are eaten in Africa), but if the two non-endemic species are racially different this is unlikely.

Such changes need many years to come about. In this case, the non-endemic terrapins must have floated there on logs, or mats of vegetation.

They are known on the islands as *torti soupap*, the Creole word for plug, which the creatures are supposed to resemble in shape. They live in freshwater pools and marshes on most of the larger granitic islands.

The **black-bellied terrapin** (*Pelusios seychellensis*) is thought to be unique to Seychelles, but as it is only known from three specimens collected in 1895 (probably on Mahé), it is either now extremely rare or extinct.

The **yellow-bellied terrapin** (*Pelusios castanoides*) and **star-bellied terrapin** (*Pelusios subniger*) are found in the marshes of some of the smaller islands, as well as on Mahé and La Digue. The yellow-bellied terrapin is also found on Praslin.

Terrapins are carnivorous, taking snails and carrion, but occasionally eat plants; the Seychelles' species probably keep to a similar diet. They can bury themselves in the mud of drying marshes and emerge when the rains return. Although protected by law, they are under pressure due to the drainage of marshes by man.

Amphibians

The existence of amphibians in Seychelles is remarkable in itself. Alfred Russell Wallace, a naturalist who developed theories of evolution similar to those of Charles Darwin at about the same time, defined oceanic islands as being "entirely without indigenous land mammalia or amphibia".

Seychelles passes on the first count, but fails on the second. Twelve species of amphibia, eleven of which are unique to Seychelles, demand an explanation.

In fact, both Darwin and Wallace classified Seychelles as "continental islands". The presence of these amphibia was vital evidence in establishing the uniqueness of Seychelles as a continental fragment in mid-ocean.

Caecilians

Caecilians are an ancient race — blind, legless amphibians, resembling earthworms, but with a backbone, mouth, jaws, and teeth. They are completely harmless to man.

Caecilians are well adapted for a burrowing life, with small pointed heads, elongated bodies, and mouths below the head (to prevent soil from entering).

Eyes, which are little use underground, are either very small or absent. Sensory tentacles either side of the mouth help these creatures explore their subterranean environment.

Seven species occur in Seychelles, all of them unique to the islands. The largest of these, the **swimming caecilian** (*Hypogeophis rostratus*), often enters streams at night, and is sometimes disturbed there by bathers or washerwomen.

They grow to thirty-seven centimetres (15 inches). The second largest species, the **big-headed caecilian** (*Grandisonia alternans*), reaches twenty-eight centimetres (11 inches). Smallest of all is the **small-headed caecilian** (*Grandisonia brevis*), being less than twelve centimetres (five inches).

Six of the seven species can be found on Mahé, the only exception being the **Praslin flat-headed caecilian** (*Grandisonia diminutiva*), which is similar to another species, the **flat-headed caecilian** (*Grandisonia larvata*). The two are difficult to distinguish and may represent a single species.

The other two species to complete the list are **pin-headed caecilian** (*Grandisonia sechellensis*) and, rarest of all, the **toothy caecilian** (*Praslinia cooperi*).

Frogs

Five species of frogs occur and, apart from the **Mascarene frog** (*Ptychadena mascareniensis*), they are unique to Seychelles. The largest is the **Seychelles tree frog** (*Tachycnemis seychellensis*).

The bright green females grow to nearly twenty centimetres (eight inches) in length, while the brown males are less than forty-five millimetres (two inches). The chorusing of the males — especially in rainy weather — sounds like ducks quacking.

The other frogs do not have English names in common usage, but the following descriptive names are suggested.

The **pygmy piping frog** (*Sooglossus gardineri*) is one of the smallest frogs in the world. Fully grown specimens, no bigger than a finger-

Above: Unique Seychelles tree frog.

nail, can be heard in the mountains, and many people mistake their call for that of a bird or cricket.

They are fairly common in damp leaf litter where they feed on tiny invertebrates and try to avoid wolf snakes. Apart from the songs of the ubiquitous mynahs and bulbuls, their call is often the only sound in the mountains.

Thomasset's tocking rock frog (*Nesomantis thomasseti*) is a rare, mostly nocturnal rock-climbing species, hardly ever found on trees or shrubs.

The **croaking carry-cot frog** (*Sooglossus sechellensis*) has developed an amazing habit. The tadpoles climb onto their mother's back until they develop into young frogs and hop off. This form of parental care is extremely rare and, apart from this unique Seychelles example, occurs only in a few species in tropical South America and New Zealand.

However, it is the male that carries the young American and New Zealand frogs, and they are in no way related to the Seychelles species. This is a fascinating example of unusual behaviour evolving entirely independently in different parts of the world.

Maestros of Disguise

There are at least five times as many species of insects in the world than all other creatures combined. And in a warm, humid, tropical climate you would expect insects to proliferate, and they certainly do — often in surprising ways.

Of the 3,500 insect species to be found in Seychelles, the majority are unique to the islands. Many of these unique forms may have come from ancient Gondwanaland, or from a time when the islands were not so isolated, the remainder arriving as transoceanic colonizers.

Although there is a strong Oriental and Malagasy-African influence, to have so many unique forms suggests that Seychelles should perhaps be classified as a region in its own right rather than in either one of these two great regions.

The **Aldabra** group — much younger in origin than the granitic islands — has a totally different insect fauna. Indeed, only about four per cent of species are common to both

areas. You might imagine that the relatively young age of Aldabra — about 125,000 years — would be insufficient for endemic forms to emerge yet, even so, it has many unique species.

One study put it at nearly forty per cent of the 700 species present, but this figure may be on the high side due to lack of knowledge concerning what exists in nearby Africa. In origin, however, Aldabran insects are firmly part of the African region.

To most people insects are pests. Yet the flies which can spoil a picnic on a European summer's day are uncommon in Seychelles. Even the mosquitoes are less trouble than elsewhere; active mainly at dusk, they can make their presence felt on overcast days, however, and when walking in the undergrowth or near water.

Introduced species represent a tiny proportion of the total but they contain one of the most noticeable of all insect pests — the **American cockroach**. No visitor will fail to encounter this beast on a Seychelles night.

Another unwanted immigrant is the **crazy ant** — also known as **Maldive ant** — after an area of North Mahé where they were first reported. This large ant has spread unchecked due to the lack of predators. Control measures have been taken, but it is firmly established. Its bite is fairly painful and if left uncontrolled the ant could wreak havoc on Seychelles' endemic invertebrate fauna.

White ants, or **termites**, are extremely common. In fact, they are related to cockroaches and may have been the first creatures on earth to establish a social system. One species builds a mud-like nest on coconut palms, from which tunnels radiate up and down the tree, enabling the occupants to rove under cover. They are ultra-sensitive to sunlight.

Deep in the centre of the nest, firmly cemented into the royal cell, the gigantic queen spends her life tended by an army of workers and well-armed guards, producing eggs at the rate of about one every two seconds.

At the onset of the rainy season (October-November) you may see swarms emerging from the nest to fly briefly around a light. They then alight, shed their wings, and search for a suitable site for a new colony. Unlike bees and ants, there are equal numbers

Above: One of the islands' maestros of disguise — the Seychelles leaf insect.

of males and females in a colony. Termites can destroy or damage untreated wood and furniture.

Most insect species are small and inconspicuous, but there are some notable exceptions. The **giant tenebrionid beetle**, unique to **Frégate Island** where it can be seen during the daytime on tree trunks, is extraordinary. It has a lumpy back and spidery legs, quite unlike anything else you may encounter.

Another unmistakable beetle is the large flying **rhinoceros beetle** that can disturb the tranquillity of a tropical evening by flying in through open windows like a bomber plane.

This shiny black monster will then dive-bomb the light bulb and land on its back with an apparent headache. Its rhinoceros-like horn gives the beetle its name. It is quite harmless, but the larvae do great damage to young coconut palms by burrowing into the living shoots.

Surviving trees often bear witness to rhinoceros beetle infestation. You will see many a coconut palm leaf with a V-shape cut out of it, showing where larvae lunched, prior to the leaf opening up. Another pest, the

melittomma beetle, also does serious damage to coconut palms.

Two blackish wasps are common. The female **potter** or **mason wasp** constructs a little mud pot that any potter would be proud of — spherical with a lipped opening at the top — for a nest which is usually attached to walls or vegetation and stocked with caterpillars paralysed by the wasp's sting.

A single egg is hung from the roof of the pot, and the opening sealed with mud. When the larvae hatches, it feeds on the larder of caterpillars in the privacy of its own home.

The other, smaller wasp — the **mud dauber** — makes a string of cylindrical, untidy pots, and preys on several species of spider. Mud dauber nests are common on house walls and the underside of overhanging granite rocks.

The **yellow wasp**, which has an extremely painful sting, can be very aggressive if you accidentally approach its nest and should be avoided. Look out for its hanging nest — lamp-like paper structures with honeycomb cylinders on the underside — and keep well clear.

Some insects are masters of disguise, and the prize for champion of them all should go

244

to the **Seychelles leaf insect**. Its body and legs are perfectly disguised as green leaves, with blotches of brown. There are even irregular shapes on the legs, resembling leaves which have been nibbled by insects, while the head looks like a bud.

The female is about ten centimetres (four inches) long, the male a little smaller, with gauzy wings. Despite their size they are almost invisible in the vegetation. Even their eggs are camouflaged: they resemble a winged seed, brown with ribs.

Another cunning camouflage maestro is the **stick insect** of which there are at least five species, all endemic, varying in colour from green to brown to brick-red.

Most live in the high hills and it needs a keen eye to pick them out. Sometimes they align themselves with the midrib of fern fronds, or the veins of a leaf. As with many endemic insects, there is a close association with endemic plants.

The **praying mantis** is not such a master of disguise, but its cryptic colouring and stationary posture enable it to go unnoticed. The front legs are held in a praying position. When an unfortunate victim passes by they grab it and eat it.

Mantids have fascinated man since earliest times due to their human-like postures, and many cultures regard them with great reverence. "Mantis", indeed, is Greek for "soothsayer", "prophet", or "diviner". Many Muslims still believe a mantis faces Mecca in its reverential pose.

Cannibalism is common, and sex is a risky business for the smaller male, which is often eaten by the mate after coupling. Looking on the bright side, some now suggest the male benefits its offspring by providing valuable protein for the female during egg production.

Visitors are often surprised at the paucity of butterflies. Perhaps there were more species before the destruction of the original forests, or perhaps ocean islands are not the best places for the evolution of highly active, winged insects.

In the mountain forests you may see one of the largest, the **King of Seychelles**. An endemic butterfly of Oriental origin, it is brown with white circles on the forewing. Only found on **Mahé** and **Silhouette**, it is much more sedentary than its Oriental cousin,

a habit which is advantageous to an island species, and lessens the risk of being blown out to sea.

Large hawk moths often fly into brightly lit buildings at night. One of these, the **death's head hawk moth**, is sometimes seen on tree trunks during the daytime.

If alarmed, they make a surprising rattling noise, lifting their wings to reveal a startling yellow-striped body and hindwings—enough to deter even a curious cat. Other hawk moths include the beautiful green **oleander hawk moth** and the rather smaller **hummingbird hawk moth** and **bee hawk moth**.

To most insects, seawater is as fatal as an insecticide, yet the **ocean skater,** with its long delicate legs, has adapted to life on the high seas. They have even been found hundreds of kilometres from land, and could be an important food item for some seabirds.

In dry, soily areas, look out for the small round pits of the amazing **antlion**. If an ant passes this way, the antlion will fire particles of dry soil or sand at the victim, causing it to fall down the sloping sides of the pit towards its waiting jaws.

Spiders, scorpions, and others

Spiders are the second-largest group of land animals after the insects. More than seventy species have been described, most of them unique to the islands.

The enormous but harmless **palm spider** is commonly seen on telegraph wires and in the undergrowth. Their huge, extremely strong webs are constructed remarkably quickly.

Overnight a web can appear from nowhere. The females grow to ten centimetres (four inches) or more across, yet you have to look closely at the web to detect the tiny males.

Another large species, the **wolf spider**, is blackish-brown and fast-moving. It builds no web, but relies on speed, and a powerful bite. It should be treated with respect. The same applies to the fatter, hairier **tarantula**. If in doubt, err on the side of caution.

Except on **Frégate**, scorpions are rare. There are three species, but two are small and inconspicuous. The other grows to about eight centimetres (three inches). All have a nasty sting.

As they are nocturnal, never walk around at night without shoes. There are also four endemic species of **whip scorpion,** fearsome-looking but harmless creatures.

Giant millipedes are common on **Cousin, La Digue,** and **Aride** where they grow to about twenty-five centimetres (10 inches) in length. They protect themselves by rolling into a ball or secreting unpleasant hydrogen cyanide. However, they are harmless creatures if left alone.

Centipedes also reach great lengths. They are found in disturbed soils, or in piles of rotting coconut husks. Large, colourful, but menacing-looking, centipedes emerge at night and scurry from one shelter to the next.

They should never be handled, as the front legs are adapted for biting and the poison injected can cause severe swelling. Even the small species should be treated with respect.

Above: The palm spider, one of seventy species found in Seychelles, crafts a silken web overnight.

Flora: Forests of Mist and Rain

Although the visitor's eye may be drawn at once to the showy exotics such as **bougain-villaea, hibiscus,** and **frangipani,** the true magic of Seychelles' flora lies in its endemic plants. Few of these are as spectacular, perhaps, but they have their own fascination.

Seychelles can boast species dramatically different from anything found in the rest of the world. Some are so rare that the numbers of known individuals are counted in tens and twenties. Others survive only on certain islands, or high up in relict mountain forest, existing as they have done for centuries, long before man was there to see them.

These islands must have been beautiful indeed when the crew of the *Ascension* first gazed upon them. In 1609 the sheltered bays of the east coast were thickly girdled with mangrove swamp, **takamaka** trees shaded the beaches, and delicate **casuarina** pines soughed in the wind.

In this lowland forest — none of which survives today — were giant trees twenty-one metres (70 feet) tall and 4.5 metres (15 feet) in circumference. Among them were evocative names from a lost past — **bwa-d-fer, bwa-d-nat, bwa-d-tab,** and **gayak.**

For the most part, the descendants of these magnificent trees are now reduced to spindly specimens, clinging to survival in the higher hills. Their very excellence was their death warrant.

The navies of the day, enmeshed in the Seven Years and Napoleonic wars, needed wood for shipbuilding. Naturally the lowland forests, most easily accessible, were cleared first.

The only compensation perhaps is that, because of this preoccupation with wood supply, early European travellers documented the forests they found in detail. Maybe one day some areas will be restored to their former beauty.

As the mountains rose and the soil grew deeper, a second type of forest could be found. There, **northea** (named after the botanical artist Marianne North who visited Seychelles) and **bwa rouz** dominated, tall

Above: One of the world's rarest plants — Wright's gardenia (*bwa citron*) — found only on Aride Island.

straight trees spaced at wide intervals, whose eighteen-metre (60-foot) canopy sheltered the now extinct Seychelles green parakeet.

In the eerie stillness of the glades and ravines below the leafy ceiling, **screwpines** and **lataniers** thrust their stilt roots many feet down steep ledges in search of water. These forests were soon diminished.

Higher still, on the mountain tops, lost in almost permanent cloud, were the strangely silent moss forests. Few birds except the bulbuls came so high, and the silence would be broken only by the croaking of frogs and the steady dripping of moisture from the thick wadding of moss which grew over everything.

The trees there, such as **manglye-d-gran-bwa**, and **bwa kasan**, were smaller, reaching only between twelve and fifteen metres (40-50 feet) high, often twisted into strange forms. The undergrowth was so luxuriant that small trees took root in the moss which festooned the larger trees.

Tangled roots trapped soil and provided impromptu flowerpots for ferns, tiny native **begonias**, and **melastomas**. Shy **orchids** perched in niches in the trunks and an

endemic **pitcher plant** trailed and draped its way through the undergrowth.

Some remnants of this mysterious, primaeval forest may be seen in the high hills of **Mahé** and **Silhouette**, but much is lost for as the lowland forests disappeared man climbed higher for his timber.

One introduced tree has largely altered the appearance of Seychelles' forests. From sea level to the top of **Morne Seychellois** you will find **cinnamon**.

Cinnamon plants were brought to Seychelles in the days when spices were a valuable commodity and spice plants were stolen and smuggled out to botanists eager to try and grow them for themselves, in an attempt to break the monopoly the Dutch held on the rest of the world.

Pierre Poivre, intendant of Mauritius (then the Île de France) hoped to grow spices in secrecy and security in Seychelles. The plantation, located at **Anse Royale**, was later destroyed when, in an act of panic, the garrison officer set fire to the plants thinking that a ship sighted on the horizon was a British frigate because she flew the British ensign.

The ship, which turned out to be French, had raised the enemy flag thinking the British had occupied the islands. The spice garden was gone, but the birds had already begun to spread the cinnamon seeds throughout the island.

It thrives, and now dominates at all levels, except in the mist forest, where *northea* holds on to its tenuous predominance. This "blanket coverage" is due mostly to the coppicing of the cinnamon trees during the 1930s, when cinnamon, oil and bark topped the list of Seychelles' exports.

Despite the efforts of the first settlers, and because of the shade cover provided by the cinnamon, Seychelles did not lose its forests entirely, nor all its endemic species.

Above: Mangrove *Ceriopstagal*.

Opposite top left: Hibiscus.

Opposite top: *Crinum* lily.

Opposite left: Coleus plant.

Opposite: Glorious "Pride of Barbados" flower.

The visitor will still find the granite hills swathed in thick vegetation. It is the forest content which has changed, with flat-topped **albizia** stepping its way up the valleys, and other aggressive species making the most of new opportunities.

Praslin's green coat looks a little more threadbare, perhaps because its mountains were more accessible to the tree fellers, although it is possible that, attracting less cloud and rainfall, Praslin's forests were dominated by the native palms and, such forest being drier, fires could have been a part of their natural cycle.

The cathedral hush of the **Vallée de Mai World Heritage Site**, opens a window on Praslin's remote past for the visitor. Truly antediluvian in atmosphere, one almost expects a dinosaur to lumber into view around every corner.

There the **coco de mer** dominates. Much has been written about this amazing palm, which is represented on Seychelles' coat of arms, its currency, and in its songs. Legends about this palm abound (See "Valley of The Forbidden Fruit," Part Two).

Appropriately, the nut produced by the female tree resembles in shape the female pelvis. What the catkin of the male tree is said to resemble you may well imagine. Naturally the myth grew up that *coco de mer* trees move about on stormy nights and mate in the moonlight. Anybody who sees the act is doomed.

General Gordon, later to die in the defence of Khartoum, was so struck by this valley that he thought he had discovered the site of the Garden of Eden. And the forbidden fruit? The *coco de mer*, of course.

From this point, the rest is all awesome statistics. The *coco de mer* nut takes seven years to mature, weighs up to eighteen kilos (40 lbs), and grows more than half a metre (two feet) long.

Germination takes two years, then the immense leaves with a span of six metres (20 feet) appear, pushing upwards on the longest leaf stalks in the plant kingdom. The female trees produce a zigzag flowering stalk more than half-a-metre (two feet) long.

This usually bears three or four nuts, although up to ten nuts can be produced, weighing altogether about 180 kilos (400 pounds). The female tree does not fruit until it is twenty-five years old, and the trees live to a great age, reaching up to thirty metres (100 feet) in the case of the male tree, and twenty-four metres (80 feet) in the case of the female.

Coco de mer nuts were once thought to grow on trees which lived under the sea, hence their name. Due to their rarity they commanded high prices. Kings decorated the hollowed-out shells with fabulous encrustations of gold and gems, and used them as cups.

The coco de mer was said to protect against poisons. It was thought that the nuts were found washed up on beaches in Maldives, and since the tree could be found nowhere else in the world other than remote, as yet unexplored, Praslin, their origins were a mystery which increased the awe of those who owned them.

This story is romantic, but the realist may prefer another theory — that Arab or Indian traders, who had sailed this ocean for centuries, knew about the coco de mer and where to find it. They jealously guarded their secret, and limited supplies, enhancing the mystique of the nut to keep the price high.

This idea could be supported by the fact that a newly fallen nut soon sinks in sea water. Whatever the truth, once Europeans discovered the origins of the nut in 1768, the legends died, and soon the only market for a coco de mer shell was in Mauritius, where shopkeepers used them as sugar scoops.

This remarkable tree occurs naturally only on Praslin and **Curieuse**. The nuts are killed by sea water, and so the species could not spread as the coconut did.

The timber is little used, but the leaves provide fine wall liners and are extremely long lasting. Hollowed-out, the shells are used as balers in fishing boats, and serve as kitchen utensils.

An immature nut contains a jelly, which is sometimes served as a dessert, but the tourist's most likely encounter with a coco de mer is as a souvenir, highly polished or decorated. If you do buy a coco de mer, remember that you need a permit to get it out of the country, and this should be obtained from the vendor.

Seychelles has more than one unique palm to its name. In fact there are six endemic species, including the coco de mer. Four of the palms are known locally as lataniers: **latannyen milpat**, **latannyen oban**, **latannyen fey**, and **latannyen lat**. The sixth is the **palmis**.

Latannyen milpat is so called because when the breeze catches its finely fringed leaves, they look like the legs of a millipede, rippling with motion.

Latannyen oban is a pretty, delicate palm, which only grows to about 7.6 metres (25 feet) high. The ends of the deeply divided leaves look as if they have been snipped off, giving a blunted appearance.

Latannyen fey has wide, undivided leaves, excellent for thatching. Its English name is **thief palm**. It seems that in 1857 some botanically-minded thief stole the first specimen grown at Kew Gardens.

Latannyen lat grows tall, up to twenty-five metres (80 feet). Laths for walling can be made from its trunk.

All these palms grow in the mountain forests, though occasionally they occur at lower altitudes, especially in gardens.

Should you wish to become an instant "palm expert" remember that latannyen lat has the most impressive stilt roots, latannyen milpat has the long "millipede leg" leaves, latannyen oban has the leaves with "snipped off" ends, and latannyen fey has undivided leaves.

Palmis, the last endemic palm, is also extremely distinctive. There is a smooth, pale column above the trunk, before the leafy crown of the tree. Here is the living shoot of the plant, eaten as a delicacy and known as "millionaire's salad".

It was given this name because, to obtain the salad, the tree must be killed. Palmis is delicious served with a squeeze of lime, or in a cheese sauce, but the heart of an ordinary coconut palm serves just as well, and does not endanger one of Seychelles' unique species.

All these unique palms are protected by spines around the base of the trunk, perhaps to prevent young seedlings from being eaten by giant land tortoises.

Should you visit the Vallée de Mai, you will notice other palm-like trees with leathery leaves which share the coco de mer's habitat. Five species of pandanus are endemic to

Seychelles, but one occurs only on **Aldabra**.

Horne's pandanus and Seychelles pandanus occur in this sort of mountain habitat. Horne's pandanus, or *vacoa parasol*, is named after a former director of the Mauritian botanical gardens. It grows eighteen metres (60 feet) tall, and has a crown of large leaves.

Seychelles pandanus has a smaller trunk, and grows in the more remote mountain regions. Its stilt roots grow as long as thirty metres (100 feet), reaching down cliff faces to form amazing natural archways.

Balfour's screwpine, named after another botanist, grows from sea level up through the mountains. It perches on ledges, sending out small exploratory stilt roots in search of soil and moisture. The crown is a ball of strap-like leaves.

The final endemic pandanus has no English name, but the local name is *vakwa rivyer*. It is a low-growing, widely spreading plant which likes high, rocky ledges. Only the more adventurous visitor will encounter this, and may have cause to curse it.

It is armed with nasty spikes all along the edges of its long leaves, and just to make sure it gets you, the prickles face alternately front and back. It can be most painful to walk through and well deserves its scientific name of *Multispicatus*.

The introduced pandanus, **vakwa sak**, is a native of Madagascar. Its leaves can be used to weave baskets and ropes.

Should you tire of puzzling over palms and pandanus, Seychelles also has some beautiful endemic flowers and shrubs. The **Wright's gardenia**, or *bwa sitron*, now occurs naturally only on **Aride Island**, although there are several introduced specimens on Mahé, notably those by the **Sans Souci forestry station**.

After rain this small tree is covered in lovely, creamy, gardenia-like flowers, which are spotted with magenta. The flowers give off a beautiful perfume. The fruit is round, smooth, and bright green, hence the local name.

There are many orchids in the mist forests of Seychelles, most of which have a timid beauty not normally associated with the exotic blooms found in expensive florists.

Anyone who stops at Sans Souci, the spot where the cliff drops away from below the road, may see what is perhaps Seychelles' loveliest orchid.

This is the **wild vanilla**. Its thick, fleshy, leafless stems scramble over small trees and shrubs, sending out wiry brown aerial roots. What may attract your attention at first are the large white flowers which have a delicate apricot flush in the throat of the trumpet-like centre.

In shape, the flowers bear some resemblance to daffodils and exude a sweet perfume. They open and die all in a day. They produce a pod, but it is not used as a flavouring.

Another striking orchid, often found in gardens, as well as the forests, is the **payanke**, or tropicbird orchid, so named because the waxy white and green flowers have a long spur like the tail of a tropicbird. This is the national flower of Seychelles. It is indigenous there, in Madagascar, and the Comoros.

On exposed areas of red soil, you might notice the sweet little **pat-d-poul orchid**, with its cream and purple flowers. Most of the other orchids, living in remote habitats and flowering sporadically, are hard to find. Few have more than a Latin name, and perhaps

Above: The marvellous fantasia of *Barringtonia* or fish poison tree.

high in the hills, new species still await discovery.

Turning from the beautiful to the strange, the **lyann potao** is a **pitcher plant**. Worldwide there are about seventy species of pitcher plants. All have tendrils modified to form small pitchers which secrete a sugary solution that attracts insects.

The insects slip on the smooth sides, and are digested in a liquid in the base of the pitcher, which contains enzymes. Pitcher plants grow on poor soils, and the insects provide extra nutrients. Interestingly, not all insects fall foul of the pitcher plant. There is a species of mosquito whose larvae live in the digestive fluid.

Although locally common, the plant's "estimated area of dispersal . . . totals a mere forty-seven hectares (116 acres) and hence justifies the IUCN *Red Data Book*'s category of vulnerable".

The Seychelles pitcher plant is a reminder of the islands' unique Afro-Asian heritage. Much of Seychelles' flora is African in origin, but *all* pitcher plants, with the exceptions of the Madagascan and Seychelles' species, are Asian, another echo of that ancient land link between the continents.

The pitcher plant is a climber, some leaves ending in tendrils, and it drapes itself over

Above: Sweet-scented frangipani.

shrubs, and amongst the lower branches of trees. The tiny white flowers are inconspicuous and in colour the pitchers resemble that of apple-skin, green and russet. They grow in the hills of Mahé and Silhouette.

The **Seychelles jellyfish tree** can perhaps only truly delight the eye of a botanist. Only a few specimens of this tree, which had to have a separate genus created for it, survive high up on just two remote Mahé mountaintops. It is one of the most primitive flowering plants in the world, distantly related to tea.

The jellyfish tree, *bwa mediz*, is so called because when its fruit opens up it resembles jellyfish. The tree has dainty leaves, among them many that are orange-red in colour.

The flowers, small and white with a tinge of pink, are not spectacular. The tree only grows about nine metres (30 feet) tall, and is now extremely rare. At one time, in fact, it was thought extinct. Its rediscovery as recently as 1970 was cause for celebration.

Any visitor who walks around the market will notice some unusual fruits and vegetables. These are almost all produced by introduced trees or plants, but still hold a great deal of interest, for this is the bounty of the tropics.

Mention of the **coconut** may seem obvious, but many people do not realise that the familiar nut is encased in a fibrous green or brown case, and it is this which will withstand amateur attacks with rocks and knives.

Ask a local to show you how it should be done. The drink obtained from a fresh, unripe coconut, though quite pleasant, is not actually coconut milk. To obtain this you must soak grated coconut in hot water for half an hour, squeeze out the liquid and let the resulting cream come to the top.

General Gordon decided that the Tree of Life in his Garden of Eden was the **breadfruit** tree. The locals say that those who eat a Seychelles' breadfruit must return one day, so it may be worth experimenting. The taste itself is reward enough.

It can be treated like potato — fried, baked, or boiled — and cooked with coconut milk it makes a very filling desert called *la daube*. Breadfruit looks like a green football, weighing up to two kilos (4.5 lbs), turning yellow as it ripens. It is borne on a handsome tree with dark, glossy green leaves, commonly seen in inhabited areas. Another staple is **cassava**, a long, tough-skinned tuber bigger than the pink or yellow skinned sweet potatoes. The plant itself consists of a tall, spindly stalk with hand-like leaves.

The flesh of cassava is actually poisonous until cooked, or grated and washed through with water. If you buy a bag of local crisps and find them amazingly hard, they have been made from cassava.

At certain times of the year, particularly after the rains, you will find the mountain roads splattered with squashed fruit from **santol**, a common tree up in the hills. The orange-yellow fruit is enclosed in a hard, felted case. The taste is neither unpleasant nor exciting — hence the numbers left lying about.

Another fruit which floods the market at certain times is the **jamalac**. These heart-shaped fruits can be white or rose-pink in colour, and are again produced on a tree. The flesh is juicy and refreshing, but not sweet. Locally it is used to make jam, and added to fruit salad.

For many people the idea of breakfasting off exotic fruits is the true tropical idyll. There are many varieties of pawpaw: the small, dark-orange fleshed ones being the most delicious.

They are produced on a small "tree" with a trunk covered in heart-shaped scars, with a crown of leaves at the top, beneath which the fruits cluster. Pawpaw contains a powerful enzyme, papain, which dissolves protein.

For this reason, it is used in contact lens cleaning fluids but a more local adaptation is its value in removing the spines of sea urchins, should you happen to get these under your skin while diving. The papain in a slice of pawpaw simply dissolves them.

Continuing with fruit salad ingredients, everyone will recognize the **banana**, even though there are about twenty-five varieties in Seychelles.

The small, very sweet ones are called *banan mil*. The very large green ones are *banan san zak*, which are not eaten raw but do make excellent crisps. There is even a red variety. These familiar hands of fruit grow on a medium-sized "tree" with large leaves like banners.

Each plant (they are not trees at all, but related to grasses) produces a long stalk with a strange, purple, cone-shaped "flower". Each night a lip of this peels back to reveal the true flowers beneath, a row of creamy tubes which are the beginnings of the banana hand. Once the fruit is harvested, the plant dies.

Mangoes abound in Seychelles, and there are many types. Some are rounded, yellow, and sweet, others elongated, reddish-green, and excellent grated as salad or chutneys.

Pineapples grow wild in cracks in the granite glacis in the hills. The fruit, red at first, burgeons in the centre of a rosette of stiff, pointed leaves. Purple flowers are produced around the fruit. These wild examples are fine to eat, but not, of course, as sweet and juicy as the cultivated varieties.

Passion fruit is delicious in drinks or fruit salads. The smooth, yellow, oval fruits are opened to reveal an orange jelly full of dark seeds. The fruit is grown on a creeper, often used to cover ugly fences.

At the market you will see vanilla pods, ginger root, and cinnamon bark on sale. Seychelles has a unique **vanilla orchid**, but the pods produced commercially grow on a different species.

It is also a climber with very regularly spaced leaves on either side of a long stalk which clings to tree trunks. You may notice escaped vanilla vines running up trees like ladders.

Pollination in Seychelles is done by hand because the hummingbirds and insects the plant relies on in its native tropical America are not found there. The pods are cured using steam or boiling water, then left to dry in the sun. The process takes about a month.

Ginger root is taken from beneath a tall, leafy plant which produces a cone-shaped flowering spike. There are many ornamental gingers which produce the same tall leaves, but varied stalks. Some bear orchid-like, fragrant flowers, some spikes of red flowers like a flaming torch, and others a pyramid-shaped, pink flower with white margins to the petals. The roots of these plants are not used in cookery.

Cinnamon is common in the hills. The tree's leaves are distinctive, having three vertical, parallel veins. If you chew a leaf you will taste the cinnamon oil which once formed a large part of Seychelles' exports. The "quills" you find on the market are made by peeling off the bark of young trees.

Other spices grow there. You may find the purple fruits of **clove trees** on mountain paths.

Cardamom is produced at the base of enormous green leaves, similar to ginger. The pretty white and mauve flowers, which also nestle close to the ground, are orchid-like.

Lemon grass grows abundantly in mountain clearings. You will recognize it by its delicious smell when you brush past it or rub it in your fingers. It is the basis for a locally-made insect repellent, and when infused with boiling water makes a refreshing digestive tea called *citronelle*, the local name for the grass.

Another grass, on a bigger scale, is **sugar-cane**, which is also grown, but not on any commercial scale. It is more commonly seen in the lower hills of south Mahé, and Praslin, near to the houses. Cut into sections, children chew the cane, but the reason for its cultivation is more probably the production of *bacca*, a raw, potent local brew.

The largest grass in Seychelles is **bamboo** and there are several species, including a yellow variety. Bamboo grows on mountain paths, in towering stands thirty metres (100 feet) tall, flowering extremely occasionally.

In some species the interval is 120 years, and yet almost every plant around the world will flower at exactly the same time. A section from a large bamboo is a popular container for the collection of toddy from the palm tree.

Should you take a drive over the mountain passes, you are certain to notice a shrub with many pink or white round fruits. The **coco plum**, originally planted as an anti-erosion measure, is now extremely widespread in open areas. The fruit is harmless, but can best be described as tasting like soggy cotton-wool.

In the ditches you will see a pretty yellow flower, called **koket**, which is used in local herbal medicines. The spikes of deep purple blue flowers are **epe ble**, of which there are several varieties, including a pink one.

Not far away you will probably see the white flowers of the **Star of Bethlehem**. Attractive as it is with its white, star-like flower, beware. It is extremely poisonous, the juice causing skin problems and, if you should get any in your eyes, possibly blindness.

Another extremely poisonous plant is the **thorn apple**, which deserves its local name of *feydyab* (devil leaf). This is a woody shrub that grows up to two metres (seven feet) or more high, with white or mauve trumpet-shaped flowers.

The plant contains an hallucinogen, daturine, and giddiness can result simply from smelling the flowers. It is thought that the oracles at Delphi used daturine to help them make their prophecies.

Bwa tangin, which also has the ominous name of "ordeal plant", is a small, pretty tree which has lovely white flowers with mauve throats. The fruit, a shiny rose-pink oval, looks delicious, but *tangin* is extremely poisonous.

It was used in Madagascar for trial by ordeal in an effort to make the suspect confess during the agony caused by the poison, or, rather like old English witch-dunking, to prove guilt or innocence, depending on whether the victim survived or not.

In shady ditches you will see the attractive green and white leaves of **dumb cane**, now known to many as a "pot plant". It has a poisonous sap which causes swelling of the mouth and throat if taken orally, hence the name.

Dianella has grass-like leaves, at the centre of which grows a flowering stalk. The flowers are blue and small, but the berry eventually produced is a beautiful midnight blue. It is poisonous but, like many such plants, in skilled hands it has medicinal value and is used locally in this way.

An unlikely source of danger is the **cashew nut** tree. These grow not uncommonly on the granitic islands, but the nuts are not exploited commercially. The nut, with its distinctive shape, can be seen growing under a large pink fruit, the cashew apple.

The nut is edible and can be made into wine or jam, but the shell in which the nut is encased contains a very corrosive oil, which can burn the skin off the fingers and lips of an unwary cashew nut fan. In fact the shell must be carefully burnt off, for even the fumes are poisonous.

Turning away from the sinister and back to the beautiful, most people will recognize the hibiscus growing in almost every garden. This shrub, with its distinctive trumpet-like

Above: Tropical rainforest of Congo Rouge in Mahé's Morne Seychellois National Park.

flowers, and long protruding stamen, comes in several varieties.

Some flowers are orange, some scarlet, and some white. **Coral hibiscus** has pink flowers with very frilly petals, and these grow facing downwards. **Sleeping hibiscus** has bright red flowers which never open up.

Frangipani is a small tree with spongy branches. The flowers have fleshy, waxy petals, most commonly white with margins of pink, and a yellow centre. Yellow and pink varieties also exist. The flowers give off a heady perfume.

Allamanda is another common shrub which has yellow or purple trumpet-shaped flowers. The **poinsettia**, known as a popular pot plant at Christmas time in Britain and the USA, is a shrub some 1.4 metres (four to five feet) tall in Seychelles, and is a blaze of scarlet at certain times of year.

Bougainvillaea grows in a riot of colours: orange, pink, purple, and white. One variety bears white and purple "flowers" on the same bush. In fact the colourful "flowers" are bracts, modified leaves protecting the true but insignificant, tubular flowers.

The plant is named after the eighteenth-century French explorer Louis de Bougainville who found the plant in Brazil. He also visited Seychelles.

In plant pots and old paint or milk tins, neatly laid out in some gardens, you may notice the pink or white flowers of **Madagascar periwinkle**. Not only is this a pretty border plant, it has also been discovered to have remarkable medicinal properties, used in the treatment of childhood leukaemia with great success.

Portulacas, with their fleshy leaves and bright flowers of myriad different colours, are also popular. A local species which does not have the spectacular flowers, makes a tasty, peppery salad.

Another garden favourite is the **canna lily**. These stand around a metre (three feet) tall, and have showy red or yellow flowers, rather like an iris. The leaves can be green, purple, red, or variegated.

It is related to the banana, as is the **bird of paradise plant**, with its orange flowers shaped like the head of a bird with a sharp beak and a crest at the back.

Lobster claw is another unlikely banana relative, although you will notice the similarity of the tall leaves. The strange "flower" consists of crimson bracts, like boats, with green or yellow margins, which grow alternately up a spike. These bracts hide the real purple flowers inside. A larger relative of the banana is the **traveller's palm**, of Madagascan origin. This has a very distinctive shape, the large leaves being spread like an open fan. Its name comes about because if a thirsty traveller cuts off one of these leaves he will find the hollow stalk contains about two litres (four pints) of water.

The **rain lily** or "flower of the west wind" is often planted in public gardens such as those at the airport, and around the **Zom Lib monument**. As their name implies, they flower almost immediately after rain, opening their crocus-like pink, white, or yellow flowers at the end of slender stalks. Their leaves resemble grass.

In marshy areas you might find the lovely **water hyacinth**. The spikes of lilac flowers, streaked with yellow, are extremely pretty, but the plant has the reputation of a pest because it spreads rapidly, clogging waterways.

In damp areas at the edges of marshes, or in shady ditches, you will also find several types of **crinum lily**. All have strap-like leaves, but the flowers vary from white, bell-shaped blooms to more feathery ones. Some crinums have pink stripes, but most are pure white.

The **spider lily** will tolerate drier conditions. These flowers resemble spiders, as the name suggests, having long, trailing extensions to the white petals.

Entwined in the hedgerows you will see the drooping bunches of orange-red **Rangoon creeper**, the purple bells of **railway creeper**, the sprays of pink **coral creeper**, and the beautiful sky blue trumpets of **sky flower**.

The lovely **ipomoea** hangs in curtains from telephone wires, and in some areas of Sans Souci it cloaks everything, even large trees, with its dark green leaves and white-throated flowers.

There are many species of tree in Seychelles, but among the most distinctive are **casuarina, badamier, takamaka, kalis d pap**, **Nile tulip tree**, and **banyan**. Growing most commonly in coastal areas, the **casuarina** has feathery silver-green leaves. **Bodanmyen** is remarkable for its shape. Young trees produce branches horizontal to the trunk, which ring the tree, making circles at different levels up the tree. The trees shed their leaves, which turn bright red before dropping off. The purple-pink fruits, popular with fruit bats, contain an edible nut which gives the tree its other name of "Indian almond".

Takamakas are the silver-trunked trees which lean out almost horizontally over many Seychelles' beaches, providing welcome shade. Their hard, round, green fruits are often found floating in the sea.

Kalis d pap has delicate pink flowers which are supposed to resemble the pope's headgear. Calice yields a lovely silvery-blonde timber, very popular with local furniture makers.

The **Nile tulip tree's** fiery orange flowers, with yellow margins to the petals, are more noticeable. The local name, *pis pis*, arises from the fact that the unopened flowers, when squeezed, spurt out a jet of water.

Equally unmistakable is the **banyan**. The key to identification is the rope-like aerial roots which grow downwards from the branches. These roots thicken until they look like additional trunks. Banyans often cover large areas and are sacred to Buddhists. There is a fine example in the Botanical Gardens and a large specimen at the foot of **Ma Constance** (on the north-west coast just beyond Victoria).

Banyans seem to be engulfed in Tarzan-style creepers, but these are the aerial roots. Other trees, however, are draped, and sometimes strangled by several species of creeper, now known the world over as pot plants. The **philodendron** has heart-shaped, deep-green, velvety leaves. Those of **fruit salad vine** are larger, variegated green and yellow.

This has been a whistle-stop tour of just some of the more interesting plants and trees found in Seychelles, both endemic and newcomer. There are many, many more. Most of the more noticeable ones are pan-tropical plants and can be identified using guides from Africa, Asia, or South America. The endemics can be trickier to find and name, but the reward is greater. What you will see are totally unique species found nowhere else but on these remote scraps of land — all that remains of an ancient world, now almost completely lost forever.

Island Cruises

The 115 islands of Seychelles may be among the jewels of the Indian Ocean, but only half a dozen are served by air and even fewer by boat. The only regular ferry services run between just three islands — **Mahé**, **Praslin**, and **La Digue**.

For the real island lover, whose idea of an ideal vacation is to visit as many islands as he can, Seychelles has a great deal to offer. Probably the best way to visit and enjoy many of the more remote islands is from the comfort of your own floating hotel, a large sail-driven or motor-powered yacht.

The joy of chartering is that it gives you the versatility and freedom to go where you want and drop anchor at any time — in deserted idyllic coves or just offshore — to follow your own pursuits, a walk ashore to investigate the local flora and fauna or a stroll along the beach.

These craft are expensive, but they do accommodate up to ten passengers and arranged on a group basis the cost is shared. If you are on your own most operators will coordinate to fill vacant cabins, so do not think it is beyond your pocket. All it needs is time and a little organisation.

The Marine Charter Association on Mahé also represents many owners and skippers whose boats are available for game fishing, day cruises or longer charters to the near or distant islands.

The variety and range of charter vessels based in the islands is impressive — from luxury yachts to catamarans. The largest charter yacht operating out of Victoria, and among the best known is the twenty-one-metre-long (70-foot) *My Way*, with a seventy tonne displacement. Others include *Laura B*, the seventeen-metre (55-foot) yacht *Bie*, two catamarans — *Encounter* and *King Bambo* — *Escapade*, a fourteen-metre (45-foot) cruiser and, based in Praslin, the twelve-metre (40-foot) catamaran *Stephanie*.

My Way accommodates up to forty people for day trips, or ten on overnight or longer cruises. *Encounter*, a 13.5-metre (44-foot) catamaran built in 1983, accommodates four in two large double cabins with queen size beds. It is equipped with electricity, cooker, refrig-erator, icebox, outside shower, and toilet.

The other catamaran, thirteen-metre-long (40-foot) *King Bambo*, is a perfect balance of space, luxury, and stability. Guests travel leisurely throughout the islands, pausing for snorkeling and windsurfing ably assisted by the crew led by the skipper and a hostess.

Four ample double-berth cabins below deck, all with private shower and head, ensure undisturbed nights of sound sleep. The roomy deck areas make an ideal sun deck when the sail is hoisted each morning.

Departures are throughout the year, and visitors can choose to take the whole boat with a party of friends or join a group to sail to destinations most people can only dream about — Praslin, **Bird Island**, La Digue, **Silhouette**, and **Curieuse** on a one-week cruise; the remote **Amirantes** on a two-week cruise.

Snorkeling and scuba diving feature prominently in *King Bambo*'s charter programme. She has been carefully designed with diving and safety in mind — from stepped decks with built-in swim platforms to two concealed Bauer compressors.

Her skipper is a PADI-qualified dive-master with many years experience in Seychelles waters. *King Bambo* is a splendid example of the skills of the island boat builders.

The rhythmic syllables that form the word "takamaka" are sounds that you come across often during your stay on the islands. It is the name of one of the islands' sturdiest trees, often found skirting the shoreline.

The Seychellois carve the huge trunks into the graceful bows and hulls of the ships that ply the Indian Ocean carrying passengers and cargo between the islands.

Now at the end of the twentieth century the traditional *pirogue* with oars has given way to custom-built schooners. These graceful vessels in varnished dark wood leaning full sail against the force of the south-east trade wind are a pleasure to watch.

Another splendid example of the craftsmanship of Seychelles boat builders is the schooner *Silhouette* which serves the growing passenger traffic between Praslin and La Digue.

Every day another stately schooner, *La Belle Praslinoise*, leaves the old pier at **Victoria**, Mahé, carrying cargo and passengers to

Baie St. Anne Jetty on Praslin and the cargo schooner *La Belle Vue* plies between Mahé and the inner islands.

On La Digue, *La Feline*, and *La Curieuse* are available for charter cruises and diving trips to the Amirantes.

For those not in that bracket there is still plenty of choice among the other yachts and catamarans — of both price and comfort. Once you have cruised Seychelles' waters you will find it difficult to enjoy them any other way.

Fighting Fish of the Deep Ocean

The delights of deep-sea fishing are still relatively unexplored in Seychelles, despite the knowing smiles of the local people when you ask about the prospects of landing sailfish, barracuda, and the like.

But this mid-oceanic group of islands has some quite remarkable fish and "Big Game Fishing" is dedicated to the art of catching some of the bigger scaly monsters that roam the Indian Ocean.

Generally speaking these are not sharks, which are not really considered game fish, but the big, fast-swimming predators with such evocative names as **kingfish**, **sailfish**, **marlin**, and **tuna** — all excellent eating fish — but regarded so highly by sport fishermen because they are difficult to catch and even more difficult to land: the fight to bring a marlin to the boat can take several hours.

The best fishing grounds are at the very edge of the **Seychelles Bank**, a submarine plateau where the sea suddenly plunges to a depth of more than 1,830 metres (6,000 feet), which is generally fifty kilometres (30 miles) or more from Mahé. The islands of **Denis** and **Bird** are on the northernmost edge and thus closest to the best fishing and return impressive catches.

However, as any fisherman will tell you, fish do not read the same books as anglers. The records show that the most productive sailfish area is around **Silhouette Island**, which is well inside the main plateau.

They are there in plenty. And even as more and more visitors discover the thrill of this particular chase, it is still possible for anyone, experienced angler or beginner, to establish a Seychelles record during a day's fishing.

Less than an hour by boat from Mahé you may encounter kingfish and sailfish weighing up to forty kilos (88 lbs), and the ever present bonitos. Naturally you will also find many species of tuna ranging from the yellow-fin to the big-eyed variety, as well as barracuda and shark.

The waters round the coral islands of Bird and Denis provide a home for a large variety of game fish, including dog-tooth tuna as well as marlin.

Sailfish, famous for their aerobatics, abound from March to June as well as in October and November. The yellow-fin tuna, skipjack tuna, and dog-tooth tuna may be caught during the season of the south-east trade winds.

Bonito, or little tuna, are common to the islands, and Seychelles has long been a noted source of record bonito. Dorado and wahoo run throughout the winter season.

The king of game fish, the marlin, has been seen throughout the year, and they still tell of the 240-kilo (530-lb) black marlin boated on a handline within six kilometres (four miles) of **Beau Vallon Beach** on Mahé.

Enthusiasts will quickly recognise a sharp contrast in conditions around Seychelles. The **Amirantes** to the south, and around the islands of Bird, Denis, and Frégate to the north are always exciting for fishermen.

The waters covering the Seychelles Bank itself are never much more than seventy metres (230 feet) deep. From November to May these huge areas become the territory for deep-sea fishing. April to October are not the best months because the sea becomes too rough.

Whichever area you choose, experience suggests you are unlikely to come away disappointed.

The boats used for big game fishing range from high-speed outboard powered boats of

Opposite: Fountain of surf cascades over granite rocks.

seven metres (23 feet) to twenty-metre (65-foot) diesel-powered motor cruisers. All these types of craft will use a considerable amount of fuel in a day's fishing and the price of a charter reflects this.

The trips usually include lunch and soft drinks and the crew will generally prepare at least one of your catch as a snack to help you concentrate on catching more. Charters can be booked either through the **Marine Charter Association** in the **yacht basin** in **Victoria** or through one of the travel agents.

The operators of these boats also offer day cruises to the various islands, such as **Aride**, Silhouette, **North**, and many others; so if you fancy a day trip to the island you have seen on the horizon for the past week this may be the way.

They are always pleased to help and make suggestions as to the suitability of your requests in relation to the prevailing sea and weather conditions.

Charter boats are fully licensed, with properly qualified skippers and mechanics aboard; their crews also know who to contact on the various islands for landing permission and which islands they can visit during certain weather conditions.

It is this experience and safety that you pay for, besides the fuel that you use. If you are offered a super cheap deal, the chances are that this is not a licensed operator and probably does not have the appropriate safety equipment or experience required to offer these services.

Very few of these "cowboys" are still in operation as the authorities have acted against most of them. Should you be approached with such an offer you should consider firstly that your safety could be in jeopardy and secondly that you do not really want to spend days of your vacation appearing in court as a material witness in a prosecution case if they get caught operating without a licence.

Deep-sea fishing and angling tours can be booked through the Marine Charter Association in Mahé and many of the hotels on **Praslin** and **La Digue** as well as Denis and Bird.

Opposite: Hobie Cat enthusiasts off Beau Vallon.

Watersports: Sun and Sand, Sea and Fun

No other place in the world offers the watersports enthusiast so much freedom, variety, and challenge as the Seychelles.

Close to the Equator, widely scattered over thousands of kilometres of the Indian Ocean, these islands provide the perfect environment for virtually every form of watersports enjoyed by mankind — from parasailing behind a powerboat to simply sailing leisurely from one island to another.

In between, the Seychelles offers one location after another in which to enjoy all watersports: swimming, water-skiing, windsurfing, surfing, sailing (from dinghies and catamarans to ocean going yachts and schooners), scuba diving, snorkeling, and big game fishing. There is even a strongly contested canoe polo league, a new kind of sport, in the **yacht basin** of the capital, **Victoria**.

The granite plateau on which the islands stand offer safe shallow waters, teeming with myriad fish and corals, and visibility of up to forty metres (130 feet).

Yet close by the margin of the plateau the depths sometimes plunge vertically as much as 1,800 metres (6,000 feet) to the ocean bed — hosting complementary but contrasting species of tropical deep-sea fish.

Four hotels on **Mahé**, one on **Praslin**, one on **La Digue**, and one on **Desroches** have facilities for scuba diving. Glass bottom boats and semi-submersibles are run by major tour operators and attract the largest numbers of tourists.

Snorkeling

Snorkeling is an ideal way to explore the shallow reef areas and many hotels have excellent snorkeling areas within swimming or walking distance. Almost anyone who swims can snorkel but while some take to it straight away, others often need a helping hand.

Most scuba diving centres offer short, inexpensive snorkeling courses and, if you are apprehensive about throwing yourself into an Indian Ocean teeming with fish, it is well worth taking one.

Snorkeling is easy, relatively cheap, and allows you to spend hours watching the world of the coral reefs. Equipment is available from the **Underwater Centre**, at the **Coral Strand Hotel,** at much lower prices than in most European countries — a combination of prudent buying by the Centre and strict government price controls.

If you take note of a few tips you will find it even more enjoyable: buy, borrow, or rent a mask that fits snugly. You test this by putting it to your face without using the strap and breathing in through the nose. If it fits properly it will stick. If it is loose, try another one and keep trying until you find one that does fit.

Ask any of the boat guides, watersports staff, or dive centre instructors for a basic introduction on the proper way to use the equipment: this is normally given when you collect the equipment.

Anyone who feels at all nervous, or young children, should take a snorkeling course to learn the tricks of the trade. It is also a great way to keep the kids occupied and makes for real fun family outings.

After this initial introduction you must now find out which are the best places in your locality to go snorkeling, how to reach them, and what are the potential problems — such as waves, currents, or difficult entries and exits.

Always take adequate precautions against the sun: snorkeling keeps you cool, but the water does not stop you from burning. T-shirts help, but remember the sensitive skin on the back of your knees and neck. Waterproof sunscreen cream or the full protection of Lycra body suits provide ideal protection.

Lycra suits also protect you from minor scrapes against the coral and you can always use them afterwards for aerobics at home.

Finally, whenever possible, swim — rather than walk — around the reef edge. Walking over shallow coral not only results in cuts and scrapes, but more importantly damages the corals, often severely.

Scuba diving

Snorkeling allows you to watch most of the shallow-water fish in detail, and see many different coral formations. But you are restricted by the length of time you can hold your breath and for many this becomes more than a little frustrating.

For those who just have to get down there with the fish, scuba diving is the only way to really enjoy the undersea world.

Diving has come a long way in the last three decades: modern equipment is lighter and easier to use and professional dive instructors make learning remarkably easy.

So long as you are healthy and able to swim, you can be taught to dive. If you have longed to follow in Cousteau's footsteps (or bubbles) there is no better place to do it than Seychelles.

Many dive centres in the islands belong to the **Association of Professional Divers, Seychelles**, and their staff and instructors have international qualifications — your guarantee of a safe and enjoyable diving experience. Most centres are on **Mahé**, but there are some on the other resort islands of the archipelago.

The largest and oldest established diving operation, the Underwater Centre, at the Coral Strand Hotel, **Beau Vallon Beach,** offers a number of courses throughout the year geared to your own requirements.

Although not a licence course, for many, the one-day introductory course is the key to the door of the underwater world. It will get you diving safely and comfortably in just one day.

It starts with a short theoretical lesson on what you need to know *before* going underwater, followed by a training session in the swimming pool where you will learn the basic skills to be safe and comfortable.

Provided that you feel at ease and that your instructor considers you capable, then off you go to the reef with your instructor to guide you around and introduce you to some of the multitude of marine creatures.

For those who want a recognised diving qualification, there is a five-day International Open Water Diver course, which will give you a full diving licence on completion.

The course involves five theoretical lessons, five training sessions in the swimming pool, and four open-water dives under supervision. The fees cover the cost of renting all the equipment you need, your own diving manual, log book — and your international licence.

It means you have to study in the evenings and also sit a multi-choice theory examination as well as practical diving but for most people all this is remarkably enjoyable and rewarding and well within their capacity.

Once qualified, you can continue your diving education, either in the form of advanced courses up to the level of Assistant Instructor or in special interest areas such as night diving or wreck diving.

Underwater photography, another popular course, takes you from happy snapshots on the reef right up to learning the advanced techniques for underwater video.

If this all sounds too extreme, hire a "photo buddy" to photograph or video film your underwater exploits for you to show your friends back home. The main thing is that once you have your licence the sea is your oyster.

Diving excursions are available daily from most centres. Their boats take you to the best diving spots in the islands, subject only to sea conditions and your level of experience.

All the previous hints for snorkeling apply equally to diving. Your instructors or dive masters should give you a thorough briefing on each dive site you visit.

The following points are also worth noting: remember that your legs will be much longer than normal, due to your fins, so take care not to kick the corals as you swim past. It only takes a few seconds to destroy decades of coral growth.

Never touch or handle coral structures. Their surfaces are covered by a thin, delicate skin and if they feel slimy it could mean you have ruptured the protective membrane.

Never touch or handle unfamiliar marine life. Not all are as harmless as at first they might seem. Long-spined sea urchins are particularly unforgiving.

Never remove corals or shells for even dead coral is important to the development of the reef — and "empty" shells are home to many different creatures.

Move slowly around the reef. Swimming fast allows you to see more coral, but this way fish sense you long before you approach and many go into hiding. Gentle swimmers inevitably see more fish as they do not pose a potential threat or disturbance.

You should also take time to look for smaller reef fish and other creatures as it will make your dive all the more rewarding.

Above: Fascinated tourists aboard a semi-submersible enjoy the underwater spectacle of St. Anne's Marine National Park.

Surface watersports

Wherever you happen to be staying, most watersports can be savoured from the beach of your own self-catering chalet or your hotel. The major tourist hotels all provide the necessary equipment for such sports as surfing, water-skiing, windsurfing, and snorkeling at free or nominal charges.

In the cases where the beach closest to the hotel is not ideally suitable, arrangements are made for hotel guests to use the facilities of the watersports operators elsewhere.

Most watersports centres are located at hotels or nearby premises. These facilities are normally offered to hotel residents at special rates — and some are free. All these centres are open to nonresidents as well.

At most watersports centres a deposit system is operated. The deposit is refunded when the customer returns the equipment undamaged. The deposit varies between 200 and 500 rupees depending on the equipment and may be paid in cash, by credit card, hotel credit card, or signed hotel deposit form to be added to your room bill.

Make sure that you know the period and conditions of the rental, just as you would for a rental car, together with any special restrictions on use: paying for a jet ski that ran over a submerged reef could make a big hole in your holiday budget.

Always inspect the equipment thoroughly before leaving the premises. You should ensure that any defects are either corrected or noted on the rental form.

If you are unfamiliar with the equipment ask for instruction on how to use it — almost certainly it will be worth paying for a beginner's lesson if you have never tried the activity.

Ensure that you know the opening and closing times of the centre or, at least, the time you are required to return the hire equipment; they may not necessarily be the same.

The range of activities and facilities offered by each centre is similar so long as sea and weather conditions allow. Normally hotel residents are allowed free use of snorkeling equipment but nonresidents may find it cheaper to buy if they intend to rent it for a week or longer.

Windsurfers also are normally a free facility, but most operators will check your experience before letting you out on high performance equipment.

Windsurfing fanatics should compare the location of their hotel and the date of their visit with the trade winds to make the most of their holiday.

Generally, April–May and October–November experience extremely light winds; between December and March the winds are north-west and blow onshore at Beau Vallon and offshore at the **Reef Hotel**.

From June to September they are south-east and offshore at Beau Vallon but onshore at the Reef Hotel. The **Sheraton Island resort** tends to be sheltered during the north-west season but gusty during the south-east.

Hobie catamarans are another popular wind-powered water sport as are laser dinghies and minisails. If you have never sailed a Hobie Cat you will definitely need a lesson.

Once you have mastered them, however, you will find sailing them is exhilarating and great fun. For the uninitiated, some of their performance is both unexpected and somewhat sudden, to say the least.

Parasailing is the "sport" of being towed into the air (suspended from a parachute) by a high-speed boat. No previous experience is required but you will need lots of courage.

Given that, it is undoubtedly the best way to enjoy the splendid coastal panoramas. Undisputed masters of this particular sport are **Leisure 2000**, the watersports operators at **Coral Strand Hotel**.

They have certified instructors from both the British and American Parasailing Associations and fly most days unless the wind is too strong or gusty. Parasailing is also available at Beau Vallon Aquatic Sports.

Water-skiing is always popular but you definitely need some instruction if you have never done it before. All the centres based on sand beaches offer water-skiing at various levels and most possess a range of skis for beginners up to experts.

The "water sausage" is another "no previous knowledge required" activity, fun for both participant and spectator alike. High-speed boats tow these large inflatable sausages, about five metres (16 feet) long, around the bay.

The challenge for the rider is to stay on the sausage, fitted with hand grips and low-level inflatable foot supports which act as stabilisers, as it crosses over the wake of the boat.

The job of the boat skippers is to make sure that they don't stay on. For those who survive five minutes without a dunking there is a free repeat ride.

Wet bikes and jet skis complete the line-up of most watersports centres. These one- or two-man aquatic motor scooters are about the nearest thing to flying that the watersports centres offer that is not suspended from a parachute.

Wet bikes are powered by small outboards while jet skis are driven by water jet motors. Rented out for periods of thirty minutes, they are subject to strict controls about where you use them, to protect other water craft and swimmers from inexperienced pilots.

But they are splendid fun — all the thrill of riding a motor bike for the first time, without the pain of falling off.

Some popular resorts

A few hundred metres off the west coast lies Île Thérèse. This is the base of the **Big Game Watersports Centre.** A small landing craft ferries passengers from the mainland to spend a day either lazing on the beach or to participate in the watersports available there. This operation is run by Gonzales Rodrigues, known to all as "Speedy". The facilities include windsurfers, canoes, pedaloes, Hobie Cats, water scooters, water-skiing, and big game fishing.

At some time during their holiday, most visitors pay at least one visit to **Beau Vallon Bay** in the north-west of the island, a three-kilometre (two-mile) long curve of beach.

During both north and south trade-winds, watersports can be enjoyed there. Two operators work on this particular beach: **Beau Vallon Aquatic Watersports** and Leisure 2000 Watersports.

The former is owned and managed by France Morel, the latter being owned by an Englishman, Dennis Law, better known to the locals living and working in the area as "Blanc".

Most watersports are available throughout the islands at smaller hotel-based facilities, so there is always something to enjoy. Points to note:

• Most watersports centres do not cater for the professional windsurfer, so you may be disappointed if your idea of a holiday is a windsurfing one.

• Most hotels have an arrangement for watersports, check at the reception as information is not always readily available in your room.

• Tuition for windsurfing and water-skiing are available. The instruction is good, so the absolute beginner should get the idea by the end of their holiday.

• All watersports operators are locally licensed and insured, and strict safety regulations and rules are applied.

• Parasailing and skiing are not available at Beau Vallon Bay before midday, except on Sundays and public holidays (this protects age-old fishermen's rights, and their nets).

• Watersports (subject to weather) are available every day of the year, including Sundays and public holidays.

• Snorkeling equipment is available for hire at most watersports and diving centres.

• Game fishing is also well served.

Overleaf: Parasailer about to splash down on Beau Vallon beach.

Following page: Vacationers tackle the challenges of the water sausage.

Exploring the Silent World Beneath the Waves

The shallows of the Indian Ocean were the fascinating subject for *Silent World*, a classic documentary filmed by underwater explorer Jacques Cousteau around the remote islands of **Aldabra**, **Assumption**, and **Cosmoledo**.

He showed a world that has few equals — and one which lures more and more people each year to explore its strangely coloured treasures.

It is not just its prolific coral reefs which make Seychelles a Mecca for the underwater visitor. Its rich and varied marine landscapes are diverse and many.

One of the main areas of interest, the **Seychelles bank**, is the vast submerged plateau of a sunken mountain range which lies little more than forty metres (130 feet) beneath the crystal-clear, turquoise waters — inhabited by some magnificent fish species, sweetlips, moray eels, surgeon fish, and batfish — that provide some of the prettiest and safest diving in the world.

By contrast, for those who seek adventure and excitement, at the edge of the plateau — close to **Astove**, **Farquhar**, and **Poivre** — the Indian Ocean suddenly plunges 2,000 metres (6,500 feet) down an almost vertical precipice.

Among the most beautiful and fascinating of the world's environments, the coral reefs found there are so close to the surface that even novices can enjoy them in comparative safety but only from a schooner or chartered yacht. There are no dive centres in the south.

Many hundreds of coral species make up the living reefs of the island archipelago, teeming with marine life in all its many exquisite and exotic forms.

There, swaying in the currents and the ebb and flow of the tidal draw, stand incredible underwater gardens of red, gold, yellow, and purple corals and grasses.

Underwater adventurers wishing to explore the outer edges of the islands should consult one of the dive centres. These remote reefs are especially attractive, usually undisturbed, but the choicest dive sites are known only to the dive professionals.

There are countless ideal places, both near and far, in which to explore the underwater world — due, in one part, to the geological origins of the islands and, in the other, to the fantastic variety and wealth of marine life.

On Mahé, huge granite boulders tumble into the sea to form fascinating marine gullies, caves, and arch formations among the coral heads that rise from the level sea-bed. The coral reef that begins close inshore also provides excellent snorkeling.

Shallow-water coral species — brain, fire, table, staghorn, and soft corals — are seen in abundant communities both large and small, close together and in isolation.

Within the coral heads, groupers — a form of giant rock cod — and moray and barbel eels make their homes in massive hollows.

There are myriad fishes, large and small, that adorn these reefs with brilliant colours and exquisite and sometimes grotesque forms.

You may also find larger sea predators like the tigerish barracuda and *carang* in surprisingly large numbers for so close inshore.

Some prime dive sites

1: **Trompeuse Rocks** lie approximately twenty-four kilometres (15 miles) north of **Mahé**. The rock which breaks the surface drops down some twenty metres (65 feet) to where the rocks are broken and jumbled.

There are many large shoals of fish — fusilier, *kordonnyen,* tuna, and jack. Crayfish are seen on most dives, as are sharks. Often the current is quite strong and occasionally it prevents diving.

2: **Mamelles**, approximately twelve kilometres (seven and a half miles) north of Mahé, is a lovely uninhabited island, ideal for picnics, with a cave at the north end which runs right through from east to west — it is extremely slippery and care is needed.

The dive sites are all around the southern half of the island; hauntingly beautiful coral formations over a fairly flat reef with many different fish, especially in and around the many gullies.

The shoals of fusiliers are often so thick that they block the view to the sea-bed. Depth ranges from twelve to eighteen metres (40-60 feet).

Above: Cup coral in the tropical reefs that surround the islands.

3: **The wreck of the** *Ennerdale*, a British Royal Fleet Auxiliary tanker of 47,000 tonnes which grounded on an uncharted reef and was blown up by the Royal Navy, lies approximately two and a half kilometres (one and a half miles) south of **Mamelles Island**.

The centre section of the *Ennerdale* was badly broken up but the stern with its huge bronze propeller is still recognisable, as is the bow section. The depth to the sea bed is thirty metres (100 feet) and the wreck stands well up off the bottom.

Since the bridge is lying upside down on the sea-bed to the port side of the wreck, the stern is the usual dive site. A huge grouper lived in the stern section for many years and always greeted the divers.

Often a large endormi — or sleeping nurse shark — is lurking under the stern plates. The visibility on the wreck can be very patchy and the current can often prevent diving.

4: *Ennerdale* **Rocks**, about three kilometres (almost two miles) to the south-east of the *Ennerdale* wreck, were reduced by blasting after the grounding and now range from twelve metres (40 feet) deep to a maximum

depth of about twenty-five metres (80 feet).

It is a fine offshore dive site visited by many large, pelagic fish including tuna and kingfish. There are always octopi and usually crayfish can be seen. As with most offshore sites, the current is sometimes too strong for diving.

5: **Brissare Rocks**, approximately four and a half kilometres (two and a half miles) north of Mahé, is made up of two rocky islets. The largest, to the west, is the main dive site and — depending on the current — it can be circumnavigated in about fifty minutes without too much rush at a depth of between fifteen and twenty metres (50-65 feet).

On the south side of the islet, where a natural slotted division runs approximately east-west, a giant boulder has fallen across the slot forming a short tunnel which, because of its east-west orientation, causes a fun tidal syphon.

Divers who wait at the entrance on either side for the right moment can take an exhilarating ride through the slot on the surge with no effort at all — a ride made more exhilarating if one of the small reef sharks is

Above: The carnivorous lionfish makes its home among the rocks and reefs of the tropics.

in the tunnel at the same time.

It is probably one of the liveliest areas for fish in the whole of Seychelles. Enormous "meadows" of fire coral attract uncountable multitudes of small fish. In turn these attract bigger fish which, again in turn, seem to attract the veritable giants of the deep.

Huge humphead wrasses are often seen. Endormi sharks are seen occasionally; these are inoffensive if left unmolested.

At the north end of the islet there is nearly always a current although this rarely prevents diving. Shoals of large batfish are a feature of Brissare and small white-tip reef sharks are seen on most dives.

The east islet of Brissare is rarely dived. Being smaller, waves break over its surface and spoil underwater visibility. But when the wind or current is not too strong it offers a possible alternative.

A nice rocky site with plenty of fish and an enormous moray eel which swims with the divers.

6: **L'Ilot Island**, approximately half a kilometre (one-third of a mile) off the north-west point of Mahé, is a rocky islet with a few stunted palm trees and a glorious view south along the sweep of **Beau Vallon Bay**. There is almost inevitably a current at one end of the islet or the other.

It is possible to circumnavigate it at a depth of between fifteen and twenty metres (50–65 feet), but it is something of a rush.

Although the south side is fairly uninteresting, the east and west are spectacular, and the north, with its huge jumble of enormous boulders, is incredible.

There are huge shoals of two-spot snappers with soldier fish everywhere. You will also often see large bumphead parrotfish, monstrous creatures scraping at the coral with their beaks — the stony residue is puffed out through their gills as they move along — grazing like herds of buffalo. The east side displays one of the finest soft coral gardens found anywhere in Seychelles.

7: **Chuckles**, approximately two-thirds of a kilometre (under half a mile) south of L'Ilot is an underwater rock outcrop where the sea bed is approximately fifteen metres (50 feet).

The outcrop rises about five metres (16 feet) with a reasonably delineated edge most of the way round, except on the west side.

On occasions, because of strong currents, diving there is impossible but if the current is right it makes a superb dive. In the deep fissures which divide the rocks there are many crayfish.

Areas of the rocks are covered with soft corals like multicoloured blankets and wherever you look you will see butterflyfish, angelfish, soldierfish, and sweetlips everywhere swimming around the coral.

8: **St. Anne**, the northernmost island of **St. Anne Marine National Park,** offshore from **Victoria**, on **Mahé**, has two regular dive sites — the north-west corner and the south-east side.

Both are shallow, reaching depths of no more than ten to fifteen metres (32-50 feet), with plenty of fish but little clean, live coral. However, nothing may be taken, not even dead shells or coral.

9: **Île Sèche (Beacon Island)**, a small island lying east of the southern tip of St. Anne's Island, just outside the St. Anne Marine National Park, has a number of sites: the main ones are **The Pinnacles** and the south side.

In the north-west corner The Pinnacles is a shallow but dramatic site approximately fifteen metres (50 feet) deep. The rocks, which rise sheer to the surface, attract many species of fish, especially needlefish, which often shoal there.

The south side is about twelve to eighteen metres (40-60 feet) deep with rock gullies, overhangs, and grottoes favoured by many groupers which are always there. You can also often see crayfish and, in common with most offshore sites, occasional eagle rays and sharks. At certain seasons mullet gather in enormous shoals. Visibility is variable.

10: **Harrison Rocks**, situated two and a half kilometres (one and a half miles) south of Île Sèche, form a wild, ragged granite reef rising from the sea like the black, broken stumps of rotten teeth. Huge shoals of fusiliers gather there and shark are frequently seen.

There are many groupers and scores of crayfish make their home in the large crevices. Banner fish, a fairly unusual sight, shoal there and squadrons of spotted eagle rays are sometimes seen.

11: **Turtle Rocks**, lying some three kilometres (two miles) east of the **airport**, thrusts its pinnacle above the surface when there is a strong swell. Diving is possible all around the rock, depending on wind direction. With huge granite boulders it is an exceptional site, varying in depth from ten to twenty-two metres (30-70 feet).

Commonly seen are extremely large grey stingrays; white-tip sharks; large jacks; and shoals of yellow snappers, fusiliers, and soldierfish. But, despite their name, turtles are seen only rarely around these rocks.

12: **Airport Reef**, a large underwater granite outcrop, heavily dissected by slots and gullies, lies some seven kilometres (four miles) east of the **airport** with depths ranging from twelve to twenty-six metres (40-85 feet). Crayfish abound around this remote site and sharks are often seen. In the sand of the gullies there are many examples of horned helmet shells; vast shoals of fusiliers congregate in midwater and large groupers are commonplace.

13: **Vista Rock and inshore rocks** is perhaps one of the prettiest of all the inshore dive sites. In front of Vista Hotel at the north of **Beau Vallon Bay**, the main rock is a huge granite boulder rising about fourteen metres (46 feet) from the sea-bed to two metres (seven feet) beneath the surface.

The whole rock is covered by soft corals, sea whips, and cup corals, which attract many of the most beautiful of Seychelles' tropical fish — angelfish, butterflyfish, lionfish, banner fish, jewel fish, and damsels.

Careful searching around the base of the rock will reveal paper fish and small angler fish plus many octopi and coloured moray eels. Eagle rays often swim by.

Inshore, a collection of jumbled, tumbled rocks provide an ideal end-of-dive site, since the depth is only about twelve metres (40 feet) with crayfish, octopus, snapper, and grouper in abundance.

14: **Sunset Rocks**, just offshore from **Sunset Beach Hotel**, along the north of **Beau Vallon Bay**, are orientated at approximately 90° to the beach and the ridge-top breaks the surface about half the distance offshore.

The normal dive site, at the offshore end

Top: Divers gear up at the popular Coral Strand Hotel dive centre.

Above: Novice training session for scuba divers.

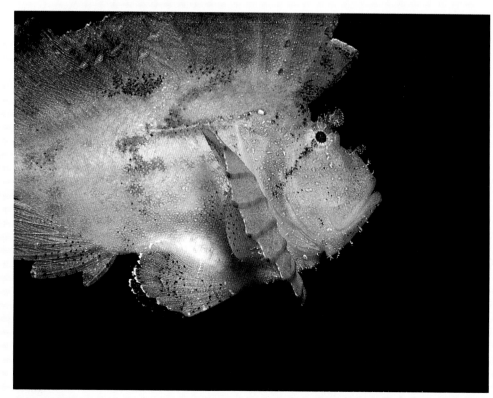

Above: Translucent against the inky-black water, the fascinating Seychelles' paper fish.

of the outcrop, suffers a little from the turbulence around those rocks which break the surface, causing a certain amount of suspended sediment which lowers visibility.

Nevertheless, it is a good dive with plenty of scorpionfish, surgeon fish, and sea cucumbers. As the maximum depth is only around twelve metres (40 feet) you can enjoy an extremely pleasant, long dive.

15: **Northolme**, about two-thirds of a kilometre (under half a mile) offshore from **Northolme Hotel**, is an extremely shallow site about ten metres (30 feet) deep, which makes it ideal for beginners.

The granite is broken ground with plenty of small areas of coral. Yellow snappers are seen in shoals and there are plenty of colourful coral fish. It is also another place where eagle rays plane over the sand.

16: **Coral Gardens**, a vast area rarely more than twelve metres (40 feet), lies almost one kilometre south-west of Northolme. But you

should note that the seaward side of the reef drops down another six metres (20 feet) to the sandy sea-bed dotted with coral-covered rocks.

The area attracts large shoals of yellow snappers, clownfish in their anemone home, angelfish, and butterflyfish. A nice easy site with much to see and enjoy.

17: **Vacoa** is an area of patchwork and coral reef, some three kilometres (two miles) offshore from **Vacoa Village** on **Beau Vallon Bay**. The depth on the inshore side is twelve metres (40 feet) and twenty metres (65 feet) on the offshore side.

The main feature of this reef is the large number of *acropora* (table) corals on the top of the reef. Fish are plentiful with some very friendly batfish awaiting the diver.

18: **BV1** is about four kilometres (two and a half miles) offshore from the police **watch station** on **Beau Vallon Bay beach**. Two large coral heads, divided by a narrow corridor and cabbage coral, are the main features.

Although the site suffers from monsoon storms, it still attracts plenty of fish, despite some areas of broken coral, and offers good opportunities for photography. The sergeant major fish come to the diver in clouds, while the batfish glide around waiting to be fed. During night dives you will see many crayfish. Depths range between twelve and fifteen metres (40–50 feet).

19: **Corsair Reef**, less than one kilometre (half a mile) offshore from the **Corsair restaurant** at **Bel Ombre**, is a coral reef running parallel to the shore. The main dive site is centred by two large coral bommies.

Soft and leather corals are one of the features of this reef which hosts many colourful tropical fish. Flying gurnards are sometimes seen, eagle rays plane by frequently, and you find some horned helmet shells on the clean sand.

The offshore edge is between seventeen and twenty-six metres (55–85 feet) deep but closer inshore it shelves rapidly becoming very shallow — from twelve to five metres (40–16 feet).

20: **Barge Wrecks** were sunk purposely by the Professional Divers Association, Seychelles, the Seychelles People's Navy and Victoria Port Authority to provide a dive site west along the reef from **Corsair**. The hulks of the two dumb barges are buoyed.

The inshore barge, which lies almost at right-angles to the reef and nearly touches it, contains the remains of an old crane. The second barge, roped to the first, is farthest from the reef, and the chain from the marker buoy is attached to the offshore end of this barge.

Depths range from about seventeen metres (56 feet) at the inshore end of the first barge to twenty-five metres (82 feet) at the deepest offshore end of the second barge. Since these barges were sunk in February 1989, they have attracted a number of fish species like *bourzwa*.

21: **Scala Reef** is a continuation of the **Corsair reef**, about one kilometre (half a mile) further west (the coast runs virtually east-west at Bel Ombre). A little deeper than Corsair, it ranges up to twenty-three metres (75 feet).

22: **Dredger Wreck (Willy's Folly)**, which lies farther offshore from **Scala** in a depth of twenty-seven metres (88 feet), was another vessel purposely sunk as a dive site in October 1989, and by 1990 had become a big attraction for larger fish.

23: **Danzilles**, a group of close inshore rocks approximately one kilometre (half a mile) east of **Scala reef**, attracts millions of tiny glass fish and for some years a large barracuda lived around the largest rock.

It offers a good combination of granite rock and coral gardens with a variety of all the different lionfish found in Seychelles. The site is often used for night dives, when the *nudibranchia* known as the Spanish Dancer can be seen; the crayfish are out feeding; and the parrotfish are asleep and approachable. A good shallow site, its depths rarely exceed ten metres (30–32 feet).

24: **Horseshoe Rock**, a roughly crescent-shaped, fully submerged rock another kilometre (half a mile) along the coast, is about three-quarters of a kilometre (one-third of a mile) offshore east of Danzille.

The inshore rock face slopes down about fourteen metres (46 feet) to a sandy sea bed. The offshore side consists of gullies surrounded by a coral garden. In a slot at the western end moray eels may be found and there are many fish, octopus — and sometimes hawksbill turtle.

25: **Whale Rock**, a little farther east of Horseshoe and closer to shore, breaks the surface like a whale's back. Below the surface the rocks form ridges and a tight corridor known as **the tunnel**.

This enclosed area, open to the surface, can be entered from arches of rock on three of its four sides and is usually rich in fish life — batfish, sweetlips, and dog puffer among them.

A jumble of granite boulders of varying sizes all around the main rocks attract fish — allowing good photographic opportunities. At the offshore edge of Whale Rock, you find another large rock site — **Castle Rock** — waiting to be explored, which can be circumnavigated easily in about fifteen minutes.

You will see many garden eels, with their

Above: Porcelain crab at rest on a carpet anemone.

heads showing out of their holes in the sand and also black pipefish, the largest pipefish found in Seychelles waters.

Although the depth is between twelve and fifteen metres (40–50 feet), take care as the currents are sometimes strong.

26: **Willy's Rock**, a small deep rock about 150 metres (500 feet) offshore approximately halfway between Whale Rock and **Baie Ternay**, offers depths up to twenty metres (65 feet). Although only a small site, such unusual creatures as angler fish, whiskered ribbon moray, and hawksbill turtle are often seen.

27: **Baie Ternay Marine National Park**, consisting mainly of coral and providing a habitat for many different coral fish, has a number of excellent dive sites ranging in depth from nine metres (30 feet) to twenty-six metres (85 feet).

Hawksbill turtle and eagle rays are frequently seen amid these coral gardens and their amazing variety of different corals. Nothing may be taken — alive or dead — from marine parks and the number of living

shells to be enjoyed makes it a popular dive site.

28: **Grouper Rock**, on the westernmost promontory of **Baie Ternay**, is named after the huge grouper which lives in the area and is seen on most dives. The depth is more than twenty-two metres (72 feet) and the site is sometimes affected by current, especially when it swirls above the main rocks.

Besides the grouper, red and yellow snapper and soldierfish abound. Hawksbill turtle also frequent this area, something of a wild site, where almost any of the large fish may be seen.

29: **Conception Island**, which lies south of **Cap Ternay** off **Port Launay Marine National Park**, is one of Seychelles' really awe-inspiring inshore dive sites; extremely deep on the north-eastern shoreline facing south with very strong currents omnipresent.

The main dive site is a pinnacle of rock in the south-west with an average depth of twenty-eight metres (92 feet). The pinnacle itself rises seventeen metres (56 feet). Tuna shoals frequently pass this rocky, rugged area and large grouper, eagle rays, barracuda, and other large fish are seen regularly.

At certain seasons, huge shoals of fusiliers cover the site. The current, however, is a problem — and must always be checked before diving.

30: **Île Thér èse**, approximately two kilometres (more than a mile) south-east of Conception Island, has a number of dive sites, both shallow — around ten metres (32 feet) — and deeper, at twenty metres (66 feet). Although some corals show damage, inevitably there is a profusion of fish life waiting around the site to greet the divers.

31: **Îsle aux Vaches**, about one kilometre (half a mile) offshore and four kilometres (two and a half miles) east of **Île Thérèse**, provides dives down to about thirty metres (100 feet) and shallower dives in the gullies.

It is another wild site where many big fish, including sharks, grey stingrays, eagle rays, and tuna are found.

At certain seasons the currents make diving impossible for many weeks at a time.

32: **Trois Bancs**, a huge area of sunken granite outcrops is between three and four kilometres (two to two and a half miles) offshore, in the west of **Boileau Bay**. The sea-bed is about thirty-three metres (110 feet) deep and the rocks rise to twelve metres (40 feet).

It is another site swept by strong currents at certain times of the year. But this dramatic site has some of the largest shoals of batfish in Seychelles and attracts eagle rays which plane by in squadron formation. You will see barracuda and shark on most dives.

33: **Shark Bank**, a set of deep-water rocks about eight kilometres (five miles) west of **Beau Vallon Bay** (towards **Silhouette Island**), rises from the sea-bed at forty-five metres (150 feet) to nineteen metres (62 feet) beneath the surface, and is often swept by strong currents.

Shark Bank is renowned for the huge grey stingrays seen on almost every dive and the numbers of large, undamaged white gorgonian fan corals.

Shoals of small barracuda often form a

wall as they follow the diver around; batfish are seen in large numbers, as are banner fish and the Moorish idol.

As with most offshore sites, almost anything big can go by and whale sharks and enormous grouper make their home in this dramatic and memorable dive site.

34: **Praslin**, with a well-equipped dive centre, offers some really spectacular diving around the islands of Praslin, **La Digue**, **Aride**, and **Frégate**. These areas are unspoilt and many of the sites are in pristine condition.

Submerged granitic rocks form a dramatic backdrop to the myriad tropical fish which surround the diver with delight.

Coupled with beautiful coral gardens and an amazing variety of invertebrate life, many of these sites are an underwater photographer's paradise. Being less exposed than many of the sites around Mahé, a variety of large, pelagic fish are regularly seen.

These sites give the diver a feeling of total isolation, moments of real solitude. It must be said, however, that the majority of these sites are weather dependent and prone to strong currents at certain times of the year.

As with the dive sites around Mahé, the depths off these islands range between ten and thirty-three metres (30-110 feet).

35: **La Digue** has a watersports centre which offers diving on occasions.

36: **Desroches** has a well-equipped dive centre. Situated approximately one hour's flying time south of Mahé, this island offers some wild, remote diving.

Schools of hammerhead sharks may be seen; manta rays, large stingrays, and turtles enchant the diver, while schools of beautiful tropical fish drift across the reefs in pursuit of their daily sustenance.

As with the more remote sites experienced from Praslin, diving there sets the adrenalin flowing. The expectation of meeting "something big" is ever present and the underwater scenery offers the photographer superb pictures.

Again, the diving is weather dependent and strong currents occur at certain times of the year.

While shallow dives of around ten metres

(33 feet) can be made on the inshore reefs, the true diving delights of Desroches are for the more experienced diver with depths regularly approaching thirty metres (98 feet) or more.

Snorkeling and Swimming

Areas along the north-west coast may be rough between December and February when the north-west monsoon blows. At this time of the year snorkeling and swimming may not be possible.

Care should always be taken and the notices posted regarding the prevailing conditions heeded.

1: **Beau Vallon Bay Area**. Although the main area of the bay in front of the Coral Strand Hotel and the Beau Vallon Bay Hotel is sandy and excellent for swimming, the far reaches of the bay offer some excellent snorkeling.

Equipment is available for hire from the various watersports and diving centres found on this beach.

The rocks to the north, beyond the **Pizzeria**, provide an area of easy access and safe snorkeling. The variety of fish and invertebrate life is excellent, giving a good introduction to the marine world of the Seychelles.

At the other end of the bay, the rocks opposite **Fisherman's Cove Hotel** offer safe and interesting snorkeling.

Further along **Bel Ombre**, by the **Auberge Club Hotel**, it is possible, with care, to enter the sea by the bus stop opposite **La Scala Restaurant**. Shoes need to be worn to walk out, however, and great care is needed. The coral is extremely sharp. But the area does provide a good mix of both coral garden and granitic rocks, although it is not always sheltered and calm. Breakers roll in there.

2: **Northolme Hotel**. There is a delightful set of rocks immediately in front of this hotel, offering safe enjoyable snorkeling with easy access.

3: **Sunset Beach Hotel**. Fingers of rock extend from this hotel (see the preceding dive guide) and there is easy access from the hotel beach.

Care should be taken, however, and only strong swimmers should venture beyond the shelter of the hotel, as strong currents are sometimes encountered.

Good snorkeling may be found too amongst the rocks at the opposite end of the hotel's small, sandy **beach**, which provides easy access for swimmers, although sometimes it can be hard to walk back due to steep shelving.

4: **Vista Bay Club**. There are several areas of rocks opposite this hotel; some of which break the surface, while others are totally submerged.

These granitic rocks offer some interesting fish life and marine scenery but if swimming a fair way offshore, care should be exercised because currents occur at certain times of the year.

The south, south-east, and eastern beaches of Mahé are susceptible to heavy seas, strong currents, and in some places undertow during the months of the south-east monsoon — usually between June and September.

Extra care should be taken during this time and the posted signs of prevailing conditions should be observed.

5: **Reef Hotel**. Snorkeling is possible directly from the beach in front of the hotel but shoes need to be worn over the coral garden and care observed during the months from June to September — the south-east monsoon.

6: **Anse Royale**. There is easy access from the small beach but shoes need to be worn across the coral garden. It is possible to snorkel out to the small island but care should be taken as a strong current may be encountered in the channel between the island and the shore.

7: **Barbarons Hotel**. Good snorkeling may be found directly in front of the hotel with easy access from the beach but shoes need to be worn. This area, however, can be rough and conditions dangerous for both swimming and snorkeling during the south-east monsoon.

8: **Île Thérèse**. A ferry carries you across from the **Sheraton Hotel** to the watersports island of **Thérèse** where it is possible to swim and snorkel from the beach.

Above: Divers return to beach after discovering the glories of the universe beneath the waves.

9: **L'Islette Island**. A ferry operates throughout the day to this small island for a relaxing away-from-it-all day. There is snorkeling on the coral gardens around this island with easy access from the beach. The marine life is not abundant, however, and shoes should be worn.

10: **Baie Lazare**. This lovely, sweeping bay is easily reached from the beach but care should be taken at certain times of the year, especially during the south-east monsoon.

11: **Takamaka Beach**. Easy access from the beach — it is a delightful place to picnic and swim. Great care is needed, however, during the south-east monsoon.

12: **Intendance Beach**. A beautiful bay with inviting white coral sand. Swimming, however, demands great care — the beach shelves steeply and the breakers crash in, creating a strong undertow. It is most susceptible to rough seas and currents during the south-east monsoon.

13: **Baie Ternay Marine National Park**. The only way to visit this area is by boat, as the road access is blocked by the National Youth Service camp at Baie Ternay.

There are regular trips to this marine park both by glass bottom boats and dive boats, available from hotels and watersports centres situated on Beau Vallon Bay. Give ample time for both swimming and snorkeling.

There is a wide-ranging variety of coral and an abundance of marine life — both fish and invertebrate.

Situated in a beautiful bay with a lovely backdrop of lush and verdant mountains, Baie Ternay Marine National Park is safe for both swimming and snorkeling.

The boat trip south down the coast passes some of the most beautiful coastline in Seychelles with fascinating coral formations and colourful birdlife.

14: **St. Anne's Marine National Park**. Round Island, Moyenne Island, and Cerf Island are all situated within this Marine Park well-served by full- and half-day excursions by glass bottom boats and semi-submersibles from **Victoria**.

Although the coral scenery underwater is

279

not as exciting as that at Baie Ternay, the fish life is still prolific.

Both swimming and snorkeling is safe and the area is pleasant and sheltered from the wind for long periods of the year.

Snorkeling equipment is usually available on the glass bottom boats, but check before booking. The watersports and dive centres have a full range of equipment for daily hire.

15: **Bird Island**. Snorkeling and swimming in the sea around Bird Island can be hazardous as some strong currents sweep by, even in the shallows.

Only strong swimmers should attempt swimming any distance offshore. In addition, the beach immediately outside the hotel shelves steeply and there is sometimes an undertow. Check with the hotel for the best areas to swim and snorkel on the day.

16: **Frégate Island**. There are several beaches accessible by foot from the hotel. Snorkeling and swimming in the sea off the **grass runway** is pleasant.

There are both rocks and coral with an abundant fish life. A word of warning — if the waves pick up at all, it can be dangerous since it is difficult to stand up and walk in these waves. As they push water over the shallows, it causes an offshore flow through the gap in the reef, in front of the small **boathouse**.

Check with the hotel for the best areas to swim and snorkel.

17: **Praslin**. There are many areas to swim and snorkel throughout the waters of Praslin, coupled with trips in glass bottom boats and dive boats.

Check with your hotel for the best areas available. Depending on the prevailing conditions and the time of year, north-west or south-east monsoons affect different parts of the island.

18: **La Digue**. There are areas both for swimming and snorkeling off **La Digue**, but check first at the hotel for the safest areas — dependent on the prevailing conditions for the day and time of the year. The north-west and south-east monsoons affect different parts of the island.

19: **Aride Island**. Both snorkeling and swimming are possible from the beach. Take care, however, as this beach shelves steeply and it is possible to be knocked over in the shallows by breakers. You need to carry snorkeling equipment with you.

Seychelles offers excellent swimming and snorkeling from white coral sand beaches in idyllic surroundings, but observe sensible safety:

• Wear shoes. The coral is sharp and can cause unpleasant cuts and scratches. Should this happen use an antiseptic cream on the wound right away.

• Beware of the black spiney sea urchins. Do not touch them or attempt to pick them up. The spines are sharp and brittle and penetrate the skin with immediate speed.

Should this happen, do **NOT** attempt to dig out the offending spines. Rub the area instead with a slice of pawpaw skin — this will dissolve the spines in a few days.

• If you must handle any marine life, be sure you **KNOW** what you are doing and always wear gloves.

Do not remove any creature from the water and remember that you are not allowed to collect anything, even a dead shell, in the national marine parks.

• Never swim too far offshore unless you are a strong swimmer, as some areas are affected by strong currents at certain times of the year.

Opposite: Watersports enthusiast revelling in one of the many challenges offered by Seychelles.

Arts and Crafts: A Heritage in the Making

Seychelles has no traditional cottage industries or indigenous handicrafts. There are, however, some well-crafted and beautiful items for tourists to take home, permanent reminders of Seychelles.

Tourism, in fact, is providing some of the stimulus for much experimentation and development in craftwork, while artists and sculptors are inspired by the new interest in a distinctly Creole culture and sometimes by the arrival of artists from overseas (who in turn are inspired by the beauty and colour of the islands).

Children are encouraged to paint and draw, create toys, musical instruments, and models from any materials at hand, their work being exhibited.

In such exhibitions it is possible to see the blend of old and new, the innovative nature of Seychelles' creative world.

The **Arts Council**, established in 1990, helps to direct this energy into the right channels, along with a new cultural heritage centre for local handicrafts.

Indigenous crafts, of course, require indigenous materials and the Seychellois are increasingly conscious of the fine line between creating objects of beauty and destroying for ever a precious natural resource.

The most obvious example of this is tortoiseshell, which is actually the shell of a hawksbill turtle. Many tourists think that this shell is in some way "harvested" and will later regrow. To obtain tortoiseshell, the creature must be killed, and in Seychelles hawksbill turtles are in danger of extinction.

It is now illegal to import tortoiseshell products into more than 100 countries. Apart from morality, buyers should be aware they are almost certainly breaking conventions and possibly national legislation when they return home. This is not a trade to encourage.

A recently established factory makes buttons from the mother-of-pearl produced by the green snail, a creature heavily exploited in the past. Indeed materials are already being imported due to depletion of local stocks.

And pieces of coral from a reef make poor ornaments. They only gather dust while their removal often spells death to delicate underwater ecosystems. By refusing to buy such products customers can help prevent the extinction of species.

Happily, many Seychellois crafts depend on renewable or carefully used resources and also display excellent craftsmanship.

One fine example of this is the work of Guy Cesar. During the 1970s, an English craftsman resident in Seychelles began making beautiful marquetry boxes inlaid with local woods. Guy Cesar has continued and expanded his tradition, creating wonderful three-dimensional designs on the lids of his splendid boxes.

Aware of the depletion of rare endemic and indigenous trees, Guy Cesar is careful in his choice of woods, and has bought up items of old furniture, old beams, and frames in order to recycle these rare woods rather than cause the destruction of existing trees.

A visit to his workshop at **Mont Buxton** is a pleasure — Guy Cesar is happy in his work and it shows. His workshop is found by taking **Button Lane** for about one kilometre out of **Victoria** to Mont Buxton, then simply ask. If the trip up the tortuous road is too daunting, you will also find his work at the **Boutique des Artisans**, the **Craft Village**, **Anse aux Pins**, and many other shops.

Indeed, the old **Plantation House** at the Craft Village bears witness to Seychellois skills in all kinds of woodwork. Love and care went into the carving, turning, and polishing of these rare Seychelles hardwoods, and in some cases still does.

Local woods are extremely unusual and beautiful, and the government keeps a careful watch on the timber felled. You need permission from the forestry department to fell almost any tree.

Another local craft based on wood is the making of model sailing ships, ranging from the rather crude but charming models which turn up occasionally on market craft stalls to meticulous, finely detailed (and quite deservedly expensive), scale models made at **La Marine**, another old Creole house at **Le Cap**. These are souvenirs to treasure for a lifetime. Hours of painstaking work goes into every model.

Woodcarving again ranges in quality from

Above: Sculptor Tom Bowers crafts another masterpiece — a delicate but detailed figurine.

the quaint to the superb. The coconut is an excellent medium, and skilful hands make ashtrays, bowls, and ornaments out of the shell.

On the other hand there are wood sculptures of dolphins, fish, turtles, and tortoises of varying quality. Some capture the spirit of the animal and reveal the grain which has been lovingly sanded and polished to produce a superb finish.

Emmanuel Figaro and Andre Farabeau are only two of Seychelles' talented woodcarvers to have won many prizes, and there are others.

Shoppers with a discerning eye will find some exceptional pieces. From time to time a wonderfully smooth and appealing tortoise, which begs to be stroked, appears in the gift shops. You will know it when you see it.

Bill Tonga, a non-Seychellois, creates sculptures in the style and traditions of another ocean, the Pacific, and may well inspire a new Seychelles style of woodcarving. Certain studios specialise in wood items which combine beauty and utility, such as unusual and attractive knife blocks and chopping boards.

Another non-Seychellois who has made the islands his home and woven their inspi-

ration into his work is former London photographer Tom Bowers. His innovative techniques involve the use of a resin developed for the space industry. At his open-air studio near **Anse à la Mouche**, Bowers shapes and moulds scenes typical of everyday Seychelles' life from the resin: a fisherman strolling home with his supper; the fun of an oxcart race before work on La Digue.

Although fashioned from late twentieth-century synthetics, the pewter-like finish of his work bears an uncanny resemblance to the bedrock which forms the foundations of the central islands. The sculptures seem to have been hewn from the living granite of Seychelles.

His work can be bought directly from his studio or through the major hotels. But it is in high demand and limited. Any of his work can be commissioned beforehand.

A cooperative **pottery** was established at **Les Mamelles** in the 1970s and now produces excellent wares with a Seychelles theme, decorated with palm trees and other tropical designs.

Many experiments have resulted in the use of clay from **Anse Soleil** and **Val d'Andorre**

on **Mahé**. You can visit the pottery to buy their products (coffee cups, vases, ashtrays, and so forth) and watch them being made.

Another craft using local materials is raffia work in palm leaf, reeds, and *tami* fibre, which is taken from the coconut palm and made into hats or flowers.

Table mats are a popular gift, or handbags made from dried vacoa leaves. These can be seen at many outlets besides the Boutique des Artisans, **Craft Village**, the **Clock Tower stalls**, and **market stalls**.

In this day and age the craft of the traditional blacksmith is perhaps rather unexpected. Gabriel Dogley (almost deaf after forty years of hammers ringing in his ears) works in a crowded forge near the Victoria **bus terminal.** He repairs metal objects and makes almost anything to order, including watering cans, cake tins, and knives.

Ron Gerlach introduced the ancient Indonesian technique of batik to Seychelles in 1969 and has taught this craft to several others over the years. It is an exacting medium, demanding self-discipline and adherence to age-old techniques with no short cuts. Each colour has to be dyed separately into the fabric — never painted on (if it is the result is not batik).

Above: Michael Adams' strong expression of Seychellois images.

Opposite top: Beautifully handcrafted replica of an inter-island schooner.

Opposite: Model boat becomes magically life-size against a Seychelles' sunset.

Above: A local craftsman fashions another work of wood art.

Gerlach's keen interest in wildlife is apparent in his lovingly created flights of tropic-birds, gentle fairy terns, and his fish — vibrant with colour and character.

If you visit his studio at Beau Vallon you can watch his pictures slowly come to life as he carefully applies wax, or pegs his work out to dry on the beach. His work is also on sale at his shop in Victoria.

Other artists also work in batik-related crafts, including David Horeau, whose subjects include Seychellois laundry women or fishermen hauling in their nets. Look out for works of these artists at **Studio Oceana** in Victoria.

The thriving clothing industry is a prime example of the way tourism has inspired innovation in local manufacture. Lena Morgan creates elegant, sophisticated evening dresses and Ron Gerlach makes beautiful batik wrap-rounds and beach wear.

T-shirts these days are an artform in themselves and some excellent locally designed and printed shirts are now produced by Sunstroke, Spectra, Oceana, and others. The vibrant colours and scenes are guaranteed to rekindle memories of Seychelles

long after the tourist is home again.

T-shirts are not the end of the story. Look for unusual dresses boldly printed with reef fish and other underwater designs. Trouser suits, evening dresses, beach wear all have a distinctive, tropical flair.

There has been a real blossoming of local artists, working either in water colours, oils, or acrylics, together with exciting work created by non-Seychellois lucky enough to live in the islands.

A visit to a local art gallery indicates what is available in the art world. The most popular media are water colour and acrylic, used to wonderful effect by Michael Adams and Christine Harter.

Michael Adams is a jungle painter — a riot of colour in every picture — where kaleidoscopic bursts of sunlight vie for attention with the dense bush, full of screaming bulbuls.

The people seem superimposed, almost supplementary. Unfortunately in many shops around Seychelles, prints of his work, produced overseas in runs of up to 500, are all that is available, but his studio at **Anse Aux Poules Bleues** may reveal the originals.

Above: Christine Harter's work reflects the pastel beauty of the islands.

Christine Harter also exhibits prints of her work, more sylvan and sunlit, evoking a gentler, quieter pace of life. Visit her charming gallery on **Praslin**.

The work of many Seychellois artists is well worth looking at. Leon Radegonde works in acrylic and water colour, his abstracts reflecting a more intimate Seychelles; old surfaces, rusty roofs, colourful shops, discarded newspapers, and tattered posters — all a part of Seychelles. Another well-known abstract artist is Peter Pierre-Louis.

Pacquerette Lablache creates dramatic, dream-like images in acrylic, and Marc Luc uses bold strokes to evoke movement and form. Donald Adelaide takes inspiration from the forests in carefully represented pictures of palm trees and screwpines with marvellous forest light and colour.

The list of exciting artists is long, but it is worth delving into their studios, at the Mahé galleries, or at **Cote D'Ôr** on Praslin.

Among them are Jacques Vidot, Serge Rouillon, Michel Desnousse, Egbert Marday, Andre Woodcock, Himier Lespoir, James Auguste, Julien Brioche, Myrna Morin, Vincent Uzice, Gerard Devoud, Emmanuel D'Offay, and from Praslin, René Ahyune, Simon Fred, and Ted Barbe. Seek out their work and make your own judgements.

Inevitably, visitors are shown much in the way of "tat", offered for sale as crafts, but if you look around you will find some beautiful work with all the skills of tradition and imagination of the present combined.

You will not fail to catch the mood of excitement in the creative world of Seychelles, where there is so much still to explore, and it is possible to take home an object or painting of real beauty without destroying the natural heritage and wonder of these islands.

Tastes of Seychelles

The Seychellois are connoisseurs of the good things the Indian Ocean has to offer the palate. A rich amalgam of influences from around the region, Creole cuisine is based on fish, and the Seychellois have some of the tastiest fish to choose from: red snapper *(bourzwa)*, mackerel, bonito, barracuda, shark, tuna, sailfish, *kordonnyen*, and parrotfish are all to be relished, in addition to lobster, shrimps, prawns and octopus, shore crabs, and clams.

The main meal of the day is taken in the evening and usually consists of grilled or curried fish with rice, cooked on a kerosene stove. Chicken or goat is more of a weekend treat.

Breakfast is a simple meal with tea, coffee, and perhaps bread — or even a sweetened condensed milk sandwich.

A visit to the market in Victoria is interesting if you want to see the newly caught fish arriving. Many vegetables are imported, but you will see local spinach, jars of chillis, bottles of coconut milk, bags of spices, bottles of vanilla essence, some local fruits which may puzzle you, and many other unusual items.

Super soups

A meal in Seychelles might begin with a soup made from lentils, well-seasoned with the inevitable garlic and ginger, or **bred (watercress) broth**. *Bred* is an umbrella term for several leafy vegetables ranging from the spinach-like leaves of the pumpkin to Chinese cabbage. There are literally dozens of varieties.

Fish soup, of course, is a speciality, usually made from the head of a large *bourzwa* with plenty of onions, tomatoes, and perhaps sour *bilimbis*, looking like miniature cucumbers. There is also *tek tek* broth, made from small clams found buried in the sand on most beaches.

Just for starters . . .

A delicious, alternative starter to soups are crisp fritters made from aubergine or octopus. Octopus is prepared with great skill in Seychelles, and is often as tender as chicken. The softening process begins when the octopus is thoroughly beaten against the rocks. One interesting formula for softening the

octopus further is to boil it with a slice of paw-paw, and an old cork from a wine bottle. The slice of pawpaw contains papain, a digestive enzyme, but I can offer no explanation for the cork. More prosaically, other Seychellois swear by the pressure cooker for really tender octopus.

You can ask for a chilli sauce to be served with your fritters but beware. This can range from the relatively harmless sauce sold locally under the brand name "Soleil", which also contains tomato, to the *"real thing"*. This will come on a small saucer and is basically chopped chillis with oil.

This is *hot*. Seychellois love chillis, including the tiny ones, known as *tipiman*, which are the hottest of the lot. Some Seychellois will pick these off the bush and eat them like sweets, but that is only for the real professional. If you are a beginner, treat chilli sauce with respect.

Salad days

If your mouth is on fire, you can cool it down with a delicious Seychelles salad or *satini*. These are usually made from sliced or grated white cabbage, tomatoes, green peppers, cucumbers, onions, and carrots with a light, refreshing dressing of squeezed lime, or lemon juice, oil, salt, and pepper.

Patol, a long cucumber-shaped vegetable, or *bilimbi*, a sour, juicy vegetable which grows directly out of the tree trunk, are also popular as salads when chopped or grated.

An unusual salad you might like to try is *palmis*, palm heart, or "millionaire's salad". Originally this was taken from the Palmis palm, an endemic species. To take the palm heart, the central core of the living shoot, means killing the whole plant, so it is now usually taken from coconut palms.

Today's "millionaire's salad" — so called because the life of a whole tree is a high price to pay for some sixty centimetres (two feet) of palm heart salad — is served with lime and oil, or sometimes cooked in a cheese sauce.

Chutneys

Cool as they may look, it could be a mistake to rush for the local chutneys. These can be made from green mango, green pawpaw, pumpkin, golden apple (a hard fruit which grows on trees and is very common at certain

Above: Tropical cornucopia of Seychelles.

times of year, known locally as *frisiter*), or *sousout* (a spiky, green vegetable which grows on a vine and is perhaps closest to the potato in texture).

The vegetable is grated and mixed with onions and lime juice and, usually . . . yes, chillis. Once you are accustomed to them they are delicious.

Fruit 'n veg?

Foods usually thought of as "fruits" are often used with excellent results as "vegetables" — for example, green mangoes served as a salad.

Bananas come in over twenty varieties in Seychelles. *Banan mil* is small and sweet, but the giant *banan san zak*, growing up to thirty centimetres (12 inches) long, never goes yellow and is used as a starch, much as potato is. It makes excellent crisps when thinly sliced.

In a banana and fish *kat kat*, *banan san zak* is simmered with the fish in coconut milk. Incidentally, coconut milk is not the watery liquid which comes out of a coconut. It is made by soaking grated coconut in hot water. When the water is drained off it settles and a rich coconut flavoured "cream" forms

on the top. Seychelles octopus curry, *zourit kari koko*, is made with coconut milk and gives the dish a delicious sweetness.

Curry favour

Curries, a local speciality, are usually spicy, fiery — and delicious. A *kari koko* will be a little milder. Fish curries are particularly good. The best fish to use is tuna or bonito.

The leaf, known locally as curry leaf, or *pile*, is used straight from the tree. It gives a distinctly aromatic flavour to local currries.

Grilled fish Creole style is usually a whole fish, such as a mackerel, or small *bourzwa*, served with a *sauce rougay*, a mixture of onions, tomatoes, chillis, ginger, garlic, and oil.

Sometimes this is wrapped in a banana leaf and baked over the grill. If you have had enough of spice, try a fish stew, made simply with onions, tomatoes, garlic, and ginger — no chillis. An unusual dish to try is shark chutney, or *satini rekin.*

The shark meat is cooked, then soaked in cold water before being squeezed dry. Chives, onions, *bilimbis*, garlic, ginger, turmeric, chillis, and oil are then added. Shark chutney has a dry texture, but is wonderful.

289

Above: Traditional and spicy Creole food — a gourmet delight.

Dried, salted fish — *pwason sale* — is also popular and is sometimes served in curry.

"What can you do with meat?"

Meat has not figured largely on our culinary tour, and indeed Seychellois inspiration seems to run out a little when they turn to pork, beef, chicken, or lamb. As one Seychellois once despairingly said to me, "what can you do with meat?" Naturally they curry it — and very good it is too.

Goat is not an uncommon item on the menu in homes, but does not often turn up in hotel restaurants. Another stand-by is beef

or pork stew, perhaps with sweet potato added. They enjoy fruit bat stewed in a similar way, or curried.

Visitors will see these large bats soaring in the sky at dusk or during dull weather. Sometimes you will see nets strung up in the trees to catch a few for the pot. Hopefully, you will not be offered any turtle meat (*kitouz* is dried, salted turtle meat), or young shearwater (*fouke*).

Remember that both are protected species, which have most likely been taken illegally. Despite their protected status, both creatures have been hunted ruthlessly for centuries so that now their numbers are dangerously low.

In the case of the green turtle, especially, your meal could literally mean the end of the species in Seychelles, so rare have they become.

Less than ten breed successfully in central Seychelles, and their only hope for survival lies in total protection. The shearwaters are protected on the island reserves where they breed, and it is illegal to take them from these sanctuaries.

The eggs of sooty terns are sold between June and July, and are harvested sensibly nowadays, unlike the past where, again, man's greed was almost responsible for wiping out the bird.

If you wish to try the seabird eggs, then you can do so with a clear conscience, but most non-Seychellois find it hard to see what the fuss is about. They are sometimes served in a curry — *kari dizef zwazo*.

Staple stand-bys

With your meal you can be served the Seychelles staple — rice, but you might also enjoy boiled or baked sweet potato or boiled cassava. One thing you should certainly try is breadfruit, if only because local legend says that he who eats Seychelles' breadfruit *must* return.

Breadfruit is a large, heavy, round fruit which grows on stately trees in almost every area of human habitation in these islands. The flesh is extremely versatile. You can boil it and mash it with butter, like potato. You can fry it and eat it as crisps or chips.

You can even eat it as a dessert, but best of all, eat it baked, preferably at a local barbecue, when it is surrounded by smouldering coconut husks and cooked in its skin. Eaten with butter and salt, this is a simple feast well *worth* returning for.

Desserts in Seychelles are usually heavy, sticky, and sweet — coconut tart, banana cake, caramel banana, and pumpkin fritters are all for those with healthy appetites.

If you are *really* hungry, then try *ladob*. This can be made from *banan san zak*, sweet potato, coco yam, breadfruit, or yams, which are simmered in coconut milk with sugar and a vanilla pod.

For a lighter alternative, a fruit salad of mango, pawpaw, jamalac (a heart-shaped, pink- or white-skinned fruit, very refreshing though not particularly flavourful), local oranges, passion fruit, and guava can be lovely with a swirl of coconut cream. *Nouga koko* (coconut nougat) is sweet and delicious.

Local sorbets or ice creams, often made of the same fruits, are a tasty end to a meal, and slip down easily between whatever gaps are left inside.

Apart from excellent locally-brewed lager, the more adventurous might like to try *toddy*, *bacca*, or *la purée*. Toddy is tapped from the living shoot of a palm tree, the dripping sap usually caught in a bamboo container at a rate of up to eight litres (1.7 gallons) a day. Innocuous when first collected, it rapidly ferments into a potent brew (up to eight per cent alcohol) and it is an acquired taste. If left, this sap becomes an excellent vinegar.

Bacca is made from sugarcane. *La purée* is made of anything that comes to hand, especially old fruit, and is extremely strong. It is not so common these days.

For those who do not care for alcohol, try a tall glass of fresh lime with a little salt or sugar added. *Citronelle* tea is made by infusing lemon grass with boiling water and is an excellent way to finish a meal, refreshingly lemon-tasting and a good digestive tisane to boot.

This has only been a brief foray into the rich, aromatic world of Seychelles cuisine. Few people leave Seychelles without at least one meal-to-remember, whether it is a simple barbecue or a night out at a restaurant. If you are willing to experiment, you should be richly rewarded.

Pirates and Plunder

"Climb the westward cliff; taking twenty five or thirty paces east . . . there you will find pirate's signs to help you trace out a circle . . . the treasure is there."

An extract from *Treasure Island*? No, these directions are taken from a letter written in 1800 by a corsair who may have hidden his treasure somewhere in the Seychelles.

Legends of pirates and pirate treasure seem more the stuff of fiction than fact. Those larger-than-life figures striding through history and into legend appeal to common admiration for the rebel. The reality is often more banal.

But for a brief period in the eighteenth century pirates did hold sway in the Indian Ocean. They did make off with fabulous treasures — and they did seek secrecy in their hide-outs in Seychelles.

Sea robbers and freebooters

The pirates who were driven away from their old Caribbean hunting grounds around the Spanish Main moved on to the Indian Ocean in search of prey and prize.

The infamous Captain Kidd, for example, was one of the first to taste its riches. He was hired by an English syndicate whose members, in fact, included the First Lord of the Admiralty, to "apprehend, seize . . . all such pirates, freebooters, sea-robbers" in the area. But Kidd had other ideas and turned pirate.

He netted booty worth £30,000, but was later caught and publicly hanged. The East India Company, who suffered the ravages of these pirates, even sent three warships to the pirate base on St. Mary's Island off Madagascar, but the expedition failed.

Kidd's change of heart was not uncommon. The "press gangs" which seized men for the European navies, were actually an effective recruitment agency for pirate crews. Disaffected seamen, who endured dreadful conditions aboard ship, were glad of any chance to escape — or make a fortune.

Crews of ships captured by pirates were usually offered the opportunity to join the pirates. Officers were welcomed for their experience and navigational skills, and artisans — sail makers, caulkers, carpenters, cordwainers — could always find a pirate berth.

One of the most famous Indian Ocean pirates, George Taylor, was a lieutenant in the British Royal Navy before he switched sides. His famous cohort-in-crime, Captain Avery (or Every), was formerly mate on a ship that escorted the Spanish treasure fleet.

Pirate ships were often run in haphazard fashion. Crew came and went, and skilled sailors were scarce. For this reason, pirate ships often foundered, due to incompetence. Damage went unrepaired for lack of artisans, lack of time, and shortage of materials. It was certainly not all "plain sailing" for sailor-turned-pirate.

Pirates had roamed the Indian Ocean as early as 1508. From 1695, Avery patrolled the seas in gentlemanly fashion. He left a warning for the captains of all English ships with the Sultan of Anjouan, giving them a signal to show if he should not pursue them, for he had "never yet wronged any English or Dutch, nor ever so intend".

Unfortunate Indians did not enjoy such exemption, and he took a ship belonging to one of the Great Mughals, which had aboard several important members of his court, "their rich Habits and Jewels, with Vessels of Gold and Silver".

This detail is from *A General History of the Pirates* by a Captain Charles Johnson, a *nom de plume* that disguised the author's identity for many years, although his amazing knowledge of pirate doings suggested he had been a pirate himself.

Despite a few "flights of fancy", much of it is accurate and can be corroborated from other sources. In fact, the author was Daniel Defoe, who took great pains to obtain eyewitness accounts of the pirates, but also used the book to make political points, thereby stretching the truth now and then.

This is how the marvellous, but unlikely story of Libertalia, the pirate republic on Madagascar, run along egalitarian principles, came into the folklore of the Indian Ocean. The episode is one of Defoe's "moral tales".

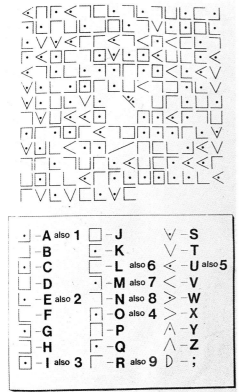

⊡ –A also 1	☐ –J	⩒ –S	
⅃ –B	⊡ –K	⅁ –T	
⊡ –C	⊏⊤ –L also 6	⩻ –U also 5	
⊔ –D	⊡ –M also 7	⟨ –V	
⊡ –E also 2	⊤ –N also 8	⟩ –W	
⌐ –F	⊡ –O also 4	⟩ –X	
⊡ –G	⊓ –P	⋏ –Y	
☐ –H	⌐⊡ –Q	⋀ –Z	
⊡ –I also 3	⌐ –R also 9	ⅅ –;	

Oliver Le Vasseur "La Buse"

Above: Cryptogram clues to La Buze's buried treasure and a portrait of the legendary pirate.

Perhaps he took his inspiration from the true story of John Plantain, a pirate who retired in Madagascar and built a fort. With a beautiful half-caste, Eleanora Brown, as his "queen", he became chief of the pirates on the island and sent ambassadors abroad to try and obtain recognition as "King of Madagascar". Only Peter the Great of Russia bothered to reply.

The pirates were at the mercy of the intermediaries, based on St. Mary's Island, who represented European and American trading houses prepared to buy pirate booty.

Arabs came from Zanzibar to do business, and a representative of Phillips Brothers, Adam Baldrige, from America. The surviving fragments of his accounts make fascinating reading.

For example, in October 1692 "arrived the *Nassau* seventy men. Captain Edward Coates to careen and share out some £500 per man". The game, though chancy, could be lucrative too.

Yet prices for loot were often low, for merchants had the advantage. Pirates needed coin, but more than that they had to have supplies: salt, beef, flour, sailcloth, wood, and hardware.

Humble items like these were often in such short supply that pirates sometimes improvised using part of their latest haul. One pirate ship once glided into harbour with its rigging adorned with tattered sails — made from silk.

When a pirate liquidated his assets, what did he do next? The real degenerates launched themselves into an orgy of drink, sex, and violence until their money ran out. Then they would look around for a ship to go out after more funds.

For every man who lost his life in swashbuckling adventure, drink, disease, or a knife in the back must have claimed three. Many a pirate who grew too old to be of any use sank into desperate poverty and starved to death.

The more far-sighted saved up their money and invested in small businesses, becoming

Above: Rusting anchor forms the cross over a forgotten pirate's grave.

traders or innkeepers. If lucky they were able to slip back into their home country without being noticed, and settle down to retirement. Periodically governments offered amnesties, and many also took advantage of this to obtain a pardon.

Some of the more flamboyant even became princes, buying themselves a Malagasy princess, and tribe to boot. One lucky man was spotted by a chieftainess and "recognized" as her long lost son. On her death, "Sam" became "King Samuel", and ruled over tribes in the area of Fort Dauphin.

The real heyday (and swan-song) of the pirates dates from the arrival of three of the least appealing; Edward England (an Irishman), George Taylor, and the Frenchman, Olivier le Vasseur, also known as "La Buze" — The Buzzard.

In 1715, le Vasseur had been given a ship by the French government to harry enemy shipping on the Spanish Main. This legalised piracy was called *privateering*, and le Vasseur drifted easily from this into piracy itself.

In 1720, Edward England arrived in the Indian Ocean aboard his ship the *Victory*. Amongst his crew was John Plantain, who decided to settle in Madagascar after dividing the spoils, but the rest were greedy for more plunder.

England was now commander of two ships. George Taylor was captain of the *Victory*, and Jasper Seager took the *Fancy*. They sailed for the Comoros, where Captain Mackra of the *Cassandra*, an East Indiaman, gave them a stiff fight off the island of Anjouan.

England's men were reinforced by le Vasseur and fourteen of his men, his own ship, the *Irish Queen*, having been "bulged and lost".

Mackra, due to the cowardice of a fellow captain aboard the *Greenwich*, lost his desperate battle, and with most of his officers dead, ran his ship aground. Though wounded in the head, he managed to escape. Incensed, the pirates offered a reward of $10,000 for Mackra, who, sure that he would be betrayed, gave himself up.

The pirates' mood had mellowed and they offered him safe conduct aboard. England felt generous, but Taylor, "a fellow of the most barbarous nature", was now in charge "by reason he was a greater brute than all the rest".

294

All England could do was suggest that liberal quantities of warm punch might "soften the beast", but "they were all in a tumult about making an end of him".

Amazingly, Mackra was saved by a pirate who had once served under him. This bizarre character, with a wooden leg, a "terrible pair of whiskers", and "stuck all over with pistols", threatened to shoot anyone who hurt his former captain.

The hot punch finally did its work, and Mackra left the ship in one piece, with the promise of a ship, the *Fancy*, and "129 bales of the Company's cloth".

On 3 September, 1720, the three pirates sailed with their joint crews of about 380 men, aboard the *Victory* and the *Cassandra*, and Mackra limped off towards Bombay a few days later.

Meanwhile the pirates, cruising off the island of Bourbon (Réunion), in April 1721, found a Portuguese ship, the *Vierege du Cap*, lying helpless in the port. It had been disabled in a storm, and most of its seventy guns thrown overboard to prevent it sinking. Taking it was a simple matter, and the pirates fell with glee on the riches aboard.

There were gold and silver bars, chests of gold coins, diamonds and pearls, and bolts of silk. Travelling with this treasure ship was the Portuguese Viceroy of Goa, the Conde de Ericeira, and the Archbishop of Goa, who had with him his fabulous regalia to which le Vasseur took a particular fancy.

Swaggering with delight at their good fortune, they invited themselves ashore to dine with the governor and his Portuguese guests. Legend has it that the pirates were so cheeky that they let the dignitaries suggest their own ransom — then paid it for them.

There was a share out, each crew member finding himself the richer by 5,000 golden guineas and forty-two diamonds. Le Vasseur opted for bullion and the regalia, which was not so readily convertible into money, but was of fabulous value.

Well-satisfied, they sailed away and into trouble. Mackra was a stubborn enemy, and he was out hunting for them with a squadron of warships.

They decided to lie low for a time off the coast of East Africa, and it is said that, for disloyalty to his fellow pirates, le Vasseur had all his booty confiscated . . . or did he? What became of that wonderful treasure? Did La Buze lose it there or bury it in the Seychelles?

At least one man was convinced that the wealth remained in the islands — and spent most of his life trying to find it, locked in what he felt was a mental struggle between himself and a wily pirate over a distance of 200 years.

Reginald Cruise-Wilkins, a Grenadier Guardsman invalided out of the army in 1941, settled for a time in Kenya where he led hunting safaris. After a bad bout of malaria in 1948, he went to Seychelles to recoup and moved into a bungalow on **Beau Vallon Bay**.

There he met a Norwegian whaling master who showed him a curious cryptogram which he had puzzled over for twenty years. Cruise-Wilkins copied it, studied it (often up to eighteen hours a day), and thought he had solved the mystery.

Meanwhile, he made other discoveries that went back to a time some years before his own interest was aroused. In 1923, he discovered, a dreadful storm lashed Mahé, and inspecting the damage afterwards, a Mr and Mrs Savy, who owned land at **Bel Ombre**, noticed strange carvings on the rocks by the beach. These crude etchings portrayed dogs, serpents, tortoises, horses, a young woman, two hearts, and a man's head. Later, beneath a carving of a large, staring eye, they discovered two coffins containing human remains.

Both skeletons had been wearing earrings when they died. Pirates? Close by was another skeleton, buried without a coffin. But there was no treasure.

The couple were approached by a local notary who had in his possession some papers which had once belonged to one Bernadin Nageon de L'Estang, also known as "Butin", which actually means "Loot": appropriate because L'Estang was a privateer.

He was also a man with a mission. The family were small Breton nobility, and it was Bernadin's dream to restore the family splendour. According to him, he was given these papers, which may have included documents belonging to La Buze himself, by the captain of the privateer, *Apollo*, on which he served. This is revealed in a letter he wrote to his brother when he was ill and felt "the fear of death".

As L'Estang tells the story, during a fight with a frigate off the coast of Hindustan, his captain was wounded, and after "first making sure that . . . (he) was a Freemason," confided to Butin "his secrets and papers for finding the sizable treasures buried in the Indian Ocean".

What exactly were these mysterious papers, and where did they come from?

La Buze, last seen off the African coast, reappears on St. Mary's Island in 1722, and spurns the offer of a pardon whose terms call for the surrender of his booty.

By 1730 he was working as a pilot in the Bay of Antongil, Madagascar. The story goes that after he was recognized by a French naval officer he decided to turn pirate again.

He fitted out his ship and set off, making such a nuisance of himself that the French navy were given orders to capture him at all costs. La Buze's luck finally ran out when he was captured by Captain L'Ermitte of the *Medusa*.

Some say that the entire crew were promptly hanged, but according to another version, le Vasseur was taken back to Bourbon to be hanged publicly as an example — on 17 July, 1730. On the scaffold he is said to have tossed a scrap of paper to the crowd with the words: "My treasure to he who can understand."

If indeed it ever existed, this original map, or cryptogram, must have vanished, but perhaps a copy did find its way into the hands of L'Estang's captain.

There are now eight documents in the archives of Mauritius, Seychelles, and France, associated with the story of La Buze and Butin.

The notary who contacted the Savys had two letters from the corsair, his will, two cryptograms, and a paper with four magical or astronomical characters inscribed on it. One of the cryptograms was encoded using an old Royal Arch Masons and Rosicrucian method.

The letters A to R are written in a grid. Each letter is represented by the part of the grid in which it appears. There are two letters in each box, so the first letter is signified by a dot. The

remaining letters — S to Z — are shown inside a cross and represented using the same method.

Thus deciphered, one of these intriguing documents begins "Apre; mey une paire de pyon tireskit deux coeurs qeseaj tete cherlaf une kort fil winshient ecu preney une culliere demi . . . "

Butin's letters, and his will, are more straightforward but cannot fail to captivate an imaginative reader. In a letter to his nephew Justin, written in May 1800, he urges him to follow his instructions and carry out his last wishes, going on to describe the burial place of one of his treasure caches on Mauritius.

"I have already removed several treasures," he tells him, "only four remain, buried in the same manner by the same pirates." He mentions a second treasure, also on Mauritius, and a third on Rodrigues.

In his will he tells how his ship foundered near Vacoa on Mauritius, and going upstream he "deposited in a cave the valuables . . . and there marked BN, my name".

In his last letter to his brother, he states that there are three treasures, the "one buried on my beloved Île de France (Mauritius) is sizable . . . three iron casks and large jars full of minted doubloons and bullion worth 30 million, and a casket crammed with diamonds".

So far no treasure has been found on Mauritius, but a cache was unearthed on the island of Pemba, close to Zanzibar, in 1966. Carved on a rock nearby were the initials BN.

Some of the treasures were undoubtedly those he had amassed himself, but did the documents given to him tell of the whereabouts of le Vasseur's treasure, and is one of these caches located somewhere on Mahé?

These islands were undoubtedly known to the pirates. They were uninhabited and far from the main shipping routes. There was water, fish and tortoise meat, timber for repairs, and quiet bays where a ship could be taken out of the water and careened or recaulked.

It was a corner of the world where they could hope for some privacy and security —

Opposite: Excavations at Bel Ombre continue in the search for buried pirate treasure said to be worth £100 million.

a good place to bury treasure.

Almost from the first occupation of the islands, there has been an **Anse Forbans** (Pirates' Bay) and a **Côte D'Or**, named for reasons long forgotten by the first settlers from Mauritius, and perhaps they had good reason to name these coves so.

Most Seychellois are convinced that several local families have established themselves secretly through lucky finds of pirate gold, though there is little, if any, tangible evidence.

There are some strange ruins on **Frégate**, and in 1911, 107 silver coins, a few forks and spoons, two shoebuckles, and a bosun's whistle were found on **Astove Island**.

A nineteenth-century visitor to Frégate left an intriguing account of that island's strange ruins. It was believed Frégate was used as a lookout by the pirates and, in August 1838, the visitor was shown "a large chest full of china from different countries, pikes from Holland, knives, boarding hatchets, broadswords, Spanish piastres . . . traces of buildings . . . ", where in 1812 they found "a cross belt and epaulette in gold".

Nearby on a rock was an inscription which "seemed to have been cut into the stone by means of a chisel".

Elsewhere on the island they found cannonballs, a lead-lined well 4.5 metres (15 feet) deep, a large teak mast which rested on a platform, the ruins of a forge, and a lead-lined drain which ran down from a nearby spring towards the remains of a settlement.

On a rise were "three tombs made of coral on which had been left copper sword hilts; a lot of bones strewn about".

The local story is that the pirates fled, fearing their hideaway had been discovered. They had amassed an enormous treasure, but because they dreaded being seized during their flight they buried some of it on the islands.

What they feared came to pass. They were taken and hanged, with the exception of one who was spared for his youth. On his eventual death, he gave a note to his friend, which revealed the location of the treasure.

At least one person who saw it was "left in no doubt of its authenticity . . . Searches made in the spots indicated have not met with success, but they often find Spanish piastres

and other coins called crusados which the sea washes up on the beach . . . "

No trace of the note, and the magnificent cross of the Archbishop of Goa has come to light — yet. In the 1960s, when Cruise-Wilkins began his search for le Vasseur's treasure in earnest, he estimated its value at £100 million.

Convinced that his study of the cryptogram and the L'Estang papers had given him the necessary clues, he returned to Nairobi to raise financial backing. By 1967 at least £10,000 of his own funds, and £24,000 from the backers, had been spent.

But the Seychelles authorities took him seriously enough to provide labourers and the site at Bel Ombre was fenced off. Bearings were taken from the marks the Savys had discovered, and six were found to intercept.

As the digging began, the first exciting discovery was made — a roughly built staircase, which was mentioned in the documents, and seemed to lead up towards the huge sheet of granite glacis which is so striking a feature of the hills overlooking Bel Ombre.

There were crude carvings on the walls of the staircase. But — whether by act of man or nature — the entrance to the underground cavern that Cruise-Wilkins believed housed the treasure was blocked.

Coming to the conclusion that le Vasseur was a more subtle opponent than he had originally thought, Cruise-Wilkins decided that the pirate had set out an elaborate game "for his own amusement and for the befuddlement of those he intended to seek the treasure. There could be no easy access . . . le Vasseur did not intend it".

He became convinced that the "game" was based on Greek legend and astronomy, played out over a "board" covering twenty-four hectares (60 acres). It seemed that anyone who wanted the treasure of La Buze had to work for it; that, in fact, they must perform the Twelve Labours of Hercules.

To support the theory, another carving was discovered, this time of a figure which seemed to represent Andromeda, chained to the Ethiopian coast waiting to be seized by the sea monster.

The beach was honeycombed with man-made tunnels in which other strange finds were made, including three round stones (the Golden Apples?), a piece of willow-pattern pottery (mentioned in the documents), the blade of a sword (the scimitar of Perseus?), sticks driven vertically into the ground (the dragon's teeth planted by Jason?), and near an underground stream, a coin, dating from le Vasseur's time (payment to Charon for crossing the Styx?).

Totally convinced that he was playing le Vasseur's game, piece by piece Cruise-Wilkins removed 700 tonnes of rock from a ledge to reveal significant carvings, diverted an underground stream (killing the water snake, Hydra), and, as the trail seemed to lead him below sea level, installed expensive pumping equipment and built sea walls to hold back the tide.

These defences, now somewhat forlorn, can still be seen at Bel Ombre. It was time for the descent into the underworld, an underground cavern below sea level, covered by a huge stone slab.

The cavern could only be approached from the north, all other approaches were booby-trapped. A dam would have to be built, and they would need more funding. "Le Vasseur has led me almost in a complete circle, but I believe that at last I have him."

Cruise-Wilkins died, still searching, still believing. In recent years his family has taken up the challenge again. But are these the dreams of an eccentric?

It is difficult to dismiss entirely all Cruise-Wilkins' discoveries, which included a flintlock pistol, pieces of a seventeenth-century wine jar, the trigger-guard of a musket, and a coin from the time of Charles I.

Though hardly the casks crammed with diamonds of which Butin wrote, they are in their own way equally exciting.

How did these oddities find their way into these tunnels? Is La Buze's treasure still out there, waiting to be discovered?

For most visitors to these islands, le Vasseur has certainly left at least one treasure there — the mystery and romance of a legend.

And an enigma yet to be solved for those who still dream of crusados and caskets crammed with diamonds.

Collected the World Over

Seychelles stamps are among the most beautiful in the world — not surprising, considering it boasts unique flora and fauna, some of the finest beaches anywhere, and a variety of exotic subjects.

Even so, a great deal of thought, inspired design, and fine detail is needed to produce such an extremely high standard of theme and finished work.

As more and more tourists take home a piece of Seychelles captured on a set of stamps, philately has become a substantial foreign exchange earner.

However, no matter how well-designed or colourful the subject, a stamp's real beauty to the philatelist lies in its value. But in recent years, the value of Seychelles stamps has failed to appreciate as rapidly as anticipated. All this should soon change.

In January 1990, the Seychelles Post Office scrapped the old system of selling stamp issues, irrespective of demand, until supplies were sold out. Stamps, blocks — even first-day covers — were available several years after their date of issue at face value. No more.

Now all unsold commemorative issues are withdrawn from the normal sales counters three months after their issue and from the philatelic bureau at **Victoria Post Office** six months after their issue. The remainders are destroyed.

No doubt this has enhanced Seychelles' reputation as producers of stamps of both beauty and value.

Post Office history

Seychelles had a post office long before it issued its own stamps. It opened in Victoria on 11 December, 1861, when Seychelles was a dependency of Mauritius and Mauritian stamps were used for almost three decades.

These first stamps, however, were cancelled by a postmark reading "B64" — and any stamps so marked, especially complete covers, are now exceptionally valuable.

To mark the centenary of the Seychelles post office, a replica of this rare and valuable cancellation was reproduced. These stamps were considered by many to be the most

Above: Some of Seychelles' old, rare, and treasured stamps.

attractive Seychelles had produced up to that time. Indeed, the set was declared the masterpiece of a London philatelic exhibition.

Almost exactly fifty years to the day after Britain's Penny Black became the world's first adhesive postage stamp, Seychelles issued its first stamps on 5 April, 1890 — a set of eight ranging in value from two to sixteen cents and now worth considerably more than their face value.

At this time the population was tiny and the irregular mail service, linked to the calls of ships at this distant outpost, limited. In fact, internal mail was virtually non-existent.

But this gave Seychelles stamps an exotic curiosity as well as a high value — a value that was enhanced by certain die changes, surcharges, overprints, and value changes.

This also meant that stamp issues were not on sale long before being withdrawn — sometimes only a few months elapsed — which in turn increased their value. Such stamps are extremely valuable today.

New stamps appeared in the colonies of Great Britain from 1 January, 1902, with the death of Queen Victoria, and the accession to the throne of King Edward VII — but they did not reach Seychelles until June 1903.

For the first time, the circular background depicting the monarch was in full colour, not line-shaded. Eleven values were issued, but one month later, the three-cent stamp was exhausted. Its popularity remained a mystery.

Other values — fifteen cents, eighteen cents, and forty-five cents — were overprinted. One theory was that speculators who knew the value of rare stamps from far-flung Seychelles bought up the supply to force an overprint.

King Edward VII died at Buckingham Palace on 6 May, 1910, but it was another two years before the King George V issue reached Seychelles.

The most fascinating issue of the first half of this century was the Silver Jubilee set of 1935. Some stamps depicted an extra flagstaff on Windsor Castle, the royal residence that illustrated all four values in the series, and this aberrant is now extremely valuable.

One year later, King George V was dead. King Edward VIII's short reign, prior to his abdication, was never commemorated in Seychelles. But the first King George VI issue of three Seychelles stamps sold in huge numbers to local speculators, encouraged by the phenomenal rise in value of the Silver Jubilee issue.

So much money was raised, in fact, that the government was able to carry out some reclamation work in the centre of Victoria. The site was named **Coronation Field.** The speculators were not so fortunate. In later years many had to sell for little or no profit.

The following year, 1938, saw Seychelles' first pictorial issue — a set of fourteen stamps illustrating aspects of Seychelles life: the *pirogue*, the giant land tortoise, and the *coco de mer*.

Above: Seychelles' special issues are avidly sought by stamp collectors all around the world.

In 1949, King George VI remarked light-heartedly that he was no longer a "callow youth" and suggested it was high time to redraw his portrait on stamp issues.

But the new portrait which appeared on Seychelles' stamps did not go on sale until after his death three years later. Speculators rushed to acquire this issue — confident that it would be on sale for an extremely limited time.

One collector, however, still burnt his fingers to the tune of 600 rupees, a tidy sum in those days. He posted sixty ten-rupee stamps to himself, then put the stamps in water to remove them from the envelopes.

Unfortunately for him, unlike earlier issues, these were not impervious to water. An unusual kind of paper had been used on this occasion — and the colour peeled off in strips.

In 1956, four years after the accession of Queen Elizabeth II, Seychelles issued the first ever commemorative stamp edition specific to Seychelles. It showed the **Possession Stone** which then stood in the grounds of State House (it was moved to the museum next to the Post Office in Victoria in 1964).

Modern Seychelles stamps

Since 1956, almost all Seychelles stamps have been unique to Seychelles, with the emphasis on both national and international anniversaries. Naturally, with such a rich and diversified nature, wildlife has been a central theme.

During the 1980s, special issues featured the *coco de mer*, Seychelles fruit bat, fairy tern, Seychelles scops owl, and Seychelles kestrel — each stamp within a set illustrating different aspects of the species it featured. Many other birds, plants, and insects have also been featured.

One attractive way to buy these sets is as commemorative blocks — for example one 1989 set depicted four of Seychelles' unique endemic birds.

Each illustrated a bird and the island with which it is associated — the **black parrot** of **Praslin**, the **sooty tern** of **Bird**, the **magpie robin** of **Frégate**, and the **roseate tern** of **Aride**. The whole set, purchased as a block, was encased by a border illustrating tropical shores and a blue sky filled with terns.

Like Seychelles, **Zil Elwannyen Sesel** — the Outer Isles — has also had some outstanding and beautiful wildlife issues.

The first was a set of five two-rupee stamps, each showing a different type of coral, the whole set joining together to illustrate a coral garden. A similar idea was used for coral fishes the next year. And in 1987, three, three-rupee stamps — illustrating the **Vallée**

301

de Mai, from a painting by local artist Christine Harter — were issued.

It seems a pity to break up such sets for the mundane purpose of posting a letter.

In 1988 a slightly different style was used when two pairs of stamps were issued show-ing the breeding aspects of green turtles. Joined in a vertical format, the two-rupee stamp showed a beach scene with the lower stamp illustrating a nesting turtle, the upper stamp a turtle emerging from the sea.

The three-rupee pair has a similar background, with baby turtles above digging their way out of the nest, and below a beach covered with other hatchlings heading for the sea.

One 1983 block, though not forming a continuous scene, is especially attractive. It illustrates four pictures of Seychelles flora drawn and painted a century before by Marianne North. Where else could you buy four such masterpieces for less than twelve rupees?

Happy anniversaries

Seychelles is an independent state, but it maintains close ties with Britain and the Commonwealth. Royal events are popular commemorative subjects and slightly different sets are usually produced by both Seychelles and *Zil Elwannyen Sesel* — Seychelles Outer Islands — to commemorate the same event.

Christmas, with a tropical flavour, is also commemorated. But no snow or robins or pieces of holly — instead, in 1989 Santa pulled a *pirogue* of presents up on Beau Vallon beach, and a stocking-shaped pitcher plant spilt over with presents.

The Olympics have always been marked by stamp issues; even the 1988 games — at which Seychelles was not represented.

Local events, especially political ones, are featured. Even the visit of notable persons is cause for a special issue — the 1986 visit of Rudolf Nureyev to perform in the ballet *Giselle*, and the Pope's visit, were commemo-rated by stamp issues and souvenir blocks.

Zil Elwannyen Sesel

From June 1980, stamps have been issued for use in the outer islands of Seychelles — **Aldabra Group**, **Coétivy**, **Farquhar Group**, and **Amirantes**. The first issue was the same as the definitives used for Seychelles, but it was inscribed *Zil Eloigne Sesel*.

The same year the first commemorative one-rupee issue featured *Cinq Juin*, the vessel that plies between Mahé and the outer islands, also used as a travelling post office.

One unusual feature of the outer islands' stamps has been how three different ways of spelling the Creole word for "outer" were used in a period of five years. The change reflects the rapid evolution of the Creole language in the first half of the 1980s — its move away from French spellings to a purely phonetic written form. In 1980, *"Eloigne"* (identical to the French word) was used. Two years later it became semi-phonetic — *"Elwagne"* — and purely phonetic — *"Elwannyen"* — in 1985.

In 1984, a special set commemorated the reopening of the **Aldabra Post Office**, when collectors from all over the world rushed to obtain first day covers bearing the postmark of one of the world's smallest, most remote post offices.

Seychelles life and culture

Big game fishing, tourism, water sports, and other aspects of island life have all been featured on Seychelles stamps. One novel 1989 four-stamp issue featured Creole cooking — each stamp showed a different local dish.

When purchased as a block, the four stamps joined together to form a typical Seychelles buffet, laid out on an hibiscus-decorated table, with a beach scene as the backdrop. To cap it all, the souvenir block even incorporated the recipe for each dish.

How to collect Seychelles stamps

Standing order forms for Seychelles and *Zil Elwannyen Sesel* can be obtained from **Seychelles Philatelic Bureau**, **Premier Building**, **Victoria**, **Seychelles**.

Orders can be placed for all stamp issues, souvenir blocks, and first day covers but a deposit is needed to cover the costs of future issues.

Opposite: *Sega* dancer performs in a whirl of colour.

Overleaf: An afternoon walk in paradise.

PART FOUR: BUSINESS SEYCHELLES

The Economy

The economy of Seychelles has been built firmly on the two "Ts": tourism and tuna. Directly, tourism alone provides about half of all foreign exchange receipts. The second-largest source of income, airlines and shipping, again includes a substantial element of tourism.

The tuna industry has witnessed a spectacular growth in recent years. Canned tuna exports, which began in 1987, now account for well over half of all physical exports. Physical exports, however, still only account for about eight per cent of foreign exchange.

Indirect earnings from the tuna industry through shipping revenues and re-export of petroleum products (primarily sales to tuna fishing vessels) are also extremely important.

Despite the severe limitations of a small island economy, Seychelles has achieved remarkable progress. Gross Domestic Product — GDP — per capita of more than US$2,600 places the nation among middle income countries.

The literacy rate is about seventy-five per cent, and there is close to full employment. Inflation has remained low and growth has been moderately good.

Seychellois society is egalitarian, based on education for all, the objective being an overall development of human resources to correspond with the country's needs. Elementary education from the age of six to twelve is free and Creole, the student's mother tongue, is taught as a language in school.

The Seychelles Polytechnic at Mahé deals with the training of technicians and specialized personnel with courses in line with national development and the working market's requirements.

The layout is extremely practical and productive, and the courses range from agriculture to building, to health, to seafaring studies.

But a population growth of 1.7 per cent, the high level of public debt servicing, and the degree of bureaucratic central control remain causes for concern.

In recent years, however, there has been a willingness on the part of the government to reduce the role of the state and encourage private sector consultation and investment.

In January 1989, a package of private sector incentives came into effect that put emphasis on the modernisation of the productive sector and the encouragement of management training.

The National Workers' Union has been asked to adapt to new work practices, and consultation at all levels with the Seychelles Federation of Employers' Associations has been actively encouraged. All these indicate a change in thinking and the government's concern to create a more vibrant mixed economy.

Opportunities

Small islands in mid-ocean present special difficulties for investors. Inevitably, Seychelles faces severe constraints to its economic development. In presenting the Seychelles Industrial Development Policy 1989-93, the Minister for National Development listed these constraints as:

• Limited natural resources.

• A small local market.

• Relatively high production costs.

• A strong and stable currency, relative to countries with low labour wages whose currencies face constant devaluation.

• Lack of sufficient qualified and experienced personnel at top and middle management levels.

• Lack of industrial infrastructure.

While acknowledging the severity of these constraints, the government also expressed its conviction that opportunities have yet to be fully explored. In particular, industries which exploit the natural resources of Seychelles, and which substitute imports or increase exports, are most welcome.

Agriculture

Despite a tropical climate, with high rainfall and long hours of sunshine, agriculture in Seychelles is limited by a shortage of land, especially flat land, and competition with building projects for the best sites.

In 1988, the CIF value of food and animal imports was twice as great as the value of all exports. As far as possible the Seychelles Marketing Board — SMB — has attempted to use local products.

Initially, a government-imposed monopoly and strict price control proved to be counter-productive, but to its credit the government was quick to acknowledge this, relax controls, and permit market forces to operate once again.

As recently as 1981 Seychelles' main export was copra. Two-thirds of all exports by value were copra. This fell to less than four per cent by value in 1988.

Similarly, volume dropped dramatically during the same period from more than 3,000 metric tonnes to little more than 1,000. Seychelles' copra is high quality, but the fall in world prices coupled with high local labour costs have rendered the importance of this crop almost negligible.

Export of cinnamon bark, another traditional crop since the early days of settlement, also fell during the same period. Both cinnamon and copra exports are controlled exclusively by SMB.

In March 1990, however, the Minister for Agriculture and Fisheries announced that the government welcomed an enhanced role for the private sector in the processing and export of coconut and cinnamon produce.

Government assistance would include infrastructure, manpower training, credit facilities, and possibly market intelligence.

Opportunities also exist for the industrialisation of artisan fishing. Canned tuna rose dramatically in importance following the establishment of a joint French–Seychelles tuna cannery which began exporting in 1987. This could possibly be a model for future joint ventures.

SMB also manufactures an excellent range of smoked fish, sausages, and other animal and fish products. One of the most recent projects has been to rear tiger prawns (*Penaeus monodon*) for both local and export markets from a prawn farm on Coétivy Island.

The project was financed on purely commercial terms, including a loan of US$3.5 million from a Swedish bank.

It is seen as a measure of the government's determination to place all new projects on solid financial foundations. Similar projects on other outer islands will also be considered once the Coétivy project is fully operational.

Another recent SMB project has been the establishment of an orchid farm at Barbarons Estate on the west coast of Mahé.

Both the prawn farm and orchid farm projects have been based on a sound commercial philosophy, together with a high degree of foreign expertise, especially in the initial stages, reflecting government determination to obtain the best possible sources to ensure commercial success.

The government has identified the following opportunities as areas for new developments:

• Higher value products in the cinnamon and coconut industries.

• Boat construction for local and export markets based on local timber.

• Exploitation of marine algae.

• Vinegar production from coconut sap.

• Increased use of medicinal plants, honey, pickles and chutneys, snacks based on local products, biscuits, pastas and noodles, and boiled sweets.

• Wood veneers from local timbers.

Manufacturing

Nowhere are the difficulties facing the constraints of a small island economy more apparent than in manufacturing, which so often depends on economies of scale, a large labour force, mass production, and large local markets.

Nevertheless, opportunities for manufacturing do exist with an emphasis on high value products and natural resources.

The government wishes to promote production of:

- Polished granite for export.

- Sanitary ware from local resources.

- Roofing tiles, corrugated sheets, nails, and crown corks.

- Paper packaging.

- Car mufflers and batteries.

The government will also encourage any investor who wishes to engage in high value export products with a significant added local value.

In an age where environmental concerns are of increasing importance, opportunities may also exist for recycling imported manufactured materials such as paper, glass, and metals.

Although the local market is limited, the high cost of imports and government determination to encourage local enterprises merit serious attention to such projects.

Tourism

Tourism is by far and away Seychelles' largest source of foreign exchange. Today, tourist arrivals are rapidly approaching 100,000 a year.

This may not be a great number compared to other countries, but it is greater than the local population, and there is a high emphasis on the promotion of Seychelles as a fairly exclusive destination, rather than simply another cheap package deal.

There are only three tour operators in Seychelles and the government has indicated that no new entrants will be allowed.

Opportunities do exist, however, in the tourism sector in areas which are not subject to the same limitation of competition. These may include hotel projects, and projects to increase the availability of marine-related tourist facilities.

Investment

Seychelles today has emerged from a period of ideologically-bound doctrines to pursue a mixed development strategy and a strengthened partnership between the public and private sectors.

There are no restrictions on share ownership and companies range from being 100 per cent Government-owned to being 100 per cent privately-owned, with joint ventures also common.

As a general rule, however, the public sector will be the majority shareholder in investments involving the exploitation of natural resources. The public sector may also seek a partnership in industrial investments exceeding one million rupees.

Private Sector

The private sector plays a vital role in the Seychelles economy. Thirty-two per cent of all formal employment is private. The Government has recently introduced fiscal and monetary incentives to broaden this role still further.

In the future, ventures will be highly selective and the size of the Seychelles economy is small enough to allow examination of each venture on its own merits.

Foreign Investment

The Government welcomes foreign investment, and offers various incentives and guarantees. However, a distinction is made between Seychellois and non-Seychellois investors and companies.

A Seychellois investor has Seychelles citizenship and resides in Seychelles. A company is considered a Seychellois investor if it is registered locally, managed and controlled locally, and at least fifty-one per cent of its shares are held by Seychelles' citizens and residents.

The absence of foreign exchange controls is a positive factor in favour of foreign investment. The Government has repeatedly committed itself to this policy.

An investment code is currently being considered to guide the potential investor through the set up and implementation of their proposals.

Incentives

Investment Priorities

Seychelles Industrial Development policy has five main objectives:

• Employment creation.

• Better utilization of local resources.

• Consolidation of existing manufacturing industries.

• Consolidation of import-substitution and export-oriented industries.

• Promotion of foreign exchange earnings.

Trades Tax Exemption

In Seychelles, customs duty is replaced by trades tax. From January 1989, for a period of five years, capital equipment for the industrial sector was free of trades tax for new ventures except for general vehicles and electricity generating equipment.

Where an existing factory is importing equipment to increase its capacity to manufacture products already produced by another company, or to replace existing equipment, trades tax shall be ten per cent on CIF.

Special consideration may be given, on request, to waive it completely.

Trades tax on imported raw and intermediate materials (except petroleum products), and parts for assembly purposes shall be nil. For petroleum products the prevailing rate applies, except for export-oriented industries.

Trades tax on exports shall be nil, while goods for the local market shall be assessed on a case by case basis.

The prevailing trades tax rate shall apply to spare parts, however, but requests for a concession may be made through the Industry Division to the Ministry of Finance. Packing materials for export-oriented products may also be exempted.

Concessions may be given on construction materials and equipment for new projects. Replacements and renovations will not normally receive concessions but major additions to existing establishments will be considered if these create their own profit centre, providing additional income and employment.

Specialised machinery and equipment for agricultural development may be exempted but spares will bear the normal rate.

Protection of Industry

The Government favours the protection of local industry and will take measures to achieve this, such as import control. Steps may be taken to ensure quality is at least as high as imported materials.

As a rule, import-substitution industries based on imported materials will not be encouraged if the foreign exchange cost of local production exceeds the cost of imports. Consideration may be given, however, to such projects if there is a significant employment creation factor.

Capital Considerations

All new investments are required to have a minimum share capital equal to at least thirty per cent of the capital investment and a percentage of working capital not exceeding thirty per cent, but subject to negotiation.

These requirements are considered necessary to provide a proper gearing ratio and to ensure the commitment and seriousness of the investor.

Capital investment may be in cash or kind. If in kind (land, buildings, technology), the value will be determined by negotiation between the Government and the investor. Second-hand equipment or buildings will generally be based on depreciated replacement cost.

Working capital shall also be valued by negotiation together with the percentage share of working capital to be contributed as equity by the investor.

Investors may raise share capital by borrowing locally up to a value equal to the product of total share capital and the percentage of shares owned by resident citizens of Seychelles. The balance must be raised externally.

All investors, having paid up share capital, may borrow locally for investment and working capital purposes. This does not apply to non-Seychellois investors in projects in which resident citizens hold less than fifty per cent of the shares and who are engaged in export-oriented industries based on imported raw materials. Such investors must borrow externally.

The interest on borrowing from banks is tax deductible, whereas interest on borrowing from shareholders is not.

Where funds are raised overseas, the rate of interest, conditions, and repayment terms must receive Government approval before project implementation.

Project Appraisal and Approval Procedures

All new industrial developments or rehabilitation and modernisation of existing ones, must be submitted to the Industry Division for investment appraisal.

Appraisal forms are available on request. If the Industry Division finds it relevant to Seychelles the project will be submitted to the Project Appraisal Committee — PAC — for consideration.

If rejected by the Industry Division, the applicant may appeal to the President's Office for a final decision on whether or not it should proceed to the PAC.

If approved by the PAC, it will be submitted to the Council of Ministers. If approved, the applicant will submit an application to the Seychelles' Licensing Authority for a licence.

All agreements relating to transfers of technology require government approval. Where the value of technology produced from overseas exceeds 500,000 rupees, unless already owned by the investor, multiple quotes must be obtained.

In considering whether to grant approval to a project, the government will be guided by the following criteria:

• Technological viability.

• Financial viability.

• Socio-economic viability when assessing its impact on balance of payments, Government revenue, local value added, distribution of value added, employment creation, the environment, and the contribution to economic self-reliance.

Business Tax

A concessionary flat rate of fifteen per cent Business Tax (i.e. tax on profits) shall apply to export-oriented industries based on imported raw materials.

Depreciation Allowances

Concessionary rates shall apply to new equipment; forty per cent for the year expenditure is incurred and twenty per cent for each of the next four years.

Losses Carried Forward

Losses may be carried forward for seven years.

Withholding Tax

There shall be no withholding tax on dividends paid to Seychellois investors or amounts distributed in a partnership. For non-Seychellois investors, withholding tax on dividends shall be nil for the first ten years, and thereafter at the prevailing rate.

Gainful Occupation Fees

Gainful Occupation Permit — GOP — fees (currently 10,000 rupees a year for all non-Seychellois) shall be waived for the following:

• Persons carrying out studies if such services cannot be obtained locally.

• For import-substitution industries based on imported raw and intermediate materials there will be no fees for managerial and technical personnel, not available locally, for a period of three years following the arrival of the person in the country after which the prevailing rate will apply, unless there is a case for prolonging the waiver period.

• For export-oriented industries based on imported raw materials there will be a waiver of fees for technical and managerial staff not available locally for a period of eight years after which the prevailing rates will apply.

• For industries based on the country's natural resources there shall be a waiver of fee for technical and managerial personnel for a period of five years after which the prevailing rate will apply. However, in all cases a permit will still have to be applied for and obtained.

Getting Started

Most business enterprises in Seychelles are limited liability companies. This includes a number of Government parastatals, wholly or partly owned by Government investment institutions or representatives.

Many smaller companies are proprietary companies, which have no more than fifty members (excluding employees other than directors), all directors and shareholders are the members of the company, the company has no preference shares, at least three-quarters of the shares are held by the directors, (if not, the company has less than twenty members), no member or director is a corporation, and there is no holding company.

Company Registration

Any two or more persons may form a company with limited liability by subscribing their names to a Memorandum of Association. The memorandum must be in English and state the name of the company with "Limited" as the last word, and, if applicable, "Proprietary" as the penultimate word.

The memorandum lays out the objects of the company and states that the registered office shall be in Seychelles and the liability of members is limited.

It may not state that the company may pursue any objects the directors or members shall think fit, or include a provision that different parts of a clause relating to objects shall be construed independently (as if each part stated the sole objects of the company), or any objects not stated with reasonable certainty. It must state full share details, and be signed by each shareholder in the presence of at least one witness.

The Articles of Association may also be produced. These must be printed in English, divided into consecutive numbered paragraphs, and be signed by each subscriber of the memorandum in the presence of at least one witness. If articles are not registered, the articles shall be deemed to be as laid out in the Companies Ordinance.

The memorandum and articles must be delivered to the Registrar of Companies, Room 8, First Floor, Kingsgate House, Victoria, for registration.

The Registrar shall ensure these comply with the Ordinance, that the objects are lawful, and the name to be registered is not undesirable. If the Registrar is not satisfied on any of these points, he shall inform the person who presented the memorandum within one month, giving reasons.

An appeal may be made within one month by any aggrieved person, the decision of the court being final. On registration, the Registrar issues a Certificate of Incorporation and the company becomes a legal entity.

Every company must make an annual return to the Registrar within forty-two days of the annual general meeting. The return must contain details of shares, shareholders, directors, and the company secretary as specified in the Companies Ordinance.

A certificate signed by a director and the company secretary confirming the accounts submitted with the return are true copies and copies of the auditors and directors reports must all be annexed to the annual return.

Restrictions on Foreign Ownership

No foreign investor may purchase immovable property, nor purchase shares in any company with an interest in immovable property, without sanction from the Seychelles Government. No foreigner may rent immovable property without sanction from the Government.

Trade Licensing

A licence from the Seychelles Licensing Authority — SLA — is required for almost any activity, and both a licence fee and a processing fee are payable at the time of application. Individuals or companies contemplating a new activity should complete an assurance form and pay a fee of 200 rupees.

The SLA will consider whether to accept the application or not, and notify the applicant. In the event it is rejected, the applicant has the right to appeal directly to the Minister of Finance for a final decision.

Import and Export Procedures

Permits are required for all imports by companies. Individuals have fewer restrictions, but will still require permits for certain items, including computer equipment and motor vehicles. Permits are also required for all exports.

Both import and export permits are issued by the Seychelles Marketing Board.

Price Controls

Retail and wholesale mark-ups are set by the Government for almost all items except certain locally produced items.

Work Permits

All foreigners working in Seychelles must possess a Gainful Occupation Permit prior to arrival in Seychelles. These must be requested a minimum of ten weeks prior to the date the permit is required.

A one-year permit costs 10,000 rupees plus a non-refundable processing fee of 600 rupees. Generally it will not be possible to obtain permits for skills deemed to be readily available amongst Seychellois. In addition, the Immigration Division will generally require a security bond from the employer to cover the cost of a return air ticket and a contract of employment attested by the Labour Commissioner in quadruplicate.

Finance

The commercial banks operating in Seychelles are Barclays Bank, Bank of Credit and Commerce, Banque Francaise Commerciale, Habib Bank Ltd, and Standard Chartered Bank of Africa.

All have their head offices in Victoria. Barclays has two offices in Victoria and others at Beau Vallon; Baie St. Anne, Praslin, Grande Anse, Praslin; and La Digue.

Banque Francaise has an office at Anse Royale. Barclays and Bank of Credit and Commerce have airport bureau open for all international flights.

The Development Bank of Seychelles is a major force in investment financing in Seychelles. It finances investment projects at concessionary rates of interest. However, the bank has to discriminate between foreign-owned and local firms and individuals.

Taxation

Business Tax

Under the Business Tax Act 1987, tax is levied on the assessable income of a business de-rived or deemed to be derived in Seychelles. Generally speaking, all expenses incurred in producing assessable income are allowable deductions, except those of a capital, private, or domestic nature.

Emoluments, royalties, and interest payable will only be allowable provided contributions have been paid under the Business Tax and Social Security Act of 1987.

Repairs are only allowable if the item under repair is used to produce assessable income and the repairs were occasioned by their use in carrying on the business. Bad debts are allowable only if the Commissioner of Taxes is satisfied every effort has been made to recover such debts.

Tax losses may be carried forward for up to seven years.

Every company carrying on a business in Seychelles must appoint a Public Officer within three months of commencement of business, to be responsible for taxation matters.

Withholding Tax

Withholding Tax is payable at fifteen per cent on the following payments to nonresidents: dividends, royalties, partnership profits, and income from trust estates.

In addition it is payable at the same rate on interest payments, except those from a bank or other lending institution. It should be noted the definition of royalties is a wide one, and may include professional fees paid by a resident to a nonresident.

Trades Tax

Trades Tax replaces customs duty and is generally levied on all imports into Seychelles, at the point of importation. In addition, goods manufactured and services provided in Seychelles are liable to trades tax.

Tax on local goods and services is payable within fifteen days of the end of the month in which it became liable. A penalty of ten per cent on late payments and additional tax is payable at twenty two per cent a year. The Commissioner of Taxes may remit the penalty or additional tax if he finds sufficient reason.

More details regarding liability, assessment, and other details are contained in the Trades Tax Regulations, 1987.

Annual Returns

All businesses must furnish the Commissioner of Taxes with a return of income by 31 March, following the tax year for which the return is made.

Collection of Tax

For existing businesses, taxation is provisionally assessed at the beginning of each tax year. The taxpayer may apply once in each tax year for a variation of the provisional assessment but the Commissioner may impose a penalty of twenty per cent of the tax avoided if the eventual assessment proves to be higher than the variation requested.

For new businesses, an estimate of net income for the first year of trading must be produced to the Commissioner of Taxes within fourteen days of commencement of business. The Commissioner will then issue a provisional assessment.

Social Security

There is no income tax in Seychelles. This is replaced by a system of social security levied on salaries and benefits. A flat rate contribution of five per cent payable by employees, while the employer pays contributions on the following scale:

First 1,000 rupees	10 per cent
Second 1,000 rupees	20 per cent
Third 1,000 rupees	40 per cent
Fourth 1,000 rupees	60 per cent
Over 4,000 rupees	80 per cent

Employers are responsible for the payment of monthly contributions fifteen days after the end of each month.

Non-monetary benefits received by an employee are subject to Social Security contributions payable at six-month intervals. Contributions are payable within fifteen days at the end of each six months. Non-monetary benefits are:

• Company car, assessable either on actual private usage at 3.30 rupees a mile or at ten per cent of the retail value of a new car, currently set at 90,000 rupees.

• Airline tickets, assessable on the lowest economy fare advertised by Air Seychelles.

• Accommodation, assessed at 2,500 rupees a month for a house of at least two bedrooms, or 2,000 rupees for a flat, maisonette, one-bedroom house, or other property.

• In-house benefits over and above 1,200 rupees a year, (e.g., for goods and services provided free or below cost by an employer).

• Living expenses, such as electricity and water.

• Entertainment allowances in excess of 400 rupees, unless supported by receipts.

• Bonuses and lump sums.

In general, all salaries and benefits relating to the employment of expatriates are subject to Social Security contributions. Expatriates employed as part of a foreign aid agreement are not subject to Social Security contributions on the portion of their contract paid by the foreign aid agency.

PART FIVE: FACTS AT YOUR FINGERTIPS

Visas and immigration regulations

Visas are not required. On arrival visitors are granted a pass valid for one month. It may be extended at three-monthly intervals for up to twelve months on production of an onward or return ticket, valid travel documents, proof of sufficient funds, and acceptability at the next port of entry.

The fee for each renewal is 200 rupees, payable at the Immigration and Civil Status Division, Independence House, Independence Avenue, Victoria, (P.O. Box 430. Tel: 25333) weekdays from 08.00-11.00 and 13.00-15.00.

Travellers by sea are exempt from these requirements provided the master of the vessel, or the shipping agent, gives the immigration authorities a written guarantee of their repatriation.

Health requirements

The Seychelles are free of tropical diseases such as malaria, bilharzia, typhoid, and dysentery. Vaccination against polio is recommended, but not essential. Tap water is safe to drink, milk is pasteurised, and all food is generally safe to eat. There are few dangerous insects and no poisonous snakes.

International flights

Air Seychelles flies three times a week from London via Paris, Frankfurt, Zurich, and Rome and once weekly from Singapore. Aeroflot, Air France, British Airways, Kenya Airways, and Lux Air also serve Seychelles.

Approximate flying time from Seychelles to London is twelve hours, Singapore seven hours, the Gulf five hours, Nairobi three hours, and Mauritius two and a half hours.

On arrival

The sole point of entry is Seychelles International Airport on Mahé. It is ten kilometres (six miles) from Victoria. It has all facilities including currency exchange at

Barclays Bank and the Bank of Credit and Commerce for flight arrivals and departures, duty-free shop, snack bar, and tourist kiosk. A porter service is available.

Tourists in groups are met on arrival and transferred to their hotels by representatives of local tour agents. There is no airline bus service.

Public buses stop at the petrol station opposite the airport for northbound passengers (to Victoria, Beau Vallon) and on the airport side of the road, a short distance to the left of the airport exit, going south (Anse Aux Pins).

All car rental agencies, tour operators, and the Tourist Board have airport representatives to meet arrivals.

There is a mailbox at the airport. There is no telephone in the departure lounge.

International Flight Inquiries: 76751/2
Cargo Enquiries: 76751
Cargo Clearance and Deliveries: 76356

Air fares

The usual range of air fares is available: first, business, and economy class, as well as excursion and APEX fares.

Fares vary according to the season, with higher fares operating during European holiday periods, which mark the "high" season in Seychelles.

You can make stopovers *en route* with all fares except APEX. Reductions are available for children.

Departure tax

There is no airport departure tax. When applicable it will be included in the cost of the air ticket.

Arrival by sea

Arrivals by sea must obtain clearance from Port Victoria on Mahé, the only port of entry. Visiting yachts under twenty Gross

Registered Tonnes — GRT — pay fifty rupees a day. Vessels between twenty to 300 GRT pay 100 rupees a day in Seychelles' waters and vessels over 300 GRT pay 6,000 rupees a day.

Domestic flights

Air Seychelles operates daily flights between Mahé, Praslin, Bird, and Frégate; Denis four times a week; and Desroches three times a week. Scenic flights and charters to the outer islands can also be arranged.

Services are operated by Islander (nine seats), Trislander (seventeen seats), and Twin Otter (twenty seats). Check-in time is thirty minutes before departure.

Inter-island flights leave from the Domestic Terminal at Pointe Larue, to the north of the International Terminal, past the snack bar and along a covered pathway in a separate building.

When arriving by car, branch left as you turn into the airport drive. The Domestic Terminal car park is on your left, the terminal on the right. It has a small kiosk-snack bar which is open when flights are operating.

Flights to Praslin and Frégate take approximately fifteen minute; flights to Bird and Denis approximately thirty minutes; and flights to Desroches approximately sixty minutes. Inter-Island Flight Inquiries: 76501.

Customs

A reasonable volume of personal effects, such as cameras and film, can be freely imported. Banned imports include any type of firearm (including air pistols, rifles, and spearguns), animals, agricultural, and horticultural produce.

Visitors are restricted to duty-free items of 200 cigarettes or fifty cigars and one litre bottle of spirits, one litre bottle of wine, one small bottle of perfume, together with other dutiable articles up to a value of 400 rupees (approximately £50 sterling).

Road services

Bus services operate on Mahé and Praslin and a minibus service on La Digue. On Mahé services run between 05.20–21.30, Sunday-Thursday, and 05.30–01.30 Friday–Saturday. On Praslin services operate between 06.00–17.30 Monday–Saturday, with a limited Sunday service. On La Digue there is a daily minibus service between 05.00–17.30.

The services are reasonably priced and fairly reliable. On Mahé the bus station is on Palm Street, Victoria. There is also a small depot at Anse Aux Pins, near the school. Fares are between two and five rupees. You must wait for buses at the authorised stops.

Taxi services

Taxi fares are standardised (on a meter system). Rates are listed at the International Airport and in many taxi cabs. On Mahé and Praslin taxis are available at the airport (when flights are in) and hotels. There are two taxi stands in Victoria — next to the new Craft Centre in Albert Street, and at the Boutique des Artisans in Independence Avenue.

Car hire

Licensed operators hire out a variety of vehicles. The price includes unlimited mileage but excludes insurance and tax. The types of car available are: Mini-moke, Ford Escort, Ford Laser, Datsun, Lancer, Toyota, Mercedes, and the one-litre Suzuki jeep.

Petrol, which is sold by the litre, cost just under five rupees a litre in June 1990. There are petrol stations in Mahé at Victoria, Beau Vallon, Anse Royale, and opposite the International Airport. There are also two in Praslin at Grande Anse and Baie St. Anne.

Driving

A valid national or international driving licence is required. Visitors without either are required to take a short driving test. Visitors may use their domestic licences for up to ninety days. Thereafter, a local licence must be obtained from the Seychelles Licensing Authority (200 rupees for five years). The speed limit is 40 kilometres (25 miles) an hour in Victoria in built up areas and 65 kilometres (40 miles) an hour for the rest of Mahé. An insurance disc and a registration certificate must be displayed on all vehicles.

Ferry services

Ferries depart daily for Praslin and La Digue from the Old Pier in Victoria. Ferries leave Baie St. Anne, Praslin, every day at 06.00, arriving Mahé around 09.00, and departing from the Inter-Island Schooner Quay on

Mahé around 12.00 for Praslin. There are regular ferries throughout the day between Praslin and La Digue.

Climate

The weather in Seychelles is generally warm and humid. The year divides into two monsoon seasons. The south-east monsoon blows fairly steadily from May until the end of September and the north-west monsoon from October to April.

The pleasant, even temperature varies all year between 24°C and 30°C (75–86°F). It is coolest from June to October and hottest from December to April. Rainfall, in sudden sweeping downpours, is high. The wettest months are December and January.

For weather forecasts, listen to RTS news broadcasts, or telephone 76494 (Meteorological Station).

Currency

The Seychelles Rupee is divided into 100 cents. Notes are issued in denominations of 100 rupees (red and orange), 50 rupees (green), 25 rupees (purple and green), and 10 rupees (blue). The coins are 5 cents, 10 cents, 25 cents, 1 rupee, and 5 rupees.

Currency regulations

There are no exchange control regulations in Seychelles, but you may not export more than 100 rupees in notes, and 10 rupees in coins. Any excess money can be exchanged at banks or the airport bank offices.

Banks

Banks in Victoria open between 08.30–13.00 Monday-Friday. Barclays in Albert Street is open for foreign exchange only from 14.00–16.00. Some banks open on Saturday from 08.30–11.00.

The banks at the airport only open for flights. On Praslin, the Baie St. Anne Barclays Branch is open Monday–Friday, 08.30–13.00, and Saturday 08.30–11.00. The Grande Anse Branch is open Monday-Friday, 09.00–12.00 and Saturday 09.00–11.45.

On La Digue, Barclays is open Tuesdays and Thursdays only, 10.30–14.00.

Credit cards

American Express, Diners Club, Visa, Barclaycard, Access, and Mastercard are accepted at hotels and some restaurants and shops, but not widely used. Check before trying to use your card. American Express has a local agent, Travel Services Seychelles Ltd., Victoria House (Tel: 22414). The agent for Diners Club is J. K. Parcou, 209 Victoria House (Tel:23303).

For Visa enquiries contact Barclays Bank (Tel: 24101), and for Mastercard contact Bank of Credit and Commerce, (Tel: 23927).

Government

Seychelles is an independent republic within the Commonwealth, a member of the United Nations Organization, and the Organization of African Unity.

There are 115 islands with a total land-mass of 453 square kilometres (175 square miles), spread over an Exclusive Economic Zone of 1,340,000 square kilometres (515,000 square miles) between 4° and 10° south of the Equator, 46° to 56° east of Greenwich. The granitic islands lie around 4° south and 56° east.

The population is approaching 70,000. Victoria, the capital, has a population of about 23,000. Sixty-seven per cent of the population is under thirty.

The government operates under an executive President who is also Secretary-General of the sole political party, the Seychelles Peoples Progressive Front — SPPF. He heads a cabinet of ten ministers.

The judiciary consists of the High Court, presided over by the Chief Justice, the Magistrates Courts, and a Court of Appeal.

Language

Seychelles is trilingual. Creole is the official language. English is the language of law and commerce and French is also spoken.

Religion

The vast majority of Seychellois are Roman Catholic. Other Christian denominations include the Church of England, Seventh Day Adventists, and Mormons. The Catholic and Anglican cathedrals are in Victoria. Other faiths include Islam, Hinduism, and Bahai.

Time

Seychelles is four hours ahead of Greenwich

Mean Time, three hours ahead of Central European Time, and one hour ahead of Kenya time.

Daylight

There is no twilight in Seychelles. The sun rises quickly at 06.15 and sets equally swiftly at about 18.30. It is dark by 19.00. This varies by only a matter of minutes throughout the year, giving twelve full hours of daylight every day.

Business hours

Most businesses operate 08.00–16.00, Monday–Friday, some opening 08.00–12.00 on Saturdays. Lunchtime is 12.00–13.00.

Shops are not generally open before 09.00, and close at around 17.00. Many close for lunch between 12.00–13.00. You will find some of the shops outside the main centre open in the evenings and during weekends and public holidays. The larger shops close for the afternoon on Saturdays and all day Sunday.

Security

Seychelles is a friendly and peaceful country, well-policed, where crime of any kind is rare. Visitors, however, are advised to lock their cars and keep a watchful eye on their belongings when swimming.

Telecommunications

Local and international satellite services are operated by Cable and Wireless. There are twenty-three telephone connections for every 100 citizens. Direct international dialling is available to more than 100 countries with new ones being added each year.

Telex and telefax services are also available in most hotels. Cable and Wireless also provides leased circuits, maritime ship-to-ship and ship-to-shore radio communication services, and aviation communications.

Media

Seychelles has one trilingual daily newspaper, *Seychelles Nation*, published by the Press Office of the Department of Information. The national Seychelles Agence Presse publishes a monthly news review in English and French for the international media. The same agency also publishes *Seychelles Today*, a quarterly magazine on island life. *The People*

is a trilingual annual magazine published by the ruling party, the Seychelles People's Progressive Front. The Roman Catholic Mission also publishes a trilingual bi-monthly paper, *L'Echo des Iles*.

Silhouette, the inflight magazine of Air Seychelles, carries many fascinating articles about life and tourism in Seychelles.

Regular trilingual radio and television services are operated by Radio Television Seychelles.

Radio Seychelles broadcasts daily in English, French, and Creole, Monday–Friday 06.30–08.00, 11.00–13.15, 18.00–22.00. Saturdays and Sundays, 06.30–22.00.

The full news is broadcast in French at 12.30, in English at 19.00, and in Creole at 20.00. Headline news is presented in Creole at 06.30 and 12.00, in French at 07.30 and 21.00, and in English at 07.00 and 13.00. The news is broadcast on 219 metres, 1368 Hz.

Television broadcasts, in Creole, English, and French, between approximately 17.30–22.30 weekdays with an intermission at 19.30.

Broadcasting hours are longer during weekends, with programmes beginning around 15.00 and going on until after 23.00. There is a news summary in English at 18.00, in Creole (main news, with some items in English and French) at 19.00, and another news summary in French at 20.30. At present, a minority of programmes are in Creole. System Pal I, 626 lines.

Energy

The electricity supply is 240 volts (50 cycles AC). Plugs used are three-point, square-pin.

Medical services

Dial 999 for fire, police, or ambulance at all hours. There is a well-equipped central hospital in Victoria and there are smaller hospital-clinics at Anse aux Pins, Anse Boileau, Anse Royale, Baie Lazare, Beau Vallon, Béolière, Corgat Estate, English River, Glacis, Les Mamelles, North Point, Port Glaud, and Takamaka on Mahé; Baie St. Anne and Grande Anse on Praslin; La Digue; and Silhouette.

Generally, the doctors speak English. Hotels may have a duty nurse. The clinics are open between 07.30–17.00 Monday–Friday and 07.30–12.00 Saturdays.

Visitors can obtain emergency treatment for illness and accidents at any time at the main hospital in Mont Fleuri, just outside Victoria. There is a basic consultation fee of seventy-five rupees for tourists.

Insurance

Cover can be bought in Seychelles from the State Assurance Company, but it is usually cheaper and more practical to buy it in your own country before departing for Seychelles.

Chemists

There are three chemists on Mahé and a central pharmacy at Victoria Hospital. The chemists are: Behram's Pharmacy, Mont Fleuri, (Tel: 23659); Fock Heng Pharmacy, Revolution Avenue, Victoria (Tel: 22751); and George Lilams, Benezet Street, Victoria (Tel: 21733).

All sell many familiar brand medicines besides filling prescriptions, and can advise on minor health problems. Hospitals and clinics also dispense prescribed medicines.

The hospital dispensary is open Monday-Friday 08.00–18.00 and Saturdays 08.30–12.30. Chemists open between 08.00–17.00 Monday-Friday, Saturday morning, and may close for lunch.

Liquor

Seychelles Breweries' Seybrew beer and soft drinks are excellent. Wines and spirits are imported and costly. There are no licensing hours in Seychelles, although premises must be licensed to sell alcohol.

Guinness is brewed locally under licence, as is Eku lager. Shop prices for beer and soft drinks are about half those charged in hotels and restaurants. Bottles carry a one-rupee refundable deposit.

Tipping

Tips are not really expected anywhere in Seychelles. Most hotels and restaurants include service in their charges. If you do wish to show particular appreciation, include ten per cent on restaurant bills, and a few rupees for porters or room service.

Taxi drivers do not expect tips, but again you may wish to show particular appreciation if you have hired a taxi for an island tour or long journey.

Clubs

The local businessmen's clubs, e.g. Rotary, Round Table, Lions, welcome visiting members. The Yacht Club, which serves excellent, reasonably-priced meals, has an exchange membership scheme for members of yacht clubs overseas. Contact the Commodore for details.

English–Creole

Hello	Bonzour
How are you?	Konman ou sava?
I am well	Byen mersi
Thank you	Mersi
(very much)	Mersi bokou
Goodbye	Orevwar
Hotel	Hotel
Room	Lasanm
Bed	Lilit
Food	Manze
Coffee	Kafe
Beer	Labyer
Cold	Fwa
Hot	So
Tea	Te
Meat	Lavian
Fish	Pwason
Bread	Dipen
Butter	Diber
Sugar	Disik
Salt	Disel
Bad	Pa bon
Today	Ozordi
Tomorrow	Demen
Now	Mantenem
Quickly	Vit
Slowly	Lentemn
Hospital	Opital
Police	Gard
Mr.	Myse
Mrs.	Madanm
Miss.	Manmzel
I	Mon
You	Ou
He, she	Li
We	Nou
They	Zot
What?	Kwa?/Ki?
Who?	Ki?/Lekel?
Where?	Kote?

When?	Kan?
How?	Ki mannyer?
Why?	Akoz?
Which?	Lekel?
Yes	Wi
No	Non
To eat	Manze
To drink	Bwar
To sleep	Dormir
To bathe	Begner/Naze
To come	Vini
To go	Ale
To stop	Arete
To buy.	Aste
To sell	Vann
Street/road	Rue
Airport	Erpor
Shop	Laboutik
Money	Larzan
Cent	Sou
One	Enn
Two	De
Three	Trwa
Four	Kat
Five	Senk
Six	Sis
Seven	Set
Eight	Wit
Nine	Nef
Ten	Dis
Eleven	Onz
Twelve	Douz
Thirteen	Trez
Fourteen	Katorz
Fifteen	Kenz
Sixteen	Sez
Seventeen	Diset
Eighteen	Diswit
Nineteen	Disznef
Twenty	Ven
Twenty-one	Venteen
Twenty-two	Vennde
Twenty-three	Venntwa
Twenty-four	Vennkat
Twenty-five	Vennsenk
Thirty	Trent
Forty	Karant
Fifty	Senkant
Sixty	Swasant
Seventy	Swasanndis
Eighty	Katreven
Ninety	Katrevendis
One hundred	San

Phrases

Where is the hotel?	Kote otel silvouple?
Good morning	Bonzour
Good afternoon	Bonapremidi
Good evening	Bonswa
Please come in	Vini silvouple
Please sit down	Asizie silvouple
You're welcome	Pa dekwa
Where do you come from?	Cote out sorti?
I come from . . .	Mon sorti . . .
What is your name?	Ki mannyer ou apele?
My name is . . .	Mon apel . . .
Can you speak Kreol?	Ou kabab kose Kreol?
Only a little	Zis en pe
I would like to learn more	Mon oule apran enkor
How do you find Seychelles?	Ki mennyer ou vwa Sesel?
I like it here	Mon konten avek Sesel
The weather is hot, isn't it?	Letan is so, wi?
Where are you going?	Cote ou pou ale?
I am going to . . .	Mon pou ale . . .
Please stop here	Arete isi silvouple
How much?	Konbyen?
Wait a minute	Esper mon enn ti momen
I have to get change	Mon fodre ganny larzan sanze
Excuse me	Ekskiz
Where is the toilet?	Cote ou kabinen silvouple?
In the back	Deryer lakour
Where may I get a drink?	Ou mon kapab ganny enn bwa?
One cup of coffee	Enn tas kafe
How much does this cost?	Konbyen i vann?
That's quite expensive	I ase ser

318

In Brief

National Parks and Reserves

The total landmass of Seychelles is 452.5 square kilometres (181.7 square miles), of which 208.16 square kilometres (80.4 square miles) — forty-six per cent — has been designated as National Parks, Reserves, or Protected Areas. A further 228 square kilometres (88 square miles) of marine areas have been designated as Marine National Parks for the conservation of marine ecosystems.

A National Park is defined as an area set aside for the propagation, protection, and preservation of wildlife or objects of aesthetic, geological, prehistoric, historical, archaeological, and scientific interest for the benefit, advantage, and enjoyment of the general public. In the case of a "marine national park", this includes an area of the shore, sea, or sea-bed together with coral reef and other marine features.

Two of these areas, Aldabra atoll and Vallée de Mai on Praslin, are World Heritage Sites, protected under international law as unique natural sites of world importance.

Three islands — Aride, Cousin, and Aldabra — are special nature reserves where flora and fauna are protected under Seychelles law.

Two other categories of parks have been defined as "areas of outstanding natural beauty" and "strict nature reserves". The latter is an area set aside to permit the free interaction of natural ecological factors without outside interference except that which is indispensable for the existence of the reserve. No such areas have yet been designated.

Marine national parks

Virtually all fishing is prohibited within Marine National Parks. All corals, shells, and other marine life are given complete protection. Anchorage is not permitted in certain zones.

Swimming, snorkeling, diving, and sailing are all permitted, but a fee may be levied on each person entering the perimeter of the park. Park rangers are engaged to ensure rules and regulations are followed.

Shell reserves

No person may collect or disturb any shell in areas designated as shell reserves, except certain ones listed in the Fisheries Regulations. It is forbidden to collect, disturb, sell, or export the Triton conch shell.

Protected areas

Where in the public interest special precautions are required to prevent unauthorised entry upon any land, an order is published in the official gazette.

Although most areas under this heading concern the supply of essential services, two areas have been designated to protect natural flora and fauna. The first is the African Banks and surrounding reefs: Île aux Cocos, Île La Fouche, Île Platte, and surrounding areas.

The second protected area is Bel Ombre, where archaeological excavations are being conducted, which has been designated because of its historical importance.

Other legislation

The Wild Birds Protection (Nature Reserves) Regulations establishes nature reserves for the protection and preservation of wild land and seabirds on various islands:

- Beacon or Île Sèche
- Booby or Île aux Fous
- Boudeuse
- Étoile
- Praslin (Vallée de Mai)
- King Ross or Lamperiaire
- Mamelles
- Cousin
- Île aux Vaches Marines

No person may harm any bird or egg in these areas. Under the Collection of Birds Eggs Regulations, sooty tern and common noddy eggs may be collected from Desnoeufs and L'Îlot (Frégate). No quota is set for Desnoeufs and a quota of 70,000 is set for L'Îlot.

Terrapins and tortoises are protected under the Wild Animals (Seychelles Pond Turtle)

319

Protection Regulations and the Wild Animals (Giant Land Tortoise) Protection Regulations.

Sea turtle legislation

There is general agreement that sea turtle populations around the world, including Seychelles', are depleted due to high exploitation levels and international trade.

In 1973, twenty-one countries signed the Convention on International Trade in Endangered Species — CITES — which went into effect on 1 July, 1975. Seychelles acceded to CITES without reservation on 26 January, 1977.

Both green and hawksbill turtles are listed in Appendix 1, which is the highest category covering species threatened with extinction for which trade must be subject to strict regulation and only authorised in exceptional circumstances.

Nevertheless, green and hawksbill turtles are heavily exploited in Seychelles. The killing of female turtles is prohibited while males may only be killed after a permit has been obtained.

However, permits are a mere formality, and there is no quota system, and little, if any control over the killing of females including those that come ashore to nest.

There are no restrictions on trade and hawksbill turtle curios are sold openly. Many are purchased by visitors who then export them to their country of residence, unaware that this is a violation of CITES, and, in many cases, national legislation. About 100 countries have ratified CITES. These include almost every country that sends tourists to Seychelles.

Seychelles is well aware of its obligations under CITES and legislation is now under review. The government has frequently repeated its commitment to conservation and there is hope that moves will be made to protect the remaining turtle population before it is too late.

Parks and Reserves Legislation

The National Parks and Nature Conservancy Ordinance of 1969 and its various amendments defines four types of protected area in Seychelles: Areas of Outstanding Natural Beauty are set aside for their preservation and maintenance for the benefit, advantage, and enjoyment of the general public; National Parks are set aside for the propagation, protection, and preservation of wildlife, or the preservation of sites of aesthetic, geological, prehistorical, archaeological, or any other scientific interest, for the benefit of the general public; Special Reserves are set aside for the protection of characteristic wildlife; and Strict Nature Reserves are set aside to permit free interaction of ecological factors without outside interference.

There are several other acts which protect wooded vegetation and forest; animals and birds; the giant land tortoise and Seychelles pond turtle; marine mammals; seashells; and several beaches.

Parks and Reserves Administration

The Seychelles National Environment Commission is responsible for developing and reviewing all policy matters relating to the environment; reviewing existing legislation, conservation, and management; coordinating all activities relating to the conservation and management of the environment; and promoting education.

The Department of the Environment is the main executive for conservation policy and responsible for the creation and management of all protected areas apart from Aldabra, Aride, and Cousin.

Aride and Cousin are owned and managed as Special Nature Reserves by the Royal Society for Nature Conservation — RSNC — and the International Council for Bird Preservation — ICBP — respectively.

Aldabra is owned by the Seychelles government but administered as a Special Nature Reserve by the Seychelles Island Foundation, an international conservation group that includes the Royal Society, the Organisation de la Recherche Scientifique et Technique Outre Mer, the RSNC, the Smithsonian Institute, and the Worldwide Fund for Nature.

Department of the Environment
Independence House
PO Box 199
Victoria
Tel: 25333
Telex: 2312

World Heritage Sites

Aldabra Atoll

Geographical location: An atoll north of the Mozambique channel, 1,090km west south-west of Mahé, 420km north-west of Madagascar, and 640km east of the East African mainland.

Altitude: Sea level to 8m.

Area: 15,380ha land, 2,000ha mangrove, and 14,200ha sea.

Physical features: Aldabra is a raised coral atoll, 34km long and 14.5km wide. It consists of four main islands of coral limestone separated by narrow passes and enclosing a shallow lagoon. The lagoon, which covers some 15,000ha, contains many small islands and the entire atoll is surrounded by an outer reef. Weathering has led to dissection of the limestones into holes and pits, along the coast there are undercut limestone cliffs. On the southern (windward) coast there is a raised beach and sand dunes. Marine habi- -tats range from mangrove mud flats to coral reefs. The tidal range is 3m which can lead to strong channel currents. The climate is semi-arid with a pronounced wet season from November to April. Average rainfall is 1,200mm.

Vegetation: An exceptionally rich flora with 273 species of flowering shrub and fern, 19 of which are endemic and 22 shared only with neighbouring islands. Much of the island is covered with dense *Pemphis acidula* thicket. The endemic species include *Peponium sublitorale*. Many of these plants are considered to be endangered. Mangroves surround the lagoon, and inshore waters support sea-grass meadows.

Fauna: This island group is one of the few areas in the world where reptiles dominate the terrestrial fauna, with the largest population of (more than 150,000) giant tortoise. Green turtle breed there with up to 2,000 females laying annually and large numbers of hawksbill turtle can also be seen. The only endemic mammal is the flying fox. About 1,000 species of insect have been found, many new and endemic. Rats, cats, and goats which have been introduced now pose a serious threat to both habitat and wildlife.

The giant robber, or coconut crab, roams the atoll at night.

Birdlife: More island forms than anywhere else in the Indian Ocean. There are 10 sub-species: the sacred ibis, green-backed heron, Malagasy white-eye, Malagasy coucal, Malagasy bulbul, Malagasy turtle dove, Comoro blue pigeon, souimanga sunbird, red-headed forest fody, and Malagasy night-jar. Pied crows also occur (possibly naturally but may have arrived by ship) and the Malagasy kestrel, though not endemic, breeds only there in Seychelles.

The islands are important breeding grounds for thousands of seabirds, including red-tailed tropicbird, white-tailed tropicbird, red-footed booby, great frigatebird, lesser frigatebird, and nesting terns. There are several hundred masked booby and 12 endemic forms of terrestrial birds, including the last representative of the western Indian Ocean flightless birds — the Aldabran white-throated rail (about 5,000 individuals). There are two endemic birds, the Aldabra warbler and the Aldabra drongo (about 1,500 individuals). The Aldabra warbler was one of the rarest and most endangered bird species in the world as only five birds were seen after its discovery in 1968. Last seen in 1983, it is now almost certainly extinct.

Visitor facilities: None, but an intensive research project extending across the whole atoll has been underway since 1967 when the Royal Society commenced work there. The research station passed to Seychelles Islands Foundation in 1980.

Vallée de Mai Nature Reserve

Geographical location: Within Praslin National Park on Praslin Island, 50km north-east of Mahé.

Altitude: Sea level to approximately 500m.

Area: 18ha, within Praslin National Park (675ha).

Physical features: A valley close to sea level in the north-eastern portion of Praslin National Park on the granitic island of Praslin. The streams originating in the valley feed into the Nouvelle Découverte River, which flows westward through the national park into the sea at Grande Anse. The other principal river, Fond B'Offay, flows eastward into Baie St. Anne. The area was untouched until the 1930s and still retains some palm forest in a near natural state.

Vegetation: Four principal vegetation types have been identified on Praslin, of which three occur in the Vallée de Mai area.

1) **lowland forest** (30–180m) once dominated by mimosa and eugenia but, following human settlement, now comprises well developed secondary forest with the endemic palm *Phoenicophorium borsigianum*, mango, cinnamon, *Sideroxylon ferrugineum*, and *Randia lancifolia*.

2) **intermediate palm forest** (30–500m), unique within the Seychelles being the only area where all six of the endemic palm species occur together.

3) **Vallée de Mai**, with monospecific palms *Dickenia nobilis*, *P. borsigianum*, *coco de mer*, *Verschaffeltia splendida*, and *Nephrosperma vanhoutteana*, which are all endemic to the Seychelles. There are also pandanus, *Dillenia*, and *Adenanthera pavonina*.

4) **eroded land** (100–500m) which has been recolonised by *Randia lancifolia*, *P. borsigiana*, *Dodonaea*, and *Dillenia ferruginea*, or planted with coco plum, mahogany, and lemon grass. In addition to the palms, there are a further 28 endemic species, including the rare vine *Toxocarpus schimperianus*. Takamaka and kalis d pap have been introduced.

Fauna: There are few mammal species on the island apart from the endemic Seychelles flying fox (which roosts in the reserve), sheath-tailed bat, and the insectivorous tenrec, which was introduced to Seychelles from Madagascar. Reptiles include the endemic chameleon, Seychelles house snake, Seychelles wolf snake, Brahminy blind snake, green and bronze geckos, and several species of skink. Six caecilians are known to occur in the deep beds of moist humus, but they are rarely seen. The streams contain freshwater crab, large freshwater prawn, shrimp, and the only species of freshwater fish endemic to Seychelles, the gourgeon.

Birdlife: The most noteworthy bird is the rare black parrot. Other birds include the barn owl, Seychelles bulbul, Seychelles blue pigeon, Seychelles sunbird, and Seychelles cave swiftlet.

Visitor facilities: Access to the valley is on foot along marked trails from the road, which divides the park in two.

Vallée de Mai sells souvenirs and refreshments. A visitors' fee of 25 rupees a person is levied, all funds going to support Seychelles Islands Foundation.

National Parks

Morne Seychellois

Geographical location: Covers most of the west and central massif of Mahé Island south of Victoria.

Altitude: Sea level to 905m.

Area: 3,045ha.

Physical features: A very rugged part of the largest granitic island, rising from sea level to 905m-high Morne Seychellois. Contains a variety of habitats. Numerous rivers drain the rugged upland region including the Mare aux Cochons, the Boulay, and Grande Anse.

Vegetation: Almost all plants endemic to Mahé are within the park. Although largely invaded by exotics, especially albizia, cinnamon, and santol, the park contains some fine areas of endemic trees, including the stronghold of the kafe maron, jellyfish tree, northea, bwa rouz, koko maron, five endemic palms, and four endemic screwpines. Other plants include payanke, orchids, tree ferns, dianella, and pitcher plant. Relict native communities include *Randia serica*, *Pervillei*, and *Northea seychellarum*. There are two large populations of the rare and endangered bwa-d-fer, *Vateria seychellarum*, and bwa mediz, *Medusagyne oppositifolia*. Other threatened species include the palm *Roscheria melanochaetes*, which is well represented, and *Toxocarpus schimperianus* which was only recently discovered at two sites. The congo rouz area from Sans Souci to Le Niol is especially rich in Seychelles' endemic flora.

Fauna: Tenrec, Brahminy blind snake, Seychelles house snake, Seychelles wolf snake, tiger chameleon, skinks, geckos, stick insects, leaf insects, all 5 frogs, and 6 out of 7 caecilians. Several large roosts of endemic fruit bat and sheath-tailed bat. Among the caecilians is the very rare *Praslinia cooperi*, which was only discovered in 1983.

Birdlife: Seven endemics out of 11 species, (including the rare and endangered Seychelles bare-legged scops owl, and Seychelles white-eye restricted to Mahé), large numbers of Seychelles blue pigeon, Seychelles kestrel, Seychelles sunbird, Seychelles bulbul, Seychelles cave swiftlet, and white-tailed tropicbird. There are also many Malagasy turtle doves.

Visitor facilities: Viewing points at Mission and well-marked footpaths to Morne Blanc, Copolia, and Trois Frères, all commencing from signboards along Sans Souci road.

Praslin

Area: 337.6ha.
Geographical location: Central hills of Praslin, including the whole of the World Heritage Site of Vallée de Mai.
Altitude: 20-360m.
Vegetation: Contains the best area of palm forest on Praslin with all 6 endemics represented. Also some fine areas of mixed forest dominated by bwa rouz.
Fauna: Tenrec, Seychelles fruit bat, tiger chameleon, Praslin green gecko, Seychelles wolf snake.
Birdlife: Seychelles black parrot, Seychelles bulbul, Seychelles blue pigeon, Seychelles sunbird.

Marine National Parks

Baie Ternay

Geographical location: A sheltered bay on the extreme western tip of Mahé.
Altitude: Sea level down to a depth of 37m.
Area: 80ha.
Physical features: A shallow lagoon approximately 800m wide, at the extreme western tip of Mahé, lying between continuous fringing reef at the head of the bay. It is grooved and cut by numerous surge channels and offers refuge to large numbers of reef fish.
Vegetation: A variety of seaweeds including stalked *Turbinaria*.
Fauna: Hawksbill turtle breed there and the reef fish are prolific. Reef development is not extensive and there are few living corals. The deeper reefs fringing the rocky headlands are in good condition, comprising soft corals that are anchored on colonies of dead *porites*.
Birdlife: Green-backed heron, waders.

Visitor facilities: It is not possible to approach from the land side as it is occupied by a National Youth Service camp. But it is accessible from Beau Vallon and popular for swimming and snorkeling. Glass bottom boats are available for hire from Beau Vallon.

Curieuse

Geographical location: Comprises the irregular-shaped Curieuse Island and its surrounding waters, including the outlying St. Pierre Islet and the entire channel between the island and Anse Boudin, Praslin, and elsewhere, to 1000m from the shoreline — the high water mark along the north-east coast of Praslin.
Altitude: 30m below sea level to 172m.
Area: 1,470ha (283ha marine).
Physical features: Comprises the rugged granitic island of Curieuse (2.83ha) which rises to the 172m-high Curieuse Peak, St. Pierre Islet, and the northern coastline of Praslin from Pointe Chevalier to Pointe Zanguilles. The marine part of the park ranges from shallow-water reefs to a 30m dropoff and includes mangrove swamp, rocky intertidal shore, and sandy beaches. A causeway has been built across the mouth of Baie Laraie creating a small lagoon known as Turtle Pond.
Vegetation: One of the two islands where *coco de mer* grows naturally. Also principal locality for the endemic vine *Toxocarpus schimperianus*. Fine specimens of *Northea seychellarum* are to be found behind Baie Laraie. Developing mangrove community on Turtle Bay. Casuarina and Takamaka.
Fauna: A population of some 300 giant tortoises introduced from Aldabra have been reduced to fewer than 100 by poachers. About 20–40 hawksbill turtles nest each year. Fish life is abundant and varied. Land crabs are common in the mangroves. Reptiles include Brahminy blind snake, gecko, and the lizards *Gehyra mutilata*, *Mabuya sechellensis*, and *Scelotes gardineri*. The marine section has good coral growth. These are especially prolific around Île St. Pierre and Anse Petit Cour, which is known for its tubular coral colonies. Most common are colonies of blue-tipped, mauve, or brown staghorn and pink *Pocillopora*. Fish include angelfish, grouper, and soldierfish. Molluscs, octopi, and lobsters were once common and only in the mangrove areas are

there significant populations of crab.
Birdlife: Seychelles sunbird, Seychelles bulbul, and fairy tern predominate.
Visitor facilities: Facilities are planned in the Anse St. Jose-Caiman plateau area. Two areas have been set aside for swimming. Some Praslin hotels organize trips with a barbecue ashore.

Port Launay

Geographical location: A small bay on the north-west coast of Mahé, south of Baie Ternay. An enclosed sandy cove, with a fringing reef.
Altitude: From sea level to a depth of 25m.
Area: 158ha.
Physical features: A sheltered cove with predominantly rocky shoreline fringed with coral reefs and interspersed with sandy beaches.
Vegetation: Onshore mangrove forests fringe steep, forested slopes. Seaweed, especially stalked *Turbinaria*, covers the back-reef zone.
Fauna: Reef development is not extensive and there are few living corals. The deeper reefs fringing the rocky headlands are in very good condition with soft coral anchored on colonies of dead *Porites*.
Birdlife: Mainly blue pigeon and green-backed heron in the mangrove forests.
Visitor facilities: None.

St. Anne

Geographical location: An area of reef surrounding a series of 6 granite islands about 5km (3 miles), east of Victoria: St. Anne, Cerf, Round, Moyenne, Long, and Cachée.
Altitude: 30m below sea level to 250m.
Area: 1,423ha.
Physical features: A group of six small rugged granitic islands together with adjacent reefs and sea. Habitats include reefs, granite boulders, sandflats, seagrass beds, intertidal rocks, and sandy beaches.
Vegetation: Among the dead reefs are extensive beds of sargasso seaweeds. The seagrass *Thalassia hemprichii* is to be found between Round and Cerf. On the islands coconuts predominate. On the north-east side of St. Anne there is a steep and rocky area which still has plenty of the native palm *Phoenicophorium* and pandanus.
Fauna: Fine marine life, especially between Moyenne and St. Anne. There are more than

150 species of reef fish, as well as crabs, sea urchins, marine worms, starfish, octopuses, sea cucumbers, and a variety of underwater life. It is probably the main breeding site for hawksbill turtle in Seychelles. Numerous fruit bats in the forests of Cerf.
Birdlife: Green-backed heron, various waders and terns. Seabirds use the sandbanks which are exposed at low tide.
Visitor facilities: The reefs attract numerous visitors and there are several glass bottom boats for hire and two semi-submersibles. Swimming, sailing, and diving are all permitted, but a national park entrance fee is payable and all marine life is protected. Seven areas of delicate shallow coral areas are viewing areas only; no anchoring is allowed. There are restaurants on Cerf, Round, and Moyenne. Tourism is prohibited on Long which is a prison, and St. Anne is reserved for National Youth Service students.

Special Reserves

Aride Island

Geographical location: Aride is the northernmost granitic island of Seychelles some nine kilometres north of the north-west tip of Praslin and 45km north north-east of Mahé.
Altitude: Sea level to 134m, plus the reef to a distance of 200 (soon to be increased to 1,000 m).
Area: 68ha.
Physical features: Some ninety per cent of the island is occupied by a rugged hill rising to 134m, while the remaining area is a flat coastal plain not more than 4m above the high-water mark. The fairly exposed fringing coral reefs around the island are proposed for inclusion in the park.
Vegetation: The vegetation is largely free of exotics and is the most natural and undisturbed of any of the islands of Seychelles. The dominant species is *Pisonia grandis*. Aride is the only known locality of Wright's gardenia. A species of peponium, unnamed and undescribed, has also been discovered. Other significant species include several species of ficus, hibiscus, *Euphorbia pyrifolia*, *Intsia bijuga*, *Hernandia nymphaefolia*, *Morinda citrifolia*, *Barringtonia*

asiatica, *Tournefortia argentea*, and Balfour's screwpine. Aride has the best mapou woodland on the hillside. The coastal plateau is dominated by takamaka, badamier, barringtonia, bwa blan, and tortoise tree, typical native coastal woodland largely destroyed in Seychelles. The beach crest is a lawn of morning glory with a hedge of half-flower *(scaevola)* and scattered specimens of cordia, tree heliotrope, (bwa tabak), bwa-d-ros, and var.

Fauna: Extremely high density of lizards, especially Wright's skink, (only found on seabird islands), and Seychelles skink. Other lizards include bronze gecko, and green gecko. Sightings of Brahminy blind snake and Seychelles wolf snake are rare. Hawksbill turtles nest during the north-west monsoon, and — very occasionally — green turtle during the south-east. Cetaceans are often seen offshore, especially bottlenose dolphin. Life is prolific on the reef, with over 150 species of fish recorded. Aride is also known for the royal tang and its groves of staghorn coral.

Birdlife: Ten nesting seabird species, which is more than any other island except Aldabra with 11. Aride is home to over a million seabirds. It has Seychelles' largest populations of white-tailed tropicbird, Audobon's shearwater, fairy tern, and roseate tern, the world's largest colony of lesser noddy, the only hilltop colony in the world of sooty tern, the only site in the granitic islands for red-tailed tropicbirds, together with common noddy, bridled tern, and wedge-tailed shearwater. There are huge numbers of roosting great frigatebirds and some lesser frigatebirds. Endemic land birds include the Seychelles warbler, while the moorhen lives in the marshy areas of the coastal plain.

Visitor facilities: No overnight accommodation but regular day trips can be organized from most Praslin hotels. The majority of visitors come to see the bird colonies. Bathing is permitted and snorkeling and diving are considered excellent.

Cousin Island

Geographical location: A small island on the shallow Seychelles Bank, 2.35km west–south-west of Miller's Point on Praslin Island.
Altitude: Below sea level to 69m.
Area: 28ha.

Physical features: The island is approximately rectangular in shape with a small group of rocks located some 200-300m offshore. About eighty per cent of the island comprises a flat coastal plain on the northern and eastern flanks of the granite hill which rises to 69m. The southern and western slopes are rocky and barren, right down to the shore, while the northern and eastern slopes support dense stands of trees. Eighty per cent of the north-west, north, and north-east shores are characterized by sandy beaches. The seasonal change in wind direction (north-west to south-east) creates a constant movement of sand between the east and north coasts. There is also a fringing coral reef which extends, on average, some 200m out from the high-water mark. The only fresh water on the island is a small, seasonal rivulet carrying run-off from the hill down the northern slope to a depression near some wells and a freshwater marsh.

Vegetation: The island supports a variety of vegetation types including coastal herb communities; mature *Pisonia grandis* forest; regenerated *Pisonia/Morinda citrifolia* woodland which is replacing abandoned coconut plantations on the coastal plain; substantial areas of mangrove swamp; and a small freshwater marsh. The hillside is dominated by *Panicum maximum*, *Cyperus polyphyllus*, *Cyperus ligularis*, *Portulaca oleracea*, and communities of *Fimbrystylis/Bulbostylis*; dense thickets of euphorbia, pandanus, and open sedge/herb communities on the granite slopes; papaya (introduced), casuarina, and *Scaevola taccata* occupy the beach zone. Other notable species include *Ficus*, *Guettarda speciosa*, and castor-oil plants. Of the 125 plant species, more than half are introduced. The ICBP is attempting to re-establish the original island vegetation which was thought to comprise forests of *Pisonia grandis* on the plateau, thickets of *Scaevola* and *Suriana maritima* along the coast, backed by a dense hedge of *Cordia subcordata*, *Guettarda speciosa*, and *Morinda citrifolia*; and dense woods of *Morinda* and *Ficus*.

Fauna: The only residential mammal is the hare, which was introduced from India in the 1920s. Fruit bats commute from nearby Praslin. Cousin has one of the largest populations of breeding hawksbill turtle in the

Seychelles and an occasional green turtle. There are also a small number of giant tortoise which have been reintroduced. Other reptiles include Seychelles terrapin, skinks, and geckos. Insects and arachnids include giant millipede, scorpion (including the tailless whip scorpion), and the Madagascar termite. Butterflies are extremely scarce with only six species including painted lady and *Parallelia torrida*. Over 230 species of reef fish and several species of crab have been recorded. Corals are represented by *Acropora, Millepora, Pocillopora*, and *Stylophora*.

Birdlife: Cousin was mainly acquired by the International Council for Bird Preservation because it was the home of three rare and endangered endemic land birds: the Seychelles warbler, the Seychelles fody, and the Seychelles turtle dove (which is believed extinct through hybridisation with an introduced race). Seabirds are by far the predominant bird species with fairy tern, Audobon's shearwater, wedge-tailed shearwater, white-tailed tropicbirds, and bridled terns nesting on the hill. Lesser noddy and common noddy prefer the coastal plain for their nesting sites. In all, 52 species have been recorded including Madagascar fody, barn owl, Indian mynah (introduced), Seychelles sunbird, great frigatebird, and lesser frigatebird.

Visitor facilities: Tourism is restricted to daytime visits. There is no overnight accommodation.

La Digue Vev Reserve

Geographical location: On western plateau of La Digue, some three hours by boat from Mahé.
Altitude: 10m.
Area: 8ha.
Physical features: A low-lying plateau bordered on two sides by a public dirt road. Part of a large freshwater swamp is contained in the north-western portion of the reserve.
Vegetation: Dominant woodland trees include takamaka and badamier. Also coconut and casuarina.
Fauna: Terrapins.
Birdlife: Seven to nine pairs of the rare and endangered Seychelles black paradise flycatcher. Other birds include Seychelles bulbul and Seychelles sunbird.
Visitor facilities: A marked pathway.

Animal Checklist

KEY
* endemic species
# endemic subspecies
+ introduced

MAMMALS

Whales and Dolphins
Fin Whale
Sei Whale
Goosebeak Whale
Dense Beaked Whale
Great Sperm Whale
Roughtooth Whale
Shortfin Pilot Whale
Great Killer Whale
False Killer Whale
Pygmy Killer Whale
Melonhead Whale
Grey Dolphin
Spinner Dolphin
Bridled Dolphin
Bottlenose Dolphin

Bats
*Seychelles Fruit Bat
*Aldabra Fruit Bat
*Sheath-Tailed Bat
#Silhouette Sheath-Tailed Bat

Land Mammals
+Tenrec
+Indian Hare

BIRDS

Shearwaters
Wedge-Tailed Shearwater
Audobon's Shearwater

Tropicbirds
Red-Tailed Tropicbird
White-Tailed Tropicbird

Boobies
Red-Footed Booby
Masked Booby
Brown Booby
Abbot's Booby

Frigates
Great Frigatebird
Lesser Frigatebird

Herons and Allies
Chinese Bittern
#Green-Backed Heron (degens)
#Green-Backed Heron (crawfordi)
#Cattle Egret (seychellarum)
Grey Heron
#Aldabra Sacred Ibis (abbotti)

Ducks
Garganey

Birds of Prey
*Seychelles Kestrel
Malagasy Kestrel
European Hobby
Eleanora's Falcon

Moorhens and Rails
Moorhen
*White-Throated Rail

Waders
Crab Plover
Kentish Plover
Lesser Sand Plover
Greater Sand Plover
Pacific Golden Plover
Grey Plover
Sanderling
Curlew Sandpiper
Bar-Tailed Godwit
Whimbrel
Greenshank
Terek Sandpiper
Common Sandpiper

Skuas
Antarctic Skua

Gulls
Brown-Headed Gull
Lesser Black-Backed Gull

Terns
Gull Billed Tern
Crested Tern
Lesser Crested Tern
Black-Naped Tern
Roseate Tern

Bridled Tern
Sooty Tern
Saunders Tern
White-Winged Black Tern
Lesser Noddy
Brown Noddy
Fairy Tern

Pigeons and Doves
+Malagasy Turtle Dove (picturata)
#Malagasy Turtle Dove (aldabrana)
#Malagasy Turtle Dove (coppingeri)
#Seychelles Turtle Dove (rostrata)
+Barred Ground Dove
*Seychelles Blue Pigeon
#Comoro Blue Pigeon (minor)

Coucals
#Malagasy Coucal (insularis)

Parrots
#Seychelles Black Parrot (barklyi)

Owls
+Barn Owl
*Seychelles Bare-Legged Scops Owl

Swiftlets
*Seychelles Cave Swiftlet

Nightjars
#Malagasy Nightjar (aldabrensis)

Thrushes and Allies
#Malagasy Bulbul (rostratus)
Red-whiskered Bulbul
*Seychelles Bulbul
*Seychelles Magpie Robin

Warblers
*Seychelles Warbler
Malagasy Grass Warbler

Flycatchers
*Seychelles Black Paradise Flycatcher

Sunbirds
#Souimanga Sunbird (aldabrensis)
#Souimanga Sunbird (buchenorum)
#Souimanga Sunbird (abbotti)
*Seychelles Sunbird

White-eyes
#Malagasy White-eye (*aldabrensis*)
*Seychelles Grey White-eye

Drongos
*Aldabra Drongo

Crows
+Indian House Crow
Pied Crow

Mynahs
+Indian Mynah

Waxbills
+Common Waxbill

Weavers and Allies
+House Sparrow
#Red-Headed Forest Fody (*aldabrana*)
+Malagasy Fody
*Seychelles Fody

REPTILES

Tortoises
*Aldabra Giant Land Tortoise

Turtles
Leatherback Turtle
Hawksbill Turtle
Green Turtle

Terrapins
*Black-Bellied Terrapin
Yellow-Bellied Terrapin
Star-Bellied Terrapin

Lizards
*Mahé Stripeless Green Gecko
#Praslin Green Gecko
Mahé Bar-Tailed Green Gecko
*Bronze Gecko
Common House Gecko
*Seychelles Skink
*Wright's Skink
Snake-Eyed Fishing Skink
*Tiger Chameleon

Snakes
*Seychelles House Snake
*Seychelles Wolf Snake
+Brahminy Blind Snake

AMPHIBIANS

Caecilians
*Big-Headed Caecilian
*Small-Headed Caecilian
*Praslin Flat-Headed Caecilian
*Flat-Headed Caecilian
*Pin-Headed Caecilian
*Swimming Caecilian
*Toothy Caecilian

Frogs
*Seychelles Tree Frog
Mascarene Frog
*Thomasset's Tocking Rock Frog
*Pygmy Piping Frog
*Croaking Carry-Cot Frog

MARINE FISH

Sharks
Sleeping Shark
Whale Shark
Grey Reef Shark
White-Tip Shark

Rays
Round Ribbontail Ray
Spotted Eagle Ray
Manta Ray
Grey Sting Ray

Morays
Zebra Moray
Geometric Moray
Leopard Moray

Lizardfish
Variegated Lizardfish

Needlefish
Crocodile Needlefish

Flyingfish
Tropical Two-Wing Flyingfish
Flying Gurnards

Squirrelfish
Yellow-Tipped Squirrelfish
Sabre Squirrelfish
Blotcheye Soldierfish
Seychelles Soldierfish

Trumpetfish and Allies
Trumpetfish
Serrate Flutemouth
Black Pipefish
Yellow-Bellied Pipefish
Razorfish

Scorpionfish and Allies
Red Firefish (Lionfish)
Long-Spined Firefish
Bearded Scorpionfish
Frogfish
Paperfish
Stonefish

Goldies
Sea Goldie

Rockcod
Slender Rockcod
Peacock Rockcod
Coral Rockcod
Potatobass

Bigeyes
Crescent-Tail Bigeye

Sweetlips
Sailfin Rubberlip
Blackspotted Sweetlips

Snappers
Green Jobfish
Dory Snapper
Red Snapper
Blue-Banded Snapper

Fusiliers
Gold Striped Fusilier
Rainbow Fusilier

Spinecheeks
Yellowstripe Spinecheek

Batfish
Orbicular Batfish
Longfin Batfish

Moonies
Diamond Fish

Goatfish
Yellowstripe Goatfish

Dashdot Goatfish
Redspot Goatfish

Angelfish
Dusky Cherub
Emperor Angelfish
Blue Angelfish
Royal Angelfish

Butterflyfish
Threadfin Butterflyfish
Saddled Butterflyfish
Gorgeous Gussy
Halfmoon Butterflyfish
Blackback Butterflyfish
Rightangle Butterflyfish
Purple Butterflyfish
Vagabond Butterflyfish
Yellowhead Butterflyfish
Zanzibar Butterflyfish
Longnose Butterflyfish
Schooling Coachman

Trevallies
Bluefin Trevally
Rainbow Runner
Golden Trevally

Pilotfish
Pilotfish

Dorado
Dorado

Sharksucker
Sharksucker

Hawkfish
Spotted Hawkfish
Freckled Hawkfish

Sweepers
Copper Sweeper

Damsels
Dusky Damsel
Sevenbar Damsel
Scissortail Sergeant
Sordid Sergeant
Sergeant Major
Dicky Damsel
Green Damsel
Skunk Clownfish

Seychelles Three-Barred Clownfish
Blue Chromis
Chocolate Dip
Golden Chromis
Domino
Zebra Humbug
Two-bar Humbug
Jewel Damsel
Blue Pete
Sulphur Damsel

Wrasses
Yellowtail Tamarin
Turncoat Hogfish
Floral Wrasse
Tripletail Wrasse
Humphead Wrasse
Queen Coris
Slingjaw
Bird Wrasse
Chessboard Wrasse
Barred Thicklip
Bluestreak Cleaner Wrasse
Sixbar Wrasse
Goldbar Wrasse
Crescent-Tail Wrasse

Parrotfish
Humphead Parrotfish
Blue-Barred Parrotfish
Dusky Parrotfish
Bullethead Parrotfish

Mullet
Fringelip Mullet

Barracudas
Great Barracuda
Pickhandle Barracuda

Rockskippers
Rippled Rockskipper
African Mudhopper

Surgeons and Unicorns
Powder-Blue Surgeon
Blue-Banded Surgeon
Convict Surgeonfish
Two-Tone Tang
Sailfin Tang
Spotted Unicorn
Orange-Spine Unicorn

Moorish Idol
Moorish Idol

Rabbitfish
Orange Rabbitfish
Fork-Tailed Rabbitfish
Star-Spotted Rabbitfish

Kingfish
Kingfish (Wahoo)

Tuna and Gamefish
Eastern Little Tuna (Bonito)
Skipjack Tuna
Indian Mackerel
King Mackerel
Yellowfin Tuna
Big-Eye Tuna
Sailfish
Blue Marlin

Triggerfish
Orangestripe Triggerfish
Black Triggerfish
Picasso Triggerfish
Chevron Triggerfish

Filefish
Honeycomb Filefish
Harlequin Filefish

Boxfish
Blue-Spotted Boxfish
White-Spotted Boxfish

Toadfish
Starry Toadfish

Puffers
Black-Spotted Puffer
Dog Puffer
Honeycomb Toby
False-Eye Toby
Model Toby

Porcupinefish
Porcupinefish

INSECTS

Beetles
Giant Tenebrionid Beetle
Melittomma Beetle
Rhinoceros Beetle

Wasps
Mud Dauber
Potter (Mason) Wasp
Yellow Wasp

Butterflies and Moths
Bee Hawk Moth
Death's Head Hawk Moth
Hummingbird Hawk Moth
King of Seychelles
Oleander Hawk Moth

Others
Antlion
American Cockroach
Crazy Ant (Maldive Ant)
Ocean Skater
Praying Mantis
Seychelles Leaf Insect
Stick Insect
Termite (White Ant)

ARACHNIDS

Spiders
Palm Spider
Tarantula
Wolf Spider

Scorpions
Whip Scorpion

ARTHROPODS

Giant Millipede
Centipede

A Demographic Profile

The population of Seychelles at the 1987 census was 68,598. Almost ninety per cent, 61,183 people, live on the main island of Mahé. A total of 5,002 persons live on the second-largest island, Praslin, constituting 7.29 per cent of the total.

Just under three per cent — 1,927 — live on La Digue, and 191 people inhabit Silhouette.

The remaining 295 Seychellois are as far-flung and widely scattered as the Outer Islands on which they live.

Gazetteer

(First line indicates kilometre distance from Victoria, Mahé.)

SEYCHELLES ISLANDS

GRANITIC ISLANDS

Mahé
Highest point: 905 metres (2,969 feet)
Area: 15,252 ha (58.9 square miles)

Praslin
45km
Highest point: 367 metres (1,204 feet)
Area: 2,756 ha (10.6 sq miles)

La Digue
50km
Highest point: 333 metres (1,093 feet)
Area: 1,010 ha (3.9 sq miles)

St. Anne
5km
Highest point: 250 metres (820 feet)
Area: 219 ha (0.84 sq miles)

Cerf Island (Île au Cerf)
5km
Highest point: 108 metres (354 feet)
Area: 127 ha (0.49 sq miles)

Long Island (Île Longue)
7km
Area: 21.2 ha (0.082 sq miles)

Round Island (Île Ronde)
6km
Area: 1.8 ha (0.007 sq miles)

Moyenne
6km
Area: 8.9 ha (0.034 sq miles)

Beacon Island (Île Sèche)
8km
Area: Unsurveyed. Approx 1.5 ha
(0.006 sq miles)

Île Cachée
7km
Area: 2.1 ha (0.008 sq miles)

Île Anonyme
9km
Area: 9.6 ha (0.037 sq miles)

Île Hodoul
0.05 km
Area: 0.1 ha (0.0004 sq miles)

Rat Island (Île aux Rats)
10km
Area: 0.8 ha (0.003 sq miles)

Île Souris
15km
Area: 0.4 ha (0.002 sq miles)

Thérèse Island (Île Thérèse)
8km
Area: 73.9 ha (0.285 sq miles)

Conception
9km
Area: 60.3 ha (0.233 sq miles)

L'Islette
7km
Area: 3.2 ha (0.012 sq miles)

Chauve Souris (Mahé)
12km
Area: 0.1 ha (0.0004 sq miles)

Île aux Vaches Marines
7km
Area: 4.7 ha (0.018 sq miles)

L'Ilot
7km
Area: 0.5 ha (0.002 sq miles)

Cousin
44km
Highest Point: 58 metres (109 feet)
Area: 28.6 ha (0.110 sq miles)

Cousine
44km
Area: 25.7 ha (0.099 sq miles)

Curieuse
52km
Highest point: 172 metres (564 feet)
Area: 286 ha (1.104 sq miles)

Île Ronde (Praslin)
46km
Area: 19.3 ha (0.075 sq miles)

Chauves Souris (Praslin)
50km
Area: 0.7 ha (0.003 sq miles)

St. Pierre (Praslin)
51km
Area: 0.5 ha (0.002 sq miles)

Booby Island (Île aux Fous)
50km
Area: Unsurveyed. Approx 0.5 ha
(0.002 sq miles)

Aride
50km
Highest point: 134 metres (440 feet)
Area: 68.3 ha (0.264 sq miles)

Zave
50km
Area: 0.7 ha (0.003 sq miles)

Félicité
55km
Highest point: 231 metres (758 feet)
Area: 268 ha (1.035 sq miles)

Marianne
60km
Area: 94.7 ha (0.377 sq miles)

Grande Soeur
60km
Area: 84 ha (0.324 sq miles)

Petite Soeur
60km
Area: 34 ha (0.131 sq miles)

Île aux Cocos
55km
Area: Unsurveyed.
Approx 2 ha
(0.008 sq miles)

Île La Fouche
55km
Area: Unsurveyed.
Approx 0.5 ha
(0.002 sq miles)

Silhouette
30km
Highest point: 740 metres (2,428 feet)
Area: 1,995 ha (7.702 sq miles)

North Island
35km
Area: 201 ha (0.776 sq miles)

Mamelles
18km
Area: 8.8 ha (0.034 sq miles)

Île aux Recifs
34km
Area: 20 ha (0.078 sq miles)

Frégate
55km
Highest point: 125 metres (410 feet)
Area: 219 ha (0.846 sq miles)

L'Ilot Frégate
50km
Area: Unsurveyed. Approx 1 ha
(0.004 sq miles)

CORALLINE ISLANDS

Bird Island (Île aux Vaches)
105km
Area: 101 ha (0.390 sq miles)

Île Denis
95km
Area: 143 ha (0.552 sq miles)

OUTER ISLANDS

Île Plate
140km
Area: 54 ha (0.209 sq miles)
Platform reef

Coétivy
290km
Area: 931 ha (3.595 sq miles)
Platform reef

AMIRANTES GROUP

Rémire (Eagle Island)
245km
Area: 27 ha (0.104 sq miles)
Platform reef

D'Arros
255km
Area: 150 ha (0.579 sq miles)
Platform reef

Desroches
230km
Area: 394 ha (1.521 sq miles)
Platform reef

Étoile
305km
Area: 1.4 ha (0.005 sq miles)
Platform reef

Boudeuse
330km
Area: 1.4 ha (0.005 sq miles)
Platform reef

Marie Louise
310km
Area: 52.5 ha (0.203 sq miles)
Platform reef

Desnoeufs
325km
Area: 35 ha (0.135 sq miles)
Platform reef

AFRICAN BANKS

African Banks
235km
Area: 30 ha (0.116 sq miles)
Platform reef

Île du Sud (South Island)
235km
Area: Unsurveyed.
Platform reef

St. Joseph's Atoll
250km

St. Joseph
Fouquet
Ressource
Petit Carcassaye
Grand Carcassaye
Benjamin
Banc Ferrari
Chien
Pélican
Vars
Île Paul
Banc de Sable
Banc Cocos
Total area: 122 ha (0.471 sq miles)

Poivre Atoll
270km

Poivre
Area: 111 ha (0.429 sq miles)

Florentin
Île du Sud
Area: 137 ha (0.529 sq miles)

Alphonse & St. François Atolls
400km

Alphonse
Area: 174 ha (0.672 sq miles)

Bijoutier
405km
Area: Unsurveyed.

St. François
410km
Area: 17 ha (0.066 sq miles)

FARQUHAR GROUP

Providence Atoll
710km

Providence
Area: 157 ha (0.606 sq miles)
Reef platform

Bancs Providence
Area: 71 ha (0.274 sq miles)
Reef platform

St. Pierre
740km
Area: 167 ha (0.645 sq miles)
Raised limestone platform reef

Farquhar Atoll
770km

Île du Nord
Île du Sud
Manaha Nord
Manaha Milieu
Manaha Sud
Goëlettes
Lapin
Île du Milieu
Depose
Banc de Sable
Total area: 799 ha (3.085 sq miles)

ALDABRA GROUP

Aldabra Atoll
1150km
Grand Terre
Picard
Polymnie
Malbar
Île au Cèdres
Île Michel
Île Esprit
Île Moustiques
Ilot Parc
Ilot Emile
Ilot Yangue
Ilot Dubois
Ilot Magnan
Ilot Lanier
Total area: 15,380 ha (59.385 sq miles)
Raised limestone atoll

Cosmoledo Atoll
1045km

Menai
Area: 241 ha (0.930 sq miles)

Île du Nord
Area: 21 ha (0.081 sq miles)

Île Nord-Est
Area: Unsurveyed

Île du Trou
Area: 0.5 ha (0.002 sq miles)

Goëlettes
Area: 3.0 ha (0.012 sq miles)

Grand Polyte
Area: Unsurveyed

Petit Polyte
Area: Unsurveyed

Grand Île (Wizard Island)
Area: 192 ha (0.741 sq miles)

Pagode
Area: Unsurveyed

Île Sud-Ouest
Area: Unsurveyed

Île Moustiques
Area: Unsurveyed

Île Baleine
Area: Unsurveyed

Île Chauve Souris
Raised limestone atoll

Astove
1,045km
Area: 661 ha (2.552 sq miles)
Raised limestone atoll

Assumption
1,140km
Area: 1,171 ha (4.521 sq miles)
Raised limestone platform reef

SEYCHELLES ROCKS

It is debatable what constitutes a "rock" and what an "island", but the following have been designated rocks by the Seychelles Government Survey Department:

Grand Rocher — 2km east of Île Longue
Roche Hodoul — off the Anse Etoile coast
Trois Dames — off the Port Glaud coast
Roche Tortue — 1km east of Île aux Rats
Roche L'Intendance — off Anse L'Intendance
Roche Mancienne — off Anse Cachée
Roche Capucin — off Pointe Police
Brizards — halfway between Mahé and Les Mamelles
Blanchisseuse & Trompeuses — between Mamelles and Cousine
Requin & Caimans — south of Pointe Consolation, Praslin
Roche Canal — between Praslin and La Digue
Lion — 1km south of Frégate
Roche Grande Maman — off Chevalier Bay, Praslin
Parisiennes — off Anse Kerlan, Praslin
Roche Baleines — 2km west of Petite Anse Kerlan, Praslin
Roche Caret — off Fond de l'Anse, Praslin
Grosse Roche — off the coast between Anse Bateau and Anse Souvenir, Praslin
Île Malice — between Petite Anse and Pointe La Farine, Praslin
Roche Boquet — east of Ponte Cabris, Praslin
Roche Canon — west of Cousin
Roche Canon — west of Curieuse
Roche Marceline — off the north west coast of Silhouette
Roche Jean Pierre — east of Île Denis
Ponte Sud — east of Frégate
Île Plate — north west of Frégate
Roche Navire — south of Félicité
Roche Marceline — north of Félicité
Chemine — north west of Frégate

Museums & Historical Sites

Man has not lived in Seychelles for much more than 220 years, so not surprisingly, the country is not rich in historical sites, although those that do exist often have a particular charm about them.

Te National Museum on Independence Avenue, Victoria, contains an interesting collection of natural history items including the Possession Stone, one of Seychelles' oldest artifacts.

It is open Monday to Friday from 09.00 to 17.00 and on Saturdays from 09.00 to 12.00.

The National Archives, at La Bastille, contains some fascinating documents, maps, and photographs. Also held there are the records of the liberated slaves brought to Seychelles by the British, some of which include photographs.

The archives are open to researchers every weekday from 09.00 until 16.00 and on Saturday from 09.00 until 12.00. The staff are very helpful.

The National Museum
Victoria
Mahé
Tel: 23653

Historical documents, maps, and photographs dating back to 1744; collections of butterflies, coins, and shells.

National Archives
Bastilles
Mahé
Tel: 21931

Historical documents, maps, and publications.

National Monuments

The following are national monuments under Seychelles' law. Those marked with an * are on private property.

Mahé

*Beauvoir Cemetery
La Misère Road
Victoria

Old cemetery.

Bel Air Cemetery
Bel Air Road
Victoria

Seychelles' first cemetery. The corsair Jean François Hodoul is buried there. There is also the tomb of the "giant", who was supposed to have been 2.74 metres tall (8 feet 11 inches). He was poisoned when other residents became afraid of his strength.

Bicentennial Monument
Roundabout at Independence Avenue and Fifth June Avenue
Victoria

Known locally as Twa Zwazo, this monument represents the three elements of Seychelles' society; Europe, Africa, and Asia.

Botanical Gardens
Mont Fleuri

Open every day between 06.00 and 18.00, the gardens have a collection of palms, including the *coco de mer*. Giant land tortoises can be seen there. Laid out in 1901 by Mr. P.R. Dupont, the mature gardens are a lovely spot.

Cascade Catholic Church
Cascade

Attractive, white church on the hill overlooking the sea.

*Ex-Chateau Des Mamelles
Les Mamelles

Fine-looking house built in 1804. Once the home of the corsair, Jean François Hodoul.

Clock Tower
Junction of Independence Avenue, Albert, and Francis Rachel Streets
Victoria

Paid for by public subscription and inaugurated in 1903, the Clock Tower commemorated Queen Victoria and Seychelles' new status as a Crown Colony, separate from Mauritius. It is a replica of a clock tower on Vauxhall Bridge Road, London, and it does not chime.

Diamond Jubilee Fountain
Corner of Independence Avenue, by the Supreme Court
Victoria.

Freedom Square
Between Francis Rachel Street
and Independence Avenue
Victoria

Formed from the mud and rubble which slid down from St. Louis during the Avalanche of 1862, this land was originally called Gordon Square, after General Gordon. Its present name was given because early political rallies were held there.

*Kenwyn House
Francis Rachel Street
Victoria

Old colonial house, now the residence of the manager of Cable & Wireless PLC.

La Bastille Building
La Bastille
Victoria

Old colonial house, now houses the Seychelles National Archives.

Les Palmes Theatre
Mont Fleuri
Victoria

Liberation Monument
Fifth June Avenue
Victoria

Known as Zomn Lib, this monument commemorates 5th June, 1977.

*Maison Blanche
Bel Eau Road
Victoria

Old colonial house.

Maison du Peuple
Latanier Road
Victoria

Seychelles' centre of government. Built at the instigation of the national party, work began in October 1979, the foundation stone being laid in June the same year. Total cost was R8.5 million, much of which was provided by Algeria. The building is faced in "red" Praslin granite.

*Ex-Maxime Jumeau's House
Anse à la Mouche

Mission Ruins
Sans Souci

Once known as Venn's Town, it was a mission and school where the children of liberated slaves were educated.

Ex-Nageon's House
Pointe Larue

National Library
State House Avenue
Victoria

Built by the Carneigie Trust in 1907.

Pierre Poivre Bust
Francis Rachel Street
Victoria

Erected by the Seychelles Society in 1972 to commemorate Pierre Poivre (1719-1786), who introduced spice plants to Seychelles, in particular cinnamon, which later became an important cash crop for the islands.

*Ex-Plantation House
La Plaine

Old colonial house, which now houses "La Marine". Extremely fine-scale models of sailing ships are made there to a very high standard.

*Roman Catholic Priest's Residence
Oliver Maradan Street
Victoria

Imposing building by the cathedral.

*St. Paul's Cathedral
Revolution Avenue
Victoria

The Anglican Cathedral was built in 1857 and consecrated by Bishop Vincent Ryan, Bishop of Mauritius, becoming a full cathedral in 1960.

*"1776"
Sans Souci Road
Victoria

This is the house in which Archbishop Makarios was accommodated during his exile here. Now the residence of the American Ambassador.

SPUP Museum
Francis Rachel Street
Victoria

Inaugurated as a museum of the Seychelles People's United Party, (now the Seychelles People's Progressive Front) in June 1984, this old building was the SPUP's headquarters for 20 years before Liberation. It is open from 09.00 to 17.00, Tuesday to Friday.

*State House
State House Avenue
Victoria

(Closed to the public, unless you have permission to visit). Completed in 1913 to replace earlier, unsatisfactory premises, it was designed by the wife of a governor who forgot to allow for a staircase, even though the building has two storeys.

*State House Cemetery
Grounds of State House
Victoria

(Closed to the public, unless you have permission to visit). Contains the graves of early Seychelles' residents, most notably Jean Baptiste Queau de Quincy (1752-1827) who was administrator during both French and British occupations.

Supreme Court
Francis Rachel Street, near Clock Tower
Victoria

Other Islands

Plantation House
La Digue

Leper Colony Ruins and Doctor's House
Curieuse

Plantation House
Silhouette

Plantation House
Farquhar

Public Holidays

January 1 & 2	New Year	June 29	Independence Day
March/April	Good Friday (variable)	August 15	Assumption of Mary (La Digue Festival)
	Easter Monday (variable)		
	Easter Sunday (variable)	November 1	All Saints' Day
May 1	Labour Day	December 8	Immaculate Conception
June 5	Liberation Day		
June	Corpus Christi (observed on the Thursday after Trinity Sunday)	December 25	Christmas Day

LISTINGS

Airlines

Victoria offices

Aeroflot
Pirates Arms Building
Tel: 25005

Air France
Victoria House
PO Box 256
Tel: 22414

Air Seychelles
Victoria House
PO Box 386
Tel: 21547

British Airways
Kingsgate House
PO Box 292
Tel: 24910

Kenya Airways
Shipping House
PO Box 288
Tel: 22989/23907

Lux Air
Victoria House
PO Box 386
Tel: 21547

The following airlines
have offices in Victoria
but do not operate
services:

Air India
Victoria House
PO Box 356
Tel: 22414

Air Mauritius
Victoria House
PO Box 356
Tel: 22414

Air Tanzania
Kingsgate House
PO Box 611
Tel: 24900

Cathay Pacific
Victoria House
PO Box 356
Tel: 22414

Ethiopian Airlines
Kingsgate House
PO Box 611
Tel: 24900

Lufthansa
Kingsgate House
PO Box 611
Tel: 24900

Air Charter

Air Seychelles
Victoria House
PO Box 386
Tel: 21547

Airport

Seychelles International
Airport
Anse des Genéts
Tel: 73001

Foreign Diplomatic Missions

AMERICAN EMBASSY
Victoria House
PO Box 251
Victoria
Tel: 23921/2
Fax: 25189

BELGIUM CONSULATE
PO Box 596
Huteau Lane
Victoria
Tel: 24434

BRITISH HIGH
COMMISSION
Victoria House
PO Box 161
Victoria
Tel: 23055/6
Fax: 25127

CHINESE EMBASSY
PO Box 680
Plaisance
Mahé
Tel: 44295

CUBAN EMBASSY
PO Box 108
Victoria
Tel: 24094

CYPRUS CONSULATE
Turtle Bay Estate 47
PO Box 450
Anse aux Pins
Tel: 76215

ROYAL DANISH
CONSULATE
PO Box 231
Victoria
Tel: 24156

FRENCH EMBASSY
PO Box 478
Mont Fleuri
Mahé
Tel: 24523
Fax: 25248

FEDERAL REPUBLIC
OF GERMANY
CONSULATE
PO Box 132
Mont Fleuri
Mahé
Tel: 22306

INDIAN HIGH
COMMISSION
PO Box 488
Le Chantier
Victoria
Tel: 24489
Fax: 24810

MADAGASCAR
CONSULATE
PO Box 68
Victoria
Tel: 44030

MAURITIAN
CONSULATE
Anse aux Pins
Mahé
Tel: 76441

MONACO
CONSULATE
Chateau de Feuilles
Praslin
Tel: 33316
Fax: 33916

NETHERLANDS
CONSULATE
PO Box 372
Glacis
Mahé
Tel: 47100

NORWAY
CONSULATE
Victoria House
PO Box 457
Mahé
Tel: 23866

SWEDISH
CONSULATE
PO Box 270
New Port
Mahé
Tel: 24710
Fax: 24065

SWISS CONSULATE
PO Box 33
Santa Maria Estate
Anse à la Mouche
Mahé
Tel: 71050

USSR EMBASSY
P.O. Box 632
Le Niol
Tel: 21590

Seychelles Missions Abroad

FRANCE
Mr. Calix D'Offay
53 rue François 1er
Paris 75008
Tel: 472 39811
Telex: 649634 AMBSUI
Fax: 472 37702

UNITED KINGDOM
Mr. Silvester
Radegonde
111 Baker Street
2nd Floor
Eros House
London W1M 1FG
Tel: 071 224 1660
Telex: 28146 SEYCOM C
Fax: 071 487 5756

UNITED NATIONS
Mr. Mark Marengo
820 Second Avenue
Suite 927F
New York, New York
10017
Tel: 212 687 9766
Telex: 220032 FMUNUR
Fax: 212 808 4975

Seychelles Consulates

AUSTRALIA
Mr Guy Robert
Hon. Consul General
271 Canning Road
Les Murdie
Perth
WA 6076
Tel: 2916570

Mr John Charody
Hon. Consul General
6th Floor
55 Macquaire Street
Sydney, NSW 2000
Tel: 2314802/2412647

AUSTRIA
Mr Karl Pisec
Hon. Consul General
Gubhausstrabe 12
A-1040 Vienna
Tel: 653215/651585
Telex: 132064 PISEC A

BELGIUM
Mr Jacques Mortelmans
Hon. Consul General
Avennue Molière 301
1060 Bruxelles
Tel: 3453423
Telex: 65235 INTOUR B

DENMARK
Mr Erling Starup
Hon. Consul
Vejleso Parken No. 16
DK-2840 Holte
Tel: 024 20001
Telex: 16600 FOTEX DK

FRANCE
Mr Adil Iskaros
Hon. Consul General
53, Rue François 1er
Paris 75008
Tel: 4720 3966
Telex: 650055 ANI F

Mr Pierre Soubiron
Hon. Consul General
375, Avenue du Prado
Marseille 13008
Tel: 91 71 66 88
Telex: 420423 CBEM F

FEDERAL REPUBLIC OF GERMANY
Mr Michael Scheele
Hon. Consul
Prinzregentenplatz 15
800 Munchen 80
Tel: 089/476057
Telex: 05215822 SHELD D

Mr Han Joachim Worms
Hon. Consul
Jungfernstieg 7
D-2000 Hamburg 36
Tel: (040) 34 66 06
Fax: (040 35 25 29

GREECE
Mr A.Pantazopoulos
Hon. Consul General
10 Tsokopoulou St
15237 Filothei, Athens
Tel: 8081509/6828766
Telex: 218821 PANT GR
222565 SEYC GR

HONG KONG
Mr Gerald Quilindo
Hon. Consul
Seychelles Trading Co.
R5203 Funghes
Commercial Building
6-8A, Prat Avenue
Tsim Shatsui, Kowloon
Tel: 3-689764/3-689753
Telex: 39311 SEYCO HX

INDIA
Mr Lalit Mohan Thapar
Hon. Consul
Tharpar House
124 Janpath
New Delhi 11001
Tel: 310411
Telex: 031-3845 BILT IN

INDONESIA
Mr S. Prawirosujanto
Hon. Consul
8, Jalan Patiunum
Kebayoran Baru
Jakarta 12120
Tel: 772313
Telex: 61696 WARISIA

IRAQ
Mr Ghasaq Fadhil Abbas
Hon. Consul
Sadoun Street
Bros Building Stane No. 3
Baghdad
Tel: 8882850

ITALY
Mr Antonio Rolfini
Hon. Consul
Viale Sandro 5
20127 Milano
Tel: 6084440
Telex: 311271 PTC I

Mr Egidio Ariosto
Hon. Consul
Via Del Tritone 46
00185 Roma
Tel: 6780530
Telex: 613469 WTD ROM I

JAPAN
Mr Atsushi Goto
Hon. Consul
Nagoya-Denki-Gakuen
Wakamizu, Chikusa,
Nagoya
Tel: 052 722 3354
Telex: 4443705 AIT AGJ

KENYA
Mr Jean Antoine
Hon. Consul
PO Box 20400
Nairobi
Tel: 748545
Telex: 22186
Fax: 740569

LEBANON
Mr Amin S. Najjar
Hon. Consul
P.O. Box 206, Beyrouth
Tel: 316316
Telex: 20820 LE (CEDRES)

MADAGASCAR
Mr S. de Commarmond
Hon. Consul
B.P. 1071, Antananarivo
Tel: 20949
Telex: 22294 DECOTA MG

MONACO
Mr Michel Chiappori
Hon. Consul
14 Boulevard Rainier III
Principauté de Monaco
Tel: (93) 302796

NETHERLANDS
Mr Jan de Hoop
Hon. Consul
1272 Huizen
Oud Bussummerweg 44
Tel: (2159) 40904
Telex: 10400

NORWAY
Mr Tore Wendelborg
Hon. Consul
C/O Vest Reisebureau
A/S Drammensveien
126
0277 Oslo 2
Tel: 2556420
Telex: 72457

SPAIN
Mr Juan Gaspar Solves
Hon. Consul General
Rambla Cataluna 20
Barcelona 7
Tel: (93) 3172700
Telex: 98671 HUSA F

Mr Benito Gil Alvaro
Hon. Consul
Gruppo Hoteles Husa
Paseo de la Castellana
1260 IZQDA
28046 Madrid
Tel: 2751200
Telex: 27521 HUSA F

SWEDEN
Mr Lars A. Kristoferson
Hon. Consul
The Beijer Institute
Box 50005
S-104/05 Stockholm
Tel: 160490
Telex: 17148 BEIJER S

SWITZERLAND
Mr Otto Meier-
Boeschenstein
Hon. Consul
Beethovenstrasse 5
BP 4782
CH 8002 Zurich
Tel: 2027871
Telex: 815818 CH

TUNISIA
Ms Claude Bauzil
Hon. Consul
Dar Chems
Route de la Corniche
Hammamet
Tel: 80448
Telex: 26464 KAMMAR

Seychelles Tourist Offices

FRANCE
Ms. Danielle Bastienne
32 Rue Ponthieu
75008 Paris
Tel: (33) (1) 42898685
Fax: (33) (1) 45638512
Telex: (7) 649140 SEYPAR

GERMANY
Mrs. Edith Hunzinger
Kleine Bockenheimer
Strasse 18A
D-6000 Frankfurt AM
Main 1
Tel: (49) (69) 292064
Fax: (49) (69) 296230
Telex: (41) 414788 SEY D

ITALY
Ms. Josée Gonthier
Centre Cooperazione
Internazionale
Piazza Giulio Cesare 1
Fiera Di Milano
20145 Milan
Tel: (39) (2) 4985795/
4692964
Fax: (39) (2) 4813943
Telex: (43) 353132 SEYMI

JAPAN
Mr. Hisayaund Nisho
Ginraku Building 7F
Ginza 2-4-1, Chuo-Ku
Tokyo 104
Tel: (81) (3) 562342
Fax: (81) (3) 5618138

KENYA
Mr. Colin Church
Jubilee Insurance
Exchange Building
P.O. Box 30702, Nairobi
Tel: (254) (2) 25103/
26744/21335
Fax: (254) (2) 728696
Telex: 22380 ENLITEN

SCANDINAVIA
Mr. Thomas Westerberg
Adolf Frediks
Kyrkosata 13
8-11137 Stockholm
Tel: (46) (8) 240716
Fax: (46) (8) 216549
Telex: 19113 VOYAGES

UNITED KINGDOM
Ms. Liz Naya
2nd Floor, Eros House
111 Baker Street
London WIM 1FE
Tel: (44) (01) 224 1670
Fax: (44) (01) 487 5756

USA
Mr. M. Marengo
Seychelles Mission (UN)
820 Second Avenue
Suite 927
New York, NY 10017
Tel: (212) 6879766
Fax: (212) 8084975

SINGAPORE
Mr. Paul Armstrong
01-56 United Square
101 Thomson Road
Singapore 1130
Tel: 2557373
Fax: 2521100
Telex: 28162 HMSIN RS

HONG KONG
Mr. Dino Capelvenere
46th Floor
Hopewell Centre
183 Queen's Road
East GPO Box 40
Tel: (5) 86526552
Telex: 65578 WTRV HX

SEYCHELLES
Independence House
PO Box 92
Victoria, Mahé
Tel: 25313/25314
Fax: 21612
Telex: 2275 SEYTOB SZ

Accommodation

Hotels, Guest Houses, and Self-Catering

Mahé

AUBERGE D'ANSE BOILEAU
PO Box 211
Anse Boileau
Tel: 76660

AUBERGE CLUB DES SEYCHELLES
PO Box 526
Danzilles
Tel: 47550

AUBERGE LOUIS XVII
PO Box 607
La Louise
Tel: 44411

BEAUFOND LANE
PO Box 140
Mont Fleuri
Tel: 22408

BEAU VALLON BAY HOTEL
PO Box 550
Beau Vallon
Tel: 47141

BEAU VALLON BUNGALOWS
Beau Vallon
Tel: 47382

BEL OMBRE HOLIDAY VILLAS
PO Box 528
Bel Ombre
Tel: 47616

BLUE LAGOON CHALETS
PO Box 442
Anse à la Mouche
Tel: 71197

BOUGAINVILLE HOTEL
PO Box 378
Bougainville
Tel: 71334

CALYPHA RELAIS DES ISLES
Ma Constance
Tel: 41157

CAREFREE GUEST HOUSE
PO Box 403
Anse Faure
Tel: 76237

CHATEAU D'EAU
PO Box 107
Barbarons Estate
Tel: 78399

CLOSE DES ROSES
Anse Étoile
Tel: 41245

COCO D'OR HOTEL
PO Box 665
Beau Vallon
Tel: 47331

CORAL STRAND HOTEL
PO Box 400
Beau Vallon Beach
Tel: 47036

EQUATOR HOTEL
PO Box 526
La Beolière
Grand Anse
Tel: 78228

LA LOUISE LODGE
PO Box 193
La Louise
Tel: 44349

HARBOUR VIEW GUEST HOUSE
PO Box 631
Mont Fleuri
Tel: 22473

HILLTOP GUEST HOUSE
Serret Road
St. Louis
Tel: 23553

HOTEL CASUARINA BEACH
PO Box 338
Anse aux Pins
Tel: 76211

LA ROUSETTE
PO Box 690
Anse aux Pins
Tel: 76245

LAZARE PICAULT CHALETS
PO Box 135
Baie Lazare
Tel: 71117

LE MERIDIEN BARBARONS BEACH HOTEL
PO Box 626
Tel: 78253

LE MERIDIEN FISHERMAN'S COVE HOTEL
PO Box 35
Bel Ombre
Tel: 47252

LE NIOL GUEST
HOUSE
PO Box 591
Le Niol
Tel: 23262

LE TAMARINIER
GUEST HOUSE
Marie Laure Drive
Bel Ombre
Tel: 47611

L'ISLETTE ISLAND
PO Box 349
Port Glaud
Tel: 78229

MANRESA GUEST
HOUSE
Anse Étoile
Tel: 41388

MICHEL HOLIDAY
APARTMENTS
PO Box 277
Les Mamelles
Tel: 44540

NORTH POINT GUEST
HOUSE
Fond des Lianes
Machabee
Tel: 41339

NORTHOLME HOTEL
PO Box 333
Glacis
Tel: 47222

PANORAMA GUEST
HOUSE
Mare Anglaise
Tel: 47300

PENSION BEL AIR
PO Box 116
Bel Air
Tel: 24416

THE PLANTATION
CLUB
PO Box 437
Baie Lazare
Tel: 71588

REEF GOLF CLUB
HOTEL
PO Box 388
Anse aux Pins
Tel: 76251

ROSE COTTAGE
GUEST HOUSE
Pointe Au Sel
Tel: 71434

SEA BREEZE GUEST
HOUSE
Pointe Conan
Tel: 41021

SEYCHELLES
SHERATON
PO Box 450
Port Glaud
Tel: 78451

SUNRISE GUEST
HOUSE
Mont Fleuri
PO Box 615
Tel: 24560/24836

SUNSET BEACH
HOTEL
PO Box 372
Glacis
Tel: 47227

VACOA VILLAGE
PO Box 401
Beau Vallon
Tel: 47130

CHEZ JEAN
PO Box 552
Glacis
Tel: 41445

VILLA MADONNA
GUEST HOUSE
Beau Vallon
Tel: 47403

VILLA MARIA
Cascade
Tel: 73046

VILLA NAPOLEON
PO Box 5
Beau Vallon
Tel: 47133

VISTA BAY CLUB
PO Box 622
Glacis
Tel: 47351

Praslin

BEACH VILLA
Grande Anse
Tel: 33445

BRITTANIA GUEST
HOUSE
Grande Anse
Tel: 33215

CHATEAU DE
FEUILLES
Pte. Cabris Estate
Baie St. Anne
Tel: 33316

CHAUVE SOURIS
ISLAND LODGE
Anse Volbert
Tel: 32003

CÔTE D'OR LODGE
PO Box 388
Tel: 32200

FLYING DUTCHMAN
Grande Anse
Tel: 33337

GRANDE ANSE
BEACH VILLA
Tel: 33445

HOTEL L'ARCHIPEL
Anse Gouvernement
Tel: 32242

INDIAN OCEAN
Grande Anse
Tel: 33324/33457

LA RESERVE HOTEL
Anse Petite Cour
Tel: 32211

MAISON DES PALMES
Amitié
Tel: 33411

ORANGE TREE GUEST
HOUSE
Baie St. Anne
Tel: 33248

PARADISE HOTEL
Anse Volbert
Tel: 32255

PRASLIN BEACH
HOTEL
Anse Volbert
Tel: 32222

VILLAGE DU
PECHEUR
Côte D'Or
Tel: 32030

La Digue

BERNIQUE'S GUEST
HOUSE
Tel: 34229

CHOPPY'S
BUNGALOWS
Anse Réunion
Tel: 34224

GREGOIRE'S ISLAND
LODGE
Tel: 34233

JOC D'OR GUEST
HOUSE
Tel: 34250/34247

LA DIGUE ISLAND
LODGE
Anse Réunion
Tel: 34232

Others

BIRD ISLAND LODGE
Kingsgate House
PO Box 404
Victoria
Booking Office: 24925

DENIS ISLAND
LODGE
Kingsgate House
PO Box 404 Victoria
Booking Office: 24913/
44143
Island: 76328

DESROCHES ISLAND
RESORTS
Oceangate House
Independence Avenue
Victoria
Tel: 24502

FRÉGATE
PLANTATION CLUB
PO Box 330
Booking Office Tel:
23123
Island Tel: 24789

SILHOUETTE LODGE
Silhouette
Tel: 24003

Business Associations

Mahé

Car Hire Operators
Association
Tel: 23747

Federation of Civil
Engineers and Building
Contractors
PO Box 214
Tel: 24710

Federation of
Employers Association
of Seychelles
Room 37
Premier Building
PO Box 599
Tel: 24710

Marine Charter
Association
Fifth of June Avenue
PO Box 469
Tel: 22126

National Workers Union
Maison du Peuple
Tel: 24030

Nurses Association
Mont Fleuri
Tel: 24820

Seychelles Chamber of
Commerce
Room 38
Premier Building
PO Box 443
Tel: 23310

Seychelles Women's
Association
Francis Rachel Street
Tel: 24218
Small Hotels and Relais
des Isles Association
PO Box 92
Tel: 22881

Taxi Owners' Drivers'
Association
PO Box 555
Oliver Maradan Street
Tel: 23895

Clubs

Happy Youth Club
La Rosiere
Tel: 23876

Lions Club of Mahé
PO Box 493
Victoria
Tel: 22173

Reef Hotel Golf Club
PO Box 388
Anse aux Pins
Tel: 76251

Rotary Club of Victoria
Coral Strand Hotel
PO Box 400
Beau Vallon
Tel: 47036

Round Table

Seychelles Yacht Club
Fifth of June Avenue
Victoria
Tel: 22362

Tour Operators and Travel Agents

Mahé

Air Bookings Ltd
Shipping House
PO Box 312
Victoria
Tel: 22536/22989/24667

Bunson Travel
Shipping House
PO Box 475
Victoria
Tel: 22682/22292

Mason's Travel
Revolution Avenue
PO Box 459
Victoria
Tel: 22642

National Travel Agency
Kingsgate House
PO Box 611
Victoria
Tel: 24900

Orchid Travel
Pirates Arms Building
PO Box 115
Victoria
Tel: 24953

Travel Services (Seychelles)
Victoria House
PO Box 356
Victoria
Tel: 22414

Praslin

Mason's Travel
Grande Anse
Tel: 33211

National Travel Agency
Amitié
Tel: 33223

Travel Services (Seychelles)
Villa de Mer
Tel: 33438

Car Hire Companies

Mahé

Alpha Rent-a-Car
PO Box 643
Victoria
Tel: 22078

Norman's Car Hire &
Travel Service
(Avis Rent-a-Car)
PO Box 224
Mont Fleuri
Tel: 24511

Budget Rent-a-Car
PO Box 72
Les Mamelles
Tel: 44280/44296

City Car Hire
Anse aux Pins
Tel: 76829

Echo (Pty) Ltd
Mont Fleuri
Tel: 21666

Europcar International
Victoria House
PO Box 559
Victoria
Tel: 23303/47018

Exoticars
PO Box 673
Mare Anglais
Tel: 47333

Hertz Leisure Cars
PO Box 600
Revolution Avenue
Victoria
Tel: 22447/22669

Island Car Hire
PO Box 635
Victoria
Tel: 76832

Jean's Car Hire
PO Box 522
St. Louis
Tel: 22278

Joe's Car Hire
Le Rocher
Tel: 23420/44239

Kobe Car Hire
PO Box 375
Le Rocher
Tel: 21888

Koko Cars
PO Box 601
Victoria
Tel: 24404/47632

Leisure Cars
PO Box 600
Victoria
Tel: 22447/22669

Mahé Cars
PO Box 361
Les Mamelles
Tel: 44566

Meins Car Hire
PO Box 169
St. Louis
Tel: 23005/22366

Nelson's Car Hire
PO Box 461
Victoria
Tel: 22923

Petite Car Hire
PO Box 83
Victoria
Tel: 44608

RAM Car Hire
Boston House
5th June Avenue
Victoria
Tel: 23443

Silversands Rent-a-Car
PO Box 279
Bel Ombre
Tel: 47060

St. Louis Motor Hire
PO Box 522
St. Louis
Tel: 22270

Sunshine Cars
PO Box 127
Victoria
Tel: 24671

Tropicar Rent-a-Car
Jivan's Building
Mont Fleuri
Tel: 23838

Union Vale Car Hire
PO Box 509
Beau Vallon
Tel: 47052

Victoria Car Hire
PO Box 640
Victoria
Tel: 76314

Praslin

Austral Car Rental
Baie St. Anne
Tel: 32015

Praslin Holiday Car
Rental
Grande Anse
Tel: 33219/33325

Prestige Car Hire
Grande Anse
Tel: 33226

Solare Car Hire
Grande Anse
Tel: 33525

Standard Car Hire
Anse Kerlan
Tel: 33555

Bus Companies

Seychelles Public
Transport Corporation
PO Box 610
Victoria
Tel: 24550

Anse Aux Pins Depot
Tel: 76492/76870

La Digue Depot
Tel: 34341

Praslin Branch
Tel: 33258

Taxis

Wilton Albest
Tel: 22518

M. Alcindor
Victoria
Tel: 22515

A.A. Leong
Taxi Stand
Victoria
Tel: 22653

B. Otar
Tel: 22763

W. Payet
Taxi Stand
Victoria
Tel: 22912

Hospitals

Mahé

Seychelles Hospital
PO Box 52
Mont Fleuri
Tel: 24400

Anse Royale Hospital
Anse Royale
Tel: 71222

North East Point
Hospital
Tel: 41044

Mental Hospital
Les Canelles
Tel: 71323

Praslin

Baie St. Anne Hospital
Tel: 33333

La Digue

Logan Hospital
Tel: 34255

Clinics

(On Mahé unless listed otherwise)

Anse aux Pins	24400/
	76535
Anse Boileau	76649
Anse Kerlan,	
Praslin	33855
Baie Lazare	71151
Beau Vallon	24400
Beolière	78259
Corgat Estate	24400
English River	24400
Glacis	24400
Grande Anse,	
Praslin	33414
Les Mamelles	24400
Port Glaud	78223
Silhouette	
Island	24110
Takamaka	71231
Family Welfare	24400
Fiennes	
Institute	44023/
	44049

Banks

Bank of Baroda
PO Box 124
Albert Street
Victoria
Tel: 23038/21533

Bank of Credit and
Commerce
PO Box 579
Victoria
Tel: 22303/22305
Airport agency
PO Box 579
Tel: 76725

Banque Française
Commerciale
PO Box 122
Albert Street
Tel: 23096
Anse Royale Branch
Tel: 71166

Barclays Bank PLC
Main Branch
Independence House
PO Box 167
Victoria
Tel: 24101
Market Street Branch
PO Box 99
Victoria
Tel: 24101
Airport Office
Tel: 73029
Beau Vallon Office
Tel: 47391
Baie St. Anne Branch
Praslin
Tel: 33344
La Digue Office
Tel: 34348

Central Bank
Central Bank Building
Independence Avenue
Victoria
Tel: 21580

Development Bank of
Seychelles
PO Box 217
Independence Avenue
Victoria
Tel: 24471

Habib Bank
PO Box 702
Francis Rachel Street
Tel: 24371/24372

Seychelles Savings Bank
Independence House
PO Box 531
Victoria
Tel: 21921

Standard Chartered
Bank of Africa, PLC
Kingsgate House
PO Box 241
Independence Avenue
Victoria
Tel: 25011

Casinos

Casino des Seychelles
Beau Vallon Bay Hotel
Tel: 47272

The Plantation Club
Baie Lazare
Tel: 71588

Night Clubs

Barrel Investments (Pty)
Victoria
Tel: 22136

Chez Rif
Pointe Larue
Tel: 76869

Flamboyant
Discotechque
Victoria

Katiolo Club
Anse Faure
Tel: 76453

Cinemas

Deepam Cinema
Victoria
Tel: 22585

Art Galleries, Studios, and Potteries

Michael Adams
Anse Aux Poules Bleues
Tel: 71106

Tom Bowers Sculpture
Anse à la Mouche
Tel: 71518

Guy Cesar
Mont Buxton

Gerard Devoud
Les Mamelles

Christine Harter
Côte D'Or
Praslin
Tel: 32131

Island Designs
Le Chantier
Tel: 24296

Pineapple Studio
Anse aux Poules Bleues
Tel: 71230

Ron Gerlach Batiks
Revolution Avenue
Victoria
Tel: 22670

Seychelles Potters
Co-Operative
Les Mamelles
Tel: 44080

Studio Oceana
PO Box 545
Victoria
Tel: 24791

Sunstroke
PO Box 237
Victoria
Tel: 24767

Seychelles Media Directory

Magazines

Seychelles Today
PO Box 321
Union Vale
Victoria
Tel: 24161

Newspapers

Seychelles Nation
Press Office
Department of
Information
PO Box 321
Union Vale
Victoria
Tel: 24161

Radio

Radio Television
Seychelles (RTS)
219 m 1368kHz
Mon-Fri 06.00–13.15
18.00–20.00
Sat–Sun 06.00–22.00
Full news bulletin:
Creole 22.00, French
12.30, English 19.00
Headlines: Creole 06.30
and 12.00, French 07.30
and 21.00, English 07.00
and 13.00
Union Vale
Tel: 24161

Far Eastern Broadcasting
Association (FEBA)
PO Box 234
Anse Étoile
Tel: 41281

Television

Radio Television
Seychelles (RTS)
Pal B, 625 lines
Mon–Fri 17.30–22.30
Sat–Sun 16.00–22.30
News summary:
English 18.00
French 20.00
Full news bulletin:
(mostly Creole) 19.00
Hermitage
PO Box 321
Tel: 24161

Cultural Centres, Libraries and Museums

American Cultural
Center
Victoria House
Victoria
Tel: 23921

Centre Culturel
Français
Pirates Arms Building
Victoria
Tel: 24611

Kreol Institute
Maison St Joseph
Anse aux Pins
Tel: 76357

National Archives
La Bastille
Victoria
Tel: 21931

National Institute of
Pedagogy
Mont Fleuri
Tel: 24777

National Library
PO Box 45
State House Avenue
Victoria
Tel: 21072

Seychelles National
Museum
Independence Avenue
Victoria
Tel: 23653

SPUP Museum
Francis Rachel Street
Victoria

Bibliography

Aldabra Alone (1970), by Tony Beamish, published by George Allen & Unwin Ltd, London.

Aride Island Nature Reserve, Seychelles, Management Plan (1989), by Ian Bullock, RSNC Internal Report.

Aride Island Nature Reserve, Scientific Report April 1987 - April 1989 (1989), by Ian. Bullock, RSNC.

Biogeography and Ecology of the Seychelles Islands (1984), edited by D.R. Stoddart, published by Dr. W. Junk Publishers, The Hague.

Birds of Seychelles (1979), by Tony Beamish, published by Government Printer, Hong Kong.

Birds of Seychelles (1989), by Ian D. Bullock, ICBP Education Project First Draft.

The Birds of Seychelles and the Outlying Islands (1974), by Malcolm Penny, published by Collins, Glasgow.

A Birdwatcher's Guide to Seychelles (1989), by Adrian Skerrett & Ian Bullock, First Draft.

Byen Manze Kreol, by Ulric Denis et al, published by Delroisse.

The Conservation of the Seychelles Warbler (Acrocephalus sechellensis) on Cousin Island, Seychelles (1990), by Jan Komdeur & Mike Rands, ICBP Internal Report.

The Doomsday Book of Animals (1981), by David Day, published by Ebury Press, London.

Environmental Legislation of Seychelles (1989), by G.H. de B. Romilly, Department of the Environment, Seychelles.

A Fish Watchers Guide to Seychelles (1989), by D.R.L. Rowat, In Press.

Flowers and Trees of Seychelles (1986), by Francis Friedmann, published by Editions Delroisse Paris.

Flowering Plants of Seychelles (1989), by S.A. Robertson, published by Royal Botanic Gardens, Kew.

Fodies of the Seychelles Islands (1961), by John Hurrell Crook.

Forgotten Eden, a View of the Seychelles Islands (1968), by Athol Thomas, published by Longmans Green & Co, London.

La Geste Francaise Aux Sechelles (1987), by Guy Lionnet, published by Collection Mascarin.

Guide to Fishes (1982), by E.M. Grant, published by Department of Harbours and Marine, Brisbane.

List of the Flowering Plants and Ferns of Seychelles by D. Bailey, published by Government Printer, Seychelles.

Histoire des Seychelles (1982), by Jean-Michel Filliot, Ministry of Education, Seychelles.

Histoires Vraies des Seychelles (1987), by John Louis Adam, published by Poligraf, Rome.

The History of Seychelles, Part One: French Occupation (1940), by John T. Bradley, printed by Clarion Press, Victoria, Seychelles.

Introduced Birds of the World (1981), by John L. Long, published by David & Charles, London.

Islands in a Forgotten Sea (1969), by T.V. Bulpin, published by Books of Africa.

Marine Turtles in the Republic of the Seychelles (1984), by Jeanne Mortimer, IUCN World Wildlife Fund.

The Natural History of the Seychelles, by Jeremy High, published by G.T. Phillips & Co, London.

Observations of Nesting and Group Behaviour of Seychelles White-Eyes, (Zosterops modesta) (1979), by P.W. Greig-Smith, British Ornithologists Union.

Oxford University Biological Expedition to the Seychelles 1985 (1986), by David Baum et al, Oxford University.

Pierre Poivre (1974), by Malleret, Mauritius.

Rare Birds of the World (1988), by Guy Mountfort, published by Collins, Glasgow.

Red Sea Reef Fishes (1986), by Dr. John E. Randall, published by IMMEL Publishing, London.

Review of the Environmental Legislation of Seychelles (1990), by G.H. de B. Romilly, Department of Environment Seychelles, Internal Report.

Seabirds, an Identification Guide (1983), by Peter Harrison, published by Croom Helm, Kent.

Sea Guide to Whales of the World (1981), by Lyall Watson, published by Hutchinson & Co, London.

Seychelles (1989), by Peter Vine, published by IMMEL Publishing, London.

The Seychelles Black Paradise Flycatcher on La Digue 1977-8 (1981) by Jeff Watson, WWF.

The Seychelles Black Paradise Flycatcher, (Terpsiphone corvina) (1988), by Ian Bullock, Jan Komdeur, Mariette Komdeur, Victorin Laboudallon, and Gill Lewis, ICBP.

Seychelles Industrial Development Policy 1989-1993 (1988), by Jacques Hodoul, Ministry for National Development Presentation.

The Stamps and Postal History of Seychelles, by Leslie Harris, published by Phillips & Co, London.

The Story of Seychelles (1965), by A.W.T. Webb, Victoria, Seychelles.

Striking Plants of Seychelles, by Guy Lionnet.

Threatened Birds of Africa and Related Islands: The ICBP/IUCN Red Data Book, Part 1 (1985), by N.J. Collar & S.N. Stuart, published by ICBP & IUCN.

The Treasure Seekers' Treasury (1978), by Roy Norvill, published by Hutchinson & Co., London.

Unpublished Documents on the History of the Seychelles Islands Anterior to 1810 (1980), compiled by A.A. Fauvel, published by Government Printing Office, Seycelles.

The Vallée de Mai, Praslin Seychelles (1973), by Nicholas Polunin & John Procter, Biological Conservation.

All pictures taken by **Mohamed Amin** and **Duncan Willetts** except the following:

Debbie Gaiger: Pages: 92-93, 100, 111, and 248 (top left) and 279.

Willy and Pam Kemp: Pages: 224 (bottom), 229, 271 and 274.

David Rowat: Pages: 214, 216, 218-219, 221, 223, 224 (top), 230 and 270.

Lindsey Chong-Seng: Pages: 124, 126, 185, 194, 195, 197, 202, and 236.

Adrian Skerrett: Pages: 6, 27, 159, 172, 193, 198, 206, 212, 227, 244, 247, 248 (top right and bottom left), 251, and 255.